JUNG AND THE EPIC OF TRANSFORMATION

Vol. 3

Nietzsche's "Thus Spoke Zarathustra" and the Challenge of Transformation

by Paul Bishop

CHIRON PUBLICATIONS • ASHEVILLE, NORTH CAROLINA

www.ChironPublications.com

Interior and cover design by Danijela Mijailovic
Printed primarily in the United States of America.

ISBN 978-1-68503-695-9 paperback
ISBN 978-1-68503-696-6 hardcover
ISBN 978-1-68503-697-3 electronic
ISBN 978-1-68503-698-0 limited edition paperback
ISBN 978-1-68503-699-7 limited edition hardcover

Library of Congress Cataloging-in-Publication Data Pending

Contents

List of Abbreviations

AP = C.G. Jung, *Analytical Psychology: Notes of the Seminar Given in 1925*, ed. William McGuire (Princeton, NJ: Princeton University Press, 1989).

BB = C.G. Jung, *The Black Books, 1913-1932: Notebooks of Transformation*, ed. Sonu Shamdasani, trans. Martin Liebscher, John Peck, and Sonu Shamdasani, 7 vols. (New York and London: Norton, 2020).

CW = C.G. Jung, *Collected Works*, ed. Sir Herbert Read, Michael Fordham, Gerhard Adler, and William McGuire, 20 vols. (London: Routledge & Kegan Paul, 1953-1983). Cited in the text with volume number and paragraph reference.

DKV = Wolfram von Eschenbach, *Parzival*, ed. Eberhard Nellmann, trans. Dieter Kühn, 2 vols. (Frankfurt am Main: Deutscher Klassiker Verlag, 2006).

ETG = *Erinnerungen, Träume, Gedanken von C.G. Jung*, ed. Aniela Jaffé (Olten and Freiburg im Breisgau: Walter-Verlag, 1990).

H = *The Holy Bible, according to the Douay and Rheims Version* [1859], ed. George Leo Haydock (Duarte, CA: Catholic Treasures, 2006).

JLW = C.G. Jung and Aniela Jaffé, *Jung's Life and Work: Interviews for "Memories, Dreams, Reflections" with Aniela Jaffé*, ed. Sonu Shamdasani with Thomas Fischer, trans. Heather McCartney and John Peck (Princeton, NJ, and Oxford: Princeton University Press, 2026).

KSA = Friedrich Nietzsche, *Sämtliche Werke: Kritische Studienausgabe*, ed. Giorgio Colli and Mazzino Montinari, 15 vols. (Berlin and New York; Munich: de Gruyter; Deutscher Taschenbuch Verlag, 1967-1977; 1988).

KSB = Friedrich Nietzsche, *Sämtliche Briefe: Kritische Studienausgabe*, ed. Giorgio Colli and Mazzino Montinari, 8 vols. (Berlin and New York; Munich: de Gruyter; Deutscher Taschenbuch Verlag, 1975-1984).

L = C.G. Jung, *Letters*, ed. Gerhard Adler and Aniela Jaffé, trans. R.F.C. Hull, 2 vols. (Princeton, NJ: Princeton University Press, 1973-1975).

MDR = *Memories, Dreams, Reflections of C.G. Jung*, ed. Aniela Jaffé, trans. Richard and Clara Winston (London: Routledge & Kegan Paul, 1963).

NJB = *The New Jerusalem Bible*, general ed. Henry Wansbrough (London: Darton, Longman & Todd, 1985).

NK = *Nietzsche-Kommentar*, i.e., *Historischer und kritischer Kommentar zu Friedrich Nietzsches Werken*, ed. Heidelberger Akademie der Wissenschaften, 13 vols. in 6. (Berlin and New York: de Gruyter, 2012-2024).

PU = C.G. Jung, *Psychology of the Unconscious: A Study of the Transformations and Symbolisms of the Libido: A Contribution to the History of the Evolution of Thought*, trans. Beatrice M. Hinkle (London: Moffat, Yard, 1916) (cited with paragraph references as reprinted [London: Routledge, 1991]).

RB = C.G. Jung, *The Red Book: Liber Novus* [Reader's Edition], ed. Sonu Shamdasani, trans. Mark Kyburz, John Peck, and Sonu Shamdasani (New York and London: Norton, 2012).

SNZ = C.G. Jung, *Jung's Seminar on Nietzsche's "Zarathustra": Abridged Edition*, ed. and abridged James L. Jarrett (Princeton, NJ: Princeton University Press, 1998).

SNZ (vol. and page number) = C.G. Jung, *Nietzsche's "Zarathustra": Notes of the Seminar given in 1935-1939*, ed. James L. Jarrett, 2 vols. (London: Routledge, 1989) (cited with volume number and page reference).

ZL = C.G. Jung, *The Zofingia Lectures*, trans. Jan van Heurck (London: Routledge, 1983).

Abbreviations of titles of Nietzsche's works

AC	*The Anti-Christ*
BT	*The Birth of Tragedy*
BGE	*Beyond Good and Evil*
CW	*The Case of Wagner*
D	*Daybreak*
EH	*Ecce Homo*
GM	*On the Genealogy of Morals*
GS	*The Gay Science*
HA	*Human, All-Too-Human*
NCW	*Nietzsche contra Wagner*
TI	*Twilight of the Idols*
UM	*Untimely Meditations*
Z	*Thus Spoke Zarathustra*
WP	*The Will to Power*

Editions of translations cited

Wolfram von Eschenbach, *Parzival: A Knightly Epic*, trans. Jessie L. Weston [1894], 2 vols (New York: Stechert, 1912).

Johann Wolfgang Goethe, *Faust: Parts I and II*, trans. Albert G. Latham (London; New York: Dent; Dutton, 1908).

Friedrich Nietzsche, *Thus Spake Zarathustra: A Book for All and None* [*Complete Works of Friedrich Nietzsche*, ed. Oscar Levy, vol. 4], trans. Thomas Common (Edinburgh and London: Foulis, 1909).

A note on translation

Nietzsche's *Zarathustra* is cited here from the translation published in 1909 by the Scottish translator and critic Thomas Common

(1850-1919). Common lived in Corstorphine, then close to (and now part of) Edinburgh on the east coast of Scotland; under the leadership of Alexander Tille (1866-1912), who lived in Glasgow on the West coast, taught at its University, and had published an earlier translation of *Zarathustra* in 1896, Common was a major figure in this Scottish project to produce a complete edition of Nietzsche's works in English. These days, Common's translation is, for various reasons, out of favor; and his association with the eugenicist and antidemocratic views of Tille also counts against him.[1] It is true that, in the meantime, numerous (and, for the most part, vastly better) translations of *Zarathustra* have appeared, notably by Walter Kaufmann (1954), R.J. Hollingdale (1961), Graham Parkes (2005), and Adrian Del Caro (2006). Yet Common's translation, which is now out of copyright, was attentive to the biblical resonance of the original German (even if sometimes at the cost of philological accuracy), and taken up in Oscar Levy's edition of Nietzsche's works (1909-1913).[2] It had become widely known by the time Jung was developing his Analytical Psychology, and it became the translation he chose for his seminars on *Zarathustra* from 1934 to 1939; hence its use here.

[1] For further discussion (and criticism) of the work of Common and Tille, see David S. Thatcher, *Nietzsche in England, 1890-1914: The Growth of a Reputation* (Toronto: University of Toronto Press, 1970), pp. 17-52; Stefan Manz, "Translating Nietzsche, Mediating Literature: Alexander Tille and the Limits of Anglo-German Intercultural Transfer," *Neophilologus*, 91 (2007), 117-134; and Ritchie Robertson, "Nietzsche in Glasgow: Alexander Tille, John Davidson and Edwin Muir," in Gerard Carruthers, David Goldie, and Alastair Renfrew (eds), *Scotland and the 19-Century World* (Amsterdam and New York: Rodopi, 2012), pp. 213-230.

[2] For further discussion, see Dan Stone, "Oscar Levy: A Nietzschean Vision," in *Breeding Superman: Nietzsche, Race and Eugenics in Edwardian and Interwar Britain* (Liverpool: Liverpool University Press, 2002), pp. 12-32; and "An 'Entirely Tactless Nietzschean Jew': Oscar Levy's Critique of Western Civilization," *Journal of Contemporary History*, vol. 36, no. 2 (April, 2001), 271-292. Lest right-wing readings of Nietzsche be seen as the preserve of Scottish intellectuals, the case of Anthony Ludovici (1882-1971) — who taught at University College, London, and translated various works by Nietzsche — proves the opposite; see Stone, "Anthony Mario Ludovici: A 'Light-Weight Superman,'" in *Breeding Superman*, pp. 33-61.

Commentaries on Nietzsche's *Zarathustra* (in alphabetical order of author)

David B. Allison, *Reading the New Nietzsche: "The Birth of Tragedy," "The Gay Science," "Thus Spoke Zarathustra," and "On the Genealogy of Morals"* (Lanham: Rowman & Littlefield, 2001).

Keith Ansell-Pearson and Paul S. Loeb (eds.), *Nietzsche's "Thus Spoke Zarathustra": A Critical Guide* (Cambridge: Cambridge University Press, 2022).

Charles Bambach, *Nietzsche's "Thus Spoke Zarathustra": A Critical Guide and Introduction* [Edinburgh Critical Guides to Nietzsche] (Edinburgh: Edinburgh University Press, forthcoming).

Paul Bishop (ed.), *A Companion to Friedrich Nietzsche: Life and Works* (Rochester, NY, and Woodbridge: Camden House, 2012), esp. Chapter 7, "Thus Spoke Zarathustra."

Douglas Burnham and Martin Jesinghausen, *Nietzsche's "Thus Spoke Zarathustra": An Edinburgh Philosophical Guide* (Edinburgh: Edinburgh University Press, 2010).

Francesca Cauchi, *Zarathustra* contra *Zarathustra: The Tragic Buffoon* (Aldershot: Ashgate, 1988; reprinted Routledge, 2018).

Francesca Cauchi, *Zarathustra's Moral Tyranny: Spectres of Kant, Hegel and Feuerbach* (Edinburgh: Edinburgh University Press, 2022).

Volker Gerhardt (ed.), *Friedrich Nietzsche: Also sprach Zarathustra* [Klassiker Auslegen, vol. 14] (Berlin: Akademie Verlag, 2000).

Robert Gooding-Williams, *Zarathustra's Dionysian Modernism* (Stanford, CA: Stanford University Press, 2001).

NK, 4/1 and 4/2 = Katharina Grätz, *Kommentar zu Nietzsches "Also sprach Zarathustra" I und II* and *Kommentar zu Nietzsches "Also sprach Zarathustra" III und IV* [Historischer und kritischer Kommentar zu Friedrich Nietzsches Werken, vols. 4/1 and 4/2] (Berlin and Boston: de Gruyter, 2024).

Karl Knortz, *Nietzsches "Zarathustra": Eine Einführung* (Halle an der Saale: Hugo Peter, 1906).

Laurence Lampert, *Nietzsche's Teaching: An Interpretation of "Thus Spoke Zarathustra"* (New Haven, CT, and London: Yale University Press, 1986).

Paul S. Loeb, *The Death of Nietzsche's Zarathustra* (New York: Cambridge University Press, 2010).

James Luchte (ed.), *Nietzsche's "Thus Spoke Zarathustra": Before Sunrise* (London and New York: Continuum, 2008).

Heinrich Meier, *What Is Nietzsche's Zarathustra? A Philosophical Confrontation* [2017], trans. Justin Gottschalk (Chicago and London: University of Chicago Press, 2021).

Matthew Meyer, *The Routledge Guidebook to Nietzsche's "Thus Spoke Zarathustra"* (London and New York: Routledge, 2025).

Graham Parkes, *Composing the Soul: Reaches of Nietzsche's Psychology* (Chicago and London: University of Chicago Press, 1994).

Bhagwan Shree Rajneesh, *Zarathustra*, 2 vols. (vol. 1, *A God that can Dance*; vol. 2, *The Laughing Prophet* (Cologne: The Rebel Publishing House, 1987).

Stanley Rosen, *The Mask of Enlightenment: Nietzsche's "Zarathustra"* (Cambridge and New York: Cambridge University Press, 1995).

Gary Shapiro, *Nietzschean Narratives* (Bloomington and Indianapolis, IN: Indiana University Press, 1989).

T.K. Seung, *Nietzsche's Epic of the Soul: "Thus Spoke Zarathustra"* (Lanham, MD: Lexington Books, 2005).

Leo Strauss, *On Nietzsche's "Thus Spoke Zarathustra,"* ed. Richard L. Velkley (Chicago and London: University of Chicago Press, 2017).

Hans Weichelt, *Zarathustra-Kommentar* (Leipzig: Felix Meiner, 1910; [2]1922).

Jungian approaches to Nietzsche (in chronological order)

Liliane Frey-Rohn, *Friedrich Nietzsche: A Psychological Approach to His Life & Work* [*Jenseits der Werte seiner Zeit: Friedrich Nietzsche im Spiegel seiner Werke*, 1984], ed. Robert Hinshaw and Lela Fischli, trans. Gary Massey (Einsiedeln: Daimon, 1998).

Paul Bishop, *The Dionysian Self: C.G. Jung's Reception of Friedrich Nietzsche* (Berlin and New York: de Gruyter, 1995).

Gerhard Schmitt, *Zyklus und Kompensation: Zur Denkfigur bei Nietzsche und Jung* (Frankfurt am Main, Berlin, Bern: Lang, 1998).

Graham Parkes, "Nietzsche and Jung: Ambivalent Appreciations," in Jacob Golomb, Weaver Santaniello, and Ronald Lehrer (eds.), *Nietzsche and Depth Psychology* (Albany, NY: State University of New York Press, 1999), pp. 205-227.

Lucy Huskinson, *Nietzsche and Jung: The Whole Self in the Union of Opposites* (Hove and New York: Brunner-Routledge, 2004).

Martin Liebscher, *Libido und Wille zur Macht: C.G. Jungs Auseinandersetzung mit Nietzsche* (Basel: Schwabe, 2012).

Paul Bishop, *On the Blissful Islands with Nietzsche & Jung: In the Shadow of the Superman* (London and New York: Routledge, 2017).

Gaia Domenici, *Jung's Nietzsche: Zarathustra, The Red Book, and "Visionary" Works* (Cham: Palgrave Macmillan, 2019).

Acknowledgements

I should like to thank colleagues at Chiron Publications, especially Len Cruz and Steve Buser, for their interest in this project at an early stage and for their support in turning it into a reality; many thanks to Jennifer Fitzgerald for her invaluable contribution to managing the project, to Robert Mikulak for his careful copyediting, and to Sophia Houmaoui for her meticulous proof-reading..

I am extremely grateful to the Academic Sub-Committee of the IAAP for its financial support for this project, without which it would not have been possible to bring it to publication. And I should like to thank Joe Cambray for his advice and support, for which I am likewise extremely grateful.

Over the years I have incurred a number of debts to innumerable colleagues in *Germanistik* and Jung Studies alike, especially Roger Stephenson; Jim Walker (at Camden House); and students and colleagues in the School of Modern Languages and Cultures (SMLC) at the University of Glasgow, where for a number of years I offered an Honors Option on *Zarathustra* (learning much from the questions and responses of those students who chose it), as well as the first-years of the Comparative Literature course on Heroes, where I presented highlights from *Zarathustra* — and again found that the text resonated with some students well beyond the confines of the lecture hall (or, in recent years, the Zoom call). In addition, I should like to thank for their for advice, conversations and support: Alan Cardew; Terence Dawson; Leslie Gardner; Phil Goss; Gottfried Heuer; Lucy Huskinson; Peter Kingsley; Laura London; Martin Liebscher; Christiana Ludwig; Roderick Main; Catriona Miller; Pamela J. Power; Susan Rowland; Andrew

Samuels (and other colleagues at the Department of Psychosocial and Psychoanalytic Studies, formerly the Centre for Psychoanalytic Studies, at the University of Essex); and Sonu Shamdasani.

In 2009, I was invited by ISAP (International School of Jungian Psychology) to be a speaker at the Jungian Odyssey, which was to take place in Sils Maria, Switzerland, from 6-13 June. The theme of the retreat was Creation and Destruction, so the presence of Nietzsche made itself felt not only in the Nietzsche-Haus and at the Zarathustra stone near Surlei, but also in the opulent surroundings of the Waldhaus Hotel, where the event was being held. Subsequently the papers from this conference were published as *Destruction and Creation: Facing the Ambiguities of Power* [Jungian Odyssey Series, vol. 2], edited by Isabelle Meier. For the discussions at the Odyssey and at other events, I should like to thank the following: John Hill, Christiana Ludwig, and Murray Stein (whose invitations to contribute to the Zurich Lecture Series and to *Jung's Red Book for Our Time* have, time and again, encouraged me to focus on various aspects of Jung's relation to German culture). In February 2016 and February 2017, I offered a course at the C.G. Jung-Institut, Zurich, on *Reading Nietzsche's "Zarathustra,"* examining the Prologue and then Part One of *Zarathustra*; I should like to thank the participants on this course for their supportive comments and engagement with Nietzsche's work — in a sense, this book was born during those two courses. And in March 2023, I was invited by the Johnson Foundation to give a lecture on "Understanding the Influences of Goethe and Nietzsche on the Ideas of C.G. Jung," which was an opportunity to revisit previous work on this area in the light of this ongoing project. I should also like to thank James Ellis of the *Hermitix* podcast and Jakob Lusensky of the *Psychology & The Cross* podcast for the opportunities to discuss with them Nietzsche, Jung, and related figures. And I am indebted to Laura London for the kind invitations she has extended to be interviewed for her *Speaking of Jung* podcast and for her interest in my work.

Above all, I am grateful as always for support from Helen, not to mention Ruben.

Preface

As we saw in Volume 1 of this series, in *Memories, Dreams, Reflections,* Jung signaled his affinity with the world of the Knights of the Grail by identifying his father as Anfortas (that is, as "a 'fisher king' whose wound would not heal") and by recounting a dream, set in front of the Grail Castle, in which he realized that he, Jung, was being called upon to play the role of a Grail Knight and to "fetch the Grail" (MDR, 241 and 311-312). In the protocols of Aniela Jaffé's original interviews for *Memories*, Jung recalls, "This dream made one of the most powerful impressions upon me of any dream," and he continues, "That is really how it's been in my life: this visibility of the Grail or of the Grail castle," adding: "One comes there, when one is it, and the Grail remains eternally *introuvable*, because one is not it. It is the mystery of individuation, and that is a *mysterium*, and there human understanding ceases. Individuation must be a mystery, for one will never understand it" (JLW, 276 and 277).[1]

Pondering a later dream of 1923, in *Memories* Jung recalled a frightening vision in which he encountered the Wild Huntsman, the "*Grünhütl,*" or Wearer of the Green Hat, identified by Jung as Wotan, the "god of [his] Alemannic forefathers," and in turn as the

[1] In this context, we can see how inspired the choice of *Memories, Dreams, Reflections* (i.e., *Erinnerungen, Träume, Gedanken*) really was. For the German word *Erinnerung* in the title of Jung's memoirs has less the sense of "memory" (or "recollection") and more the sense of *Ermahnung* ("exhortation," "admonition," or "warning"), *Einprägung ins Gedächtnis* ("imprinting on one's memory"), or *Beherzigung* ("heeding"), as it is used in Goethe's poem with that title (*Werke* [HA], vol. 1, p. 133, cf. p. 529).

Roman god Mercury or Hermes, a "nature spirit" who returned to life again in the Grail legend as—Merlin (MDR, 345).[2] In the Jung/Jaffé protocols, Jung describes Merlin as a "tremendously important figure" because he represents the "real solution." His figure, he adds, represents the "attempt of the unconscious at that time to bring forth a figure parallel to Parsifal," who "corresponds to the Christian hero." And Jung goes even further, declaring Merlin to be not just "more significant" than Parsifal, but "infinitely more significant," inasmuch as he is the "great tragic figure from this whole epic," that is, the epic of the Grail (JLW, 223). Nevertheless, an explicit identification on Jung's part with the figure of Parzival, the Grail knight at the center of Wolfram von Eschenbach's great epic, can be found in *The Red Book* (as we shall see in Volume 4.)

And we saw in Volume 2 of this series how, in *Memories, Dreams, Reflections*, Jung signaled his affinity with Goethe by talking about his "legendary kinship" with Goethe, referring to an "annoying tradition that my grandfather was a natural son of Goethe" (and so, in effect, Goethe was his great-grandfather) (MDR, 52; cf. JLW, 142-144). This story was, in fact, so "annoying" that Jung kept on repeating it, "speak[ing] of this stubbornly persistent legend"—says Aniela Jaffé—"with a certain gratified amusement" (MDR, 52)! (Jung even dropped a reference to this alleged kinship in his correspondence with Freud …).[3] Elsewhere in *Memories*, Jung adds that this "annoying story" had made such an impression on him, inasmuch as it "at once corroborated and seemed to explain my curious reactions to *Faust*" (MDR, 261).

---

[2] Other accounts of this dream or vision can be found in the entry for 2-3 January 1923 in *Black Book 7* and in the Jung/Jaffé protocols (BB7, 224-226 and JLW, 267).

[3] See Jung's letter to Freud of 18 January 1911 (*The Freud/Jung Letters: The Correspondence Between Sigmund Freud and C.G. Jung*, ed. William McGuire, trans. Ralph Manheim and R.F.C. Hull (Cambridge, MA: Harvard University Press, 1988), pp. 384-385). For Freud's eye-twinkling way of playing along, see his letters to Jung of 9 March 1909 and 22 January 1911 (pp. 210-211 and 388).

In this third volume, we shall explore the affinity between Jung and another figure—Friedrich Nietzsche, an affinity signaled by Jung when, in *Memories, Dreams, Reflections*, he recalls of his time as a student that Nietzsche had been "on my programme for some time," yet that he had been "held back by a secret fear that I might perhaps be like him" (MDR, 122). Now the notion of the "secret" is a governing idea of *Memories* and the Jung-Jaffé protocols alike, and in the case of Nietzsche, this "secret" is said to have "isolated him from his environment" and appears to be related to the fact that, like Jung, Nietzsche was the son of a clergyman. (In his Seminar on *Zarathustra*, Jung frequently reminded his audience that Nietzsche had been the son of a church minister, adding: "I know what *that* means"!)[4]

The secrecy which, until very recently, surrounded *The Red Book* is part of a strategy that Jung also learned from Nietzsche—namely, not to speak "naïvely and incautiously" about one's *arrheton* (ἄρρητον), i.e., the term for the "unspeakable" in the ancient Greek mystery cults.[5] In *Memories, Dreams, Reflections,* Jung describes himself as having been more clever than Nietzsche, inasmuch as he had quickly noticed that to speak the unspeakable could "lead to trouble" (MDR; 123). Like the educated Philistines, or *Bildungsphilister,* which, tragi-comically, he criticized—tragi-comically, because he himself was one—Nietzsche did not understand himself when he "fell into the mystery"—*das Mysterium*, the same term used by Jung in *The Red Book*—"and into the unspeakable [*das Nichtzusagende*]," and when he wanted to "sing its praises" (that is, of falling into the mystery or the

[4] Jung, SNZ, vol. 1, 31; cf. 69, 261, 429, 576; vol. 2, 961 and 1095.

[5] Note the distinction between *arrheton* (or "the ineffable," i.e., that which, in principle, *cannot* be brought to speech) and *aporrheton* (or that about which discourse is *forbidden*) (Charles Stein, "Ancient Mysteries," in Glenn Alexander Magee (ed.), *The Cambridge Handbook of Western Mysticism and Esotericism* (Cambridge: Cambridge University Press, 2016), pp. 3-12 [p. 3]).

unspeakable) to "the crowd that had been forsaken by all the gods" (MDR, 124).

Forsaken by all the gods … As we saw in Volume 1, there is good reason to believe that Jung is ultimately grappling with Parzival's question, *waz ist got*, "What is God?" (§119, l. 17; vol. 1, p. 68, and §332, l.1; vol. 1, p. 188). In Volume 2, we considered Goethe's *Faust* as formulating a key tenet of German Romanticism when he writes that "truth, identical with the divine, may never be witnessed directly; we perceive it only as reflected in the particular example, the symbol"[6] and as confirming the maxim that "the greatest gift we have received from God and Nature is life: the rotation of the monad around itself, which knows neither rest nor peace."[7] And, as we shall see in Volume 4, some of the key insights achieved in *The Red Book* involve the nature of Jung's God, a God who is emphatically "not dead," but who is "as alive as ever" (RB, 516). In so writing, Jung is positioning himself in the clearest possible way against Nietzsche, who in *The Gay Science* announces the death of God (GS §108 and §125) and in *Thus Spoke Zarathustra* assumes it as part of the background to the epic series of discourses delivered by Zarathustra.

And in this present volume of *Jung and the Epic of Transformation,* we now turn to Nietzsche's *Zarathustra*, a monumental work (and one that it took Jung five years to consider in his legendary seminar from 1934 to 1939—and even he, thanks to geopolitical events outside his control, abandoned this project before finishing the final chapters of Part Three and missing out entirely Part Four). Because of *Zarathustra*'s length and complexity,

[6] See Roger Cardinal, *German Romanics in Context* (London: Studio Vista, 1975), pp. 43-43.

[7] *Maxims and Reflections*, #1253; in *Maximen und Reflexionen*, ed. and trans. R.H. Stephenson (Glasgow: Scottish Papers in Germanic Studies, 1986), p. 124. For further discussion, see Fritz Joachim von Rintelen, "Die Gottesidee bei Johann Wolfgang von Goethe," *Philosophisches Jahrbuch*, 60 (1950), 1-7.

we shall focus on a number of key discourses, in line with the "map" set out for Chapter 1. Accordingly, we shall focus on the opening Prologue, which is rich in symbolic action; on the figures in "Of the Three Transformations" of the Camel, the Lion, and the Child, which recur in several later discourses; on the figure of the *Übermensch,* that "human-being-who-is-more-than-a-human-being" which the Earth Spirit in *Faust*, Part One, had mocked the crisis-ridden Doctor Faust for wanting to be, but whom Zarathustra describes as being the "meaning of the earth"; and on two key chapters from Part Four, "The Midnight-Song" and the concluding chapter, "The Sign."

After examining these select discourses from *Thus Spoke Zarathustra* in Chapter 1, we shall turn in Chapters 2 and 3 to the role played by Nietzsche in Jung's works, notably in *Transformations and Symbols of the Libido* (1911-12) as well as in his early systematic and typological writings. At the conclusion of Chapter 3, we look at the presentation of Nietzsche in *Memories, Dreams, Reflections*—a text with a complicated authorship, as two recent works have shown.[8] Yet *Memories, Dreams, Reflections* has proved itself over the years to be a work which serves for many as an introduction to Jung, the man and the—what? Analyst? Mystic? Prophet? Visionary? My hunch is that it is unlikely to relinquish that importance in anything like the near future. And if archival research—and what can be gleaned from fragments on the cutting-room floor—reveal that statements contained in *Memories, Dreams, Reflections* are historically untrue, then Jung himself might well retort, alluding to the phrase attributed to Hegel, "Well, so much the worse for history!"

---

[8] See Aniela Jaffé, *Streiflichter zu Leben und Denken C.G. Jungs* (Einsiedeln: Daimon, 2021), incorporating a monograph-length "Historischer Kommentar" by Elena Fischli (the entire work is translated by Caitlin Stephens as *Reflections on the Life and Dreams of C.G. Jung* [Einsiedeln: Daimon, 2023]); and JLW.

Finally, in Chapter 4, we consider Nietzsche's role in *Psychology and Alchemy* (1944) and (in the light of Sir George Ripley's *Cantilena*, sometimes called *George Ripley's Song*) in *Mysterium Coniunctionis* (1955-1956). At various moments in between—and in an excursus in Chapter 2 on the symbol of the Grail in relation to Nietzsche—we shall draw on the insights found in Jung's Seminar on *Zarathustra* (1934-1939), which despite being (or perhaps because it is) incomplete, stands as a major exercise in the analysis of Nietzsche's work; an exercise which has been recognized as "legendary" by Katharina Grätz in her own recent volumes on *Zarathustra* in the *Nietzsche-Kommentar*, even if one might take issue with her description of Jung's reading of *Zarathustra* as "not searching for philosophical insight, but trying to break down residues of the collective unconscious in analytical interpretations."[9]

After many years when it was only available in typoscript volumes to readers undergoing Jungian analysis or training, the notes of the Seminar were finally published in 1989 in two volumes edited by James L. Jarrett (1917-2015), Professor of the Philosophy of Education at the University of California, Berkeley; and subsequently in an Abridged Edition in 1998. (This Abridged Edition makes a good starting point for anyone wishing to explore the seminars, although some significant passages were, for one reason or another, omitted from it.) The reluctance to publish the Seminar on *Zarathustra* made it almost as well-kept a secret as Jung's *Red Book*, which itself was not published until 2009 (and in a Reader's Edition in 2012). Now that *The Red Book* has been published, the relative lack of attention (within and outside the Jungian community) which the *Zarathustra* Seminar has since received—albeit with notable exceptions—means that, in some respects, it is more of a secret than ever, and it remains a remarkable

[9] NK 4/1, 53.

study of an even more remarkable work which has itself the notion of the secret at its very core.[10]

Recent critics have argued that the great Homeric epics, the *Iliad* and the *Odyssey*, contain secret information—scientific (and specifically astronomical) information about the cycles of the sun, the moon, and the planet Venus;[11] and about the correspondence between the movements of stars and constellations and the battles between the Greeks and the Trojans.[12] Others have argued that the journey undertaken by Odysseus is the greatest "secret" journey of all time—the "journey back to where you are" or the journey to the Self.[13] As Alan Watts powerfully expresses this idea:

> The illusion is that change takes time. The truth is change happens the moment you decide. You don't need more time. You need a shift in being. You see, there are infinite versions of you. Each living a life shaped by a different choice. The question is: Which one will you tune into? One decision, one gentle pivot and the entire path unfolds differently. Don't underestimate how powerful one moment of clarity could be. The universe responds the second you align. So if you're wondering what to do, just listen. The version of you who already chose is calling you home.[14]

---

[10] For a fuller discussion of the Seminar, see Paul Bishop, *Jung's Seminar on Nietzsche's "Zarathustra": Birth of an Archetypal Hermeneutics* (Palgrave Macmillan, forthcoming).

[11] Florence and Kenneth Wood, *Homer's Secret Odyssey* (Stroud: The History Press, 2011).

[12] Florence and Kenneth Wood, *Homer's Secret Iliad: The Epic of the Night Skies Decoded* (London: Murray, 1999).

[13] David A. Beardsley, *The Journey Back To Where You Are: Homer's "Odyssey" as Spiritual Quest* (Highland Park, NJ: Ideograph Media, 2014). For further discussion, see Volume 1, pp. 34-62.

[14] Audio available on YouTube HTML <https://www.youtube.com/watch?v=NnA0qDCunzw>.

Or as Nietzsche subtitled his late semiautobiographical work, *Ecce Homo*, it's all about "how you become what you are." In this spirit, let us take the next step in this journey together. For *Thus Spoke Zarathustra*—which has rightly been described as Nietzsche's "epic of the soul" (T.K. Seung)—is the work which we shall now explore as the next case study in our four-stage history of the epic of transformation. Are you ready for the journey to begin? Listen …

Chapter 1

Zarathustra Highlights

1. **Part One, Prologue**	
2. **"Of the Three Transformations":**	
Camel →	**"Of the Vision and the Riddle"**
	"Of the Spirit of Heaviness," §2
Lion →	**"Of the Famous Wise"**
	"Of Old and New Tables," §1
Child →	**"The Child with the Mirror"**
	"On the Blissful Islands"
3. ***Übermensch* →**	**"On the Gift-Giving Virtue"**
	"On the Blissful Islands"
	"Of Old and New Law Tables," §3
4. **(a) "The Midnight-Song"**	
(b) "The Sign"	

1. Part One, Prologue

The opening chords of Richard Strauss's tone poem of 1896, named after Nietzsche's *Thus Spoke Zarathustra*, have—thanks largely to Stanley Kubrick's 1968 film of Arthur C. Clarke's science fiction novel *2001: A Space Odyssey*—acquired an almost iconic value. The piece opens with a sustained double low C played on the double basses, contrabassoon, and organ, before a brass fanfare of three notes in intervals of a fifth and an octave, C – G – C, introduces the "nature" or "dawn" motif that announces in shattering, ear-deafening tones the "sunrise" (*Sonnenaufgang*). The tone poem is structured by these notes which, with the two final conflicting keys

(C –G – C – B – F♯ – B), are said to represent the "world-riddle," and it is less a setting of Nietzsche's work as such and more a series of musical reflections on nine sections from it: Introduction, or Sunrise; "Of Those in Backwaters"; "Of the Great Longing"; "Of Joys and Passions"; "The Song of the Grave"; "Of Science and Learning"; "The Convalescent"; "The Dance Song"; and finally, the *Nachtwandlerlied* or "Song of the Night Wanderer." (One could, if one wanted, use these chapters as a guiding thread through the labyrinth of this fascinating, perplexing work; however, here we will choose different chapters on which to focus, reflecting the theme of transformation in the work as a whole.)

While a deeply ambiguous composition—is the "world-riddle" ever solved or not?—Strauss's tone poem captures the sheer sense of momentousness in Nietzsche's extraordinary text, which opens thus:

> When Zarathustra was thirty years old, he left his home and the lake of his home, and went into the mountains. There he enjoyed his spirit and solitude, and for ten years did not weary of it. But at last his heart changed, — and rising one morning with the rosy dawn, he went before the sun, and spake thus unto it:
>
> Thou great star! What would be thy happiness if thou hadst not those for whom thou shinest!
>
> For ten years hast thou climbed hither unto my cave: thou wouldst have wearied of thy light and of the journey, had it not been for me, mine eagle, and my serpent. (Z Prologue §1)

In fact, this entire opening section is almost exactly identical with the section (GS §342) that had concluded Nietzsche's previous work, *The Gay Science* (1882; 1887). There are only two substantive differences: In the earlier version, the lake of Zarathustra's home is called Lake Urmi (or Urmia),[1] and the episode is presented under the title "*Incipit tragoedia*"—"The tragedy begins," a way of inscribing the project of Zarathustra within the Greek tragic tradition as a whole and of linking it to Goethe's *Faust*, itself described as a *Tragödie*. (In what sense, we asked, is *Faust* a tragedy? We might ask the same question of *Zarathustra*; or, more accurately, in what sense is it a comedy?)[2] For in his Preface to the second edition of *The Gay Science*, Nietzsche wrote: "'*Incipit tragoedia*' we read at the end of this awesomely malicious book. Beware! Something downright wicked and malicious is announced here: *incipit parodia*, no doubt" (GS Preface §1). Again, in what sense is this a work a comedy or a parody? An answer is given at the end of the Preface where Nietzsche makes a crude but revealing joke: "'Is it true that God is present everywhere?' a little girl asked her mother; 'I think that's indecent'—a hint for philosophers! One should have more respect for the bashfulness with which nature has hidden behind riddles and iridescent uncertainties. Perhaps truth is a woman who has reasons for not letting us see her reasons? Perhaps her name is—to speak Greek—*Baubo*?" (GS Preface §4). Here Nietzsche is alluding to the Greek mythological figure of the goddess of mirth and liberated sexuality, often depicted as lifting

[1] Lake Urmia is a lake in northwestern Iran, between the provinces of East Azerbaijan and West Azerbaijan; its location is fitting for the figure of the historical Zarathustra (or Zoroaster), the founder of Zoroastrianism; see Walter Kaufmann's note to GS §342.

[2] For some critics, Parts One to Three of *Zarathustra* constitute a tragedy, with Part Four as a satyr play — a humorous drama performed at the annual Dionysian festival following the performance of three tragedies. (This view is shared by such critics as Matthew Meyer (2025), Douglas Burnham and Martin Jesinghausen (2010), Paul S. Loebe (2010), and Lawrence J. Hatab (2005); Loebe suggests that the idea of the satyr play as a model for Part Four of *Zarathustra* goes back to Eugene Fink's study *Nietzsches Philosophie* of [3]1973, while Meyer traces it back to Karl Knortz's study of 1906, *Nietzsches "Zarathustra": Eine Einführung.*) In *The Birth of Tragedy*, Nietzsche had argued that tragedy was a fusion of Apollonian and Dionysian forces: masked immobile actors speaking words, around which the fast-moving, almost invisible, semianimal satyr chorus whirled.

her skirt and exposing her vulva (a gesture she used to jest with Demeter when the goddess was lamenting the loss of her daughter, Persephone). With the sounds of Strauss's tone poem still ringing in our ears (or in our imagination), and these first three paragraphs in front of us, let us pause for a moment and step back. Why does Zarathustra go and live in a cave in the first place?

In his great work *Höhlenausgänge* (or *Exits from the Cave*) (1989), the German philosopher Hans Blumenberg (1920-96) presented the entirety of the Western philosophical tradition as a series of attempts to find a way out of a cave.[3] The cave in question is, of course, the one in Plato's *Republic*—the cave at the center of an allegory told by Socrates at the beginning of Book 7 (514a-519d) and related to the preceding analogy of the divided line (509d-511e) and the analogy of the sun (507b-509c) in Book 6.[4] Rightly, the famous allegory of the cave is seen by Blumenberg (as it is by, say, Martin Heidegger)[5] as being central to Western metaphysics, and it can be divided into four stages.

The first stage tells the story of a group of human beings in a subterranean cave (514a-515c). In the second stage, Socrates narrates how one of these human beings is liberated within the cave (515c-e). In the third stage, the liberation of this human being continues and, exiting the cave, he accedes to the light (515e-516c).[6] Finally,

[3] Hans Blumenberg, *Höhlenausgänge* (Frankfurt am Main: Suhrkamp, 1989).

[4] See *The Republic of Plato*, ed. and trans. Allan Bloom (New York: Basic Books, 1991). For further discussion, see Arthur Herman, *The Cave and the Light: Plato versus Aristotle and the Struggle for the Soul of Western Civilization* (New York: Random House, 2913); and Paul Bishop, *German Political Thought and the Discourse of Platonism: Finding the Way out of the Cave* (Cham: Palgrave Macmillan, 2019).

[5] Martin Heidegger, *The Essence of Truth: On Plato's Cave Allegory and "Theaetetus"* [1932], trans. Ted Sadler (London and New York: Continuum, 2002; Bloomsbury, 2013); and "On the Essence of Truth: Winter Semester 1933-1934," in *Being and Truth*, trans. Gregory Fried and Richard Polt (Bloomington and Indianapolis, IN: Indiana University Press, 2010), pp. 67-201.

[6] For discussion of the metaphorical and scientific reality of light and its cognitive significance, see Arthur Zajonc, *Catching the Light: The Entwined History of Light and Mind* (New York and Oxford: Oxford University Press, 1993).

a fourth stage follows, for the prisoner, thus liberated, must look back and attempt to return back down into the cave (516c-517b). The goal of this final stage is to attempt the liberation of those who remain in the cave, but it brings with it a great risk for the one who returns—"let them only catch the offender, and they would put him to death":

> This entire allegory, I said, you may now append, dear Glaucon, to the previous argument; the prison-house is the world of sight, the light of the fire is the sun, and you will not misapprehend me if you interpret the journey upwards to be the ascent of the soul into the intellectual world according to my poor belief, which, at your desire, I have expressed whether rightly or wrongly God knows. But, whether true or false, my opinion is that in the world of knowledge the Idea of good appears last of all, and is seen only with an effort; and, when seen, is also inferred to be the universal author of all things beautiful and right, parent of light and of the lord of light in this visible world, and the immediate source of reason and truth in the intellectual; and that this is the power upon which he who would act rationally, either in public or private life must have his eye fixed.
>
> (*The Republic*, 516c-517b; trans. Benjamin Jowett)

As one of the most fundamental texts in the tradition of Western thought, the allegory of the cave can be interpreted in a number of ways: as educational, as epistemological (or metaphysical, or ontological), or as political. How is the allegory of the cave related to two other allegories (or analogies, similes, or metaphors) in

Book 6—the analogy of the sun (507b-509c)[7] and the analogy of the divided line (509d-511e)?[8]

Imagine, says Socrates, a line divided into two uneven segments, giving us a longer segment and a shorter segment. Then, he says, subdivide these segments again in the same proportion, giving us a total of four segments in all in ever-decreasing length. This line, Socrates suggests, provides us with a matrix for classifying the kinds or degrees of knowledge illustrated figuratively in the allegory of the cave. The prisoners see the shadows of objects projected on the wall: this is the realm of images, called the domain of "opinion," or *eikasia*. Next, we have the realm of objects, seen only by the prisoners if they turn their heads around: This realm of objects is the domain of "belief," or *pistis*. In other words, Plato is distinguishing between our perceptions of objects and objects themselves. But at this stage, we are still within the cave: Audaciously, Plato proposes to duplicate this division, only not in the realm of objects and perceptions, but in the realm of the ideal.

In other words, we have to go beyond the knowledge of things and objects and acquire a more abstract kind of understanding, which Plato associates with mathematics: He calls this domain "reflection," or *dianoia*. But we can, he says, go yet further and acquire a kind of intuitive knowledge he calls "insight," or *noësis*: This is the realm of the Platonic Ideas, a realm of pure intellectual forms. Corresponding to these different sorts of objects of knowledge are two fundamentally different kinds of knowing: What the fire is to the realm of the cave ("objective" knowledge), the sun is to the outside realm ("ideal" knowledge). If the fire is the light

[7] See Robert J. Fogelin, "Three Platonic Analogies," *The Philosophical Review*, vol. 80, no. 3 (July 1971), 371-382.

[8] For further discussion, see John Malcolm, "The Line and the Cave," *Phronesis*, vol. 7, no. 1 (1962), 38-45; and "The Cave Revisited," *Classical Quarterly*, vol. 31, no. 1 (1981), 60-68.

that enables us to see the world, then the sun represents what Plato calls the Idea of the Good (507b-509c), which enables us to see the realm of the Ideas (and, on Neoplatonic readings, actually brings everything into being). Hence the keystone in the architecture of Plato's argument in the allegory of the cave is the Idea of the Good.

And it is this idea that Nietzsche apparently completely, utterly, and vehemently opposes. In the quasi-autobiographical work *Ecce Homo* (written 1888; pub. 1908), he puts it thus, indexing this rejection of the idea of the Good to the name of Zarathustra as being "the first who recognised that the optimist is just as degenerate as the pessimist, though perhaps more detrimental":

> "*Good men never speak the truth. False shores and false harbours were ye taught by the good. In the lies of the good were ye born and bred. Through the good everything hath become false and crooked from the roots.*" (EH Why I am a Destiny §4)

And we find cave metaphors elsewhere in Nietzsche's writings, notably, in the third of his *Untimely Meditations*, titled "Schopenhauer as Educator" (1874).

Here Nietzsche talks about how "philosophy offers an asylum to a man into which no tyranny can force its way, the cave of interiority [*die Höhle des Innerlichen*], the labyrinth of the heart" (UM III §3);[9] of how Schopenhauer can, after Kant, be the "leader

[9] Note here the allusion to Goethe (NK, 1/4, pp. 104-105). The profoundly psychoanalytic second version of the poem "To the Moon" (1787-1788) concludes with these two stanzas: "Bliss, to shut the world outside / Though no hate to bear, / And in dear friend confide / And the pleasure share // That, by other men not known / Or not judged aright, / Roams the labyrinthine zone / Of the heart [*das Labyrinth der Brust*] at night" (Goethe, *Selected Poems*, trans. John Whaley (London: Dent, 1998), p. 55; alternatively translated by Christopher Middleton as: "Happy man, that rancor-free / Shows the world his door; / One companion by — and both / In a glow before // Something never guessed by men / Or rejected quite: / Which, in mazes of the breast [*das Labyrinth der Brust*], / Wanders in the night" (Goethe, *Selected*

who leads us up from the caves of sceptical gloom or criticizing renunciation up to the heights of tragic contemplation, to the nocturnal sky and its stars extended endlessly above us, and who was himself the first to take this path" (UM III §3);[10] and of how "solitude," symbolized by the "desert and the cave," is the gift that such a philosopher's fellow human beings will present to him (UM III §3).[11]

In this essay, Nietzsche presents Schopenhauer as a true educator—and true education itself as a kind of liberation. "Culture" (or *Bildung*) is, Nietzsche writes, "liberation" (*Befreiung*), describing this process as the "removal of all the weeds, rubble and vermin that want to attack the tender buds of the plant, an outstreaming of light and warmth, the gentle rustling of nocturnal rain, it is imitation and worship of nature when it deflects her cruel and merciless assaults and turns them to good [...]" (UM III §1). If Schopenhauer as an educator is a liberator, then so is Zarathustra—with the difference that Zarathustra is not only an educator and a liberator; he is also a prophet.

In *Ecce Homo*, Nietzsche complains, "People have never asked me as they should have done, what the name of Zarathustra precisely meant in my mouth, in the mouth of the first immoralist; for that which distinguishes this Persian from all others in the past is the very fact that he was the exact reverse of an immoralist" (EH Why I Am a Destiny §3). Here, Nietzsche acknowledges that there *was* a historical figure called Zarathustra (or Zoroaster), as indeed there was: an ancient prophet from Persia (or what is now called Iran), who lived for an unknown period in the second millennium B.C.E., sometimes dated between 1500 and 500 B.C.E. The historical Zoroaster was the founder of Zoroastrianism, a religion that is

Poems, ed. Christopher Middleton [Goethe Edition, vol. 1] (Boston: Suhrkamp/Insel, 1983), p. 65).

[10] See NK, 1/4, pp. 110-112.

[11] See NK, 1/4, p. 120.

currently in decline and has all but disappeared from the area where it flourished, ancient Persia (or modern-day Iran).[12] (In 2020, the BBC World Service reported on how some young Zoroastrians were trying to find partners of the same faith against the background of a decline in believers.)[13]

In 19th-century Germany, the legacy of Zoroaster was being actively researched and investigated,[14] and Nietzsche would undoubtedly have been aware of this. However, in *Ecce Homo,* he sees the intellectual-historical achievement of Zoroaster as residing in one specific idea:

> Zarathustra was the first to see in the struggle between good and evil the essential wheel in the working of things. The translation of morality into the realm of metaphysics, as force, cause, end-in-itself, is his work. But the very question suggests its own answer. Zarathustra created this most portentous of all errors, — morality; therefore he must be the first to expose it. [...] Have I made myself clear? ... The overcoming of morality by itself, through truthfulness, the moralist's overcoming of himself in his opposite — in me — that is what the name Zarathustra means in my mouth. (EH Why I am a Destiny §3)

Elsewhere, Nietzsche is equally trenchant in his rejection of "idealism"; in *Twilight of the Idols*, for instance, he singles out the

[12] For further discussion, see Françoise Dastur, "Who is Nietzsche's Zarathustra? A Note on the Iranian-Persian Background," *Comparative and Continental Philosophy*, vol. 1, no. 1 (2009), 39-54.
[13] "Looking for Love: The Zoroastrian Way," *The Documentary*, BBC World Service, broadcast 20 September 2020.
[14] See Michael Stausberg, *Faszination Zarathushtra: Zoroaster und die Europäische Religionsgeschichte der Frühen Neuzeit*, 2 vols. (Berlin and New York: de Gruyter, 1998).

Athenian historian Thucydides (the author of the *History of the Peloponnesian War*) for particular praise, contrasting him to—ah! that name again—Plato as follows:

> My recreation, my predilection, my cure, after all Platonism, has always been Thucydides. Thucydides and perhaps Machiavelli's *principe* are most closely related to me owing to the absolute determination which they show of refusing to deceive themselves and of seeing reason in *reality*, — not in "rationality," and still less in "morality." [...] Greek philosophy is the decadence of the Greek instinct: Thucydides is the great summing up, the final manifestation of that strong, severe positivism which lay in the instincts of the ancient Hellene. After all, it is courage in the face of reality that distinguishes such natures as Thucydides from Plato: Plato is a coward in the face of reality — consequently he takes refuge in the ideal: Thucydides is master of himself, — consequently he is able to master life. (TI What I Owe to the Ancients §2)

Hence, by reviving the figure of the historical Zoroaster and overcoming his ideology through the words of his own literary figure of Zarathustra, Nietzsche seeks to bring about nothing less than a world-historical change, which promises to split the history of the world in two.

For in a letter of 4 October 1888, Nietzsche told Malwida von Meysenbug (1816-1903) that the "first book of my *Revaluation of All Values*"—by which he means the work known as *The Anti-Christ* — "is finished," describing it as the "great philosophical event of all times, with which the history of humankind will be broken into two halves ..." (KSB 8, 447).[15] In his letter to Paul Deussen (1845-1919) of 26 November 1888, he made remarkable claims for himself—"My life is now reaching its culmination: another couple of years, and the earth will tremble from a great lighning bolt. I swear to you that I have the power to change the *calendar*. There is nothing in existence today that will not be toppled, I am more dynamite than human being"—and for *The Anti-Christ*: "My *Revaluation of All Values*, with the main title '*The Antichrist*,' is finished. In the next two years I shall have to take steps to get the work translated into 7 languages; the *first* edition in each language circa one million copies" (KSB 8, 491-492). And in a letter to the Danish scholar and critic Georg Brandes (1842-1917) (a letter that has only survived in draft form), Nietzsche repeated his lines about splitting the history of the world into two, marking the beginning of a new calendar, and being dynamite; described the work as a "*deathblow* against *Christianity*" and as a "*judgment on the world*," albeit one over which is said to lie "a grandiose calm and sense of elevation" (KSB 8, 500-502). And Nietzsche claims that he will do this by ushering in a *transformation*—of what kind, we have yet to see.

Zarathustra's cave is both an echo of Plato's cave in *The Republic* and its inversion: for *this* cave is, after all, at the top of a mountain! Whereas Plato's cave is a place of ignorance located deep in the bowels of the earth, Zarathustra's cave is a place of enlightenment, situated on a high point of the earth's surface; whereas Plato's sun is an image of the absolutely transcendent Good, Zarathustra's sun is so immanent that it depends for its "happiness" (*Glück*) on Zarathustra and his animals.[16] Not surprisingly,

[15] For a recent discussion of these late works, see Heinrich Meier, *Nietzsche's Legacy: "Ecce Homo" and "The Antichrist," Two Books on Nature and Politics* [2019], trans. Justin Gottschalk (Chicago and London: University of Chicago Press, 2024).
[16] Graham Parkes, *Composing the Soul: Reaches of Nietzsche's Psychology* (Chicago and London: University of Chicago Press, 1994), pp. 131-132.

therefore, Martin Heidegger (1889-1976) approved of Nietzsche's description of his philosophy as "inverted Platonism" (*umgedrehter Platonismus*), while suggesting that this inversion (*Umdrehung*) was in fact more of a "twisting free" (*Herausdrehung*).[17]

Indeed, in the opening Prologue, Zarathustra makes so bold as to address the sun directly: In this anti-Platonic, post-Copernican universe, it is the human being, not the sun, that is at the center of things! As we shall see, the cyclical course of the sun structures the entire work: from the sunrise of the Prologue and the concluding chapter of Part One, via such chapters as "Before Sunrise," "At Midday," and "The Night-Wanderer Song," to the final chapter at the end of Part Four. Throughout the text, Zarathustra hails the advent of what he calls the "great midday" (*der große Mittag*).

But the echoes of the opening Prologue are not only Platonic. We are told that Zarathustra had decided to leave his home and its lake and to head for the mountains when he was 30 years old—that is, at about the same age when Christ is said to have gone into the desert to be tempted by Satan prior to beginning his ministry (Matthew 4:2, Mark 1:13, Luke 4:2). Whereas Christ went into the Judean desert to fast for a symbolic period of 40 days and 40 nights (anticipating the 40 days of the period between his Resurrection and his Ascension [Acts 1:3]), Zarathustra goes up the mountain and into his cave for—10 years! Whereas Christ's period in the

---

[17] "My philosophy is an *inverted Platonism*: the further something is from true being, the purer, the more beautiful, the better it is. Living in illusion as the goal" (KSA 7, 7[156], 199; Friedrich Nietzsche, *Writings from the Early Notebooks*, ed. Raymond Geuss and Alexander Nehamas, trans. Ladislaus Löb (Cambridge: Cambridge University Press, 2009), p. 52); see "Nietzsche's Overcoming of Platonism," in Martin Heidegger, *Nietzsche*, vols. 1 and 2, trans. David Farrell Krell (San Francisco: Harper & Row, 1979), vol. 1, *The Will to Power as Art*, pp. 200-210; cf. WP §572 = KSA 12, 7[2], 253. On Heidegger's use of the more complex term *Herausdrehung* ("twisting free"), which implies the inversion is a first move, followed by a subsequent twist onto another level of discourse, see John Sallis, *Crossings: Nietzsche and the Space of Tragedy* (Chicago and London: University of Chicago Press, 1991), pp. 2-4; cited in Parkes, *Composing the Soul*, p. 132.

desert was a time of fasting and temptation, we are told that on the mountain Zarathustra "enjoyed his spirit and solitude, and [...] did not weary of it." And whereas Christ's period in the desert was a prelude to revealing what He was (and what He had been from all eternity), that is, the Son of God, the 10 years Zarathustra spends on the mountain are the prelude to a moment of *transformation*: "But at last his heart changed" (*Endlich aber verwandelte sich sein Herz*). What does Zarathustra have to say to the sun?

> Thou great star! What would be thy happiness if thou hadst not those for whom thou shinest!
>
> For ten years hast thou climbed hither unto my cave: thou wouldst have wearied of thy light and of the journey, had it not been for me, mine eagle, and my serpent.
>
> But we awaited thee every morning, took from thee thine overflow and blessed thee for it. (Z Prologue §1)

In this address to the sun, Zarathustra foregrounds the theme of "happiness" (*Glück*), attributing the source of the sun's happiness to himself and his animals. In this exclamation, we can hear an echo (and an inversion) of words spoken by Goethe in his essay on Winckelmann—a passage which also sets out the ideal toward which Nietzsche's Zarathustra will be striving:

> When the healthy nature of man functions as a totality, when he feels himself in the world as in a vast, beautiful, worthy, and valued whole, when a harmonious sense of well-being affords him pure and free delight — then the universe, if it were capable of sensation, would exult at having reached its goal, and marvel at the culmination of its own development and being. For what is the use of all the expenditure of suns and planets and moons, of

> stars and galaxies, of comets and nebulae, of completed and developing worlds, if at the end a happy man does not unconsciously rejoice in existence?[18]

And there is another echo and another inversion—for Nietzsche, philosophy is an invitation to us to rejoice *consciously* in our existence.

Up on his mountain, Zarathustra has not been entirely alone. He is accompanied, as he is at crucial moments elsewhere in the work, by his two animals: his eagle and his serpent. Behind these animals lies a rich iconographical tradition: a tradition of emblems and alchemical symbols.[19] In biblical terms, the serpent plays a critical role in the story of Genesis (and in the Book of Revelation) as a symbol of evil, but it also represents (as in the case of the serpent of bronze [Numbers 21:4-9]) the power of salvation; and in the case of *The Red Book*, the serpent is an important symbol of the creative energies of the unconscious (see CW 9/i §291, §293, §386, §402).[20] The eagle is one of the attributes of St. John the Evangelist, and it represents one of the four creatures symbolizing the Evangelists (that is, the angel for St. Matthew, the lion for St. Mark, the ox for St. Luke, and the eagle for St. John) that are described as surrounding God's throne in the Book of Revelation (see 4:7).

[18] Goethe, "Winckelmann" [1805], trans. by H.B. Nisbet, in H.B. Nisbet (ed.), *German Aesthetic and Literary Criticism: Winckelmann, Lessing, Hamann, Herder, Schiller, Goethe* (Cambridge: Cambridge University Press, 1985), pp. 236-258 (pp. 237-238).

[19] David S. Thatcher, "Eagle and Serpent in *Zarathustra*," *Nietzsche-Studien*, 6 (1977), 240-260.

[20] For further discussion of the symbol of the serpent, see Hans Leisegang, "The Mystery of the Serpent," trans. Ralph Manheim, in *The Mysteries* [*Papers from the Eranos Yearbooks*, vol. 2], ed. Joseph Campbell (Princeton, NJ: Princeton University Press, 1955), pp. 194-260; and, most recently, Andrei A. Orlov, *Supernal Serpent: Mysteries of Leviathan in Judaism and Christianity* (Oxford: Oxford University Press, 2023); and Jordan B. Peterson, *We Who Wrestle With God: Perceptions of the Divine* (London: Allen Lane, 2024), pp. 59-64 and 445-453.

Perhaps a clue to their significance lies closer to home and is more intuitive though; and it is the interpretation offered by Jung in his seminar on Nietzsche's *Zarathustra*.[21] For Jung, the serpent represents the body, being an "age-old representative of the lower worlds, of the belly with its contents and the intestines," and it functions as a "personification of whatever comes from the body, sexuality and every vital physical function" (SNZ, 18); in short, everything that is *chthonic*. (In his seminars on dream analysis (1928-1930) Jung explains that "these cold-blooded relics [serpents, snakes, crocodiles, etc.] are, in a way, uncanny powers, because they symbolize the fundamental factors of our instinctive life, dating from Paleozoic times," and "so whenever life means business, when things are getting serious, you are likely to find a saurian on the way." When benevolent, this saurian is a "tremendous force of organized instinct and pushes you over an obstacle which you would not believe possible to climb over by will-power or conscious decision" and "there the animal proves to be helpful."[22] In short, the saurian brings to light the contents of the unconscious in a way that enables us to move forward.)[23] Can we hear an echo here of Nietzsche's aphorism in *Human, All-Too-Human*, entitled "Condition for heroism": "If a man wants to become a hero, the serpent must first have become a dragon: otherwise he will lack his proper enemy" (HA I §498)?[24]

[21] In this chapter, I shall draw in part on Jung's seminar on Nietzsche's *Zarathustra*, while leaving a fuller discussion of this seminar for another study to be titled *Jung's Seminar on Nietzsche's "Zarathustra": Birth of an Archetypal Hermeneutics*. But I shall also draw on interpretative works by Graham Parkes, *Composing the Soul*; Laurence Lampert, *Nietzsche's Teaching*; and Gary Shapiro, *Nietzschean Narratives*, as well as on the two volumes in the *Nietzsche-Kommentar* series by Katharina Grätz.

[22] C.G. Jung, *Dream Analysis: Notes of the Seminar given in 1928-1930*, ed. William McGuire (London: Routledge & Kegan Paul, 1984), pp. 645-646.

[23] "The contents of all the early manifestations of religion came, not from the mind, but from the sympathetic system. And it is the saurian, the original worm, that brings up the contents of the unconscious" (Jung, *Dream Analysis*, p. 334).

[24] I am grateful to Keith Ansell Pearson for drawing my attention to this aphorism.

By contrast, the eagle represents the spirit: it "soars high, it is near the sun," and as the "bird of light" it is the "very high thought, the great enthusiasm," symbolized in Greek legend by the story of Ganymede — who is abducted by an eagle from Mount Ida near Troy (where he had been tending sheep) and transported to Mount Olympus to serve as the cup-bearer to Zeus;[25] in contrast to the serpent, it is a "spiritual, uplifting power" (SNZ, 18). It is important that Zarathustra's animals appear *together*: the earth and the sky, the chthonic and the etherial, the vertical and the horizontal, must be thought of as belonging *together*, just as the figure of Dionysos brings together the wisdom of the serpent and the pride of the eagle.[26] (Compare with Heidegger's notion of the Fourfold (*das Geviert*), that is, the "gathering" of earth, sky, gods, and mortals.)[27] Every day Zarathustra, accompanied by his serpent and his eagle, awaits the sun, receives its "excess" (*Überfluss*), and blesses it:

> Lo! I am weary of my wisdom, like the bee that hath gathered too much honey; I need hands outstretched to take it.
>
> I would fain bestow and distribute, until the wise have once more become joyous in their folly, and the poor happy in their riches.
>
> Therefore must I descend into the deep: as thou doest in the evening, when thou goest behind the sea, and givest light also to the nether-world, thou exuberant star!

[25] "[G]odlike Ganymedes / […] was the loveliest born of the race of mortals, and therefore / the gods caught him away to themselves, to be Zeus' wine-pourer, / for the sake of his beauty, so he might be among the immortals" (Homer, *Iliad*, Book 22, ll. 233-235; in *The Iliad of Homer*, trans. Richmond Lattimore (Chicago and London: University of Chicago Press, 1961), p. 410); cf. Virgil, *Aeneid*, Book 5, ll. 250-260.

[26] Parkes, *Composing the Soul*, p. 361.

[27] For further discussion, see Andrew J. Mitchell, "The fourfold," in Bret W. Davis (ed.), *Martin Heidegger: Key Concepts* (Durham: Acumen, 2010), pp. 208-218; and "The fourfold," in François Raffoul and Eric S. Nelson (eds.), *The Bloomsbury Companion to Heidegger* (London: Bloomsbury, 2016), pp. 297-302.

> Like thee must I GO DOWN, as men say, to whom I shall descend. (Z Prologue 1)

In fact, the language of the first section of Prologue is saturated with images of excess and overflow. Just as Socrates in *The Republic* ascribes the power of vision to the "overflow from the sun's treasury" and describes the eye as the "most sunlike of organs" (508b), so Zarathustra talks about the sun's "overflow" (*Überfluss*) and addresses it as "thou exuberant star" (*du überreiches Gestirn*) and as "thou tranquil eye" (*du ruhiges Auge*).[28]

Subsequently, this imagery of excess is transferred from the visual and the luminous to the haptic and the gustatory: Zarathustra says that he has become overwise, like a bee that has collected too much honey. This apian aspect recalls Plato's image in the *Ion* of poets as bees gathering honey from the gardens of the Muses (534a-b),[29] while honey itself is one of the fluids with which Dionysos is associated (along with sap, milk, semen, blood, and wine).[30] The point about *this* wisdom and about *this* honey is that Zarathustra wants to *share* it; and, in order to do so, Zarathustra must imitate the sun in respect of its solar journey — and descend.

As well as echoing the descent of the sun, the motif of *Untergang* has other resonances as well. In Plato's *Republic*, Socrates's first words talk about him "going down" to the Piraeus (327a), and further on he commands his listeners, "you must go down" (520b-d).[31] In the image of the *Untergang*, at least three ideas merge: (a) to set like the sun does, (b) to go down from the mountain, and (c) to descend to the underworld. (In this third

[28] Parkes, *Composing the Soul*, p. 412.

[29] Parkes, *Composing the Soul*, p. 412.

[30] Plutarch, *De Iside et Osiride*, §35; cited in Parkes, *Composing the Soul*, p. 412.

[31] Socrates's descent in Book 1 and his injunction to Glaucon and Adeimantus in Book 7 of the *Republic* anticipate and echo the motif of ascent and descent in the allegory of the cave.

and final sense, to go down is to perform a kind of κατάβασις or *katábasis*.)[32] But Zarathustra goes further:

> Bless me, then, thou tranquil eye, that canst behold even the greatest happiness without envy!
>
> Bless the cup that is about to overflow, that the water may flow golden out of it, and carry everywhere the reflection of thy bliss!
>
> Lo! This cup is again going to empty itself, and Zarathustra is again going to be a man. (Z Prologue §1)

The image of the cup emptying itself recalls the Christian theological notion of "kenosis" (derived from the κένωσις, *kénōsis*, i.e., the act of emptying), or the "self-emptying" by means of which Christ, in the incarnation, divested himself of his divine nature and by means of which believers "empty" themselves or their individual will and instead embrace the divine will of God. This "self-emptying" of Christ is reflected in the words of St. Paul in a passage in his letter to the Philippians (sung every Sunday at First Vespers): "[Christ Jesus] debased himself, taking the form of a servant, being made to the likeness of men, and in shape found as a man" (cf. Philippians 2:7; DRV).

In his commentary on this verse, Haydock interprets the line as meaning that Jesus "divested himself of all the marks of greatness" and that the Greek text signifies *he made himself void*.[33] A more modern translation, the NJB, translates the verse as, "But he emptied himself, taking the form of a slave, becoming as human beings are," although it suggests that the "traditional"

[32] For further discussion, see Gunnel Ekroth and Ingela Nilsson (eds.), *Round Trip to Hades in the Eastern Mediterranean Tradition: Visits to the Underworld from Antiquity to Byzantium* (Leiden and Boston: Brill, 2018); and Paul Bishop, Terence Dawson, and Leslie Gardner (eds.), *The Descent of the Soul and the Archaic: Katábasis and Depth Psychology* (London and New York: Routledge, 2023).
[33] Haydock, 1551.

interpretation, viz., that "this emptying or *kenosis* expressed Jesus' voluntary self-deprivation, during his earthly life, of the divine glory," is "less probable."[34] And another modern Catholic study Bible, in its commentary on this verse, refers the reader to St. Gregory of Nyssa's treatise *Against Apollinarius* (and its critique of the Christological teaching of Apollinarius of Laodicaea) and to §472 of the *Catechism of the Catholic Church*.[35]

(By contrast, in Gnosticism, Christ never loses his divinity, reflected in the episode in the *Pistis Sophia*, Book 1, Chapter 6, where Jesus "drew to himself the glory of his light," withdrawing his own luminosity into himself so as no longer to dazzle his disciples.)[36] In the context of the Prologue, however, Zarathustra is not so much emptying himself of his will as assuming the task of sharing his wisdom: and, in a striking echo of the doctrine of incarnation, Zarathustra says that he wants to embark again on his *Menschwerdung* (i.e., becoming human). The logic here must surely be that, in order to preach the *Über-mensch*, Zarathustra must return to being a *Mensch*—including opening himself up to his final sin, the sin of *pity*.[37]

---

[34] NJB, NT, 1941. An Orthodox commentary on this passage insists that it "deals with the Son's will, not His nature," arguing: "He emptied Himself not by laying down His divine nature or setting it aside, but by voluntarily taking on our human nature" (*The Orthodox Study Bible*, ed. Jack Norman Sparks, et al. (Nashville, TN: Nelson, 2008), p. 1613).

[35] *The Ignatius Catholic Study Bible*, ed. Scott Hahn and Curtis J. Mitch (eds.) (San Francisco: Ignatius Press, 2024), p. 2097; and *Catechism of the Catholic Church* (New York: Doubleday, 1995), §472.

[36] *Pistis Sophia*, trans. G.R.S. Mead, Book 1, Chapter 6. Available online: http://www.sacred-texts.com/chr/ps/ps010.htm (p. 6); cf. Violet McDermot, *The Fall of Sophia: A Gnostic Text on the Redemption of Universal Consciousness* (Great Barrington, MA: Lindisfarne Books, 2001), p. 105.

[37] See "The Cry of Distress":

> "[...] My last sin which hath been reserved for me, — knowest thou what it is called?"
>
> — "PITY!" answered the soothsayer from an overflowing heart, and raised both his hands aloft — "O Zarathustra, I have come that I may seduce thee to thy last sin!" — (Z IV 2).

Yet for all this talk about excess and *Untergang*, self-emptying cups and outstretched hands, there is an emphasis on what one can only call **beauty**: Zarathustra imagines that the water about to flow out of the cup will "flow golden [...], and carry everywhere the reflection of thy bliss" — the word *Abglanz* here recalling the words from *Faust II*, *Am farbigen Abglanz haben wir das Leben* ("Life in the many-hued, reflected splendour") (l. 4727). The context of this line in *Faust II*, the opening scene of Act 1, where Faust is refreshed by the forces of nature, sounds the motif of transformation that we find at the beginning of *Zarathustra* when Zarathustra's heart is transformed. Thus "begins" Zarathustra's descent or *Untergang*, a descent that is not concluded until Chapter 13 of Part Three, "The Convalescent" (§2).

This theme of transformation is soon sounded again when, in §2 of the Prologue, Zarathustra descends from his mountain. Entering the forest, he meets an elderly hermit, who recognizes Zarathustra as the wanderer he had passed many years ago. He recognizes him as Zarathustra—*and* that he is transformed: "but he hath altered" (*aber er hat sich verwandelt*). On that earlier occasion, Zarathustra had been carrying his ashes to the mountain (a strange phrase that occurs elsewhere in this work; see Z I 3 and Z III 1), and the hermit asks him: "Wilt thou now carry thy fire into the valleys? Fearest thou not the incendiary's doom?"[38] Rather than carrying his ashes, it seems that Zarathustra has, phoenix-like, risen from them, and is intent on spreading his incendiary presence among those living at the foot of his mountain.

(Commenting on this line in his seminar, Jung suggests that "when a man consists of ashes he is a disembodied spirit," and so

[38] Francesca Cauchi suggests that carrying his "ashes to the mountains" is a metaphor, signaling Zarathustra's "*Untergang* status, namely his having burned himself/his former metaphysical comforts in his own flame" (*Zarathustra's Moral Tyranny: Spectres of Kant, Hegel and Feuerbach* (Edinburgh: Edinburgh University Press, 2022), p. 146).

Christianity "only knows of Zarathustra as a being that has gone forever; he is dead, he has carried his ashes to the mountains." If this same spirit "recognizes Zarathustra coming back rejuvenated," this suggests that Christianity now "recognizes that Zarathustra has returned and is going the opposite way, coming down from the mountains" — meaning that Zarathustra is "being incarnated again" and is "becoming modern again" [SNZ, vol. 1, 34]. Zarathustra has become "rejuvenated"; he has become *transformed.*) And the old hermit continues: "Altered [*Verwandelt*] is Zarathustra; a child hath Zarathustra become; an awakened one [*ein Erwachter*] is Zarathustra: what wilt thou do in the land of the sleepers?" The reference to the child anticipates the chapter "Of the Three Transformations," in which the Child represents the third and final transformation (see below, pp. 69-74); and the reference to the awakened one anticipates the chapter "Of the Despisers of the Body," where "the awakened one, the knowing one, saith: 'Body am I entirely, and nothing more; and soul is only the name of something in the body'" (Z I 4).

Zarathustra tells the hermit that he "loves" humankind, and that he is "bringing gifts" for them,[39] but the hermit replies that *he* does *not* love human beings and that *he* loves God instead. In fact, the hermit advises Zarathustra to give nothing to human beings and to remain in the forest; when asked what he does all day, the hermit replies, "I make hymns and sing them; and in making hymns I laugh and weep and mumble: thus do I praise God. With singing, weeping, laughing, and mumbling do I praise the God who is my God" (echoing Psalm 63:1). When the two men finally part, they do so good-naturedly and on friendly terms, "laughing like two schoolboys." But when Zarathustra is alone, he says "to his heart," as if making an aside remark on the stage to an audience: "Could it be possible! This old saint in the forest hath not yet heard of it, that GOD IS DEAD!" (Z Prologue §2). Thus Nietzsche, in a surprisingly

[39] In fact, one of his later discourses is called "Of the Gift-Giving Virtue" (Z I 22)!

casual way, introduces the theme of the death of God, not in the form of an argument, but in the form of a presupposition that is to be taken for granted.[40]

The death of God is first announced in the previous work, before *Thus Spoke Zarathustra* called *The Gay Science*. In section 125 of this work, we find the famous parable of the madman who proclaims that God is dead:

> Have you ever heard of the madman who on a bright morning lighted a lantern and ran to the market-place calling out unceasingly: "I seek God! I seek God!" As there were many people standing about who did not believe in God, he caused a great deal of amusement. Why? is he lost? said one. Has he strayed away like a child? said another. Or does he keep himself hidden? Is he afraid of us? Has he taken a sea voyage? Has he emigrated? — the people cried out laughingly, all in a hubbub. The insane man jumped into their midst and transfixed them with his glances. "Where is God gone?" he called out. "I mean to tell you! We have killed him, you and I! We are all his murderers! [...] God is dead! God remains dead! And we have killed him! How shall we console ourselves, the most murderous of all murderers? The holiest and the mightiest that the world has hitherto possessed, has bled to death under our knife — who will wipe the blood from us? With what water could we cleanse ourselves? What lustrums, what sacred games shall we have to devise? Is not the

[40] For further discussion of this dramatic declaration and its implications, see A.N. Wilson, *God's Funeral* (London: Murray, 1999); Julian Young, *The Death of God and the Meaning of Life* (London and New York: Routledge, 2003); and Ronald E. Osborn, *Humanism and the Death of God: Searching for the Good After Darwin, Marx, and Nietzsche* (Oxford: Oxford University Press, 2017).

> magnitude of this deed too great for us? Shall we not ourselves have to become Gods, merely to seem worthy of it? There never was a greater event — and on account of it, all who are born after us belong to a higher history than any history hitherto!" […] It is further stated that the madman made his way into different churches on the same day, and there intoned his *Requiem aeternam deo*. When led out and called to account, he always gave the reply: "What are these churches now, if they are not the tombs and monuments of God?" (GS §125)

It is significant that the message of this dramatic text is not simply an atheist one, that is, that God does not exist; rather, it is that God is *dead*, and that *we* have *killed* him.[41] (In this respect, the passage is not so much directed at believers, but at the atheists, who have failed to use this opportunity to make a gesture as grand as "drinking up the sea.")[42] Is, in other words, Nietzsche saying that it is simply the case that, in terms of belief and practice, human beings in the West have "killed" God—that is, as a matter of *fact* they have ceased to believe? And that they have failed to grasp the consequences of this failure of belief?

At different points in *Zarathustra,* various causes are proposed for the death of God. First, in "Of the Pitiful" in Part Two, God is said to have died of his pity for humankind. Here, the Devil is recorded as having once told Zarathustra, "Even God hath his hell:

[41] For a view that Nietzsche's parable draws on the philosophical tradition of Cynicism and has less to do with atheism than with human existential concerns, see the insightful article by Charles Bambach titled "Nietzsche's Madman Parable: A Cynical Reading," *American Catholic Philosophical Quarterly*, vol. 84, no. 2 (Spring 2010), 441-456.

[42] See Bertrand Vergely, *Notre vie a un sens!* (Paris: Albin Michel, 2019), p. 196. For further discussion, see Paul Bishop, *Discourses of Philology and Theology in Nietzsche: From the "Untimelies" to The Anti-Christ* (Cham: Palgrave Macmillan, 2023), and *Nietzsche's Writing Against Religion and the Crisis of Faith: Twentieth-Century Reactions and Responses* (Cham: Palgrave Macmillan, 2024).

it is his love for man," and "God is dead: of his pity for man hath God died" (Z II 3). This thesis is confirmed later on in Part Four in "Out of Service," where the last pope tells Zarathustra:

> "[...] When he was young, that God out of the Orient, then was he harsh and revengeful, and built himself a hell for the delight of his favourites.
>
> At last, however, he became old and soft and mellow and pitiful, more like a grandfather than a father, but most like a tottering old grandmother.
>
> There did he sit shrivelled in his chimney-corner, fretting on account of his weak legs, world-weary, will-weary, and one day he suffocated of his all-too-great pity." (Z IV 6)

Second, in "Of the Apostates" in Part Three, the monotheistic God of Judeo-Christianity is said to have been laughed to death by all the other gods:

> With the old Deities hath it long since come to an end: — and verily, a good joyful Deity-end had they!
>
> They did not "begloom" themselves to death—that do people fabricate! On the contrary, they — LAUGHED themselves to death once on a time!
>
> That took place when the unGodliest utterance came from a God himself—the utterance: "There is but one God! Thou shalt have no other Gods before me!" —
>
> — An old grim-beard of a God, a jealous one, forgot himself in such wise: —
>
> And all the Gods then laughed, and shook upon their thrones, and exclaimed: "Is it not just divinity that there are Gods, but no God?" (Z III 8)

And third, in "The Ugliest Man" in Part Four, God is said to have been killed by the Ugliest Man himself, whom Zarathustra recognizes as the "murderer of God":

> […] From the ground a noise welled up, gurgling and rattling, as water gurgleth and rattleth at night through stopped-up water-pipes; and at last it turned into human voice and human speech: — it sounded thus:
>
> "Zarathustra! Zarathustra! Read my riddle! Say, say! WHAT IS THE REVENGE ON THE WITNESS?
>
> […]
>
> Thou thinkest thyself wise, thou proud Zara-thustra! Read then the riddle, thou hard nut-cracker, — the riddle that I am! Say then: who am *I*!"
>
> — When however Zarathustra had heard these words,—what think ye then took place in his soul? PITY OVERCAME HIM; and he sank down all at once, like an oak that hath long withstood many tree-fellers, — heavily, suddenly, to the terror even of those who meant to fell it. But immediately he got up again from the ground, and his countenance became stern.
>
> "I know thee well," said he, with a brazen voice, "THOU ART THE MURDERER OF GOD! Let me go.
>
> Thou couldst not ENDURE him who beheld THEE, — who ever beheld thee through and through, thou ugliest man. Thou tookest revenge on this witness!" (Z IV 7)

Whatever the reason for the death of God, this death is taken as the starting point of *Zarathustra*, not as an outcome from narrative or its argumentational logic. In turn, Jung will respond to this claim in his *Red Book* in the episode in *Scrutinies* (or "Prüfungen") when

ΦΙΛΗΜΩΝ stands beside Jung and the dead draw near, lining the walls and crying out, "We want to know about God. Where is God? Is God dead?" (RB, 515). In response, ΦΙΛΗΜΩΝ rises and utters the words that constitute the beginning of the second of the *VII Sermones ad mortuos*, "God is not dead. He is as alive as ever" (*Gott ist nicht tot, er ist so lebendig wie je*) (RB, 516). In this way, Jung reverses the announcement of the death of God, exploiting a loophole in the following logic from "On the Blissful Islands":

> Once did people say God, when they looked out upon distant seas; now, however, have I taught you to say, Superman.
>
> God is a conjecture: but I do not wish your conjecturing to reach beyond your creating will.
>
> Could ye CREATE a God? — Then, I pray you, be silent about all Gods! But ye could well create the Superman.
>
> Not perhaps ye yourselves, my brethren! But into fathers and forefathers of the Superman could ye transform yourselves: and let that be your best creating! —
>
> God is a conjecture: but I should like your conjecturing restricted to the conceivable.
>
> Could ye CONCEIVE a God? — But let this mean Will to Truth unto you, that everything be transformed into the humanly conceivable, the humanly visible, the humanly sensible! Your own discernment shall ye follow out to the end!
>
> And what ye have called the world shall but be created by you: your reason, your likeness, your will, your love, shall it itself become! And verily, for your bliss, ye discerning ones!

> And how would ye endure life without that hope, ye discerning ones? Neither in the inconceivable could ye have been born, nor in the irrational.
>
> But that I may reveal my heart entirely unto you, my friends: IF there were gods, how could I endure it to be no God! THEREFORE there are no Gods.
>
> Yea, I have drawn the conclusion; now, however, doth it draw me. — (Z II 1)

In "First Day" in *Liber Secundus* in *The Red Book*, Jung phrases this point a different way: in his language, "our God is sick"; indeed, "we have seen him dead with the venomous gaze of the Basilisk on his face, and we have understood that he is dead" (RB, 291). And yet — not *quite* dead, because "we must think of his healing," and by reducing Izdubar to the size of an egg, Jung is able to undertake this healing, declaring in "Second Day" that "my God found salvation" (RB, 291 and 295). The nature of this healing and this salvation will be discussed further in Volume 4 in this series.

After leaving the forest and its hermit, Zarathustra comes to the nearby town, where he finds the people gathered in the marketplace, awaiting a performance by a rope dancer. This setting is significant; for, after all, these days the market is everything! Zarathustra is going to bring his teachings, not just to the "marketplace of ideas," but to the very emblem of modern, secular life—its commercial center: the market. The other side of modern, secular life is, of course, the world of mass entertainment, symbolized here by the rope dancer. Economic activity and the organized fun ethic—talk about "bread and circuses"! This is the world—*our* world—which Zarathustra will seek to acquaint with his teachings: How will he get on?

In fact, the theme of communication is an important one within Nietzsche's writings in general and within *Thus Spoke Zarathustra* in particular; "it should have *sung*, this 'new soul'—

and not spoken!" as Nietzsche ruefully put it, looking back on his first book, *The Birth of Tragedy* (1872), in his "Attempt at a Self-Criticism" in 1866. The poet Stefan George (1868-1933) was to pick up on this line in his poem entitled "Nietzsche,"[43] and one of Nietzsche's greatest readers, Martin Heidegger, once wrote:

> [A] man who teaches must at times grow noisy. In fact, he may have to scream and scream, although his aim is to make his students learn so quiet a thing as thinking. Nietzsche, most quiet and shiest of men, knew of this necessity. He endured the agony of having to scream. In a decade when the world at large still knew nothing of world wars, when faith in "progress" was viritually *the* religion of the civilized peoples and nations, Nietzsche screamed out into the world: "The wasteland grows …".[44]

This theme of communication is one that can be found in Jung as well. In a letter of 3 February 1933 to E. Sabott, Jung compared himself to the pre-Socratic philosopher Heraclitus, who was dubbed "the Obscure"; time and again, Jung complained, he had had the "unfortunate experience—which also befell my illustrious predecessor Heraclitus—of being named 'the Dark'" and that, as a consequence, he had got used to thinking that either his views or

---

[43] "Nietzsche," in *The Works of Stefan George rendered into English*, trans. Olga Marx and Ernst Morwitz (Chapel Hill, NC: University of North Carolina, 1949), p. 159. For further discussion, see Paul Bishop, "Nietzsche aus der Sicht Stefan Georges: Ein Horizont, vor dem ein Licht aufgeht?", in Jutta Georg, Renate Reschke, and Vivetta Vivaretti (eds.), *Nietzsche im Horizont der Literatur* (Leiden: Brill; Fink, 2022), pp. 61-79.

[44] Martin Heidegger, *What Is Called Thinking?* [1951/1952], trans. J. Glenn Gray (New York: Harper & Row, 1968), pp. 48-49; cf. "The Desert Grows: Woe to Him, Who Harbours Deserts," in Friedrich Nietzsche, *Dithyrambs of Dionysus: Bi-Lingual Edition*, trans. R.J. Hollingdale (London: Anvil Press Poetry, 1984), pp. 28-37.

his style "must be so involved that they confront ordinary so-called commonsense with insoluble riddles" (L1, 116).

In the context of discussing the intellectual development (or lack of it) of an unidentified colleague in Berlin, Jung went on to articulate the principle that "where there are teachers there must also be students," and that "all learning was originally imitation" (L1, 116). These two facts had, Jung argued, three important consequences. First, that "it is not always indolence on the part of the student if he renounces his individuality and effaces himself in favour of the *verbum magistri*," that is, the word of the master. Second, that without such followers, "the voice of the teacher would be too weak to be heard above the hubbub of the crowd." So third (and finally), that "*many must repeat the bare word even though this repetition is not a new birth sprung from the heart*" (L1, 117; my italics). Thus, for every Goethe, Jung concluded, there had to be an Eckermann — "to cite a famous example (no presumption intended)," he added (L1, 117). This is almost exactly the reverse of the notion of discipleship espoused by Zarathustra who, in "Of the Gift-Giving Virtue," observed, "One requiteth a teacher badly if one remain merely a scholar" (Z I 22 §3). Jung certainly knew this passage; after all, he famously quoted it in his letter to Freud of 3 March 1912![45]

Then again, on several occasions Jung alluded to the experiential dimension of the sources of his psychology and foregrounded the problem of communicative strategy. For instance, in a letter to Bernhard Baur-Celio of 30 January 1934, Jung wrote that he had had "experiences which are, so to speak, 'ineffable,' 'secret' because they can never be told properly and because nobody can understand them." Describing these experiences as "taboo-ed," because they are an ἄδυτον (*adyton*, that is, something "not to be

[45] *The Freud/Jung Letters: The Correspondence between Sigmund Freud and C.G. Jung*, ed. William McGuire, trans. Ralph Manheim and R.F.C. Hull (Cambridge, MA: Harvard University Press, 1988), p. 491.

entered," an "innermost sanctuary or shrine") that is protectively surrounded by δεισιδαιμονία (*deisidaimonía*, that is, "fearing or reverencing the divine") "as faithfully described by Goethe" — at which point he cited some lines from the conclusion of *Faust II*:

Shelters the deepest cave;	*Höhle, die tiefste, schützt.*
Softly the lions, dumb-	*Löwen, sie schleichen stumm-*
Friendly about us come,	*Freundlich um uns herum,*
Honour the holy seat,	*Ehren geweihten Ort,*
Sanctified love-retreat.	*Heiligen Liebeshort.*

(ll. 11847-11853)

and he concluded: "And already too much has been said" (L1, 140-141).

Then again, in his letter of 17 June 1952 to the Israeli religious scholar R.J. Zwi Werblowksy (1924-2015), Jung wrote that the language he spoke "must be ambiguous, must have two meanings [*zweideutig, bzw. doppelsinnig sein*], in order to do justice to the dual aspect of our psychic nature," and that he strove "quite consciously and deliberately for ambiguity of expression [*nach dem doppelsinnnigen Ausdruck*], because it is superior to unequivocalness [*der Eindeutigkeit überlegen*] and reflects the nature of life [*der Natur des Seins entspricht*]"; indeed, he said, while his whole temperament inclined him to be "very unequivocal indeed" (*sehr gut eindeutig*), that was not difficult, but it would be "at the cost of truth" (*auf Kosten der Wahrheit*) (L2, 70). On other occasions, however, Jung suggested that his efforts at communication had been a failure.

As early as 1926, for instance, in a letter not included in the published correspondence, Jung wrote: "[…] I consciously and intentionally made my life miserable, because I wanted God to be alive and free from this suffering man has put on him by loving his own reason more than God's secret intentions," and that "there is a mystical fool in me that proved to be stronger than all my science."[46] And over 30 years later, in what Gerhard Adler describes as a "short and uncharacteristic bout of depression," Jung wrote in another unpublished letter, this time of November 1960, that he had been "unable to make the people see" what he had been after, and that he had "failed" in his "inmost task," namely: to "open people's eyes to the fact that man has a soul and that there is a buried treasure in the field and that our religion and philosophy are in a lamentable state [...]."[47] In a way, one can see the work on *The Red Book* as a search for the right style, or for what in *Memories, Dreams, Reflections* is called the "right language" (MDR, 213). Elsewhere in *Memories, Dreams, Reflections*, the highly problematic nature of his "confrontation with the unconscious" in *The Red Book* is foregrounded in the admission that "high-flown language" corresponds to the style of the archetypes, and that archetypes "speak the language of high rhetoric, even of bombast" (MDR, 202). As a style, it is said to be "embarrassing," or awkward, or even painful—it "grates" on one's "nerves," "as when someone draws his nails down a plaster wall, or scrapes his knife against a plate" (MDR, 202). Yet it is said that Jung found himself with "no choice"—he had had to "write everything down in the style selected by the unconscious itself" (MDR, 202; cf. JWL, 149). For his part, in *Thus Spoke Zarathustra,* Nietzsche is going to enact a massive failure on Zarathustra's part to communicate, as we can see from his performance in this marketplace.

For Zarathustra now turns to the people assembled in the marketplace, awaiting the rope dancer, and he addresses them as follows:

> I TEACH YOU THE SUPERMAN. Man is something that is to be surpassed. What have ye done to surpass man?

[46] Gerhard Adler, "Aspects of Jung's Personality and Work," *Psychological Perspectives*, vol. 6, no. 1 (1975), 11-21 (p. 12).
[47] Adler, "Aspects of Jung's Personality and Work," p. 14.

> All beings hitherto have created something beyond themselves: and ye want to be the ebb of that great tide, and would rather go back to the beast than surpass man?
>
> What is the ape to man? A laughing-stock, a thing of shame. And just the same shall man be to the Superman: a laughing-stock, a thing of shame.
>
> Ye have made your way from the worm to man, and much within you is still worm. Once were ye apes, and even yet man is more of an ape than any of the apes.
>
> Even the wisest among you is only a disharmony and hybrid of plant and phantom. But do I bid you become phantoms or plants?
>
> Lo, I teach you the Superman!
>
> The Superman is the meaning of the earth. Let your will say: The Superman SHALL BE the meaning of the earth! (Z Prologue §3)

Zarathustra's language here echoes Goethe in two significant respects. Recall that, in the opening Night scene in *Faust I*, Faust espies the sign of the Earth Spirit and conjures up the Earth Spirit, who sarcastically addresses Faust thus: "What mortal dread, thou man of more than mortal essence, / Gets hold on thee?" (ll. 489-490)—the word translated here by Albert G. Latham as "man of more than mortal essence" being, of course, *Übermensch*. Going on to castigate Faust further, the Earth Spirit taunts him, accusing him of "shrink[ing] away" and calling him "a timorous, writhing worm" (l. 498). (This scene echoes the one in Byron's *Manfred* (1817), where the Seventh Spirit cries, "Thou worm!")[48]

Although Zarathustra uses the language of evolution, pointing to the link between the ape and the human being, his

[48] See Byron, *Manfred: A Dramatic Poem*, Act 1, Scene 1 (l. 125), in Byron, *Complete Poetical Works*, ed. Frederick Page, revised John Jump (Oxford and New York: Oxford University Press, 1970), p. 391.

argument is by no means Darwinian. True, in *Daybreak* Nietzsche acknowledged the validity of Darwin's evolutionary insights, but he was always interested in the implications of these insights for how humankind saw itself: "Formerly one sought the feeling of grandeur of humankind by pointing to its divine *origin*: this now has become a forbidden way, for at its portal stands the ape, together with other gruesome beasts, grinning knowingly as if to say: no further in this direction!" (D §49). Later on, Sigmund Freud would talk about his theory of psychoanalysis as a third intellectual revolution, complementing those of Copernicus and Darwin before him.[49] In his paper "A Difficulty in the Path of Psycho-Analysis" (1917), Freud symbolically placed his own ideas alongside those of Copernicus and Darwin, arguing:

> Psycho-analysis has sought to educate the ego. But these two discoveries — that the life of our sexual instincts cannot be wholly tamed, and that mental processes are in themselves unconscious and only reach the ego and come under its control through incomplete and untrustworthy perceptions — these two discoveries amount to a statement that *the ego is not master in its own house*. Together they represent the third blow to man's self love, what I may call the *psychological* one. No wonder then that the ego does not look favourably upon psycho-analysis and obstinately refuses to believe in it.[50]

[49] For further discussion, see Friedel Weinert, *Copernicus, Darwin, & Freud: Revolutions in the history and philosophy of science* (Chichester; Malden, MA: Wiley-Blackswell, 2009).

[50] Sigmund Freud, "A Difficulty in the Path of Psycho-Analysis" [1917], in the *Standard Edition of the Complete Psychological Works of Sigmund Freud*, vol. 17 (London: Hogarth Press; Institute of Psycho-Analysis, 1943), pp. 135-144 (p. 143).

What makes Nietzsche's position post-Darwinian (rather than simply and straightforwardly Darwinian) is the way in which Zarathustra links the *Übermensch*, not to biological evolution through natural selection, but rather to the question of meaning—and to the will: "The Superman is the meaning of the earth. Let your will say: The Superman SHALL BE the meaning of the earth!" Through Zarathustra, Nietzsche is seeking to bring about a *transformation* in the way human beings see themselves; and, through their will, a transformation not just in how they see themselves, but a transformation in what they actually *are*. Inasmuch as the *Übermensch* is a goal of evolution (if, indeed, evolution can be said to have goals …), it is a goal of a *willed* evolution.

Zarathustra implores his listeners, *remain true to the earth*, and not to listen to those who speak of "superearthly hopes": in so speaking, Zarathustra is rejecting not just the Judeo-Christian tradition (with its various conceptions of the afterlife), but the entire tradition of Western metaphysics. Zarathustra describes it as a "blasphemy" to deem the "heart of the unknowable" (in fact, he says *die Eingeweide des Unerforschlichen*, i.e., the "bowels of the inscrutable") to be more significant than the meaning of the earth, and he portrays the *Übermensch* as a kind of cleansing sea into which a polluted humankind streams:[51] "Verily, a polluted stream is man. One must be a sea, to receive a polluted stream without becoming impure. Lo, I teach you the Superman: he is that sea; in him can your great contempt be submerged."

But what does it mean to remain true to the earth? And what does an *Übermensch* actually look like? Zarathustra does not say, perhaps because, a bit like the Jewish notion of the *Bilderverbot* which forbids the depiction of the divine, the *Übermensch* inevitably lies so far beyond our present state of being that we would simply lack the capacity to imagine one. In this sense, an *Übermensch* that

[51] Lampert, *Nietzsche's Teaching*, p. 19.

we could imagine would not really be an *Übermensch* at all. Yet Nietzsche does make one exception as far as the question of what an *Übermensch* would like is concerned. For in *Twilight of the Idols,* he describes someone in terms that make him sound like an *Übermensch*, and that person is Goethe:

> *Goethe.* — No mere German, but a European event: a magnificent attempt to overcome the eighteenth century by means of a return to nature, by means of an ascent to the naturalness of the Renaissance, a kind of self-overcoming on the part of the century in question. — He bore the strongest instincts of this century in his breast: its sentimentality, and idolatry of nature, its anti-historic, idealistic, unreal, and revolutionary spirit (— the latter is only a form of the unreal). He enlisted history, natural science, antiquity, as well as Spinoza, and above all practical activity, in his service. He drew a host of very definite horizons around him; far from liberating himself from life, he plunged right into it; he did not give in; he took as much as he could on his own shoulders, and into his heart. That to which he aspired was *totality*; he was opposed to the sundering of reason, sensuality, feeling and will (as preached with most repulsive scholasticism by Kant, the antipodes of Goethe); he disciplined himself into a harmonious whole, he *created* himself. [...] Such a spirit, *become free*, appears in the middle of the universe with a feeling of cheerful and confident fatalism; he believes that only individual things are bad, and that as a whole the universe justifies and, affirms itself — *He no longer denies*.... But such a faith is the highest of all faiths: I christened it with the name of Dionysus. (TI Skirmisches of an Untimely Man §49)

And in his address to the doubtless somewhat bewildered townsfolk in the marketplace, Zarathustra goes on to present the *Übermensch* as a reinstatement of the importance of the body and the life of the senses, and as having implications for all aspects of our life—for our "happiness," for our "reason," for our "virtue," our "justice," and our "pity." And Zarathustra concludes his impassioned discourse with a startling image, imagining the *Übermensch* as a bolt of lightning that kindles the greatest experience for humankind:[52]

> Where is the lightning to lick you with its tongue? Where is the frenzy with which ye should be inoculated?
>
> Lo, I teach you the Superman: he is that lightning, he is that frenzy! — (Z Prologue §3)

The response of the townsfolk is not to be wondered at, and their response is a simple one. They laugh! A voice cries out from the crowd, "We have now heard enough of the rope-dancer; it is time now for us to see him!" And at this point, the action of the Prologue splits into two: Zarathustra takes the remark as the starting point for a second discourse, while higher up above the marketplace, the rope dancer for whom the crowd has been waiting now slowly begins his work.

Seizing the moment and making the most of the situation, Zarathustra comes up with the following striking image to describe the *Übermensch*:

> Man is a rope stretched between the animal and the Superman — a rope over an abyss.
>
> A dangerous crossing, a dangerous wayfaring, a dangerous looking-back, a dangerous trembling and halting.

[52] Lampert, *Nietzsche's Teaching*, p. 19.

> What is great in man is that he is a bridge and not a goal: what is lovable in man is that he is an OVER-GOING and a DOWN-GOING. (Z Prologue §4)

This is a powerful image: It suggests that to be a human being is not to occupy a fixed position as the outcome of the evolutionary process; rather, it is a transitory position on the way to something else—in Zarathustra's terms, a staging post on the way to the *Übermensch.* This passage introduces one of the key images of *Thus Spoke Zarathustra*, the image of the bridge: In "On the Despisers of the Body," Zarathustra cries, "I go not your way, ye despisers of the body! Ye are no bridges for me to the Superman!—"(Z I 4); in "On Joys and Passions," he observes, "My brother, if thou be fortunate, then wilt thou have *one* virtue and no more: thus goest thou easier over the bridge" (Z I 5); in "Of the Tarantulas," he says, "Because, FOR MAN TO BE REDEEMED FROM REVENGE—that is for me the bridge to the highest hope, and a rainbow after long storms" (Z II 7); while in "On Redemption" (a chapter which begins with Zarathustra literally crossing a bridge), he describes himself as "[a] seer, a purposer, a creator, a future itself, and a bridge to the future — and alas! also as it were a cripple on this bridge: all that is Zarathustra" (Z II 20); and in "The Greeting," he tells the Higher Men, "Ye are only bridges: may higher ones pass over upon you! Ye signify steps: so do not upbraid him who ascendeth beyond you into HIS height!" (Z IV 11).

As if to emphasize the positive content of his teaching—after all, Zarathustra did describe it as a gift for humankind—he goes on to tell his audience about the kind of people he loves: There are, in fact, no fewer than 18 of these, including the following that incorporate some of the key images one finds in *Zarathustra* (notably those of the arrow and of the bridge):

> I love those that know not how to live except as down-goers, for they are the over-goers.
>
> I love the great despisers, because they are the great adorers, and arrows of longing for the other shore.
>
> [...]
>
> I love him who loveth his virtue: for virtue is the will to down-going, and an arrow of longing.
>
> I love him who reserveth no share of spirit for himself, but wanteth to be wholly the spirit of his virtue: thus walketh he as spirit over the bridge.
>
> [...]
>
> I love him who justifieth the future ones, and redeemeth the past ones: for he is willing to succumb through the present ones.
>
> [...]
>
> I love him whose soul is deep even in the wounding, and may succumb through a small matter: thus goeth he willingly over the bridge.
>
> [...]
>
> I love him who is of a free spirit and a free heart: thus is his head only the bowels of his heart; his heart, however, causeth his down-going. (Z Prologue §4)

Moreover, this passage demonstrates the philological symbolism that one finds throughout *Zarathustra*: the play on *Übergang* and *Untergang*, *übergehen* and *untergehen*, and the paradoxical idea that *Untergehende* (those who descend) are *Hinübergehende* (those who go across) and hence a bridge to the *Übermensch* (that is, to the human being beyond humankind). The discourse concludes by returning to the final image of the previous discourse, the image of the *Übermensch* as like a bolt of lightning:

> I love all who are like heavy drops falling one by one out of the dark cloud that lowereth over man: they herald the coming of the lightning, and succumb as heralds.
>
> Lo, I am a herald of the lightning, and a heavy drop out of the cloud: the lightning, however, is the SUPERMAN. — (Z Prologue §4)

This second discourse produces a similar response: more laughter! Zarathustra says to himself, "There they stand, […] there they laugh: they understand me not; I am not the mouth for these ears."

This problem of communication, shared by Nietzsche and by Jung, is also a core biblical theme: In the story of the call of Isaiah, the prophet has a vision in the last year of the reign of King Uzziah (in the eighth century B.C.E.) of God seated on a high and lofty throne, his train filling the sanctuary of the Temple. "Holy, holy, holy, Yahweh Sabaoth," shout the six-winged seraphs, and after he has been symbolically cleansed by a piece of hot coal held in a pair of tongs being touched on his lips, Isaiah declares his readiness to announce the Lord's message to the people. To this declaration, Yahweh responds as follows: "Go, and thou shalt say to this people: Hearing, hear, and understand not: and see the vision, and know it not. Blind the heart of this people, and make their ears heavy, and shut their eyes: lest they see with their eyes, and hear with their ears, and understand with their heart, and be converted and I heal them" (Isaiah 6:9-10). As the commentary in the NJB makes clear, Isaiah's commission to speak is accompanied by a recognition—indeed, the promise—that the prophet's preaching will be met by incomprehension on the part of the audience.[53] Yet

[53] NJB, OT, 1199. For other texts on the theme of divine hardening, see Isaiah 63:17 and Exodus 4:21 et seq., while a prophecy of the siege of Jerusalem links the advent of a "spirit of deep sleep" to the loss of ability to see: "[The Lord] has closed your eyes, the prophets, and covered your heads, the seers" (Isaiah 29:10, RSV).

this passage becomes a key reference point in the New Testament as well, particularly in relation to Jesus's technique of using parables: In Matthew (as in Mark), Jesus explains that he speaks to the multitude in parables, so that "the prophecy of Isaias is fulfilled in them, who saith: By hearing you shall hear, and shall not understand: and seeing you shall see, and shall not perceive" (13:14, cf. Mark 4:12), while in Luke the distinction is made between the disciples, "to [whom] it is given to know the mystery of the kingdom of God," and the rest, to whom this mystery is given "in parables, that seeing, they may not see, and hearing, they may not understand" (Luke 8:10). In John, this point is indexed to the multitude's disbelief, despite the many miracles, and to Jesus's decision to "go away" and "hide himself from them," because the Lord "hath blinded their eyes, and hardened their hearts, that they should not see with their eyes, nor understand with their heart, and be converted" (John 12:36-37 and 41). In his last words in the Acts of the Apostles, Paul makes a declaration to the Roman Jews, citing this passage from Isaiah (Acts 28:23-28), and in his Letter to the Romans, it is reiterated in the context of the argument that although the Jews—in contrast to the Gentiles—currently reject the gospel, yet the Jews remain the chosen people and will one day be converted (Romans 11). Correspondingly, Zarathustra decides to change his communication strategy. Rather than appealing to his audience's sense of "contempt" (*Verachtung*) for what they are, he decides instead to appeal to their pride (*Stolze*) and to speak to them of the "most contemptible thing"—the *Last Man*.

Now the figure of the Last Man (*der letzte Mensch*) has been described by Leo Strauss as modern "psychological" or "therapeutic man." According to Strauss, "the last man, the lowest and most decayed man, the herd man without any ideals and aspirations, but well fed, well clothed, well housed, well medicated by ordinary physicians and by psychiatrists is Marx's man of the future seen from an anti-Marx point of view."[54] It is, one might say, the human being that, in the century or so since Nietzsche wrote his *Zarathustra*, we ourselves have all, in one way or another, become. Even now, however, Zarathustra cannot restrain himself from saying something positive about our human potential:

> It is time for man to fix his goal. It is time for man to plant the germ of his highest hope.
>
> Still is his soil rich enough for it. But that soil will one day be poor and exhausted, and no lofty tree will any longer be able to grow thereon.
>
> Alas! there cometh the time when man will no longer launch the arrow of his longing beyond man — and the string of his bow will have unlearned to whizz!
>
> I tell you: one must still have chaos in one, to give birth to a dancing star. I tell you: ye have still chaos in you.
>
> Alas! There cometh the time when man will no longer give birth to any star. Alas! There cometh the time of the most despicable man, who can no longer despise himself. (Z Prologue §5)

But Zarathustra also speaks, as Jung puts it, of "the last man who is not able to individuate, who has no chaos in himself and therefore no motive to give birth to a star," and this would be "the man who is completely exhausted, who is absolutely satisfied, and who doesn't know of any further evolution" (SNZ, 53). While it is true that, in alchemical terms, the *massa confusa* (or the chaos of the nigredo stage) represents the beginning of the alchemical transformation, here we have an acquiescence in chaos, a delighting in *massa*

[54] Cited in Lampert, *Nietzsche's Teaching*, p. 25; cf. Leo Strauss, *On Nietzsche's "Thus Spoke Zarathustra,"* ed. Richard L. Velkley (Chicago and London: University of Chicago Press, 2017), pp. 23-24 and 33-34.

confusa, and a reluctance—indeed, a refusal—to embark on the process of transformation of the *magnum opus* via the subsequent stages of albedo, citrinitas, and rubedo. (And today, as we look around us, we might wonder: Is the chaos getting any better?)

Zarathustra's new communication strategy backfires spectacularly, however: "Give us this last man, O Zarathustra," the townspeople call out, "make us into these last men! Then will we make thee a present of the Superman!" The people are nothing less than jubilant in their rejection of Zarathustra's teaching: "They understand me not," he sadly reflects, "I am not the mouth for these ears." Like the philosopher who exits the cave in Plato's allegory but returns to liberate the others left there, Zarathustra becomes an object of laughter and mockery—and of hatred as well; "there is ice in their laughter," he says. The people think that he is "cold, and a mocker with terrible jests"; but in the next section, we see an actual jester in action.

For, high above the marketplace, the rope dancer has begun his performance. Between two towers in the marketplace, a rope has been stretched, so that it hangs above the marketplace and the people. The rope dancer is going along the rope above the marketplace and has just gotten midway across, when another figure suddenly emerges from one of the towers: "a gaudily-dressed fellow, like a buffoon" (*ein bunter Gesell, einem Possenreißer gleich*). "Go on, halt-foot [*Lahmfuß*]," he cries,[55] and moves rapidly toward the rope dancer, until he is right behind him, at which point the *Possenreißer* utters a devilish cry and leaps over the rope dancer. The rope dancer loses his footing, throws away his pole, and plummets down into the

[55] Is there a link here between this insult, calling the rope dancer "halt-foot" (*Lahmfuß*) and the figure of Oedipus, whose name in Greek, Οἰδίπους, means "with swollen foot"? For psychoanalytic approaches to the Oedipus legend, see Patrick Mullahy, *Oedipus: Myth and Complex: A Review of Psychoanalytic Theory* (New York: Hermitage Press, 1948); and Peter L. Rudnytsky, *Freud and Oedipus* (New York: Columbia Press, 1987). As we shall see in Volume 4, ΦΙΛΗΜΩΝ is a "winged spirit," but also has a "lame foot" (MDR, 209).

marketplace. Everyone rushes away—except for Zarathustra, who approaches the gruesome spectacle of the rope dancer's shattered body. When his consciousness returns, he sees Zarathustra kneeling beside him. "What art thou doing there?" he says to Zarathustra, "I knew long ago that the devil would trip me up. Now he draggeth me to hell: wilt thou prevent him?" Zarathustra replies with the following reassuring words—well, sort of: "On mine honour, my friend," he replies, "there is nothing of all that whereof thou speakest: there is no devil and no hell. Thy soul will be dead even sooner than thy body: fear, therefore, nothing any more!" (Z Prologue §6). The rope dancer is not persuaded: If what Zarathustra says is true, has his life been in vain? Is he little better than some kind of performing animal, rewarded and punished by carrots and sticks? "Not at all," responds Zarathustra, for the rope dancer has made danger his calling, and there is nothing contemptible about that. Now the rope dancer will perish as a result of his calling; he is literally an *Untergehender*, and Zarathustra promises to bury him with his own hands.

That there is a relation between these events and Zarathustra's second discourse to the people in the marketplace seems clear: The rope stretched between the two towers symbolizes the rope stretched between the animal and the *Übermensch*, that is, the rope across which humankind must cross. This rope is stretched over an abyss: the abyss of nothingness, meaninglessness, nihilism, into which we risk falling on this perilous journey. When the rope dancer falls, he does not just fall into the marketplace; he falls "into the depths" (*in die Tiefe*), a term rich in mythological (and archetypal) associations.

In the following section (§7), Zarathustra reflects on the significance of what has happened. "Uncanny is human existence and still without meaning: a buffoon can be fatal to it," he says, and he adds: "Many things are uncanny: but none more uncanny than man," thus echoing the words of the chorus in *Antigone*, "There is much that is strange, but nothing that is stranger than human being."[56] Yet this insight only serves to confirm Zarathustra in his sense of mission: "I want to teach men the sense [*den Sinn*] of their existence [*ihres Seins*], which is the Superman, the lightning out of the dark cloud — man," he affirms. Nevertheless, he has not yet found the right way to do this, and he seems to many to be "something between a fool and a corpse," thus identifying himself both with the *Possenreißer* and with the rope dancer. "Dark is the night, dark are the ways of Zarathustra," he gloomily remarks, as he carries off the rope dancer to bury him.

Section 8 opens with Zarathustra somewhat unceremoniously carrying the rope dancer's corpse over his shoulders. Suddenly, the buffoon from the earlier scene appears and whispers in Zarathustra's ear. "Leave this town, O Zarathustra," he says, "there are too many here who hate thee," and he goes on:

> "The good and just hate thee, and call thee their enemy and despiser; the believers in the orthodox belief hate thee, and call thee a danger to the multitude. It was thy good fortune to be laughed at: and verily thou spakest like a buffoon. It was thy good fortune to associate with the dead dog; by so humiliating thyself thou hast saved thy life to-day. Depart, however, from this town, — or tomorrow I shall jump over thee, a living man over a dead one." (Z Prologue §8)

[56] Sophocles, *Antigone*, l. 332-333: "Many the wonders but nothing walks stranger than man" (David Grene and Richmond Lattimore (eds.), *Greek Tragedies*, vol. 1 (Chicago and London: University of Chicago Press, 1960), p. 192). This passage also caught the interest of Heidegger; see the passage in his *An Introduction to Metaphysics*, also available as "The Ode on Man in Sophocles' *Antigone*," in Thomas Woodward (ed.), *Sophocles: A Collection of Critical Essays* (Eaglewood Cliffs: Prentice, 1966), pp. 86-100. For further discussion, see Dennis J. Schmidt, *On Germans and Other Greeks: Tragedy and Ethical Life* (Bloomington and Indianapolis: Indiana University Press, 2001), Chapter 6, "Heidegger," pp. 225-270.

This passage arguably raises more questions than it answers about how to interpret the episode in the marketplace. For one thing, it points to a convergence between the figures of Zarathustra and the buffoon, since the former is said to speak like the latter (*gleich einem Possenreißer*). For another, however, it points to a divergence between them, because the buffoon threatens in turn to leap over Zarathustra, "a living man over a dead one" (*ein Lebendiger über einen Toten*). In what sense is Zarathustra a dead man—or a dead man walking?[57] In his seminar, Jung interprets the carrying of the rope dancer's corpse as a symbol of the *transitus* (comparable to the carrying of the Cross in the Christian mystery, or the carrying of the tree in the Attis mystery, or Mithras carrying the bull) (SNZ, vol. 1, 157).[58] On Jung's account, this is a "very peculiar *transitus*," inasmuch as Zarathustra "would be in the place of the god of the antique mysteries, […] of Christ the man-god, or Mithras the hero god, or Attis the son god" and carrying the "human body, the corpse — or the humanity, one can say — which really carries him" (ibid., 160-161). But what if Zarathustra himself might be the corpse, as the buffoon suggests? After all, this would explain why, in "The Grave-Song" in Part Two, Zarathustra visits the "grave-island, the silent isle"; or, for that matter, why in Part Two there is a discourse entitled "On the Blissful Islands," the traditional place of the heroic dead in Hesiod, Homer, and Pindar?

[57] In a remarkable study, Paul S. Loeb has argued that the plot of *Zarathustra* is constructed around the death of its protagonist, his deathbed revelation of his endlessly recurring life, and his return to an identical life in order to recollect this revelation, thereby acquiring power over time itself—and transcending the human; see Paul S. Loeb, *The Death of Nietzsche's Zarathustra* (New York: Cambridge University Press, 2010).

[58] As always, Jung gets very excited by the Mithras cult; he waxes lyrical about a head of Mithras in the British Museum with a "strange hysterical expression" — "like that of a person who ought to do something which he doesn't like" (SNZ, vol. 1, 157). Jung is probably thinking of the head of Mithras from the Walbrook Mithraeum, London (item CIMRM 815).

But perhaps this is to pay too much attention to the words of a buffoon: At any rate, Zarathustra earns further mockery from the gravediggers, whom he encounters at the gate of the town. "Will Zarathustra steal the bite from the devil?" they joke: good luck with that! Trudging on for a couple of hours through the forests and swamps with the sound of howling wolves in his ears, Zarathustra comes across a lonely house with a light on, and he knocks at the door. An old man opens it—another hermit, who offers both Zarathustra and the corpse a meal of bread and wine. Is this a picnic, a Holy Communion, or a requiem Mass for the dead? It is hard to tell. Refreshed by this humble repast, Zarathustra walks on for another two hours, "trusting to the path and the light from the stars." By the time the dawn comes, Zarathustra finds that he is in a thick forest and that the path has disappeared. (This is a motif we earlier found in Book 5 of *Parzival* when, the morning after he has failed to ask the question, he discovers that Anfortas and his court have left Monsalvaesche and sets off, following the tracks of those who have departed, until they become fainter and finally disappear:

> Then he turned him, the free from falsehood, where the hoof-tracks still met his sight,
>
> [...]
>
> They had parted who rode before him, and their track he might scarcely trace,
>
> What aforetime was broad waxed narrow till he lost it nor found it more.
>
> [§249, ll. 1-2 and 5-8]

And in Book 6, Sigune advises Parzival to follow the tracks left by Cundrie that might lead him to Munsalvaesche, but again the tracks disappear, and he loses his way:

[…] And he followed the woodland way,
And fresh were the tracks before him, but such pathway the mule must choose
Thro' the depths of the dusky thicket that its traces he soon must lose.
As the Grail he had lost of aforetime, so he lost It again to-day,
And joy and delight fled with It — […].

[§442, l. 26-§443, l. 1; vol. 1, p. 256]

Conversely, there are those moments where the path suddenly becomes clear: as in Book 5, for example, when Parzival unexpectedly rediscovers the way to go, *er kom ûf eine niuwe slâ*, "Then he saw a fresh track" [§256, l. 11], or in Book 9 when Gabenis (the gray knight) encourages Parzival, *rîtet vürbaz ûf unser spor*, "ride on along our tracks" [§448, l. 21], before pointing him in the direction of Trevrizent, the holy hermit. While it may be true that, as Zarathustra says, there is not *one* single path (*den Weg* […]—*den gibt es nicht*) (Z III 11 §2), this does not mean that each individual does not have their own path which they must follow. And so, placing the corpse in a hollow tree to protect it from the wolves, Zarathustra falls asleep.

* * * * *

A brief excursus on sleep and dreams in "Zarathustra": Sleep (and, along with sleep, dreams)—the topic of sleep and dreams in *Zarathustra* deserves an entire volume of its own, not a mere excursus. Within the limitations of the space available to us here, however, let us note that *Zarathustra* contains four dreams:

- Part Two opens in "The Child with the Mirror" with Zarathustra's dream of a child with a mirror (Z II 1);

- in "The Prophet," Zarathustra has a dream (or, rather, a nightmare) about being on the *Berg-Burg des Todes* (Z II 19);
- in the concluding chapter of Part Two, "The Stillest Hour," he dreams of how a voiceless silence speaks to him (Z II 22);
- and finally, in Part Three in "Of the Three Evil Things," Zarathustra has a dream in which he is holding a scale and weighing the world (Z III 10 §1).

One could, therefore, investigate these dreams as a constitutive sequence within the overarching architecture of *Thus Spoke Zarathustra*; something one might have expected Jung to do, but he did not. Nevertheless, in his seminar, he once described *Zarathustra* as being "like a dream in its representation of events"—events expressing "renewal and self-destruction" (SNZ, 275).

* * * * *

The next morning, Zarathustra awakes late: not only after the break of day (or *Morgenröte*, the title of one of Nietzsche's previous works, as well as the title of a work by Jacob Boehme) but after the early morning (and so, it seems, he awakes just before midday). But when he awakes, he is full of amazement: "Amazedly he gazed into the forest and the stillness, amazedly he gazed into himself." And jumping to his feet, "like a seafarer who all at once seeth the land," he shouts with joy, for he has discovered a "new truth," namely: "A light hath dawned upon me: I need companions — living ones; not dead companions and corpses, which I carry with me where I will. But I need living companions, who will follow me because they want to follow themselves — and to the place where I will" (Z Prologue §9). Whereas Christ came to find the lost sheep and return them to the flock, Zarathustra has come "to allure many from the flock," and for this reason "a robber shall Zarathustra be called by the shepherds"—those hypocritical shepherds who call themselves "the good and the just" (*die Guten und Gerechten*). (But as Nietzsche tells us elsewhere: "*Good men never speak the truth. False shores and false harbours were ye taught by the good. In the lies of the good were ye born and bred. Through the good everything hath become false and crooked from the roots*" [EH Why I am a Destiny §4].)

What Zarathustra needs are those described as companions who are also creators, and to describe them, he uses a symbolically significant agricultural language:

> companions, the creator seeketh, not corpses — and not herds or believers either. Fellow-creators the creator seeketh — those who grave new values on new tables.
>
> Companions, the creator seeketh, and fellow-reapers: for everything is ripe for the harvest with him. But he lacketh the hundred sickles: so he plucketh the ears of corn and is vexed.
>
> Companions, the creator seeketh, and such as know how to whet their sickles. Destroyers, will they be called, and despisers of good and evil. But they are the reapers and rejoicers. (Z Prologue §9)

The sickles are a symbol of the goddess Demeter,[59] and in a later chapter, "Of the Great Longing" in Part Three, an analogous symbol will be used, the "vintager who waiteth with the diamond vintage-knife" or Dionysos.[60] And despite his setback in the marketplace and his exhausting journey with the corpse, Zarathustra expresses a

[59] Parkes, *Composing the Soul*, pp. 187 and 424.

[60] Parkes, *Composing the Soul*, pp. 200 and 424. For discussion of a similar imagery of vegetal husbandry as found in Plato's *Phaedrus* (275e-277c), see Marcel Detienne, *The Gardens of Adonis: Spices in Greek Mythology* [1972], trans. Janet Lloyd [1977] (Princeton, NJ: Princeton University Press, 1994), Chapter 5, "The Seed of Adonis" (pp. 99-121); and Anne Lebeck, "The Central Myth of Plato's *Phaedrus*," *Greek, Roman, and Byzantine Studies*, 13 (1972), 267-290.

renewed sense of commitment to his mission, for "twixt rosy dawn [*Morgenröte*] and rosy dawn [*Morgenröte*] there came unto me a new truth":

> But I part from thee; the time hath arrived. [...] I am not to be a herdsman, I am not to be a grave-digger. Not any more will I discourse unto the people; for the last time have I spoken unto the dead.
>
> With the creators, the reapers, and the rejoicers will I associate: the rainbow will I show them, and all the stairs to the Superman.
>
> To the lone-dwellers will I sing my song, and to the twain-dwellers; and unto him who hath still ears for the unheard, will I make the heart heavy with my happiness.
>
> I make for my goal, I follow my course; over the loitering and tardy will I leap. Thus let my on-going [*mein Gang*] be their down-going [*ihr Untergang*]! (Z Prologue §9)

Here, Zarathustra reclaims the image of the *Possenreißer,* or buffoon, and applies it to himself; yet he later comes to realize in "Of Old and New Tables" in Part Three: "There are many divers ways and modes of surpassing: see THOU thereto! But only a buffoon thinketh: 'man can also be OVERLEAPT'" (Z III 12 §4). Even a new truth, it seems, can be replaced by an even newer truth.

By the time that Zarathustra has arrived at his "new truth," decided on a new recruitment strategy, and left the corpse of the rope dancer buried in the tree (a common choice of burial place in Nordic or Norse culture),[61] it has become midday, and the sun

[61] See G. Ronald Murphy, S.J., *Tree of Salvation: Yggdrasil and the Cross in the North* (New York: Oxford University Press, 2013), pp. 98-123.

is standing "at noon-tide"—a symbolic time of day (as becomes clear in "Of the Gift-Giving Virtue," the chapter that concludes Part One). Equally, as Jung points out in his seminar, Nietzsche began writing *Zarathustra* when he had just turned 39 years old, that is, at noontide, the beginning of the afternoon of life (SNZ, vol. 1, 226).[62] Hearing the cry of a bird, Zarathustra looks up and sees his eagle, flying through the air in wide circles, and coiled around its neck is the serpent—coiled, that is, "not like a prey, but like a friend" (Z Prologue §10). "'They are mine animals,' said Zarathustra, and rejoiced in his heart" (§10). The close—indeed, amical—proximity of Zarathustra's animals prompts us to reconsider their significance. In the pagan tradition, they are the symbolic animals of Zeus (the eagle) and Apollo (the serpent); in the Christian tradition, they are the symbols of pride and cleverness; and in the Zoroastrian tradition, the eagle is the animal of Ormuzd (and a symbol of light) while the serpent is the animal of Ahriman (and a symbol of darkness).[63] So what does their intertwining mean? As Laurence Lampert has suggested, the way that the serpent wraps itself around the eagle's neck does not merely symbolize the overcoming of the epoch of Zoroaster and a new epoch in its own right, it also symbolizes the overcoming of such old dualisms as light and darkness, heaven and earth, going beyond good and evil to establish a new harmony of earth and sky.[64] Lampert's interpretation confirms that offered by Jung in his seminar of 7 November 1934, when he says that the eagle, as an animal living in the air, has the quality of spirit (or

[62] Compare with Nietzsche's letter to Carl von Gersdorff of 20 December 1887: "In a significant sense my life now stands as if *at high noon*: one door is closing, another opening" (KSB 8, 214; cf. SNZ, vol. 1, 227).

[63] Lampert, *Nietzsche's Teaching*, p. 29.

[64] Lampert, *Nietzsche's Teaching*, p. 29. For discussion of Nietzsche's research into these and other symbols in Friedrich Creuzer's *Symbolik und Mythologie der alten Völker, besonders der Griechen* (1810-1812; [2]1819; [3]1837), see Curt Paul Jantz, *Friedrich Nietzsche: Biographie*, 3 vols. (Frankfurt am Main and Vienna: Hanser, 1978), vol. 2, pp. 230-232.

that, psychologically, it is "like thought, a messenger of the highest god"), while the serpent is the symbol for the "heaviness of the earth [...] for things chthonic" (or a personification of the "physiological instincts, [...] sexuality, [...] the low instinctive cunning of the primitive or animal mind of man"):

> Zarathustra sees those two animals together, representing pairs of opposites, because spirit is always supposed to be the irreconcilable opponent of the chthonic, eternally fighting against the earth according to the dogmatic idea and the idea of old philosophies in general. (SNZ, vol. 1, 227)

And in the circling flight of the eagle and the circularity of the coiled serpent, it is surely not wrong to see a prefiguration of the doctrine of eternal recurrence?[65]

No wonder Zarathustra is pleased: for the "proudest animal under the sun, and the wisest animal under the sun," he says, "they have come out to reconnoitre." What have they set out to reconnoiter? "They want to know whether Zarathustra still liveth," and Zarathustra himself pauses to wonder: "Verily, do I still live?" (§10). (This and related questions are insistently posed throughout the entire work.) The ways of Zarathustra, which he had earlier described as "dark" (§7), he now describes as "dangerous," for it is "more dangerous," he says, "among men than among animals" (§10). "Let mine animals lead me!" he declares, and then, remembering the words of the saint in the forest and his highly negative view of humankind—"Give them nothing [...] Take rather part of their load, and carry it along with them

[65] This motif seems to be reenacted in the episode which is said to have occurred on 3 June 1915 when Jung, out on Lake Zurich, saw an osprey plunge down, seize a large fish, and rise up again with it; the interpretation offered by Jung's soul of this incident, "This is a sign that what is below is borne upward" (RB, 475), could surely also be applied to the motif of the eagle and the snake in *Zarathustra*.

— that will be most agreeable unto them: if only it be agreeable unto thee!" (§2)—he sighs, and wishes: "Would that I were wiser [*klüger*]! Would that I were wise [*klug*] from the very heart, like my serpent!" (a wish which confirms the reputation of the serpent as a symbol of prudence).[66] Is this, as Zarathustra wonders, asking for the impossible (*Unmögliches*)? (For Manto, in Goethe's *Faust*, this would not be a problem; after all, as she says, "Him I love whom the impossible doth lure" (*Den lieb ich, der Unmögliches begehrt*) (l. 7488); both Faust and Zarathustra could say, in the words inscribed above Jung's fireplace in Bollingen, *quaero quod impossibile* ["I seek what is impossible"].)[67] Even if it *is* impossible, Zarathustra opts to make the following request: "Therefore do I ask my pride to go always with my wisdom!" (§10). In the end, Zarathustra is prepared to renounce wisdom and pride alike: "And if my wisdom should some day forsake me: — alas! it loveth to fly away! — may my pride then fly with my folly!" (§10). For the transformative process on which he is embarked (and on which Nietzsche hopes that, *mutatis mutandis*, the reader is embarked as well), Zarathustra is willing to sacrifice everything. And *thus* begins his "down-going" (*Untergang*): the descent from the mountain has been but a prelude to the ups and downs (but mainly the downs…) of the rest of the work.

For it is important to appreciate that *Thus Spoke Zarathustra* has a simple, if somewhat diffuse, plot and hence a clearly discernible narrative structure.[68] For in Part One Zarathustra leaves his cave on

[66] Lampert, *Nietzsche's Teaching*, pp. 29-30. As Lampert notes, Zarathustra has to abandon one kind of prudence which would hold him back (Z II 21), and cultivate a different kind of prudence, the absence of which would endanger him (Z III 5 and 6). For Zarathustra, "learning the place of prudence means learning the immoderation of thought and the moderation of speech" (30); in other words, accommodating oneself to the limitations of communication.

[67] As Peter Kingsley has pointed out, this text is the inspiration behind the inscription Jung had carved over the stone fireplace of his retreat at Bollingen, *Quaero quod impossibile* (Kingsley, *Catafalque: Carl Jung and the End of Humanity*, 2 vols. (London: Catafalque Press, 2018), vol. 1, p. 104 and vol. 2, pp. 528-529).

[68] According to Claus-Artur Scheier, the division of the Prologue into 10 sections

his mountain and goes to the town known as the Colorful Cow; by Part Two, he has returned to his mountain and his cave but he descends again and visits the Blissful Islands; in Part Three, he sails from the Blissful Islands and travels cross-country via the Great City and the Colorful Cow back to his mountain; and in Part Four, he wanders through the mountains and forests, in search of the elusive source of a cry of distress, and encountering the various Higher Men (including the Prophet, the Last Pope, and the Ugliest Man) whom he invites back to his cave. The final chapter of Part Four, "The Sign," closes the narrative circle by restaging the moment at the beginning of the Prologue, as Zarathustra again addresses the sun, calls on the Great Midday to "rise up" and commences his own final descent. This time, however, Zarathustra himself is identified with the sun, for he leaves his cave "glowing and strong, like a morning sun coming out of dark mountains" (Z IV 20).

So there is a clear narrative structure of descent, ascent, and descent again, onto which Nietzsche maps an overarching narrative of **crisis and resolution**.[69] The following episodes form the critical moments in this narrative structure: the decision at the end of Part One in "On the Bestowing Virtue" to leave his disciplines, bidding them "Lose me and find yourselves; and only when you have all denied me will I return to you,"[70] and proclaiming the Great Noontide, the moment when "man is in the middle of his course

establishes a pattern repeated by further divisions of ten throughout the rest of the work (*Nietzsches Labyrinth: Das ursprüngliche Denken und die Seele* (Freiburg and Munich: Karl Alber, 1985), pp. 147-153 and 167-170).

[69] I borrow this phrase from Alan Cardew; see his "'Only a God Can Save Us': Crisis and Resolution," in Linda H. Woodward (ed.), *Selections from the Prometheus Trust Conferences 2006-2010* (Dilton Marsh, Westbury: Prometheus Trust, 2013), pp. 171-190.

[70] Cf. Pascal, *Pensées*, §553 (ed. Brunschvicg), "You would not seek me if you had not already found me"; and St. Augustine, *Confessions*, Book 10, Chapter 27, "You were with me, and I was not with you." For the suggestion that behind such statements lies a passage found in Plotinus (*Enneads*, 6 Ennead, treatise 5, §12, 13-29), see Pierre Hadot, *Plotinus or the Simplicity of Vision* [1989], trans. Michael Chase (Chicago and London: University of Chicago Press, 1993), p. 47.

between animal and Superman, and celebrateth his advance to the evening as his highest hope: for it is the advance to a new morning" (Z I 22 §3); his flight to the fire mountain (that is, the volcano) and his descent through the gate to the underworld where he converses with the fire hound, followed by his subsequent return five days later ("On Great Events"); the terrifying moment when he hears the voice of his "terrible mistress" speaking to him in "The Stillest Hour"; the intuition of the eternal recurrence recounted to his fellow travelers in "On the Vision and the Riddle" and the exposition of the thought of eternal recurrence to his animals in "The Convalescent"; and the deep calm and tranquility of Zarathustra's vision in "At Midday" when the world "becomes perfect" (Z IV 10).

In addition to explicit echoes of *Thus Spoke Zarathustra*—most obviously the verbal echo of Nietzsche's philological symbolism in such expressions as *Übermensch*, *Überwindung*, etc., and the neologism coined in *The Red Book* by Jung, *Übersinn*—[71] there is thus a deep affinity between Nietzsche's *Zarathustra* and Jung's *Red Book* in terms of a narrative structure that emphasizes the theme of transformation (as we shall see in Volume 4 in this series). And the notion of the transformation lies at the very heart of the first of the post-Prologue discourses spoken by Zarathustra in Part One proper.

2. "Of the Three Transformations"

Nietzsche could not have signaled the importance of the theme of *transformation* more clearly than he does by giving to Zarathustra's first discourse after the Prologue the title of "On the Three

[71] For further discussion, see Gerhard Schmitt, "Vom Übermensch und Übersinn: Nietzsches Metaphorik im *Roten Buch*," *Recherches germaniques* 8 (2011) [*Art, sciences et psychologie: Autour du "Livre Rouge" de Carl Gustav Jung (1914-1930)*; *Kunst, Wissenschaften und Psychologie. Über das "Rote Buch" von C. G. Jung (1914-1930)*, ed. Christine Maillard], 117-133.

Transformations." The significance of transformation *as a concept* is made clear in the second chapter of Part Two, "On the Blissful Islands," when Zarathustra says, "Creating — that is the great salvation from suffering, and life's alleviation. But for the creator to appear, suffering itself is needed, and much transformation" (Z II 2). Transformation for Nietzsche is never merely simply for transformation's sake: It is, in his view, an essentially *creative* dynamic. What are the three transformations of which Zarathustra speaks? He sets them out in the very first sentence of his very first discourse: "Three metamorphoses of the spirit do I designate to you: how the spirit becometh a Camel, the Camel a Lion, and the Lion at last a Child" (Z I 1). What does this mean?

From the outset it is important to note *what* is being transformed in this discourse: It is *der Geist*—a simple yet virtually untranslatable word, covering a range of meanings from "mind" and "intellect" to "spirit"; in Christian theology, there is the "Holy Ghost" or "Holy Spirit" (*Heiliger Geist*); and G.W.F. Hegel wrote a book about the phenomenology of the "spirit" (*Phänomenologie des Geistes*, pub. 1807), sometimes translated as *Phenomenology of Spirit* (trans. A.V. Miller, 1977; trans. Terry Pinkard, 2018), sometimes translated as *Phenomenology of Mind* (trans. J. B. Baillie, 1910; 2nd ed. 1931). So, this series of transformations sits somewhat uneasily between the phenomenological and the psychological; it is at once both, and neither, inasmuch as its appeal is first and foremost to the imagination of the listener (or reader). Yet this chapter can be read as a key to unlock Nietzsche's transformational argument in the work as a whole.

In the first transformation, the spirit becomes a Camel—"the strong load-bearing spirit in which reverence dwelleth: for the heavy and the heaviest longeth its strength," and "many heavy things [*vieles Schwere*] are there for the spirit." The aptness of the choice of camel for this transformation of the spirit is revealed in this line: "What is heavy [*Was ist schwer*]? so asketh the load-bearing spirit; then kneeleth it down like the Camel, and wanteth to be well laden"; and in the following, "What is the heaviest thing [*Was ist das Schwerste*], ye heroes? asketh the load-bearing spirit, that I may take it upon me and rejoice in my strength" (Z I 1).[72] What, in this context, does Zarathustra mean by heaviness?

Later in the work, Zarathustra encounters a figure called the "Spirit of Gravity" (*der Geist der Schwere*), which could also be translated the "Spirit of Heaviness," described as a someone (or something) that is "half-dwarf, half-mole," and which sits on Zarathustra as he marches "gloomily and sternly, with compressed lips," along a lonely mountain path "in corpse-coloured twilight"; and sitting on him, "paralysed, paralysing; dripping lead in mine ear, and thoughts like drops of lead into my brain":

> "O Zarathustra," it whispered scornfully, syllable by syllable, "thou stone of wisdom! Thou threwest thyself high, but every thrown stone must — fall!
>
> O Zarathustra, thou stone of wisdom, thou sling-stone, thou star-destroyer! Thyself threwest thou so high, — but every thrown stone — must fall! (Z III 2 §1)[73]

This is the "vision of the lonesomest one," and it is with this Spirit of Gravity or Heaviness squatting on his shoulder that Zarathustra arrives at a gateway:

> "Look at this gateway! Dwarf!" I continued, "it hath two faces. Two roads come together here: these hath no one yet gone to the end of.

[72] There may be a philological aptness here, too, since the Avestan version of Zarathustra's name derives from an Old Iranian word containing *–uštra*, the Indo-Iranian root of the word for "camel"; Zarathustra's full name thus means, "someone who can manage camels"!

[73] Is there, in these words spoken by the Spirit of Gravity, an echo of the biblical precept found in the Old Testament apocryphal book of Ecclesiasticus, attributed to Jesus Ben Sirach, "If one cast a stone on high, it will fall upon his own head" (27:28 [25])?

> This long lane backwards: it continueth for an eternity. And that long lane forward — that is another eternity.
>
> They are antithetical to one another, these roads; they directly abut on one another: — and it is here, at this gateway, that they come together. The name of the gateway is inscribed above: 'This Moment.'
>
> But should one follow them further — and ever further and further on, thinkest thou, dwarf, that these roads would be eternally antithetical?" — (Z III 2 §2)

The dwarflike Spirit of Gravity responds with contempt to this suggestion: "Everything straight lieth," he says, "All truth is crooked; time itself is a circle." But Zarathustra insists on his point, "Thou spirit of gravity! [*Du Geist der Schwere!*] [...] do not take it too lightly [*mache dir es nicht zu leicht*]! Or I shall let thee squat where thou squattest, Haltfoot [*Lahmfuß*], — and I carried thee HIGH!" (We should note that Zarathustra addresses the Spirit of Gravity using the same epithet with which the buffoon addresses the rope dancer, a point not noticed by Jung in his seminar on *Zarathustra* nor by most critics.) And Zarathustra continues:

> "Observe," continued I, "This Moment! From the gateway, This Moment, there runneth a long eternal lane BACKWARDS: behind us lieth an eternity.
>
> Must not whatever CAN run its course of all things, have already run along that lane? Must not whatever CAN happen of all things have already happened, resulted, and gone by?
>
> And if everything have already existed, what thinkest thou, dwarf, of This Moment? Must not this gateway also — have already existed?
>
> And are not all things closely bound together in such wise that This Moment draweth all coming things after it? CONSEQUENTLY — itself also?

> For whatever CAN run its course of all things, also in this long lane OUTWARD — MUST it once more run! —
>
> And this slow spider which creepeth in the moonlight, and this moonlight itself, and thou and I in this gateway whispering together, whispering of eternal things — must we not all have already existed?
>
> — And must we not return and run in that other lane out before us, that long weird lane — must we not eternally return?" — (Z III 2 §2)

Here we find the idea of the eternal recurrence, first mooted in a section in *The Gay Science* called "The Greatest Weight" (*Das größte Schwergewicht*) and which includes the detail of the spider and the moonlight which Zarathustra mentions here (GS §341). Jung is, however, bang on the button when he points out: (a) that "all truth is crooked, the snake's way is the right way, every straight way lieth, time itself is a circle" is precisely the idea of the eternal recurrence and thus the teaching of Zarathustra himself (SNZ, vol. 2, 1271); (b) that in the text we have already met the idea of the eternal recurrence, which was "hovering over" Zarathustra (in the circling flight of the eagle and the serpent, itself coiled into a circle) but he "has not yet a realization of it," going to suggest that the dwarf represents the "higher mind which Zarathustra will come to soon after," and this is why Zarathustra talks to the Spirit of Gravity "as if he were on a mighty high horse in order not to recognize his defeat" (ibid., 1271); and (c) that what the Spirit of Gravity says is "great language," and Zarathustra "assimilates it, and he thinks that they are his own ideas" (ibid., 1271). Thus, on Jung's account the idea of eternal recurrence is something that really belongs to the Spirit of Gravity, and hence the dwarf is the "originator of this idea, which is perfectly paradoxical"—paradoxical, because "just the thing which he reviles as the spirit of gravity is the originator of this most inspiring wisdom" (ibid., 1273). One might therefore compare the dwarflike figure of the Spirit of Gravity to the "little people" exemplified by the elves and pixies of *Faust II*, Tom Thumb or the Cabiri.[74]

"Of the Vision and the Riddle" unfolds further, against the childhood memory of a howling dog,[75] revealing the vision proper itself:

> BUT THERE LAY A MAN! And there! The dog leaping, bristling, whining—now did it see me coming — then did it howl again, then did it CRY: — had I ever heard a dog cry so for help?
>
> And verily, what I saw, the like had I never seen. A young shepherd did I see, writhing, choking, quivering, with distorted countenance, and with a heavy black serpent hanging out of his mouth.
>
> Had I ever seen so much loathing and pale horror on one countenance? He had perhaps gone to sleep? Then had the serpent crawled into his throat — there had it bitten itself fast.
>
> My hand pulled at the serpent, and pulled: — in vain! I failed to pull the serpent out of his throat. Then there cried out of me: "Bite! Bite!
>
> Its head off! Bite!" — so cried it out of me; my horror, my hatred, my loathing, my pity, all my good and my bad cried with one voice out of me. —
>
> Ye daring ones around me! Ye venturers and adventurers, and whoever of you have embarked with cunning sails on unexplored seas! Ye enigma-enjoyers!

[74] For further discussion, see Volume 2, pp. 56 and 66-67 (cf. pp. 131 and 367-368).
[75] According to R.J. Hollingdale, Nietzsche's father had died following a fall, and Nietzsche had discovered him lying there unconscious, after being attracted to the scene by the barking of dog (see Hollingdale's note in his translation).

> Solve unto me the enigma that I then beheld, interpret unto me the vision of the lonesomest one!
>
> For it was a vision and a foresight: — WHAT did I then behold in parable? And WHO is it that must come some day?
>
> WHO is the shepherd into whose throat the serpent thus crawled? WHO is the man into whose throat all the heaviest and blackest will thus crawl?
>
> — The shepherd however bit as my cry had admonished him; he bit with a strong bite! Far away did he spit the head of the serpent —: and sprang up. —
>
> No longer shepherd, no longer man — a transfigured being, a light-surrounded being, that LAUGHED! Never on earth laughed a man as HE laughed!
>
> O my brethren, I heard a laughter which was no human laughter, — and now gnaweth a thirst at me, a longing that is never allayed.
>
> My longing for that laughter gnaweth at me: oh, how can I still endure to live! And how could I endure to die at present! — (Z III 2 §2)

The dialogue with the Spirit of Heaviness thus leads directly to the doctrine of eternal recurrence, and to this enigmatic vision, which may be resolved thus: for the shepherd into whose throat the serpent crawled is surely none other than Zarathustra himself (in "The Convalescent," §2, Zarathustra identifies himself as the shepherd); and one notes, amid the gloom and horror of this passage, the emphasis on the *transformative* effect of the vision—when he leaps up, the man is no longer a shepherd or even a human being, he is a "transfigured being, a light-surrounded being" (*ein Verwandelter, ein Umleuchteter*)—just like someone in the ancient initiation mysteries. (One might recall Plutarch's description of what the soul experiences at the moment of death in terms of what the initiate underwent in the Eleusinian Mysteries.[76] Indeed, Laurence Lampert claims that "The Convalescent," "Of the Great Longing," "The Second Dance Song," and "The Seven Seals," taken together, "contain the event for the sake of which the whole book exists," namely: the "event of redemption or Zarathustra's deed of willing eternal return" (210, cf. 211-244), while Matthew Meyer describes these four chapters as Zarathustra's "initiation into the Dionysian mysteries" [236, cf. 236-257].)

In his *Guidebook* to *Thus Spoke Zarathustra*, Meyer underscores the profound ambiguity of the action in "Of the Vision and the Riddle" and "The Convalescent." In the latter, is Zarathustra "disgusted" by humankind in general or only the "small man" (*der kleine Mensch*)? And in the former, does the snake—or, as Paul S. Loeb translates *die Schlange*, the "serpent"—represent Zarathustra's disgust or nausea with humankind or with the "small human," and does biting off the head of the snake represent Zarathustra's overcoming of this disgust or nausea? Or does the snake represent disgust or nausea about eternal recurrence or eternal recurrence itself? As Meyer wisely notes, "there is a lot hanging on how we interpret Zarathustra's biting off the head of the snake" (240)!

The significance within *Zarathustra* of the Spirit of Heaviness is often overlooked by commentators (although, as we have seen, not by Jung), and later in Part Three an entire section is called "Of

[76] "In the beginning there is straying and wandering, the weariness of running this way and that, and nervous journeys through darkness that reach no goal, and then immediately before the consummation every possible terror, shivering and trembling and sweating and amazement. But after this a marvellous light meets the wanderer, and open country and meadow lands welcome him; and in that place there are voices and dancing and the solemn majesty of sacred music and holy visions. And amidst these, he walks at large in new freedom, now perfect and fully initiated, celebrating the sacred rites, a garland upon his head, and converses with pure and holy men [...]" (Stobaeus, *Anthologium*, 4. 52.49; in Plutarch, *Moralia*, vol. 15, *Fragments from Other Named Works*, trans. F.H. Sandbach (Cambridge, MA: Harvard University Press, 1969), pp. 317-19 [Fragment 178]). For further discussion, see Helene P. Foley (ed.), *The Homeric Hymn to Demeter: Translation, Commentary, and Interpretive Essays* (Princeton, NJ: Princeton University Press, 1994), pp. 70-75.

the Spirit of Gravity." In the first section of this chapter, Zarathustra identifies further with the buffoon, or *Possenreißer*, describing his way of speaking as "of the people: too coarsely and cordially do I talk," his hand as "a fool's hand" (*eine Narrenhand*), and his foot as "a horse-foot" (*ein Pferdefuß*), thus linking him (as Jung notes) with the traditional iconography of the Devil (SNZ, vol. 2, 1464). Inasmuch as he is "hostile"—"verily, deadly hostile, supremely hostile, originally hostile!"—to the Spirit of Gravity, Zarathustra also reveals his own "bird-nature" (*Vogelart*), and in a line to which Nietzsche subsequently alludes in his "Attempt at a Self-Criticism" in the second edition of *The Birth of Tragedy*, he adds: "Thereof could I sing a song — and WILL sing it!" (Z III 11 §1).

The second section of this chapter "Of the Spirit of Gravity" makes clear the link between, on the one hand, the vision of the Loneliest Man and the riddle of the shepherd at which the dwarflike Spirit of Heaviness is present and, on the other, the first of the transformations under discussion, that is, the transformation of the spirit into the Camel. For in this section, which plays with the phonetic similarity between *lehren* ("teach") and *lernen* ("learn"), *lieben* ("love") and *leben* ("live"), as well as images of verticality and flight, Zarathustra clarifies what is at stake in the transformation into the Camel. For ultimately, he suggests, our heaviest burden is in fact *ourselves*:

> Almost in the cradle are we apportioned with heavy words and worths: "good" and "evil" — so calleth itself this dowry. For the sake of it we are forgiven for living.
>
> And therefore suffereth one little children to come unto one, to forbid them betimes to love themselves — so causeth the spirit of gravity.
>
> And we — we bear loyally what is apportioned unto us, on hard shoulders, over rugged mountains! And

> when we sweat, then do people say to us: "Yea, life is hard to bear!"
>
> But man himself only is hard to bear! The reason thereof is that he carrieth too many extraneous things on his shoulders. Like the Camel kneeleth he down, and letteth himself be well laden.
>
> Especially the strong load-bearing man in whom reverence resideth. Too many EXTRANEOUS heavy words and worths loadeth he upon himself — then seemeth life to him a desert!
>
> And verily! Many a thing also that is OUR OWN is hard to bear! And many internal things in man are like the oyster — repulsive and slippery and hard to grasp; —
>
> So that an elegant shell, with elegant adornment, must plead for them. But this art also must one learn: to HAVE a shell, and a fine appearance, and sagacious blindness! (Z III 11 §2)

In so saying, Zarathustra identifies *us* as our own moral burden, and it is carrying this burden that turns *us* all into camels—and turns our life into a desert. And yet at the same time, Zarathustra proposes a solution: to have a "noble shell" (*edle Schale*), to have a "beautiful appearance" (*schöner Schein*) (see "On Immaculate Perception," where Zarathustra asks: "Where is innocence [*Unschuld*]? Where there is will to procreation. And he who seeketh to create beyond himself, hath for me the purest will. Where is beauty [*Schönheit*]? Where I MUST WILL with my whole Will; where I will love and perish, that an image may not remain merely an image" (Z II 15]), and to have "prudent blindness" (or as Nietzsche puts it in *The Gay Science*, "*Looking away* shall be my only negation" [GS §276]). Yet the fact remains that "Man is difficult to discover [*Der Mensch ist schwer zu entdecken*], and unto himself most difficult of all [*sich selber noch am schwersten*]; often lieth the spirit [*der Geist*] concerning the soul [*die Seele*]. So causeth the spirit of gravity" (Z III 11 §2). However, there are two more transformative stages to come.

The second transformation occurs in the desert, into which the laden Camel has hurried, where it next becomes a Lion:

> All these heaviest things the load-bearing spirit taketh upon itself: and like the Camel, which, when laden, hasteneth into the wilderness, so hasteneth the spirit into its wilderness.
>
> But in the loneliest wilderness happeneth the second metamorphosis: here the spirit becometh a Lion; freedom will it capture, and lordship in its own wilderness. (Z I 1)

Now the lion is the symbol of Dionysos (cf. *Homeric Hymns*, VII, ll. 44-54), as well as an animal associated in Plato's *Republic* with courage.[77] (In Book 9, Socrates proposes the following metaphor for the human soul: It consists, he says, of a manifold and many-headed beast, a lion, and a human being, representing respectively "unlawful desires," spiritedness [or *thumos*, θυμός], and reason.)[78] The chief characteristic of this Nietzschean Lion is, as Michel Onfray has pointed out, to create freedom (*se créer liberté*),[79] and it does so by taking on its enemy, the great dragon:

> What is the great dragon which the spirit is no longer inclined to call Lord and God? "Thou-shalt," is

[77] Parkes, *Composing the Soul*, p. 227; cf. *Republic*, 588b-589b.

[78] For further discussion, see Laurence D. Cooper, "Beyond the Tripartite Soul: The Dynamic Psychology of the *Republic*," *The Review of Politics*, vol. 63, no. 2 (Spring, 2001), 341-372.

[79] See the title of the *bande dessinée* authored by Michel Onfray and illustrated by Maximilien Le Roy, entitled *Nietzsche: Se créer liberté* (Brussels: Lombard, 2010).

> the great dragon called. But the spirit of the Lion saith, "I will."
>
> "Thou-shalt," lieth in its path, sparkling with gold — a scale-covered beast; and on every scale glittereth golden, "Thou shalt!"
>
> The values of a thousand years glitter on those scales, and thus speaketh the mightiest of all dragons: "All the values of things — glitter on me.
>
> All values have already been created, and all created values — do I represent. Verily, there shall be no 'I will' any more." Thus speaketh the dragon.
>
> My brethren, wherefore is there need of the Lion in the spirit? Why sufficeth not the beast of burden, which renounceth and is reverent?
>
> To create new values — that, even the Lion cannot yet accomplish: but to create itself freedom for new creating — that can the might of the Lion do. (Z I 1)

Thus the Lion is a necessary but not a sufficient stage in the transformation of the spirit: It can negate the moral code of the Ten Commandments ("Thou shalt," "Thou shalt not") and the Judeo-Christian tradition; it can create the freedom (*se créer liberté*) to create new values, but it cannot actually create those new values itself.

Nevertheless, the Lion remains an iconic animal within *Zarathustra*. In "Of the Famous Wise Ones," the first part of a critique of the philosophers that is continued in "Of Self-Overcoming," Zarathustra describes the philosophers as asses and donkeys—

> Stiff-necked and artful, like the ass, have ye always been, as the advocates of the people.

> And many a powerful one who wanted to run well with the people, hath harnessed in front of his horses — a donkey, a famous wise man.
>
> [...]
>
> Ah! for me to learn to believe in your "conscientiousness," ye would first have to break your venerating will.
>
> [...]
>
> In the wilderness have ever dwelt the conscientious, the free spirits, as lords of the wilderness; but in the cities dwell the well-foddered, famous wise ones—the draught-beasts.
>
> For, always, do they draw, as asses — the PEOPLE'S carts! (Z II 8)

—and contrasts them with the lions they *pretend* to be but are not:

> And now, ye famous wise ones, I would have you finally throw off entirely the skin of the lion!
>
> The skin of the beast of prey, the speckled skin, and the dishevelled locks of the investigator, the searcher, and the conqueror!
>
> [...]
>
> Conscientious [*Wahrhaftig*] — so call I him who goeth into God-forsaken wildernesses, and hath broken his venerating heart.
>
> In the yellow sands and burnt by the sun, he doubtless peereth thirstily at the isles rich in fountains, where life reposeth under shady trees.
>
> But his thirst doth not persuade him to become like those comfortable ones: for where there are oases, there are also idols [*Götzenbilder*].
>
> [...]

> Hungry, fierce, lonesome, God-forsaken: so doth the lion-will [*der Löwen-Wille*] wish itself.
>
> Free from the happiness of slaves, redeemed from Deities and adorations, fearless and fear-inspiring, grand and lonesome: so is the will of the conscientious [*der Wille des Wahrhaftigen*]. (Z II 8)

In "Of Old and New Tables" in Part Three, a gentler, less ferocious side of the Lion is on display, as the *laughing* Lion is used as a sign that Zarathustra's time has come:

> Here do I sit and wait, old broken tables around me and also new half-written tables. When cometh mine hour?
>
> — The hour of my descent, of my down-going: for once more will I go unto men.
>
> For that hour do I now wait: for first must the signs come unto me that it is MINE hour — namely, the laughing Lion with the flock of doves. (Z III 12 §1)

In Part Four, Zarathustra recalls this image in "The Greeting" when he says:

> Not for you do I wait here in these mountains; not with you may I descend for the last time. Ye have come unto me only as a presage that higher ones are on the way to me, —
>
> — NOT the men of great longing, of great loathing, of great satiety, and that which ye call the remnant of God;
>
> — Nay! Nay! Three times Nay! For OTHERS do I wait here in these mountains, and will not lift my foot from thence without them;

> — For higher ones, stronger ones, triumphanter ones, merrier ones, for such as are built squarely in body and soul: LAUGHING LIONS must come! (Z IV 11)

To the figure of the Lion thus accrues a special and noble significance.[80] Yet the Lion is not the destiny of the spirit but one of its staging posts. In "Of The Three Transformations," Zarathustra explains why it is not enough for the spirit to become a Lion:

> To create itself freedom, and give a holy Nay even unto duty: for that, my brethren, there is need of the Lion.
>
> To assume the right to new values — that is the most formidable assumption for a load-bearing and reverent spirit. Verily, unto such a spirit it is preying, and the work of a beast of prey.
>
> As its holiest, it once loved "Thou-shalt": now is it forced to find illusion and arbitrariness even in the holiest things, that it may capture freedom from its love: the Lion is needed for this capture.

[80] According to E.R. Dodds, the vivid image of the lion whom society seeks in vain to tame "may fairly be said to haunt the pages of Nietzsche," being found in the "blond beast" of *On the Genealogy of Morals* (GM I 11), *Twilight of the Idols* (TI "Improvers" §2), and *The Will to Power* (WP §237 and §871 = KSA 13, 15[62], 448-449 and 11[153], 72-73) as well as the "laughing lions" of *Zarathustra*, which Dodds associates with a speech by Callias in Plato's *Gorgias*, 483e-484a (see E.R. Dodds, "Appendix: Socrates, Callicles, and Nietzsche," in *Plato Gorgias: A Revised Text with Introduction and Commentary* (Oxford: Clarendon Press, 1959), pp. 387-391). According to William M. Calder III, the lions and doves, "united in their love of a prophet," recalls the "Peaceable Kingdom" of Isaiah 11:6-9, as well as a famous scholium to Thucydides 1.126.3, where the historian describes how Cylon of Athens attempted to seize the city during a festival of Zeus, only to fail miserably: "One should know that some, who admired the clarity of the story about Kylon, said 'the lion laughed here,' meaning Thucydides," i.e., he relaxed when writing this passage (William M. Calder III, "The Lion Laughed," *Nietzsche-Studien*, 14 (1985), 357-359).

> But tell me, my brethren, what the Child can do, which even the Lion could not do? Why hath the preying Lion still to become a Child? (Z I 1)

So the Camel affirms the old values of good and bad, and laden down with this burden, it hurries into the desert, where it shies away from the right to new values (*neue Werte*). By contrast, the Lion—as a beast of prey, and hence literally the "blond beast" for which Nietzsche is notoriously known—[81]attacks the dragon of monotheistic morality, negates the values of Judeo-Christianity with its "sacred Nay," and creates the space and the freedom with which new values may emerge. For those new values themselves, however, actually to emerge, a third and final transformation is necessary—the transformation of the Lion into the Child.

Zarathustra presents the Child as an emblem of ludic creativity in the following, highly evocative words:

> Innocence is the Child, and forgetfulness, a new beginning, a game, a self-rolling wheel, a first movement, a holy Yea.
>
> Aye, for the game of creating, my brethren, there is needed a holy Yea unto life: ITS OWN will, willeth now the spirit; HIS OWN world winneth the world's outcast. (Z I 1)

[81] Clearly, the lion is an example of a "blond beast," but the term acquired widely misunderstood political, even racist connotations, when in the first essay in *On the Genealogy of Morals* (1887), he writes about "the beast of prey, the splendid *blond beast* prowling about avidly in search of spoil and victory," adding that "this hidden core needs to errupt from time to time, the animal has to get out again and go back to the wilderness" (GM I §11). He concludes this sentence by referring to "the Roman, Arabian, Germanic, Japanese nobility, the Homeric heroes, the Scandinavian Vikings—they all shared this need," which makes it clear he is talking about a certain type, not a racial concept; however, this provocative term has slipped well beyond its author's control.

In what can be read as an extended gloss on these words in *Zarathustra*, Nietzsche writes in *Twilight of the Idols*:

> What then, alone, can our teaching be? — That no one gives man his qualities, neither God, society, his parents, his ancestors, nor himself (— this non-sensical idea which is at last refuted here, was taught as "intelligible freedom" by Kant, and perhaps even as early as Plato himself). No one is responsible for the fact that he exists at all, that he is constituted as he is, and that he happens to be in certain circumstances and in a particular environment. The fatality of his being cannot be divorced from the fatality of all that which has been and will be. This is not the result of an individual intention, of a will, of an aim, there is no attempt at attaining to any "ideal man," or "ideal happiness" or "ideal morality" with him, — it is absurd to wish him to be careering towards some sort of purpose. *We* invented the concept "purpose"; in reality purpose is altogether lacking. One is necessary, one is a piece of fate, one belongs to the whole, one is in the whole, — there is nothing that could judge, measure, compare, and condemn our existence, for that would mean judging, measuring, comparing and condemning the whole. *But there is nothing outside the whole!* The fact that no one shall any longer be made responsible, that the nature of existence may not be traced to a *causa prima*, that the world is an entity neither as a sensorium nor as a spirit — *this alone is the great deliverance*, — thus alone is the innocence of Becoming restored.... The concept "God" has been the greatest objection to existence hitherto.... We deny God, we deny responsibility in God: thus alone do we save the world. — (TI The Four Great Errors §8)

For his part, to describe the Child, Zarathustra uses the striking imagery of a "new beginning" (*ein Neubeginnen*), a "game" (*ein Spiel*), a "self-rolling wheel" (*ein aus sich rollendes Rad*), terms which are used again in "Of the Way of the Creating One" when he asks, "Art thou a new strength and a new authority? A first motion? A self-rolling wheel? Canst thou also compel stars to revolve around thee?" (Z I 17), and again in "Of Child and Marriage" when he declares, "A higher body shalt thou create, a first movement, a spontaneously rolling wheel — a creating one shalt thou create" (Z I 20).

These chapters illustrate well how Nietzsche proceeds with an imagistic or emblematic, rather than argumentational, logic, creating a dense network of symbols. Accordingly, the question, "Canst thou also compel stars to revolve around thee?" becomes linked to the idea of solitude, "Terrible is aloneness with the judge and avenger of one's own law. Thus is a star projected into desert space, and into the icy breath of aloneness," which in turn becomes linked to the idea of creativity:

> Ready must thou be to burn thyself in thine own flame; how couldst thou become new if thou have not first become ashes!
>
> Thou lonesome one, thou goest the way of the creating one: a God wilt thou create for thyself out of thy seven devils! (Z I 17)

This almost alchemical image of transformation is echoed elsewhere: in "Of Joys and Passions," where Zarathustra declares, "All thy passions in the end became virtues, and all thy devils angels. Once hadst thou wild dogs in thy cellar: but they changed at last into birds and charming songstresses" (Z I 5), or in the passage examined earlier, "one must still have chaos in one, to give birth to a dancing star" (Z Prologue §5).

By the same token, the sheer delight that the Zarathustrian Child takes in its ludic existence can be compared to the view of the child expressed by Friedrich Schiller (1759-1805) in his poem, "The Child at Play" (*Der spielende Knabe*):[82]

Sport, Infant, on thy Mother's breast
— that sacred isle of rest —
Where troublous grief and carking
care thy peace can ne'er molest.
Her arm supports thee safe where
yawns the dread abyss below,
And, smiling in thy guiltless joy,
thou mark'st the billows flow.
Sport, lovely innocence ! — while
yet Arcadia blooms around,
And Nature owns for thee no law
but thy heart's unfettered bound;
While thy strength in wanton pride
may still its own restraints invent,
And thy willing spirit knows not yet
grave duty's sterner bent.
Sport while thou may'st — for all too
soon will come hard Labor's day,
And Joy and Pleasure tail to
welcome Duty's sovereign sway.

Spiele, Kind, in der Mutter
Schoß! Auf der heiligen Insel
Findet der trübe Gram,
findet die Sorge dich nicht
Liebend halten die Arme der
Mutter dich über dem Abgrund,
Und in das flutende Grab
lächelst du schuldlos hinab.
Spiele, liebliche Unschuld!
Noch ist Arkadien um dich,
Und die freie Natur folgt
nur dem fröhlichen Trieb,
Noch erschafft sich die üppige
Kraft erdichtete Schranken,
Und dem willigen Mut fehlt
noch die Pflicht und der Zweck.
Spiele, bald wird die Arbeit
kommen, die hag're, die ernste,
Und der gebietenden Pflicht
mangeln die Lust und der Mut.

[82] *The Minor Poems of Schiller*, trans. John Herman Merivale (London: Pickering, 1844), p. 126; and Schiller, *Sämtliche Gedichte und Balladen*, ed. Georg Kurscheidt (Frankfurt am Main and Leipzig: Insel, 2004). As Merivale notes, "in this beautiful little poem there is no deeply hidden meaning or allegory [...] it is merely the quiet expression of a most natural sentiment — the more interesting as having been called forth from the poet, it is said, by the actual contemplation of his own infant while playing on the lap of its mother" (ibid.). The image of the child at play is also found in the poem "Nature and the School" (*Natur und Schule*), later renamed "The Genius" (*Der Genius*), which includes these lines: "But you achieve blind what we cannot do in the daylight, / And the child at play does successfully what the wise man fails to do" (*Aber blind erringst du, was wir im Lichte verfehlen, / Und dem spielenden Kind glückt, was dem Weisen mißlingt*). Lesley Sharpe notes how these lines "capture the guilelessness and apparent ease of true genius," yet Schiller subsequently abandoned these two lines, leaving as the perfect final line, "Simple and silent thou go'st

Now this symbol of the Child is, like all symbols, inherently ambiguous (or, as Jung would put it, bipolar or antithetical),[83] and it must always be read in context. In "Of the Despisers of the Body," Zarathustra quotes the following view of the body-soul relation, "'Body am I, and soul' — so saith the child. And why should one not speak like children?" and contrasts it with the view of "the awakened one, the knowing one," who says, "'Body am I entirely, and nothing more; and soul is only the name of something in the body'" (Z I 4). This is clearly *not* the ludic, creative Child of the third transformation, whereas when, in the chapter "Of Old and Young Women"—leaving on one side for a moment the complicated gender politics of this chapter— Zarathustra says, "In the true man there is a child hidden: it wanteth to play," it arguably *is*.

Two other chapters develop the significance of the Child within *Thus Spoke Zarathustra*. Part Two opens with a chapter entitled "The Child with the Mirror," and a narrative segment describing how Zarathustra, after his leave-taking from his disciplines at the end of Part One in "Of the Gift-Giving Virtue," returns to his cave and withdraws from other people; he is compared, in a quasi-biblical fashion, to a sower who has gone out and sown his seed. The months and years go past, until one morning, he awakes before daybreak from a dream. This is the first of his four dreams (see above), and he describes it as follows:

---

through the wide world thou hast won" (*Einfach gehst du und still durch die eroberte Welt*)—the caesura emphasizing the second adjective *still* and balancing it with the first, *einfach*, and thereby recalling Winckelmann's notion of "noble simplicity and tranquil greatnesss" (*edle Einfalt und stille Größe*), while adding movement in a characteristically Schillerian way (Leslie Sharpe, *Friedrich Schiller: Drama, Thought and Politics* (Cambridge: Cambridge University Press, 1991), p. 206). So why did Schiller drop the original final couplet? Sharpe suggests that this decision may have been motivated by the simple perfection of this concluding line, or by Schiller's sense that the image of a child at play might seem inappropriate after the poem's earlier evocation of Greek manhood — by contrast, Nietzsche has no such qualms.

[83] See CW 6 §823-§824; CW 15 §213.

> Why did I startle in my dream, so that I awoke? Did not a Child come to me, carrying a mirror?
>
> "O Zarathustra" — said the Child unto me — "look at thyself in the mirror!"
>
> But when I looked into the mirror, I shrieked, and my heart throbbed: for not myself did I see therein, but a devil's grimace and derision.
>
> Verily, all too well do I understand the dream's portent and monition: my DOCTRINE is in danger; tares want to be called wheat! (Z II 1)

On Lampert's account, this episode refers to one of Zarathustra's disciples who has undergone the three transformations, but only in an incomplete way. As such, this child is an emblem of "immature creativity," which seeks to reflect Zarathustra's teaching but does so in a way that transforms Zarathustra into a devil.[84] The realization that this has happened—and that, as a consequence, his teaching is in danger—prompts Zarathustra himself to undergo a *further* transformation and to revise his communicative strategy, as he explains to his animals:

> What hath happened unto me, mine animals? — said Zarathustra. Am I not transformed? Hath not bliss come unto me like a whirlwind?
>
> […]
>
> Utterance have I become altogether [*Mund bin ich geworden ganz und gar*], and the brawling of a brook from high rocks: downward into the valleys will I hurl my speech.

[84] Lampert, *Nietzsche's Teaching*, p. 86.

> And let the stream of my love sweep into unfrequented channels! How should a stream not finally find its way to the sea!
>
> Forsooth, there is a lake in me, sequestered and self-sufficing; but the stream of my love beareth this along with it, down — to the sea!
>
> New paths do I tread, a new speech cometh unto me [*Neue Wege gehe ich, eine neue Rede kommt mir*] [...]. (Z II 1)

Even in this new speech, however, there is a wistful echo of the second stage of the three transformations, and a nod toward the affinity between Zarathustra and the buffoon:

> Verily, like a storm cometh my happiness, and my freedom! But mine enemies shall think that THE EVIL ONE [*der Böse*] roareth over their heads.
>
> Yea, ye also, my friends, will be alarmed by my wild wisdom [*ob meiner wilden Weisheit*]; and perhaps ye will flee therefrom, along with mine enemies.
>
> Ah, that I knew how to lure you back with shepherds' flutes! Ah, that my lioness wisdom [*meine Löwen-Weisheit*] would learn to roar softly! And much have we already learned with one another!
>
> My wild wisdom [*Meine wilde Weisheit*] became pregnant on the lonesome mountains; on the rough stones did she bear the youngest of her young.
>
> Now runneth she foolishly [*närrisch*] in the arid wilderness, and seeketh and seeketh the soft sward — mine old, wild wisdom [*meine alte wilde Weisheit*]! (Z II 1)

Inasmuch as Part Two appears to show a number of episodes from Zarathustra's second journey, the first stop on his itinerary are those blissful islands of which Hesiod, Homer, and Pindar (among others) speak.[85] One of this chapter's themes, its replacement of God by the *Übermensch*, we have already mentioned, and we shall return to its presentation of the *Übermensch* below; another of its themes is the importance of creativity or *Schaffen*, which is indexed here to the symbol of the Child:

> Creating — that is the great salvation from suffering, and life's alleviation. But for the creator to appear, suffering itself is needed, and much transformation [*Verwandelung*].
>
> Yea, much bitter dying must there be in your life, ye creators! Thus are ye advocates and justifiers of all perishableness.
>
> For the creator himself to be the new-born Child, he must also be willing to be the child-bearer, and endure the pangs of the child-bearer.
>
> Verily, through a hundred souls went I my way, and through a hundred cradles and birth-throes. Many a farewell have I taken; I know the heart-breaking last hours. (Z II 2)

This passage reminds us that, despite (or because of) Nietzsche's critique of Christianity, Zarathustra is still concerned one way or another with the question of "salvation" or "redemption" (*Erlösung*) (a question that is also in play in Wolfram's *Parzival*, Goethe's *Faust*, and Jung's *Red Book*). Zarathustra places equal emphasis on creativity as a source of redemption from suffering, and as a

---

[85] For further discussion of the motif of the blissful islands, see Paul Bishop, *On the Blissful Islands with Nietzsche & Jung: In the Shadow of the Superman* (London and New York: Routledge, 2017).

way of embracing or even *increasing* suffering. For, in order for the creator to become a newly born Child, he must go through the pains of childbearing. In "The Seven Seals," the image of pregnancy is fused with the earlier imagery of lightning:

> Ready for lightning in its dark bosom, and for the redeeming flash of light, charged with lightnings which say Yea! which laugh Yea! ready for divining flashes of lightning: —
>
> — Blessed, however, is he who is thus charged! (Z III 16 §1)

while in "Of the Higher Men," he declares:

> Ye creating ones, ye higher men! One is only pregnant with one's own Child.
>
> [...] In your self-seeking, ye creating ones, there is the foresight and foreseeing of the pregnant! What no one's eye hath yet seen, namely, the fruit — this, sheltereth and saveth and nourisheth your entire love.
>
> Where your entire love is, namely, with your Child, there is also your entire virtue! (Z IV 13 §10)

Analogously, in the *Symposium,* Socrates recalls how Diotima had once told him,[86] "[...] All men are bringing to the birth in their bodies and in their souls":

> There is a certain age at which human nature is desirous of procreation — procreation which must be in beauty and not in deformity; and this procreation is

[86] Parkes, *Composing the Soul*, p. 236.

> the union of man and woman, and is a divine thing; for conception and generation are an immortal principle in the mortal creature, and in the inharmonious they can never be. But the deformed is always inharmonious with the divine, and the beautiful harmonious. Beauty, then, is the destiny or goddess of parturition who presides at birth, and therefore, when approaching beauty, the conceiving power is propitious, and diffusive, and benign, and begets and bears fruit: at the sight of ugliness she frowns and contracts and has a sense of pain, and turns away, and shrivels up, and not without a pang refrains from conception. And this is the reason why, when the hour of conception arrives, and the teeming nature is full, there is such a flutter and ecstasy about beauty whose approach is the alleviation of the pain of travail. For love, Socrates, is not, as you imagine, the love of the beautiful only. (206c-e; trans. Benjamin Jowett)

And Diotima continues, "[…] All men do all things, and the better they are the more they do them, in hope of the glorious fame of immortal virtue; for they desire the immortal":

> Those who are pregnant in the body only, betake themselves to women and beget children — this is the character of their love; their offspring, as they hope, will preserve their memory and giving them the blessedness and immortality which they desire in the future. But souls which are pregnant — for there certainly are men who are more creative in their souls than in their bodies conceive that which is proper for the soul to conceive or contain. And what are these conceptions? — wisdom and virtue in general. And such creators are poets and

> all artists who are deserving of the name inventor. But the greatest and fairest sort of wisdom by far is that which is concerned with the ordering of states and families, and which is called temperance and justice. (208e-209a; trans. Jowett)

Similarly, in the *Theaetetus,* Socrates is presented as a "wet-nurse," yet one who is himself not pregnant (with wisdom) (149b, 150c-e),[87] whereas Zarathustra himself is full of wisdom and, moreover, also helps others to give birth—to themselves:

> **Socrates:** Such are the mid-wives, whose task is a very important one but not so important as mine; for women do not bring into the world at one time real children, and at another time counterfeits which are with difficulty distinguished from them; if they did, then the discernment of the true and false birth would be the crowning achievement of the art of midwifery — you would think so?
> **Theaetetus:** Indeed I should.
> **Socrates:** Well, my art of midwifery is in most respects like theirs; but differs, in that I attend men and not women; and look after their souls when they are in labour, and not after their bodies: and the triumph of my art is in thoroughly examining whether the thought which the mind of the young man brings forth is a false idol or a noble and true birth. And like the mid-wives, I am barren, and the reproach which is often made against me, that I ask questions of others and have not the wit to answer them myself, is very just — the reason is, that the god compels me to be a midwife, but does not allow me to bring forth. And therefore I am not myself at all

[87] Parkes, *Composing the Soul*, pp. 243-244.

> wise, nor have I anything to show which is the invention or birth of my own soul, but those who converse with me profit. Some of them appear dull enough at first, but afterwards, as our acquaintance ripens, if the god is gracious to them, they all make astonishing progress; and this in the opinion of others as well as in their own. (150a-d; trans. Jowett)

Even though in their respective philosophies, Plato places emphasis on the transcendent and Nietzsche on the immanent, both thinkers are logically consistent in their pursuit of the implications of the imagery of childbirth.[88] In the next section of "On the Higher Men," Zarathustra exclaims:

> Ye creating ones, ye higher men! Whoever hath to give birth is sick; whoever hath given birth, however, is unclean.
>
> Ask women: one giveth birth, not because it giveth pleasure. The pain maketh hens and poets cackle.
>
> Ye creating ones, in you there is much uncleanliness. That is because ye have had to be mothers.
>
> A new Child: oh, how much new filth hath also come into the world! Go apart! He who hath given birth shall wash his soul! (Z IV 13 §12)[89]

It is a pity that Jung never got as far as Part Four in his seminar on *Zarathustra*, and that many other commentators on Nietzsche seem

[88] For further discussion of Nietzsche and Plato, see Mark Anderson, *Plato and Nietzsche: Their Philosophical Art* (London and New York: Bloomsbury Academic, 2014); and Richard Bett, "Nietzsche and Plato," in Alan Kim (ed.), *Brill's Companion to German Platonism* (Leiden and Boston: Brill, 2019), pp. 249-270.

[89] In so exclaiming, Zarathustra offers a paraphrase of the dictum attributed to St. Augustine, *Inter faeces et urinam nascimur*, that is, "We are born between feces and urine."

to overlook the deconstruction of stereotypical gender roles that Zarathustra *appears* to reassert in Part One in "Of Old and Young Women" (whereas, in that chapter, the source of its misogynistic comments is not Zarathustra himself, but the old woman whom he encounters in the twilight, who is carrying "a little truth" under her mantle, holding its mouth like a naughty young child, lest it start screaming).

For all their differences, which in the defining contrast between the emphasis on the transcendent and on the immanent, *could* not be greater, there is nevertheless a striking overlap between Plato and Nietzsche in their shared emphasis on the importance of beauty. At the end of "On the Blissful Islands," Zarathustra declares, "The beauty of the Superman came unto me as a shadow" (*Des Übermenschen Schönheit kam zu mir als Schatten*) (Z II 2). This enigmatic statement should give us reason to pause and to consider those passages where Zarathustra discusses the outcome of the three transformations at greater length. For with these three transformations—"Three metamorphoses of the spirit have I designated to you: how the spirit became a Camel, the Camel a Lion, and the Lion at last a Child. —" (Z I 1) —Zarathustra has given us, so to speak, a kind of instruction booklet on how to become an *Übermensch*. And there are three chapters in particular which can help us understand what Zarathustra means by this (often misunderstood) term.

3. *Übermensch*

Many of Zarathustra's discourses are given in or around the town called *die bunte Kuh*, variously translated as "The Colorful Cow," "The Pied Cow," "The Motley Cow," or "The Dappled Cow." (In an editorial note to Jung's Nietzsche seminar, James L. Jarrett points out that, according to Freny Mistry, this name is a literal translation of the name of the town Kalmasadalmya (or, in Pali:

Kammasuddamam), visited by the Buddha on his wanderings [SNZ, vol. 1, 272].[90] Perhaps more realistically, however, Jung suggests that the "Colorful Cow" refers to Basel, with its "chairs of virtue," its "traditional morality" (and hence its "little real morality"), and a way of life which is said to have impressed the English historian Edward Gibbon (1737-94) as being similar to that from the time of Erasmus [vol. 1, p. 273].)[91] In the preceding chapter, "Of Voluntary Death," Zarathustra had told his disciples, "Verily, a goal had Zarathustra; he threw his ball. Now be ye friends the heirs of my goal; to you throw I the golden ball. Best of all, do I see you, my friends, throw the golden ball!" (Z I 21), and in his seminar Jung initially interpreted this golden ball as a "symbol of individuation" (SNZ, 52) and later as an "entirely round thing which expresses the state of perfection, of the highest value, of gold" (SNZ, vol. 2, 781-782), prompting a host of Vedic, alchemical, Platonic, and

---

[90] Freny Mistry, *Nietzsche and Buddhism: Prolegomenon to a Comparative Study* (Berlin and New York: de Gruyter, 1981), p. 17. Mistry cites Nietzsche's letter to Gersdorff of 13 December 1875 as evidence of Nietzsche's admiration for the Buddhist scripture, the *Sutta Nipāta* (a collection of suttas in the Khuddaka Nikaya, part of the Pali Canon of Theravada Buddhism): "[...] In the past two months I looked around at India with a kind of growing thirst. I borrowed [...] the English translation of the *Sutta Nipata*, something from the Buddhist scriptures, and have already made domestic use of one of the refrains of a Sutta: 'Thus I wander, lonely as the rhinoceros.' The rendering of the unworthiness of life and of the deception of all goals often impresses itself upon me so strongly, particularly when I am lying ill in bed, that I long to hear something more of it, unadulterated, however, by Jewish-Christian idioms... The will to cognition may remain as the last domain of the will to life, as a kind of interim realm between willing and willing-no-more, a kind of *purgatory* insofar as we look back upon life with dissatisfaction and contempt, and a piece of nirvana insofar as the soul approaches therewith the state of pure vision" (KSB 5, 127-128; translated in Mistry, p. 17). On the unidentifiability of a precise textual source, however, see Grätz, NK 4/1, p. 249.

[91] Gibbon lived for five years in Lausanne (from 1751 to 1756), recording his fascination for Switzerland and its federal political structures in *Introduction à l'Histoire Générale de la République des Suisses* (1815); for further discussion, see Brian Norman, *The Influence of Switzerland on the life and writing of Edward Gibbon* (Oxford: Voltaire Foundation, 2002).

Presocratic parallels, and finally as a symbol of "the self" (SNZ, vol. 2, 787 and 792).

From the perspective of this final chapter of Part One, Jung suggests, one can look back and see in the previous chapters a "sort of preparation, like a preparatory initiation," for the idea of the self: in Chapter 15, "Of the Thousand and One Goals," where we find the idea of "many goals with no certainty as to which is the right one"; in Chapter 16, "Of Neighbourly Love," which suggests that "something else must come in, a partner, a relationship"; in Chapter 17, "Of the Way of the Creating One," which proposes that "something must be created"; in Chapter 18, "Of Old and Young Women," which offers one way of creation; in Chapter 19, "Of the Bite of the Adder," in which to be bitten by the snake symbolizes poisoning or a kind of "reversed impregnation"; in Chapter 20, "Of Child and Marriage," which has the result of this impregnation as its subject (reflected in its title); and finally Chapter 21, "Of Voluntary Death," exploring how one "go[es] under in that relationship" and "reappear[s] as a child"—in other words, an unfolding sketch of "all the interior drama of the unconscious development" which leads to this symbol of the golden ball (SNZ, vol. 2, 787-788). (This style of reading confirms the thesis proposed in this series of studies that it is in the narrative structure of these epic works that their greatest significance is to be found.)[92]

[92] This method of reading can be regarded as having Jung's own *imprimatur*, inasmuch as he links the name of the town called "The Colorful Cow" to this line in the following chapter, "But I think of what I have done and thought during the day. Thus ruminating, patient as a cow, I ask myself: What were thy ten overcomings?" (Z I 2), and makes the following methodological point: "Very often when you encounter a rather striking word, you find it again coming up from the unconscious, hovering below the threshold of the conscious, and then coming up again after a while in a new connection," and "that sometimes helps one to eludicate the meaning of a word"—"So I think one should lay stress here upon the rumination" (SNZ, vol. 1, 272-273). In this particular case, however, Jung—perhaps jokingly—suggests that this town refers to Basel with its "tremendous conservatism and a particularly rigid set of values," adding: "And at that time, the beginning of the [18]80s, it really was ruminating on the values of the past" (ibid., 273).

Yet surely what is important about the symbol of the golden ball is not just the ball itself, but the gesture of reciprocity: When he came down from his mountain at the beginning of the Prologue, Zarathustra said he was "bringing gifts unto men" (Z Prologue §2), and those gifts are surely his teaching, which he has bestowed on his disciples, in order that they may pass them on to others. Jung himself seems to say as much (see below), and in this sense Zarathustra himself really *is* the "gift that keeps on giving," and so it is appropriate that the final chapter of Part One is entitled "Of the Gift-Giving Virtue."[93]

"Of the Gift-Giving Virtue"

Originally, Nietzsche had referred to the text of what is now Part One as constituting the entirety of *Thus Spoke Zarathustra*. In other words, Part One was intended to be the whole work, beginning with Zarathustra's descent from the mountain where he had lived for 10 years and ending with the dramatic words of his departure from his disciples: "'*All gods are dead: now we want the Superman to live*'—let this be our last will at the great noontide!" (Z I 22 §3). Yet in the first half of 1883, we find the curious idea emerging in his correspondence that the protagonist of *Zarathustra* should replace its author (KSB 6, 379 and 381). At the same time, simultaneous with this "disappearance," Nietzsche's own silence will come to an end: As he told Carl von Gersdorff in June 1883, his "true" identity would now be revealed (KSB 6, 386). In this letter, we also find the first indication in his correspondence that there might be more of *Zarathustra* to come: "Oh, how everything still lies hidden in me and wants to become word and form!" (KSB 6, 386).

[93] On the centrality of the notion of the gift in this work, see Emilio Carlo Corriero, *"The Gift" in Nietzsche's Zarathustra: Affirmative Love and Friendship*, trans. Vanessa di Stefano (London: Bloomsbury Academic, 2021).

In the notebooks for the winter of 1884-85 (KSA 11), we find sketch after sketch relating to Part Four of *Zarathustra*, including several fragments which returned to an earlier title envisaged in 1881, "Noontide and Eternity." Nietzsche's decision to turn to writing a fourth part is consistent with this plan of 1881, but what of his talk of "the now inevitable fifth and sixth parts"? What made these further parts (which had not formed part of the original scheme) "inevitable" was, it seems, Nietzsche's desire to bring the work to a different kind of conclusion, with the death of Zarathustra—a conclusion following the logic of narrative structure, rather than the ecstatic affirmation of the idea of eternal recurrence. "It's no use," he told his sister, "I must first help my son Zarathustra to his beautiful *death*, otherwise he will give me no peace" (KSB 6, 557). Correspondingly, the *Nachlass* from this period (KSA 10) contains various sketches for the death of Zarathustra. This desire, never carried out in any published version, to see Zarathustra "killed off" was, perhaps, related in part to a possible fatigue on Nietzsche's part with his "son." In the *Nachlass* for spring 1884, for example, we find the note: "*Decision*: I want to speak, and no longer Zarathustra" (KSA 11, 25[277], 83).

Turning to the substance of this final chapter in Part One, we read that, when Zarathustra had taken leave of the town called "The Pied Cow," his disciples followed him and kept his company, until they came to a crossroads—a location associated in Greek mythology with Hecate and Hermes alike, and the place where, in the parable attributed to Prodicus of Ceos and related by Xenophon of Athens, Hercules had to make his choice between vice (*kakía*, κακία) and virtue (*areté*, ἀρετή).[94] At this point, Zarathustra tells

[94] See Xenophon, *Memorabilia*, 2.1.21-34; for further discussion, see Erwin Panofsky, *Hercules am Scheidewege und andere antike Bildstoffe in der neueren Kunst* [Studien der Bibliothek Warburg, 18] [1930] (Berlin: Gebr. Mann, 1997). On Hecate, see Sarah Iles Johnston, *Hekate Soteira: A Study of Hekate's Role in the Chaldean Oracles and Related Literature* [American Classical Studies, 21] (Atlanta, GA: Scholars Press, 1990); Donna Wilshire, *Virgin, Mother, Crone: Myths & Mysteries of the Triple*

them that he wishes to go on alone, for he was a "friend of going alone" (*ein Freund des Alleingehens*). The symbolic significance of the crossroads is ancient; and of all the liminal deities associated with them, the most famous is Hecate, often depicted in triplicate or trimorphic form as *Hecate Triodia* or *Trioditis*, "the one who frequents crossroads." Why do crossroads matter? Because they represent a moment of decision: Which way shall one choose to go? And because a choice is unavoidable, at a crossroads, one cannot choose *not* to choose. It is at this point the disciples make *their* choice, which is to give Zarathustra himself a gift—"a staff, on the golden handle of which a serpent twined round the sun" (Z I 22 §1).

In his Nietzsche seminar, Jung equates the symbol of the golden ball with the divine symbol of the sun, recalling from the *Upanishads* the dialogue in Book 4, Chapter 3, of the Brihadaranyaka Upanishad between Yājñavalkya and King Janaka about consciousness and the nature of existence: "Yājñavalkya, what is the light of man (*puruṣa*)?" the king asks, to which the answers are respectively the sun, the moon, fire, the voice, and finally the self, for "[abiding] among the senses there is a 'person' who consists of understanding (*vijñāna*), a light within the heart."[95] Or in Jung's own words, the "light of the self [...] is the supreme light" and this is the "exact parallel of the idea of the golden ball":

> So in giving such teaching to his disciples, Zarathustra really gives them a golden present. And whatever you give returns to you; what you give, you have gained, but what you have acquired is lost. He gives a present to his disciples, and then it returns to him. This is not said by

Goddess (Rochester, VT: Inner Traditions, 1994); and Sarah Iles Johnston, *Restless Dead: Encounters Between the Living and the Dead in Ancient Greece* (Berkeley and Los Angeles: University of California Press, 1999), Chapter 6, "Hecate and the Dying Maiden: How the Mistress of Ghosts Earned Her Title," pp. 203-249.

[95] R.C. Zaehner (ed. and trans.), *Hindu Scriptures* (New York: Everyman, 1992), pp. 81-82.

> Nietzsche in so many words. I am not even convinced that he was conscious of it; it simply happens that his disciples are able to give him that present, and they would not have been able if they had not the means. Through the gold he has given to them, they can return in kind, and with an addition which comes really from them, the serpent twined round the golden ball. (SNZ, vol. 2, 792-793)

(We should note here Jung's emphasis that Nietzsche may not have been conscious of making—or, in the language of literary theory, may not have intended to make—this point about how the gift of Zarathustra's teaching returns to him. As it stands, Jung's interpretation in these lines places him among such theorists of reciprocity as René Girard, Marcel Mauss, Claude Lévi-Strauss, and Jean-Pierre Dupuy.)

Equally, the gift of this highly symbolic staff recalls a thyrsus (that is, a wand or staff covered with ivy vines and leaves, sometimes wound round with ribbons or taenia, and topped with a pine cone or a bunch of vine leaves), associated with Dionysos (or Bacchus) and his followers, the satyrs and maenads (or bacchants), as well as the rod of Asclepius (that is, the serpent-entwined staff held by the Greek god of healing and medicine) and the caduceus (that is, the wand or staff carried by Hermes, the messenger god, consisting of a short staff entwined by two serpents and sometimes surmounted by wings):

caduceus

rod of Asclepius

thyrsus

Significantly, in his Nietzsche seminar, Jung does not pursue these specific iconographical associations, but instead he thinks through the implications of his definition of the self as "relatedness" (SNZ, vol. 2, 795). When Zarathustra is "in the circle of his disciples," Jung argues, he himself represents the symbolism of the sun (that is, the masculine, the *pneuma*) and the serpent (that is, the earth, the darkness, the female principle), in the sense that the "sun and the serpent symbolized his relation to his disciples." On this reading, Zarathustra is "in the center, the *pneuma* surrounded by the circle of mankind, and mankind is the earth; so his disciples are his earth," and he is "rooted in his disciples." "In throwing the golden ball to them, [Zarathustra] gives them himself, his own principle, and they receive it as the earth receives the seed" (ibid., 794-795).

This is a remarkably *political* reading of this passage, in some ways closer to the theory of the *Männerbund* proposed by Alfred Baeumler (1887-1968)—namely, that the basis for a new kind of state was formed by an ideologically united band or *Bund* of like-thinking men—[96] than to Jung's usual flair for spotting mythological allusions or archetypal associations. In fact, for someone who is often accused of turning his back on the real world in favor of the archaic and the archetypal, Jung could not be more emphatic about the interpersonal dimension of his psychology when he says, "The self *is* relatedness," adding: "There really could be no self if it were not in relation [...] Not that you *are*, but that you *do* is the self" (SNZ, vol. 2, 795). He even warns that it is futile to build a meditation hut on the top of Mount Everest—"you will only be visited by your own ghosts," he says, "and that is not individuation."[97] In terms of

[96] See Alfred Baeumler, *Männerbund und Wissenschaft* (Berlin: Junker & Dünnhaupt, 1934).

[97] In clarification of this point, Jung adds later in this seminar that when he said one couldn't find the self without relationship, he did not intend to "exclude the other side," and explained: "I could say just as well that you could never attain the self without isolation; *it is both being alone and in relationship*" (SNZ, vol. 2, 797; my emphasis).

the imagery of *Zarathustra*, the "symbol is the sun encoiled by the serpent," for "that is what the disciples give back to him"—thus the staff is the "answer of the disciples, and [...] a symbol of the union of Zarathustra and his disciplines" (ibid., 795).

An equally shrewd reading of this passage has been offered by Gary Shapiro, who suggests that the gold orb on the staff is reminiscent of the beginning of the prologue and Zarathustra's praise for the sun and its ever-renewed power to give.[98] Hence, the golden orb itself suggests the bestowing virtue, since it is itself a *metaphor* of such virtue. Thus, the entire staff is not only a gift but a metaphor for gift-giving itself. In his speech in the Prologue, Zarathustra sets up a metaphorical identification between himself and the sun; in this final chapter of Part One, by their choice of gift, his disciples display their recognition of that association—and thus their understanding of the meaning of at least one metaphor in Zarathustra's discourse. By taking possession of the staff with the golden orb, as well as by his interpretation of it that follows, Zarathustra reveals himself to be the "master of metaphor."[99] For the image of the staff prompts Zarathustra to reflect on selfishness and on gift-giving in general, in which it turns out that giving is a virtue in the Greek sense of *areté* (ἀρετή) or Renaissance *virtù*, a term associated with Machiavelli (1469-1527); gift-giving, it is suggested, is a power, in contrast with the weakness or sickliness of miserly selfishness.[100]

Within the text itself, the symbolic or metaphorical aspect of gold is explored by Zarathustra at some length. "Tell me, pray: how came gold to the highest value?", he asks, before answering,

[98] Shapiro, *Nietzschean Narratives*, p. 55.
[99] Shapiro, *Nietzschean Narratives*, p. 55; cf. Corriero, *"The Gift" in Nietzsche's Zarathustra* (see above).
[100] Shapiro, *Nietzschean Narratives*, p. 55. For further discussion, see Harvey C. Mansfield, *Machiavelli's Virtue* [1996] (Chicago and London: University of Chicago Press, 1998).

"Because it is uncommon, and unprofiting, and beaming, and soft in lustre; it always bestoweth itself [*es schenkt sich immer*]" (Z I 22 §1). According to Zarathustra, it is precisely because of its essentially symbolic quality that gold has this property: "Only as image [*als Abild*] of the highest virtue came gold to the highest value. Goldlike, beameth the glance of the bestower. Gold-lustre maketh peace between moon and sun" (Z I 22 §1). Not surprisingly, Jung emphasizes the *alchemical* dimension of this symbolism, inasmuch as the "uncommon gold, the philosophical gold, is the child of the sun and the moon, the male and the female" (SNZ, vol. 2, 796). Alchemical gold is special: *aurum nostrum non est aurem vulgari* ("our gold is not the vulgar gold") (cf. ibid., 796),[101] and it is often symbolized by the hermaphroditic union of male and female. Jung points to two further analogies: to the *Hiranyagarbha* (i.e, the "golden seed," "golden foetus," "golden womb") in the Vedic tradition, a "golden Child" or "god" born if the lonely Zarathustra can be united to a circle of human beings; and to *Phanēs*, the primordial deity of procreation in Orphism, sometimes called Protogonos (i.e., the "first-born"), and depicted as a deity, entwined by a serpent, who emerges from a cosmic egg.

Phanēs, whose name means the "appearing one" or the "shining one," is identified here by Jung with the rising sun (as is also the case in *The Red Book*), and described as "the one that is born at the beginning" and as "the god of the beginning, hermaphroditic, with two bodies, and there are four symbolic animals" (SNZ, vol. 2, 796). In the Orphic tradition, the four animal heads of Eros-Phanēs (that is, the ram, the lion, the bull, and the snake) correspond to the

[101] Sometimes attributed to Gerhard Dorn, in *The Psychology of the Transference* Jung notes that in the *Rosarium Philosophorum* Arnold de Villanova cites as the source of this aphoristic statement Senior, the Latin name for the Arab alchemist Muhammad Ibn Umail (CW 16 §418; cf. C.G. Jung, *Psychology of Yoga and Meditation: Lectures delivered at the ETH Zurich*, ed. Martin Liebscher (Princeton, NJ, and Oxford: Princeton University Press, 2020), p. 152; and CW 12 §40).

four seasons of spring (birth), summer (maturity), autumn (decline), and winter (death);[102] iconographically similar to the tetramorph as found in the Book of Ezekiel that later came to be associated in Christian art with the four Evangelists (Matthew = man, Mark = lion, Like = ox, John = eagle; see above), the figure of Phanēs had special associations for Jung, given the role played by this deity in his *Red Book*, where he is depicted as the "image of the divine Child" who is the "newly appearing god" (RB, 358), although his full significance is clearer in *The Black Books*.[103]

(Here Phanēs appears in the entry for 28 September 1916 as "a golden bird" who emerges from "the tree of light" (BB6, 260); and on 20 February 1917, Jung begs Phanes as the "one above" (*Oberes*) and his soul as the "one below" (*Unteres*) not to be angry with him, because the "Above and the Below [*Oberes und Unteres*] are more powerful" than he (BB6, 280). On 11 September and 11 October 1917, Philemon sings the praises of Phanēs in two hymns (BB7, 158-159), while on 31 July 1918 and on 2 August 1918 Phanēs (ΦΛ) himself speaks: "The one voice of all beings speaks in you. / The sun of all suns shines in you. / You go the way of all ways,

---

[102] Matilde Battistini, *Symbols and Allegories in Art*, trans. Stephen Sartarelli (Los Angeles: The J. Paul Getty Museum, 2005), p. 32.

[103] In the autumn of 1916 he appears in Jung's *Black Books* as a god of beauty and light. In September 1916, he is described as a golden bird (BB6, 260-261) and on February 20, 1917, as the messenger of the world-embracing Abraxas (BB6, 280). On 20 May 1917, Philemon, Jung's guide in *The Red Book*, says that he will become Phanēs, "the eternal fire, the encompassing blaze, that ~~has~~ will become invisible and visible, the eternal dawning" (BB6, 297), and on 11 September and 11 October 1917 in *Black Book 7* Philemon offers a long, litany-like, laudatory description of Phanēs (BB7, 158-159). On 31 July and 2 August 1918, in *Black Book 7* Phanēs himself speaks, concluding with the following remarkably Orphic echoes (BB7, 192-194). In April 1919, Jung painted his portrait in the calligraphic volume of *The Red Book*, describing him as the divine child and as the newly appearing god (Image 113). In other words, Phanēs was the god that had been reborn through Jung's soul (RB, 358-359, editorial footnote 211). For further discussion of Phanēs as Jung's god, see Murray Stein, "How to Read the *Red Book* and Why," *Journal of Analytical Psychology*, vol. 57, no. 3 (June 2012), 280-298 (esp. pp. 291-294); and Volume 4 in this series.

alone with all. / […] He who is complete [*Der Vollendete*] knows man and woman, but I am the human being [*ich bin der Mensch*], ~~and of the human being~~ his father and son beyond masculine and feminine [*jenseits von Mannheit und Weibheit*], beyond child and the aged [*jenseits von Kind und Greis*]. / He who is complete knows rise and fall, but I am the center beyond dawn and dusk [*der Mittelpunkt jenseits von Morgenröthe und Abendröthe*]. / He who is complete knows me and hence he is different from me" [BB7, 192-194; cf. RB, 358-359, fn. 211]. Unmistakably here one hears the Nietzschean echo, *beyond good and evil …*)

In his final discourse in Part One, Zarathustra highlights the self-performative value of gold, which "always bestoweth itself" (*es schenkt sich immer*), when he says: "Uncommon is the highest virtue [*die höchste Tugend*], and unprofiting, beaming is it, and soft of lustre: a bestowing virtue is the highest virtue [*eine schenkende Tugend ist die höchste Tugend*]" (Z I 22 §1). And just as he had thrown the golden ball back to his disciples at the end of the previous discourse, so he turns back to his disciples with this insight when he says, "Verily, I divine you well, my disciples: ye strive like me for the bestowing virtue. What should ye have in common with cats and wolves?" (Z I 22 §1), for he expects that they are (in Jung's words) striving like him for the "bestowing virtue, the virtue of the gold that is shining, beaming, radiating, giving its beauty and its fascination to everybody" (SNZ, vol. 2, 798). Rather than to be cats and wolves (that is, predatory animals), his disciples are thirsting themselves to become "sacrifices and gifts," or (in Jung's words) "to give and give to the utmost, to give oneself as a sacrifice"—an idea which is, as Jung shrewdly notes, close to the Christian ideal, in that "as Christ has given himself to mankind so Zarathustra and his disciples strive to become sacrifices to mankind" (ibid., 798). This is a side to Nietzsche that is often overlooked: Here the disciples are praised for *not* becoming cats and wolves, for *not* becoming "blond beasts"; and yet there is an important distinction to be noted vis-à-vis Christianity: After all, Zarathustra says, "It is your thirst to become sacrifices and gifts yourselves: and therefore have ye the thirst to accumulate all riches in your soul" (Z I 22 §1). For whereas Christ says, "For where your treasure is, there will also your heart be also" (Matthew 6:21), Zarathustra locates these riches and treasures *not* in the kingdom of heaven, but in the individual's soul—"Insatiably striveth your soul for treasures and jewels, because your virtue is insatiable in desiring to bestow"—in order to be able to bestow them: "Ye constrain all things to flow towards you and into you, so that they shall flow back again out of your fountain as the gifts of your love" (Z I 22 §1).

In this respect, Zarathustra is espousing an *inversion* of the Christian ideal, professing not an abnegation of the self, but rather a *Selbst-sucht*, that is, a yearning or desire for the self, misleadingly called in English (where this philological symbolism is missing) *selfishness*: "Verily, an appropriator of all values must such bestowing love become; but healthy and holy, call I this selfishness.—" (Z I 22 §1). This is why elsewhere Zarathustra says:

- in "Of Neighbourly Love," "Ye crowd around your neighbour, and have fine words for it. But I say unto you: your neighbour-love is your bad love of yourselves" (Z I 16);[104]
- in "Of the Virtuous," "It is your dearest Self, your virtue [*Es ist euer liebstes Selbst, eure Tugend*].[105] The ring's thirst is in

[104] Compare with Jung's remark in *The Red Book*, "There is a true love that does not concern itself with neighbors" ("The Conception of the God"; RB, 170).

[105] Some editions read this line as *Es ist euer Liebstes selbst, eure Tugend*, and in this phrase one can also hear an echo of Kant, who wryly noted in his *Groundwork of the Metaphysics of Morals* (1785): "From love of humankind I am willing to admit that even most of our actions are in conformity with duty; but if we look more closely at the intentions and aspirations in them we everywhere come upon the dear self [*das liebe Selbst*], which is always turning up; and it is on this that their purpose is based, not on the strict command of duty, which would often require self-denial" (AA 4, 407; *Groundwork of the Metaphysics of Morals*, trans. Mary Gregor (Cambridge: Cambridge University Press, 1998), p. 20).

you: to reach itself again struggleth every ring, and turneth itself'" (Z II 5);

- in "Of the Three Evil Things," "'Bestowing virtue' [*"Schenkende Tugend"*] — thus did Zarathustra once name the unnamable. / And then it happened also,—and verily, it happened for the first time! — that his word blessed SELFISHNESS [*die Selbstsucht*], the wholesome, healthy selfishness, that springeth from the powerful soul: — / — From the powerful soul, to which the high body appertaineth, the handsome, triumphing, refreshing body, around which everything becometh a mirror: / — The pliant, persuasive body, the dancer, whose symbol and epitome is the self-enjoying soul. Of such bodies and souls the self-enjoyment calleth itself 'virtue'" (Z III 10 §2);
- and in "Of the Spirit of Gravity," "One must learn to love oneself [*Man muß sich selber lieben lernen*] — thus do I teach — with a wholesome and healthy love: that one may endure to be with oneself, and not go roving about. / Such roving about christeneth itself 'brotherly love'; with these words hath there hitherto been the best lying and dissembling, and especially by those who have been burdensome to every one. / And verily, it is no commandment for to-day and to-morrow to LEARN to love oneself. Rather is it of all arts the finest, subtlest, last and patientest" (Z III 11 §2).

Consequently, at the end of this first section of his final discourse in Part One, Zarathustra finds a new word for this virtue which he espouses (a word which lies at the heart of many of the misunderstandings about Nietzsche)—power (*Macht*): "Power is it, this new virtue; a ruling thought is it, and around it a subtle soul: a golden sun, with the serpent of knowledge around it" (Z I 22 §1). Now, earlier I quoted Gary Shapiro's view that, by taking possession of the orbed staff and offering an interpretation of it, Zarathustra shows himself to be the "master of metaphor." This metaphorical aspect of Zarathustra's thinking is highlighted by Zarathustra himself when he says, "Upward soareth our sense: thus is it a simile of our body, a simile of an elevation. Such similes of elevations are the names of the virtues. / Thus goeth the body through history, a becomer and fighter. And the spirit — what is it to the body? Its fights' and victories' herald, its companion and echo" (Z I 22 §1). Jung, too, is interested in these lines (see SNZ, vol. 2, pp. 806-807), but Shapiro goes into greater detail, showing how the metaphorical relation between, on the one hand, the mind (*der Geist*) and the virtues (*Tugenden*) and, on the other, the body (*der Leib*) and its "elevations" (*Erhöhungen*) is, in turn, linked to the previous one of the gold orb as a metaphor of the bestowing virtue.[106] This juxtaposition of metaphors is, he explains, an example of a rhetorical device identified by Aristotle and known as a *proportional metaphor*, and it may be represented thus:

$$\frac{\text{gold}}{\text{the bestowing virtue}} = \frac{\text{mind and virtue}}{\text{body (bodily power)}}$$

In other words, gold is to the bestowing virtue as virtue is to the body. (In his *Rhetoric*, Aristotle gives the example, "the cup is the shield of Dionysos," that is, just as the wine cup is the symbol of Dionysos, so the shield is the symbol of Ares.)[107] At the end of the first part of his discourse, Zarathustra links this proportion to a second one by taking one of the elements of the previous proportion and placing it in a new one, which may be represented thus:

[106] Shapiro, *Nietzschean Narratives*, p. 55.

[107] See Aristotle, *Rhetoric*, book 3, §4 (1407a 10), in *Complete Works*, ed. Jonathan Barnes, 2 vols. (Princeton, NJ: Princeton University Press, 1984), vol. 2, p. 2244. For further discussion, see Steve Nimis, "Aristotle's Analogical Metaphor," *Arethusa*, vol. 21, no. 2 (Fall 1988), 215-266.

$$\frac{\text{power (new virtue)}}{\text{subtle soul}} = \frac{\text{golden sun}}{\text{serpent of knowledge}}$$

By reinforcing the parallel between power (in a bodily sense) and the golden sun, Zarathustra does not merely remind us, his audience, of the visual image of his staff that he was given by his disciples at the beginning of this discourse; in drawing out the consequences of the original proportional metaphor by means of a new one, he demonstrates (in Shapiro's words) the "indefinitely generative principle of metaphor and the powerful body themselves."[108]

At this point in his final discourse in Part One, Zarathustra pauses; and, when he speaks again, his voice has changed—it has been transformed (*verwandelt*) (Z I 22 §2). He repeats his earlier injunction from the Prologue—"Remain true to the earth, my brethren"—and links it with the first part of his discourse—"with the power of your virtue!"; he enjoins his disciples, "Lead, like me, the flown-away virtue back to the earth — yea, back to body and life: that it may give to the earth its meaning, a human meaning!" the meaning which is, of course, the *Übermensch*; and he reaffirms the central importance of the body and clarifies what it means to be a "knowing one" (*ein Erkennender*) when he says, "Intelligently [*Wissend*] doth the body purify itself; attempting with intelligence [*mit Wissen*] it exalteth itself; to the discerners [*dem Erkennenden*] all impulses sanctify themselves; to the exalted [*dem Erhöhten*] the soul becometh joyful" (Z I 22 §2). As in Goethe's his late, great poem *Urworte Orphisch* (*Primal Words. Orphic*), "chance" (*Tyche*) has to be transformed into "necessity" (*Ananke*),[109] or as Zarathustra

[108] Shapiro, *Nietzschean Narratives*, p. 56. For Aristotle, the greatest power of poet or rhetorician is to be metaphorical, for it is a sign of genius, implying an intuitive perception of the "similarity in dissimilarities" (cf. *Poetics*, 1459a 3-8; and *Rhetoric*, 1412a 10).

[109] See Goethe, *Selected Poems*, ed. Middleton, pp. 230-233; and *Selected Poems*, trans. Whaley, pp. 122-125. For further discussion, see Paul Bishop, *Reading Goethe at Midlife: Ancient Wisdom, German Classicism, and Jung* [Zürich Lecture Series, 3] [2011] (Asheville, NC: Chiron, 2020), pp. 173-249.

says, "Still fight we step by step with the giant Chance [*Zufall*], and over all mankind hath hitherto ruled nonsense, the lack-of-sense" (cf. Z II 20, "Of Redemption"); and there remain many paths that have yet to be trodden: "A thousand paths are there which have never yet been trodden; a thousand salubrities and hidden islands of life. Unexhausted and undiscovered is still man and man's world [*Mensch und Menschen-Erde*]" (Z I 22 §2). On Zarathustra's account, the world has gone mad: "Not only the rationality of millenniums — also their madness, breaketh out in us. Dangerous is it to be an heir"; and he offers his philosophy as a therapy for this madness, and as a way to a "new hope" (*eine neue Hoffnung*): "Verily, a place of healing shall the earth become! And already is a new odour diffused around it, a salvation-bringing odour — and a new hope!" (Z I 22 §2).

And Zarathustra pauses again, weighing the staff in his hand; and when he speaks for the third time, his voice has changed (*verwandelt*) yet again. He announces his intention to go on alone, and he orders his disciples to leave him and go away. Zarathustra explains his desire for solitude in a couple of aphoristic statements: first, "The man of knowledge must be able not only to love his enemies, but also to hate his friends"; and second, "One requiteth a teacher badly if one remains merely a scholar" (Z I 22 §3). (The second of these was, as noted above, cited by Jung to Freud in his famous letter of 3 March 1912, but Jung makes no mention of this in his seminar!). Zarathustra promises to return, and to join them for a third time (the first time was when he descended at the beginning of the Prologue, and the second was at the end of the Prologue): "And once again shall ye have become friends unto me, and children of one hope: then will I be with you for the third time, to celebrate the great noontide with you." And so Part One closes with a climactic passage that brings together the core imagery and the central themes of the work so far:

> And it is the great noontide, when man is in the middle of his course between animal and Superman, and celebrateth his advance to the evening as his highest hope: for it is the advance to a new morning.
>
> At such time will the down-goer bless himself, that he should be an over-goer; and the sun of his knowledge will be at noontide.
>
> "DEAD ARE ALL THE GODS: NOW DO WE DESIRE THE SUPERMAN TO LIVE." — Let this be our final will at the great noontide! —
>
> Thus spake Zarathustra. (Z I 22 §3)

This passage offers a reprise of the allegorical events above the marketplace in the Prologue: the great midday as a symbol of the dangerous midpoint of the rope stretched between the towers when we realize that "sombre is human life, and as yet without meaning: a buffoon may be fateful to it," and of the moment when humankind is midway between the animal and the *Übermensch*; the play on *untergehen* and *übergehen*, as the *Untergehender* blesses himself for being an *Übergehender*; and the solar imagery of midday as the zenith, the point to which the sun climbs that also marks the beginning of its descent.

The key message could not be clearer: *God is dead*, indeed *all the gods are dead*; in this post-deicidal world, there is only one hope, only one desire, only one final will — *let the Übermensch live*! Yet it is precisely over this message that Jung's *Red Book* places a question mark when, in the second of the *VII Sermones ad mortuos*, ΦΙΛΗΜΩΝ declares, "God is not dead. He is as alive as ever" (RB, 516). And in his Nietzsche seminar, Jung detects within the imagery of this final passage an echo of the Christian symbolism of the *parousia* or the apocalyptic vision of the Second Coming of Christ and the reconciliation of all things (*apocatastasis*).[110] On this account, the "great noontide is the midday meal" and, over and above this "Christian analogy of the communion," its "real message" is that "'the great noontide' when man is in the middle of his course between animal and Superhuman" is when one "celebrates that communion with Zarathustra — with the self" (SNZ, vol. 2, 838). For his part, Jung could not be more explicit: What is being described here is "psychological," and he points to a literary analogue, Dante's *Divine Comedy*: "For in the middle of their way, Dante's adventure happens to certain people, if not consciously, then at least unconsciously," [111] and Jung beautifully describes this experience as *the touch of the self* (SNZ, vol. 2, 838). In fact, Jung offers nothing less than a full-blown interpretation of these concluding lines of Part One in essentially *psychological* terms. On the one hand, there is the animal—which, for Jung, represents *unconscious existence*: the "merely biological, personal ego existence"; on the other, there is the *Übermensch*. But there is a problem: How to get from the former to the latter? And so Jung goes on to say that the "evening is the problem of individuation, the becoming of the self or the Superman [i.e., *Übermensch*]; and this

[110] This theological doctrine of the restoration of all things to the original state of perfection is associated with the Church Father Origen of Alexandria. On the life, writings, and teachings of Origen, see the catechesis given by Pope Benedict XVI on 25 April 2007 (*The Fathers* (Huntington, IN: Our Sunday Visitor Publishing, 2008), pp. 35-45).

[111] For further discussion of Jung's use of Dante, see Tommaso Priviero, "C.G. Jung's *Liber novus* and Dante's *Commedia*," *Phanês*, 1 (2018), 28-57; Daniela Boccassini, "Down to the Father's Womb: Jung's and Dante's Encounters with the Dead," *Jung Journal: Culture and Psyche*, vol. 13, no. 2 (2019), 46-81; Claudio Widmann (ed.), *Dante e Jung: Una relazione a distanza* (Rome: Magi Edizioni, 2021); and Tommaso Priviero, *Jung, Dante, and the Making of the "Red Book": Of Fire and Form* (London and New York: Routledge, 2023). For a Jungian reading of the *Divina Commedia*, see Helen M. Luke, *Dark Wood to White Rose: A Study of Meanings in Dante's Divine Comedy* (Pecos, New Mexico: Dove Publications, 1975), published in its fifth edition as *Dark Wood to White Rose: Journey and Transformation in Dante's Divine Comedy* (New York: Parabola Books, 1993); and Mark Vernon, *Dante's Divine Comedy: A Guide for the Spiritual Journey* (Brooklyn, NY: Angelico Press, 2021).

is not the going down to the evening, but is the advance to a new morning," and this can in Jungian terms mean only one thing — the "idea of rebirth in the self or *to the self*" (SNZ, vol. 2, 839; my emphasis). Thus, this passage from Nietzsche's *Zarathustra* could be said to contain *in nuce* the very core of Analytical Psychology:

- (a) in the first part of life, there is "nothing but animal purpose, unconsciousnesss, and ego existence," and as a consequence "the gods are projected: they are outside because they are not integrated";
- (b) then comes the noontide of life, when "the gods will be integrated in man" and we "recognize them as projections";
- (c) but now that we have "lost the gods," there is "the danger of inflation, of identification with the image of the divine," and as a consequence we have "to *realize the Superman* [i.e., *Übermensch*]" (my emphasis);
- (d) the Superman (or *Übermensch*) is "superconsciousness and this is now the problem," for "what is this super-consciousness that has integrated even those psychological facts which formerly were projected as gods," and "what happens then to consciousness and what will that Superman [*Übermensch*] be?" (SNZ, vol. 2, 839)

For Jung, these questions constitute nothing less than the "drama which will be enacted in the next part of *Zarathustra*"; and, in a sense, he is right, demonstrating a sensitivity to the structural significance of *Zarathustra* as an epic of transformation. Yet he is right in another sense, too: For these questions also constitute the drama that is enacted in the next step of the German epic of transformation as it takes shape in Jung's own *Red Book*.

"On the Blissful Islands"

As we have seen, the opening lines of "On the Blissful Islands" in Part Two recapitulate *in nuce* the "action" of the Prologue to

Thus Spoke Zarathustra: namely, the proclamation—in fact, the taking-for-granted—of the "death of God," and the concomitant announcement of the doctrine of the "Superman"—that is, of the *Übermensch*, the "human-who-is-more-than-(just)-human," the human who is not (in the words of the title of one of Nietzsche's early works) "human, all-*too*-human." And they do so in a way that is eminently poetic or aesthetic:

> The figs fall from the trees, they are good and sweet; and in falling the red skins of them break. A north wind am I to ripe figs.
>
> Thus, like figs, do these doctrines fall for you, my friends: imbibe now their juice and their sweet substance! It is autumn all around, and clear sky, and afternoon.
>
> Lo, what fullness is around us! And out of the midst of superabundance, it is delightful to look out upon distant seas.
>
> Once did people say God, when they looked out upon distant seas; now, however, have I taught you to say, Superman [*Übermensch*]. (Z II 2)

The notion of the superman has been much understood: Indeed, there is much in its formulation that would appear positively to invite misunderstanding! As Michel Onfray has glossed the term, the *Übermensch* represents "the individual who understands the tragic nature of reality, because he understands the mechanism of the eternal return of all things under the sign of the same; as a consequence, emancipated from the question of free will which he knows is an illusion, he understands there is no other solution than to consent to this tragedy, to love it; henceforth, he attains joy"...[112] Then again, as

[112] Michel Onfray, *Le crépuscule d'un idole: L'affabulation freudienne* (Paris: Grasset, 2010), p. 542.

Sheridan Hough has suggested, "the Übermensch is above all some sort of ideal, a 'goal' the free spirit restlessly moves toward" and, as such, "not an ideal for everyone, but only for those exceptional individuals who are his rightful genealogical predecessors"; she concludes that "there is not a discrete character called the Übermensch" and "in fact the name 'Übermensch' designates a particular dimension of the experience of the free spirits."[113]

Correspondingly, as Herbert Theierl has also argued, Nietzsche "demands a 'going-under' [*"Untergang"*], in order that the 'superman' [*"Übermensch"*] come into being," giving rise to the conclusion that both terms, "going-under" and "Superman," refer to one and the same thing, namely: to a "mystical expansion of consciousness, which is experienced as redemption"; correspondingly, the "Superman" refers, not to an individual, but to "a state of mystical ecstasy"....[114] In this context, perhaps it is significant that this chapter of *Zarathustra* mixes classical and Christian imagery: classical, because its subject is the blissful islands, an essentially pagan motif; Christian, because much of the imagery alludes to a passage from the Book of Revelation. For in his vision experienced on Patmos of the end of the world, John the Apostle and the Evangelist sees the stars falling from the heavens, "as the fig-tree casteth its green figs when it is shaken by a great wind" (Apocalypse 6:13). In turn, this passage echoes the apocalyptic imagery of the prophet Nahum—"All thy strong holds shall be like fig-trees with their green figs: if they be shaken, they shall fall into the mouth of the eater" (Nahum 3:12). (Whereas the figs of Judeo-Christianity are green, Zarathustra's figs are dark and luscious: Their red skins are ready to break, and they are juicily full of delicious sweetness.) Why, as a passionate disbeliever in God,

[113] Sheridan Hough, *Nietzsche's Noontide Friend: The Self as Metaphoric Double* (University Park, PA: Pennsylvania State University Press, 1997), pp. 100 and 89-90.
[114] Herbert Theierl, *Nietzsche—Mystik als Selbstversuch* (Würzburg: Königshausen & Neumann, 2000), pp. 13-14; cf. pp. 47-48 and 90.

would Nietzsche choose to use an image that echoes the Christian bible? Surely because, in his eyes, Zarathustra ushers in the end of the Christian (conception of the) world.

At the conclusion to this remarkable chapter, we find the following passage:

> But to man doth it ever impel me anew, my fervent creative will; thus impelleth it the hammer to the stone.
>
> Ah, ye men, within the stone slumbereth an image for me, the image of my visions! Ah, that it should slumber in the hardest, ugliest stone!
>
> Now rageth my hammer ruthlessly against its prison. From the stone fly the fragments: what's that to me?
>
> I will complete it: for a shadow came unto me—the stillest and lightest of all things once came unto me!
>
> The beauty of the Superman came unto me as a shadow. Ah, my brethren! Of what account now are — the Gods to me! — (Z II 2)

In his seminar on Nietzsche's *Zarathustra*, Jung devoted no fewer than five sessions to the chapter entitled "On the Blissful Islands" (discussing it in the final seminar of the Winter Term 1936 on 4 March 1936, and again in the early seminars of the Spring Term 1936 on 6 May, 13 May, 20 May, and 27 May 1936). In the last of these seminars, he equates Nietzsche's idea of the *Übermensch* with the "term of *the self*," explaining that it would "naturally" appear "under the cloak of the shadow" (in an archetypal sense), inasmuch as it appears "in what has been rejected," and in this sense is assimilable to the alchemical idea of the *lapis philosophorum*, or the "stone of greatest price, […] the corner-stone first rejected by the builders" (SNZ, vol. 2, 953). In psychological terms, Jung explains, this means that the "thing which we think the least of" or "that part of ourselves which we repress […] or despise" is "just the part which contains the mystery" (ibid., 953), echoing the episode called the *Mysterium* in *Liber Primus* in *The Red Book*, consisting of the "Encounter," the "Instruction," and the "Resolution"— the mystery which "showed" Jung "in images" what he should "afterward live" (RB, 207).

There are important links between the *lapis philosophorum* and the biblical tradition of the "stone rejected by the builders."[115] It also plays a significant role in Patristic sources too.[116] Prior to this

[115] For this second image, see Psalm 117 (118): 22, "The stone which the builders rejected; the same is become the head of the corner"; cited by Christ in Matthew 21:42, Mark 12:10, Luke 20:17, and applied to Christ by St. Peter in Acts 4: 11 and 1 Peter 2: 7. In Ephesians 2: 19-22, St. Paul uses the metaphor of the Church as a "holy temple," built "on the foundation of the apostles and prophets, Jesus Christ himself being the chief cornerstone." For the messianic theme of the "keystone" that becomes the "stone of stumbling" (NJB commentary), see Isaiah 8:14 and 28:16—"Therefore, thus saith the Lord God: Behold, I will lay a stone in the foundations of Sion, a tried stone, a corner-stone, a precious stone, founded in the foundation"—, Zechariah 3:9 and 47; cf. St. Paul to the Romans 9:33, and 1 Peter 2:8.

[116] In his letter to the Ephesians, §9, St. Ignatius of Antioch alludes to this Petrine and Pauline motif when he writes: "You are stones of the Father's temple, prepared for the building of God the Father" (Bart D. Ehrman [ed.], *The Apostolic Fathers*, vol. 1, *I Clement; II Clement; Ignatius; Polycarp; Didache* (Cambridge, MA, and London: Harvard University Press, 2003), p. 229). And in the 10th of his *Catechetical Lectures*, St Cyril of Jerusalem drew a link between Christ's status as the Son of God and the description of him as a stone: "We say One Lord Jesus Christ, to signify that God's Son is Only-begotten; we say, One, lest thou shouldest suppose another […] He is called a Stone; not a lifeless one, quarried by men's hands: but the chief cornerstone, on whom whosoever believeth shall not be ashamed" (*The Catechetical Lectures of S. Cyril, Archbishop of Jerusalem* [Library of Fathers of the Holy Catholic Church, vol. 2] (Oxford: Parker, 1839), p. 99). In his sermons on the occasion of church dedications (cf. Sermons §336, §337, and §338), Augustine made extensive use of the Petrine (1 Peter 2: 5) and Pauline (1 Corinthians 3:10-11) imagery of ecclesiastical construction out of stones (see Finbarr G. Clancy, "Augustine's Sermons for the Dedication of a Church," in Maurice F. Wiles, Edward J. Yarnold, and Paul M. Parvis (eds.), *St Augustine and His Opponents* [*Studia Patristica*, vol. 38] (Louvain: Peeters, 2001), pp. 48-55; and J.E. Merdinger, "Building God's House: Augustine's Homilies at Episcopal Consecrations, Church Dedications, and Funerals," in Frances Margaret Young, Michael Edwards, and Paul M. Parvis (eds.), *Augustine* [*Studia Patristica*, vol. 42] (Louvain: Peeters, 2006), pp. 195-200 [pp. 197-98]). In a sermon for the Sunday after Ascension, Johannes Tauler refers to the Gospel allusions and Paul's letter to the Ephesians, adding that "if you are not sharpened thoroughly by this stone, all Solomon's wisdom and all Solomon's strength will be of no avail" (*Sermons*, trans. Maria Shrady (New York and Mahwah: Paulist Press, 1985), p. 83).

Patristic tradition, Socrates describes the dialectic as "set above all other studies to be as it were the coping stone" (*Republic*, 534e). And for the alchemical equivalent of the Petrine metaphor, "Be you also as living stones built up, a spiritual house" (1 Peter 2:5), one might recall Gerard Dorn's injunction, "transform yourselves into living philosophical stones!" (*transmutemini de lapidibus mortuis in vivos lapides philosophicos!*).[117] If, in this alchemical-cum-psychological sense, "that part of ourselves which we repress perhaps the most" is "just the part which contains the mystery," this insight offers us a "test": "When you can accept yourself in your totality, then you have brought together the four elements — all the parts of yourself have come together from the four corners of the earth" (SNZ, vol. 2, 953). Here—as elsewhere—Jung places great emphasis on the notion of *totality*, and it is this totality that is embodied by the *Übermensch*.

"Of Old and New Law Tables," §3

Turning to Part Three, the third section of the chapter "Of Old and New Law Tables" reads like a summary of much of what we have been discussing so far. In Section 1, Zarathustra wonders if it will soon be his time—the "hour of my descent, of my down-going: for once more will I go unto men" (Z III 12 §1). He is keenly awaiting the "signs"—namely, the laughing Lion with the flock of doves. And in Section 2, Zarathustra recalls how he had sat down on "their great grave-highway" (or the end, as he sees it, of academia) when his "wise longing" ("a wild wisdom, verily! — my great pinion-rustling longing") carried him "off and up and away [...] out into distant futures, which no dream hath yet seen, into warmer souths than ever sculptor conceived, — where gods in their dancing are

[117] See Dorn's *Speculativa philosophia*, in *Theatrum chemicum* [1602], vol. 1, p. 267; cited by Jung in his Eranos lecture on "Religious Ideas in Alchemy" (1937), in CW 12 §378.

ashamed of all clothes," as he puts it (Z III 12 §2). In this strange location, he continues, he found again his "old devil and arch-enemy, the Spirit of Gravity [*den Geist der Schwere*], and all that it created: constraint, law, necessity and consequence and purpose and will and good and evil," which prompts him to ask: "For must there not be that which is danced OVER, danced beyond? Must there not, for the sake of the nimble, the nimblest, — be moles and clumsy dwarfs? —" (Z III 12 §2).

And it was also—moving into Section 3—in these "distant futures, which no dream hath yet seen" that Zarathustra now says he "picked up from the path the word 'Superman,'" and that man is something that must be surpassed. He explains this doctrine in terms that will have become familiar from our discussion: namely, "that man is a bridge and not a goal — rejoicing over his noontides and evenings, as advances to new rosy dawns" (Z III 12 §3). The dawn (*Morgenröte*) presages, of course, the arrival of the new day, which reaches its high point when the sun is at the zenith at midday, and consequently he invokes the "Zarathustra word of the great noontide, and whatever else I have hung up over men like purple evening-afterglows" (Z III 12 §3). The solar image also recurs in another form, and another nod in the direction of Goethe's encomium of Winckelmann and the image of a rejoicing universe (see pp. 13-14 above): "Verily, also new stars did I make them see, along with new nights; and over cloud and day and night, did I spread out laughter like a gay-coloured canopy" (Z III 12 §3). There follows a passage which repeats what Zarathustra has earlier said in "Of Redemption" (see Z II 20) and which, although it does not actually mention the word *Übermensch*, nevertheless expresses the essence of what Zarathustra means by this word:

> I taught them all MY poetisation and aspiration: to compose and collect into unity what is fragment in man, and riddle and fearful chance; —

> — As composer, riddle-reader, and redeemer of chance, did I teach them to create the future, and all that HATH BEEN — to redeem by creating.
>
> The past of man to redeem, and every "It was" to transform, until the Will saith: "But so did I will it! So shall I will it —"
>
> — This did I call redemption; this alone taught I them to call redemption. —
>
> Now do I await MY redemption — that I may go unto them for the last time. (Z III 18 §3)

For Zarathustra is aware that his mission to transform humankind is still not yet achieved or still not yet complete, and here he uses, once again, another version of the solar motif, in a passage which offers a variant of the conclusion to section 337 of *The Gay Science*:

> For once more will I go unto men: AMONGST them will my sun set; in dying will I give them my choicest gift!
>
> From the sun did I learn this, when it goeth down, the exuberant one: gold doth it then pour into the sea, out of inexhaustible riches, —
>
> — So that the poorest fisherman roweth even with GOLDEN oars! For this did I once see, and did not tire of weeping in beholding it. —
>
> Like the sun will also Zarathustra go down: now sitteth he here and waiteth, old broken tables around him, and also new tables — half-written. (Z III 18 §3)

In *The Gay Science* similar lines about the rays of the evening sun and the reflection of this light on the oars of the fisherman brings to a close an aphorism entitled "The 'humaneness' of the future," which concludes as follows: "This godlike feeling would then be called — humaneness" (*Dieses göttliche Gefühl hiesse dann — Menschlichkeit*) (GS §337).[118] In the context of the philosophical and poetic argument of *Zarathustra*, this feeling could also be called: *Übermenschlichkeit …*

4. (a) "The Midnight Song"

As it unfolds across its no fewer than 30 sections, the chapter "Of Old and New Law Tables" becomes increasingly lyrical; indeed, dithyrambic (to use one of Nietzsche's favorite adjectives). (The dithyramb is an ancient Greek hymn, performed with singing and dancing in honor of the god Dionysos; in his *Laws*, Plato notes the link between Dionysos and the dithyramb [700b].) As well as recapitulating some of the motifs and themes from earlier in

[118] In this aphorism of *The Gay Science* entitled "The 'humaneness' of the future," Nietzsche contemplates—from a putative standpoint several centuries in the future—the humanity of the present and its distinctive characteristic, its "historical sense." Suppose, Nietzsche argues, one could accede to some kind of archetypical insight, might the individual be able to "experience the history of humanity as a whole as *his own* history"? And what would *that* feel like? At the conclusion of this aphorism, Nietzsche suggests that such a human being would feel nothing less than divine, experiencing "a happiness that humanity has not known so far: the happiness of a god full of power and love, full of tears and laughter, a happiness that"—and here begins a section of the passage quoted by the vitalist philosopher Ludwig Klages (1872-1956) in *Of Cosmogonic Eros* (1922; 1926)—"like the sun in the evening, continually bestows its inexhaustible riches, pouring them into the sea, feeling richest, as the sun does, only when even the poorest fisherman is still rowing with golden oars!" (GS §337). For Klages, this passage serves as an expression of what he calls "cosmic," "cosmogonic," or "elemental" Eros — an Eros which is "elemental" or "cosmic," inasmuch as "the individuals who are in its grip experience themselves as pulsed through and flooded through as if were by an electrical current, which—similar in its essence to magnetism—allows the most distant souls, irrespective of their limits, to feel a unifying pull bringing them together, the means itself by which everything happens, which separates bodies, transforms space and time into the omnipresent element of an embracing and swirling ocean, and"—he adds—"in this way, regardless of their never-lessening difference, joins together the *poles of the world*"; and "cosmogonic," because it is "a state of fullness pouring out of itself, according to which the inner—inasmuch as it gives birth to itself—becomes in a moment something external, world, and phenomenal reality" (Ludwig Klages, *Vom kosmogonischen Eros*, 2nd edn. (Jena: Diederichs, 1926), p. 58; cf. *Of Cosmogonic Eros*, trans. Mav Kuhn, 2nd edn. (Munich: Theion, 2022), p. 111).

the work (for example, the notion of the *Übermensch* [§3; cf. Z Prologue §3], the figure of the buffoon or *Possenreißer* [§4; cf. Z Prologue §6], the figure of the priest [§6; cf. Z I I 4], the relation between man and woman [§23-§24; cf. Z I 18], and the figure of the creator or *der Schaffende* [§26; cf. Z I 17]), this impassioned discourse paves the way for the pivotal moment in the plot of Part Three when, in "The Convalescent," Zarathustra's identity as the teacher of eternal recurrence is confirmed for him by his animals:

> [...] Behold, THOU ART THE TEACHER OF THE ETERNAL RETURN, — that is now THY fate!
>
> That thou must be the first to teach this teaching — how could this great fate not be thy greatest danger and infirmity!
>
> Behold, we know what thou teachest: that all things eternally return, and ourselves with them, and that we have already existed times without number, and all things with us.
>
> Thou teachest that there is a great year of Becoming, a prodigy of a great year; it must, like a sand-glass, ever turn up anew, that it may anew run down and run out: —
>
> — So that all those years are like one another in the greatest and also in the smallest, so that we ourselves, in every great year, are like ourselves in the greatest and also in the smallest. (Z III 13 §2)[119]

[119] In his essay "Who is Nietzsche's Zarathustra" (1953), Heidegger affirmed that the animals had correctly identified Zarathustra (see Martin Heidegger, "Wer ist Nietzsches Zarathustra?", in *Vorträge und Aufsätze* (Pfullingen: Neske, 1954), pp. 101-126; translated by David Farrell Krell in Heidegger, *Nietzsche*, vols. 1-2 (San Francisco: Harper & Row, 1979), vol. 2, pp. 209-233; and by Bernd Magnus in David B. Allison (ed.), *The New Nietzsche: Contemporary Styles of Interpretation* (Cambridge, MA, and London: MIT Press, 1985), pp. 64-79). By contrast, others have argued that the animals are wrong (see Maudemarie Clark, *Nietzsche on Truth*

Their proclamation of the doctrine of eternal recurrence is linked to the imagery of the "great noontide of earth and man," to Zarathustra's announcement of the *Übermensch*, and to the moment anticipated in "The Gift-Giving Virtue," that is, as "the hour [which] hath now come for the down-goer to bless himself. Thus — ENDETH Zarathustra's down-going" (Z III 13 §2).

In its turn, "The Convalescent" is followed by a discourse "Of the Great Longing," in which Zarathustra addresses his soul (in much the same way that, repeatedly in *The Red Book*, Jung addresses *his*); and then by "The Other Dance-Song" (the previous dance-song having been the first of a series of three songs sung by Zarathustra during his stay on the blissful islands [Z II 9-11]), at the conclusion of which is an 11-line-long poem, interspersed with the striking of a bell as it rings in midnight:

> *One!*
> O man! Take heed!
> *Two!*
> What saith deep midnight's voice indeed?
> *Three!*
> "I slept my sleep—
> *Four!*
> "From deepest dream I've woke and plead:—
> *Five!*
> "The world is deep,
> *Six!*
> "And deeper than the day could read.

and Philosophy (Cambridge: Cambridge University Press, 1990), p. 256), that they have not grasped the implications of this teaching (Meyer, pp. 238-239), or that between Zarathustra and his animals there is no real communication; instead, they are talking past each other (Grätz, NK 4/2, pp. 340-341). What seems clear, however, is that the problem of communication and the proclamation of the doctrine of eternal recurrence are inextricably intertwined.

Seven!
"Deep is its woe —
Eight!
"Joy — deeper still than grief can be:
Nine!
"Woe saith: Hence! Go!
Ten!
"But joys all want eternity—
Eleven!
"Want deep profound eternity!"
Twelve!
(Z III 15 §3)[120]

This text is taken up again in Part Four in "The Drunken Song," where its lines are given an extensive lyrical gloss before it is given one further reprise in the conclusion to that chapter where it is hailed as "Zarathustra's Roundelay" and as a song, "the name of which is 'Once more,' the signification of which is 'Unto all eternity!'" (Z IV 19 §12).[121] In Part Three, the concluding chapter entitled "The

[120] Compare with the translation of this song offered by Alexander Tille (1886-1912):
O man! Lose not sight!
What saith the deep midnight?
"I lay in sleep, in sleep;
From deep dream I come to light.
The world is deep,
And deeper than ever day thought it might.
Deep is its woe —
And deeper still than woe — delight.
Saith woe: 'Pass, go!
Eternity's sought by all delight —,
Eternity deep — by all delight!'"
(Nietzsche, *Thus Spake Zarathustra: A Book for All and None* (New York: Macmillan, 1896), pp. 331-332). The poem is used by Mahler in the fourth movement of his Third Symphony (1893-1896), and by Delius in his cantata based on settings of extracts from Zarathustra, *A Mass of Life* (1905).
[121] For further discussion, see the recently published extensive commentary on this text by Konrad Paul Liessmann, *Alle Lust will Ewigkeit: Mitternächtliche Untersuchungen* (Vienna: Szolnay, 2021). I should like to thank Christiana Ludwig

Seven Seals (Or: the Yes-and-Amen-Song)" affirms the central message of the midnight song in its repeated cry, "FOR I LOVE THEE, O ETERNITY!" (Z III 16), whereas in Part Four the midnight song offers an affirmative counterpoint to the braying "I-A" of the ass in "The Awakening" and the subsequent blasphemous parody of the Mass in "The Ass-Festival," in which Zarathustra addresses the Higher Men as "ye wags" (*ihr Schalks-Narren*) and "ye buffoons" (*ihr Possenreißer*), "Why do ye dissemble and disguise yourselves before me!" (Z IV 18 §2), and institutes the Ass-Festival as a kind of anti-Eucharist:

> [...] "O my new friends," said he, — "ye strange ones, ye higher men, how well do ye now please me, —
>
> — Since ye have again become joyful! Ye have, verily, all blossomed forth: it seemeth to me that for such flowers as you, NEW FESTIVALS are required.
>
> — A little valiant nonsense, some divine service and ass-festival, some old joyful Zarathustra fool, some blusterer to blow your souls bright.
>
> Forget not this night and this ass-festival, ye higher men! THAT did ye devise when with me, that do I take as a good omen, — such things only the convalescents devise!
>
> And should ye celebrate it again, this ass-festival, do it from love to yourselves, do it also from love to me! And in remembrance of me!" (Z IV 18 §3)

for numerous discussions about Nietzsche and for bringing this work to my attention (and doing so in the most generous and immediate way possible). For Jung's attachment to a phrase from this poem, *Die Welt ist tief und tiefer als der Tag gedacht* (which he modifies to: *tiefer als der Mensch gedacht*), see Aniela Jaffé, *Streiflichter zu Leben und Denken C.G. Jungs* (Einsiedeln: Daimon, 2021), p. 138.

The emphasis on eternity in the midnight song is brought out in its elaborated form in "The Drunken Song," but so at the same time are its echoes of Goethe's *Faust*. In section 9, Zarathustra—who has gestured to the Higher Men to follow him and, accompanied by his eagle and his serpent, now stands at the mouth of the cave, beneath the large, round moon—sings:

> Woe saith: "Hence! Go! Away, thou woe!" But everything that suffereth wanteth to live, that it may become mature and lively and longing,
>
> — Longing for the further, the higher, the brighter. "I want heirs," so saith everything that suffereth, "I want children, I do not want MYSELF," —
>
> Joy, however, doth not want heirs, it doth not want children, — joy wanteth itself, it wanteth eternity, it wanteth recurrence, it wanteth everything eternally-like-itself. (Z IV 19 §9)

As we recalled in Volume 2, pp. 35-37 and 166-168, a desire for eternity forms a key motif in Goethe's *Faust*, both in the formulation in Part One of the wager:

> When to the moment fleeting past me,
> Tarry! I cry, so fair thou art !
> [*Werd ich zum Augenblicke sagen:*
> *Verweile doch! du bist so schön!*]
> Then into fetters mayst thou cast me,
> Then let come doom, with all my heart!
> Then toll the death-bell, do not linger,
> Then be thy bondage o'er and done,
> Let the clock stop, let fall the finger,
> Let Time for me be past and gone!
> (ll. 1699-1705)

and in Act 5 of Part Two where Faust appears—but does he really?—to fulfill the conditions of the wager, when he says:

> My will from this design not swerveth,
> The last resolve of human wit,
> For liberty, as life, alone deserveth
> He daily that must conquer it.
> Thus childhood, manhood, and grey old age here,
> With peril girt, shall spend their strenuous year.
> Fain would I see such glad turmoil,
> With a free people stand on a free soil.
> To such a moment past me fleeing,
> Tarry, I'd cry, thou art so fair!
> The traces of mine earthly being
> Not countless aeons can outwear.
> Now, in the presage of such lofty bliss,
> The highest moment I enjoy, e'en this.
> (ll. 11573-11586)

In Faust's wager with Mephistopheles, everything turns on the status of the moment or the *Augenblick*, a moment which is (in Goethe's words in his poem, "Testament" or *Vermächtnis*) "eternity" (*Der Augenblick ist Ewigkeit*),[122] and the moment is central to Zarathustra's conception of eternity as well. In verses which echo Zarathustra's (and, *mutatis mutandis*, Heidegger's)

[122] For the stanza in question, see:

"Let moderation's joys sustain you	[*Genieße völlig Füll und Segen:*
And reason's presence entertain you	*Vernunft sei überall zugegen,*
Where life is life's felicity.	*Wo Leben sich des Lebens freut.*
The past's forever re-created,	*Dann ist Vergangenheit beständig,*
The future is anticipated,	*Das Künftige voraus lebendig,*
The moment is eternity."	*Der Augenblick ist Ewigkeit.*]

(Goethe, *Selected Poems*, trans. John Whaley (London: Dent, 1998), p. 151).

previous questioning of his identity in "Of Redemption" (Z II 20), and indirectly also Christ's insistent question, "who dost thou say I am" (Matthew 16:13-20), and which reprise the opposites of midnight and midday, pain and pleasure, wisdom and folly, Zarathustra jubilantly declares in an ecstatic expression of the *coniunctio oppositorum*:

> Ye higher men, what think ye? Am I a soothsayer? Or a dreamer? Or a drunkard? Or a dream-reader? Or a midnight-bell?
>
> Or a drop of dew? Or a fume and fragrance of eternity? Hear ye it not? Smell ye it not? Just now hath my world become perfect, midnight is also mid-day, —
>
> Pain is also a joy, curse is also a blessing, night is also a sun, — go away! or ye will learn that a sage is also a fool [*ein Weiser ist auch ein Narr*].
>
> Said ye ever Yea to one joy? O my friends, then said ye Yea also unto ALL woe. All things are enlinked, enlaced and enamoured, —
>
> — Wanted ye ever once to come twice; said ye ever: "Thou pleasest me, happiness! Instant! Moment!" then wanted ye ALL to come back again!
>
> — All anew, all eternal, all enlinked, enlaced and enamoured, Oh, then did ye LOVE the world,—
>
> — Ye eternal ones, ye love it eternally and for all time: and also unto woe do ye say: Hence! Go! but come back! FOR JOYS ALL WANT — ETERNITY! (Z IV 19 §10).

In his first book, *The Birth of Tragedy* (1872), Nietzsche had distinguished between two kinds of "Greek cheerfulness": first, an un-Dionysian cheerfulness, that is, a "senile, unproductive love of existence," and as such "opposed to the splendid 'naïveté' of the earlier Greeks," which he described as the "blossom of the Apollonian culture springing from the dark abyss, as the victory which the Hellenic will, through its mirroring of beauty, obtains over suffering and the wisdom of suffering"; and second, the Alexandrian cheerfulness of the theoretical individual (BT §17). Like the first kind of "cheerfulness," this kind is thoroughly un-Dionysian: It "combats Dionysian wisdom and art, [...] seeks to dissolve myth, [...] substitutes for a metaphysical comfort an earthly consonance, in fact, a *deus ex machina* of its own, the god of machines and crucibles [...]; believes that it can correct the world by knowledge, guide life by science, and actually confine the individual" — and here comes the positively Faustian bit — "within a limited sphere of solvable problems, from which he can cheerfully say to life: 'I desire you; you are worth knowing' [*»Ich will dich: du bist werth erkannt zu werden«*]" (BT §17).

Could the search for "happiness," for *Glück*, for the desire for that moment to last forever, be the true Faustian "sin," from which redemption or salvation (*Erlösung*) lies in the insight that the moment *is* already eternal, and it is precisely this *eternal* quality that makes it worthy of love? As opposed to the Faustian quest for the *moment*, Nietzsche's Zarathustra urges us to embrace the *eternal*, reflected in a different Goethean text:

The gods give everything, the infinite ones,	[*Alles geben die Götter, die unendlichen,*
To their beloved, completely,	*Ihren Lieblingen ganz.*
Every pleasure, the infinite ones,	*Alle Freuden, die unendlichen,*
Every suffering, the infinite ones, [completely.	*Alle Schmerzen, die unendlichen, ganz.*][123]

[123] Translated by Stephen Spender, in Robert M. Browning (ed.), *German Poetry from 1750 to 1900* (New York: Continuum, 1984), pp. 57-58.

Nietzsche's Zarathustra intensifies this language even further: Instead of *Freude* and *Schmerz*, he talks about *Lust* as opposed to *Weh* and *Herzeleid*.[124]

The final reprise of this roundelay (*Rundgesang*), here used in the general sense of a song that accompanies drinking, rather than the technical sense of a *rondelet* (consisting of a strict metrical pattern and rhyme scheme, including a refrain), precedes the final chapter of *Thus Spoke Zarathustra* entitled "The Sign."

4. (b) "The Sign"

Sadly, we shall never know what Jung would have made of the final chapter of *Thus Spoke Zarathustra* entitled "The Sign," because—after what was to be the final seminar of 15 February 1939 (which continued a discussion of "On Old and New Law Tables")—the seminar series abruptly came to an end. Not that

[124] For a one-time Lutheran such as Nietzsche, the word *Herzeleid* would have triggered numerous associations, not least the old German hymn, *O Traurigkeit, o Herzeleid* — attributed to the Jesuit, Friedrich Spee (1591-1635), adapted for Protestant use by Johann Rist (1607-1667), and turned into a chorale by J.S. Bach (BWV 404) and into a chorale prelude and fugue by Brahms — which contains these lines:

O great woe!	[*O große Not!*
God Himself lies dead.	*Gott selbst liegt tot.*
On the Cross he has died;	*Am Kreuz ist er gestorben:*
And thus He has gained for us	*hat dadurch das Himmelreich*
By love the kingdom of Heaven.	*Uns aus Lieb' erworben.*]

Certainly these lines also left their mark on Hegel, who remarked in his *Faith and Knowledge* (1802) that "Good Friday must be speculatively re-established in the whole truth and harshness of its God-forsakenness" (see Hegel, *Faith and Knowledge*, ed. and trans. Walter Cerf and H.S. Harris (Albany, NY: State University of New York Press, 1977), p. 181). The term *herzeleit* is frequently used in Mechthild of Magdeburg's *The Flowing Light of the Godhead*, a work cited by Jung at several points in *Transformations and Symbols of the Libido* (see PU §107, fn. 78; §154; §160, fn. 28; and §431). And the term *Herzeleid* is cognate with *Herzeloyde*, who—as Parzival's mother by Gahmuret; as sister of Anfortas, Trevrizent, Schoysiane, and Repanse de Schoye; and as daughter of Frimutel and granddaughter of Titurel—is closely bound up with the Grail in Wolfram von Eschenbach's epic.

this mammoth exercise in textual interpretation simply petered out; rather, it was overtaken by the global political events to which it had, with increasing urgency, been alluding in previous sessions. For, despite the occasional expression of *Zarathustra*-fatigue—for instance, Jung himself opened the Spring Term of May-June 1938 by confessing, "And when I looked through the chapters we have dealt with and those we have still to deal with, I must tell you frankly, I got bored stiff, chiefly by the style" (SNZ, vol. 2, 1209)—there was plenty of interpretative vitality left in the group, which bore out Jung's earlier remarks at the opening of the Spring Term of May-June 1936, when he said that he had "agreed to risk the analysis of *Zarathustra*"—rather than looking at, for instance, Goethe's *The Fairytale* (*Das Märchen*)—"chiefly because it is a very modern piece of work which has much to do with what is happening in our time" (that is, the mid to late 1930s). It was, Jung maintained, of "great interest to look into the actual working of the unconscious mind, which has anticipated all the great political and historical events of our days"; even if, he added, *Thus Spoke Zarathustra* itself was a kind of work which "stirs the unconscious of modern man to an uncanny degree, all the more because one doesn't notice the way in which [...] it works secretly and at times even in a poisonous way" (SNZ, vol. 2, 893). As the final chapter of *Zarathustra* as Nietzsche had left the work standing, however, "The Sign" pulls together the narrative and imagistic threads that we have been following in our study of this epic of transformation.

Now the notion of the sign is itself a biblical one. In the Gospel of Matthew, some of the scribes and the Pharisees approach Jesus and ask for a sign. In response, Jesus replies, "An evil and adulterous generation seeketh for a sign: and a sign shall not be given to it, bit the sign of Jonas, the prophet. For as Jonas was in the whale's belly three days and three nights: so shall the Son of Man be in the heart of the earth three days and three nights. The men of Ninive shall rise in judgment with this generation, and shall condemn it: because they did penance at the preaching of Jonas.

And behold a greater than Jonas is here" (Matthew 12:39-41). In other words, the sign here will be the death and resurrection of Jesus (that is, his descent into Hell and his being raised from the dead).

In a later discourse in this same gospel, Jesus responds to the request of the disciples for information about the signs of his coming (*parousia*), but his advice is as much a warning about the avoidance of false signs as it is a description of what the signs of those end times will be. In those final days, "the sign of the Son of Man shall appear in heaven" (Matthew 24:30), a statement that is generally expounded in the Patristic tradition as the Cross of Christ that shall be seen in the air (Haydock, 1301). In the words of St. John Chrysostom (in a homily against Marcionists and Manichæans), "the cross is that which is brighter than the sun, more brilliant than the sunbeam: for when the sun is darkened, then the cross shines brightly; and the sun is darkened, not because it is extinguished, but because it is overpowered by the brilliancy of the cross."[125] This sign announces the imminence of the Last Judgment, when "the Son of Man shall come in his majesty" (Matthew 25:31). In the case of Nietzsche's *Zarathustra*, however, a very different kind of sign (and a correspondingly different kind of *parousia*) is announced.

This chapter's title, "The Sign," recalls both this biblical motif and Zarathustra's words in the opening chapter of Part Four, "The Honey Sacrifice," "For THIS am I from the heart and from the beginning — drawing, hither-drawing, upward-drawing, upbringing; a drawer, a trainer, a training-master, who not in vain counselled himself once on a time: 'Become what thou art!' / Thus may men now come UP to me; for as yet do I await the signs that

[125] See "Homily on the Passage 'Father, if it be possible, let this cup pass from me, nevertheless not as I will but as thou wilt:' and against Marcionists and Manichæans: Also, that we ought not to rush into danger, but to prefer the will of God before every other will," in Philip Schaff (ed.), *Nicene and Post-Nicene Fathers*, First Series, vol. 9, *Chrysostom: On the Priesthood, Ascetic Treatises, Select Homilies and Letters, Homilies on the Statutes* (Grand Rapids, MI: Eerdmans, 1889), pp. 201-207 (p. 203).

it is time for my down-going; as yet do I not myself go down, as I must do, amongst men. / Therefore do I here wait, crafty and scornful upon high mountains [...]" (Z IV 1). After carousing with the Higher Men until midnight when he invited them to join in the singing of his roundelay, Zarathustra wakes up—as Socrates is reported to have been able to do (*Symposium*, 223c-d)—completely refreshed, "jump[ing] up from his couch, and, having girded his loins, [...] [coming] came out of his cave," where he is described as "glowing and strong, like a morning sun coming out of gloomy mountains" (Z IV 20).

In a reversal of the opening section of the Prologue, Zarathustra himself is now identified with the sun; in a repetition of the opening section, however, he repeats (in a slightly modified form) what he had said to the sun then, "'Thou great star,' spake he, as he had spoken once before, 'thou deep eye of happiness, what would be all thy happiness if thou hadst not THOSE for whom thou shinest!'" (Z IV 20). Contrasting himself, who is awake, to the Higher Men, who are still asleep, Zarathustra now doubts whether they really are his "proper companions" and whether it is for *them* he is waiting in his mountains. Just as, in the Prologue, Zarathustra had recognized that he was not "the mouth" for "these ears" of the people in the marketplace (Z I Prologue §5), so he realizes that "the audient ear for ME — the OBEDIENT ear, is yet lacking in their limbs" (Z IV 20). Hearing the cry of his eagle, Zarathustra looks up, and he is pleased to see one of his animals is also awake and honoring the sun. Yet his "love" for his animals cannot disguise a sense of bitter disappointment: "'[...] But still do I lack my proper men!'—" (Z IV 20).

Then, suddenly, something happens: a flock of innumerable birds descends on him, "as it were a cloud, like a cloud of arrows which poureth upon a new enemy," but on this occasion, it was "a cloud of love, [...] showered upon a new friend." And as he brushes the birds away so he can open his eyes, he puts out his hands and finds himself grasping "a mass of thick, warm, shaggy hair," while "a roar, — a long, soft lion-roar" fills the air. Zarathustra's response is threefold: first, he is astonished and wonders what is happening to him; second, he recognizes that "*the sign cometh,*" and "a change came over his heart"; and third, he declares, "MY CHILDREN ARE NIGH, MY CHILDREN," and he falls silent.

The sign that he recognizes as coming acquires in the way that it is described a veritably emblematic form: "And in truth, when it turned clear before him, there lay a yellow, powerful animal at his feet, resting its head on his knee, — unwilling to leave him out of love, and doing like a dog which again findeth its old master." (Shades, here, of Argos's recognition of Odysseus, in Book 17 of Homer's *Odyssey*; after twenty years of waiting, this faithful dog recognizes his master, wags his tail, and dies…) "The doves, however, were no less eager with their love than the Lion; and whenever a dove whisked over its nose, the Lion shook its head and wondered and laughed" (Z IV 20). Zarathustra's reaction to this scene is one of intense emotion: He falls silent, his heart is "loosed" (*gelöst*), and he begins to cry: "And he took no further notice of anything, but sat there motionless, without repelling the animals further" (Z IV 20). Not for the first time in this work, we have reached a turning point; we are on the cusp of (yet) another transformation, the backdrop to which is this iconic scene: "Then flew the doves to and fro, and perched on his shoulder, and caressed his white hair, and did not tire of their tenderness and joyousness. The strong Lion, however, licked always the tears that fell on Zarathustra's hands, and roared and growled shyly. Thus did these animals do. —" (Z IV 20).

Iconic maybe, but what does it *mean*? The dove is an ancient symbol, associated in ancient Mesopotamia with Inanna or Ishtar, the goddess of sex, love, and war; in ancient Greece, the dove was sacred to the goddess Aphrodite, during whose main festival, the Aphrodisia, doves would be sacrificed on her altars; while in Roman mythology, doves were likewise associated with the goddesses Venus and Fortuna. In the story of the Flood in the Hebrew bible, Noah sends a dove out of the ark: The first time it returns, because the water has not receded, but the second time it returns with a sprig of an olive tree in its mouth. Within the tradition of Christian iconography, the dove is a symbol of the Holy Spirit, and it is in this form that he descends on Jesus at his baptism in the River Jordan by the hands of John the Baptist. Writing in the Grail tradition, moreover, Wolfram explains how, every Good Friday, a host is placed by a dove on the Grail, which accordingly acquires a "wishing character": "And the stone from the Host receiveth all good that on earth may be / Of food or of drink, the earth beareth as the fulness of Paradise" (Book 9, §470, ll. 11-14; vol. 1, p. 271). According to Emma Jung and Marie-Louise von Franz in their study of the Grail, the motif of the stone and the phoenix in Wolfram "links the image of the Grail with ideas of a decidedly alchemical nature," adding that "it has been further surmised that the conception of the Grail as a stone arose through some confusion over the figure of the stone table [...] or because the Grail had been imagined as a sort of portable altar on which the Host brought by the dove was laid":

> This conception of the stone as an altar paten associates it once again with the stone used to close Christ's sepulchre. According to Eastern legends this was said to be the same stone struck by Moses in the desert to provide water for the Children of Israel (Exodus 17:6; I. Corinthians 10:4). The alchemists compared it to their *lapis*. Thus the *Aurora consurgens* describes the lapis as a treasure house "founded upon a sure rock." This rock "cannot be split unless it be . . . smitten three times with the rod of Moses, that waters may flow forth in great abundance, that all the people both men and

women drink thereof."[126]

Indeed, in the alchemical tradition, the dove represents the soul bird, as found in Matthieu Merian's engraving "The Tree of the Soul" in the *Philosophia Reformata* (1622) of Johann Daniel Mylius (1585-1628), reprinted in the *Musaeum Hermeticum* (published in Frankfurt in 1625). On the title page of his *Send-brieffe* in Jacob Boehme's *Theosophische Werke* (published in Amsterdam in 1682), three doves are depicted—Noah's dove with its olive branch, a messenger dove (or pigeon), and above them the dove of the Holy Spirit, with "24 pentecostal flames or fiery tongues of the spirits of the letter"; together these three doves, in view of Johann Georg Gichtel (1638-1710), represent the "threefold spirit — of God, of nature, of art."[127] In his discussion in *Mysterium Coniunctionis* of Abraham Eleazar's *Uraltes Chymisches Werck* (Leipzig, 1760), Jung highlights the passage where the Shulamite (or the "black mother") declares, "But I must be like a dove with wings, and I shall come and be free at vespertime, when the waters of impurity are abated, with a green olive leaf" (cited CW 14 §624).[128] Commenting on this passage, Edward F. Edinger (1922-98) argues that Eleazer's whole text has as its "basic psychological reference" an "inundation by the unconscious, which corresponds to Noah's flood":

> Now when the inner greenness has been discovered from out of the blackness, the Shulamite speaks of

[126] Emma Jung and Marie-Louise von Franz, *The Grail Legend*, trans. Andrea Dykes, 2nd edn. (Boston, London: Sigo Press; Coventure, 1986), pp. 118 and 153.

[127] Alexander Roob, *Alchemy and Mysticism*, trans. Shaun Whiteside (Cologne and London: Taschen, 2001), p. 355.

[128] The mysterious Shulamite derives from a figure in the Song of Solomon (6:13), whose names is variously interpreted as (a) a girl or woman from the town of Shulam; (b) a variant spelling of the girl from Shunem, Abishag, who kept the elderly King David warm (1 Kings 1:2-4); (c) a feminine form of the name Solomon, i.e., the figure of the Lover in the Song (NJB, OT, 1039; *Ignatius Catholic Study Bible*, 1031. According to Jung, the Shulamite "comes into the same category as those black goddesses (Isis, Artemis, Parvati, Mary) whose names mean 'earth'" (CW 14 §607).

> being like Noah's dove, with the green olive leaf in her mouth. The Shulamite has been transformed into the dove of the Holy Ghost, or the dove of Aphrodite; those are two aspects of the same thing. She is a bringer of good tidings, green good tidings. She is "the thing with feathers", the green-feathered one, bringing good tidings to the beleaguered alchemist who is in the position of Noah in his ark, hoping that maybe the waters are finally abating and there's going to be some respite. The olive branch signifies that the flood is over and God's covenant, with its rainbow, is about to come. The *nekyia*, or inundation from the unconscious, is over.[129]

As it happens, the Shulamite in Eleazer's *Uraltes Chymisches Werck* goes on to describe her "cleans[ing]" transformation from something "poisonous, black, and hateful without" into "the food of heroes" in terms borrowed from the Book of Job as "out of my [earth] shall come forth blood [...] for it is all as [fire], shining red Adamah [i.e., red earth], mingled with a glowing [fire],"[130] just as "out of the lion which Samson slew there afterward came forth honey" (cited CW 14 §624). In fact, the image of a (green) lion consuming the sun is frequently found in alchemical texts such as the *Rosarium philosophorum*, the green lion symbolizing the so-called *aqua regia* (that is, "regal" or "royal water"), a mixture of hydrochloric acid and nitric acid (and hence capable of dissolving metals), which "consumes" the sun—that is, gold. (We shall return to this symbol of the green lion in Chapter 4 below, pp. 315-321.)

[129] Edward F. Edinger, *The Mysterium Lectures: A Journey through C.G. Jung's "Mysterium Coniunctionis"* (Toronto: Inner City Books, 1995), p. 269.

[130] Cf. Job 28:5: "The land, out of which bread grew in its place, hath been overturned with fire" (DRV), which Haydock paraphrases with reference to the Hebrew and the Septuagint as, "and under it is turned up as it were fire" (Haydock, 662).

Here as elsewhere, however, it is not a question of simply identifying parallels (or identifying simplistic parallels), but of uncovering the deeper *structural* affinities between individual texts or between textual traditions. For the epiphany of the doves and the Lion marks a moment of transformation, analogous to the moment in "Of the Vision and the Riddle" where the shepherd bites off the head of the snake, leaps up, and laughs (Z III 2 §2), or the moment in Zarathustra's midday vision when he falls "into the well of eternity," a moment when "the world just now become[s] perfect" (Z IV 10). In such moments, Zarathustra realizes that he is "of to-day and heretofore" (*heute und ehedem*) but also that "something is in [him] that is of the morrow, and the day following, and the hereafter" (Z II 17); he does not "talk to the Present, neither [...] talk to the Never: for talking we have patience and time [*Zeit*] and more than time [*Überzeit*]" (Z IV 1); and likewise in this final chapter, when Zarathustra understands that, as he puts it, "MY CHILDREN ARE NIGH, MY CHILDREN," and the Lion licks his tears away, we are told that "all this went on for a long time, or a short time: for properly speaking, there is NO time on earth for such things —" (Z IV 20).

What has happened to the Higher Men? In the meantime, they have woken up, and "marshalled themselves for a procession to go to meet Zarathustra, and give him their morning greeting," but on reaching the door of the cave, the noise of their steps startles the Lion, which "turned away all at once from Zarathustra, and roaring wildly, sprang towards the cave." On hearing the roar of the Lion, the Higher Men "cried all aloud as with one voice, fled back and vanished in an instant" (Z IV 20), and it is surely to this moment that Jung refers when, in "The Psychology of the Unconscious" (1917; 1926; 1943), he writes that the "roaring of the Zarathustrian lion drove back into the cavern of the unconscious all the 'higher' men who were clamouring to live" (CW 7 §37) (even if the detail is not quite accurate and the interpretation is imprecise). At around the same time, in "The Transcendent Function" (a work written in 1916 but not published until 1957), Jung goes into more detail about how Nietzsche's *Zarathustra* offers a "good example of the suppression of the unconscious regulating influence."

On this account, the discovery of the Higher Men (including in some way the Ugliest Man) expresses this regulating influence, inasmuch as the Higher Men "want to drag Zarathustra down to the collective sphere of average humanity as it always has been," while the Ugliest Man is "actually the personification of the counteraction" (CW 8 §162). (Intriguingly, Jung thus sees the Higher Men as something essentially positive, whereas in Zarathustra's eyes, they are not even worthy of pity; see below.) In a phrase that echoes what he writes in "The Psychology of the Unconscious," Jung adds that the "roaring lion of Zarathustra's moral conviction forces all these influences, above all the feeling of pity, back again into the cave of the unconscious" (CW 8 §162). In this way "the regulating influence is suppressed, *but not the secret counteraction of the unconscious*" (CW 8 §162; my emphasis)—and in Jung's eyes this counteraction makes itself apparent, not in *Zarathustra* itself, but in Nietzsche's later writings (notably *The Case of Wagner* [1888], *Nietzsche contra Wagner* [1888], and *Ecce Homo* [1888; pub. 1908]).

In these writings, Jung suggests, two trends are discernible: first, Nietzsche "seeks his adversary in Wagner, whom he cannot forgive for *Parsifal*"; and second, "his whole wrath turns against Christianity and in particular against St Paul" (as reflected in Nietzsche's comments on Paul in *The Antichrist* [1888], but also in fact in *Dawn* [1881], written *before Zarathustra*) (CW 8 §162). Here as elsewhere, Jung is seemingly relentless in reading Nietzsche in biographical terms, reflected in his view that "Nietzsche's psychosis first produced an identification with the 'Crucified Christ' and then with the dismembered Dionysos"—a "catastrophe," with which "the counteraction at last broke through to the surface" (CW 8

162).[131] Or as Jung put it in in Faustian terms in "The Psychology of the Unconscious," "a whole man [...] knows that his bitterest foe, or indeed a host of enemies, does not equal that one worst adversary, the 'other self' who dwells in his bosom [*»ihm im Busen wohnt«*]":[132] Nietzsche became "one stigmatized by the spirit [*ein Stigmatisierter des Geistes*]; like Saul he had to experience Christification, when the 'other' whispered the 'Ecce Homo' in his ear" (CW 7 §43). On Jung's account, it all boiled down to one question, throwing back at Nietzsche an accusation that he himself had made in *Nietzsche contra Wagner*:[133] "Who 'broke before the cross' — Wagner or Nietzsche?" (ibid., §43).

(Subsequent commentators in the Jungian tradition have tended to follow this line of interpretation. In her account (of Jung's account), Marie-Louise von Franz argues that Jung's analysis of *Zarathustra* arrives at a "clear distinction" between what is "genuine inspiration" in the work and what appears to be "distorted as a result of Nietzsche's unresolved personal problems, chiefly those due to his inflation"; thus, she argues, Nietzsche "identified with the Superman," as a result of which the Higher Men want to drag him "down to the collective sphere of average humanity," until the Ugliest Man emerges "as an expression of the regulating influence of the unconscious." Likewise, von Franz agrees with Jung with regard to the causes of Nietzsche's alleged psychosis: "In reality," she writes, Nietzsche "identified with the adversary of the official Christ-figure, which explains his 'pagan' and anti-Christian

[131] For further discussion of this interpretation and its equation of the cave with the unconscious in the light of Jung's marginalia, see Paul Bishop, *The Dionysian Self*, pp. 118-120.

[132] Note another Faustian echo here in the allusion to *der Gott, der* [*ihm*] *im Busen wohnt*: in the second Study scene, Faust says: "The god that in my breast abides / Stirs to its depths mine inmost passion" (ll. 1566-1567).

[133] "Richard Wagner, apparently most triumphant, but in truth a decaying and despairing decadent, suddenly sank down, helpless and broken, before the Christian cross ..." (NCW How I Broke Away from Wagner §2).

leanings," since he had been "overwhelmed by the unconscious, which in his day was surging up with great power.")[134]

Yet Jung is surely also right to detect a significant shift in this episode: So what, in the context of *our* reading of *Zarathustra* as an epic of transformation, is this significance? It is precisely that Zarathustra—whose discourse in the marketplace urged his listeners to transform themselves into *Übermenschen,* whose opening discourse in Part One featured the transformation of the spirit (into the Camel, then the Lion, and then the Child), and whose discourse on the vision and the riddle featured the shepherd who bit off the head of the snake and became "no longer man" but a "transfigured being, a light-surrounded being, that LAUGHED!" (Z III 2 §2); and who himself has undergone numerous transformations, numerous ascents and descents, in the course of the epic narrative, notably in the chapter of Part Three called "The Convalescent" (Z III 13)—is transformed for one more (and final?) time. "Stunned and strange" (*betäubt und fremd*), Zarathustra now rises from his seat: he is "astonished" or amazed (*staunend*), he inquires of his heart (*fragte sein Herz*), he reflects (*besann sich*), he is alone (*allein*). He asks himself two questions, "What did I hear?" and "what happened unto me just now?" (*was geschah mir eben?*), a question he has been repeatedly asking himself in the course of the preceding narrative.[135] And then—as if all that has gone before had been a kind of series of psychoanalytic sessions—he understands: "But soon there came to him his recollection, and he took in at a glance [*mit e i n e m Blick*] all that had taken place between yesterday and

[134] Marie-Louise von Franz, *C.G. Jung: His Myth in Our Time*, trans. William H. Kennedy (New York: Putnam, 1975), pp. 43-44. According to von Franz, a similar lack of differentiation between consciousness and the unconscious can be found in the thought of Hegel.

[135] For further discussion of the notion of pure psychic process-event or happening, see John Peck, "*Etwas geschah:* Orphaned Event and Its Adoptions," *Spring* 84 (Fall 2010), 143-162.

to-day" (Z IV 20). And what he understands has to do, significantly enough, with a stone.

Now we have already met the image of a stone in another context, one whose significance Jung discerns as essentially biographical in relation to Nietzsche. In the conclusion to the episode involving the fatal fall of the rope dancer, the "man who would not be 'surpassed' [*»übersprungen«*]" (CW 7 §36) (or the man who rather *was literally* "surpassed" by the buffoon or *Possenreißer*), Zarathustra says to the dying rope dancer, "Thy soul will be dead even sooner than thy body" (Z I Prologue §6), a passage which in "The Psychology of the Unconscious" Jung reads as prophetic of Nietzsche's own fate. Jung links this passage to the later episode in "Of the Vision and the Riddle" when the dwarflike Spirit of Gravity warns Zarathustra, "O Zarathustra, [...] thou stone of wisdom! Thou threwest thyself high, but every thrown stone must — fall! / O Zarathustra, thou stone of wisdom, thou sling-stone, thou star-destroyer! Thyself threwest thou so high, — but every thrown stone — must fall!" (Z III 2 §2). ("And when he cried his 'Ecce Homo' over himself," Jung wryly adds, "again it was too late, as once before when this saying was uttered, and the crucifixion of the soul"—one of the central episodes in *The Red Book*, as we shall see in Volume 4—"began before the body was dead" [CW 7 §36].)

Yet the stone in this final chapter is a specific stone, and one that we have met before. At the opening of Part Four, Zarathustra was sitting on "a stone in front of his cave" and "gaz[ing] calmly into the distance" before he reaffirmed his mission, "I have long ceased to strive any more for happiness, I strive for my work," and—seeing that "honey is there ready to hand, yellow, white, good, ice-cool, golden-comb-honey"—promised to make the honey sacrifice (but never actually makes it: For the *real* honey and the *real* sacrifice involves something else, "Drip thy sweetest dew, thou honey of my heart!"). After the "many seas" *around* him and the "dawning human futures," the "rosy red stillness" and the "unclouded silence" *above* him, the next day Zarathustra was sitting on this stone in front of his cave when suddenly he saw, next to his own shadow, the shadow of the old Prophet (a figure whose message, "All is alike, nothing is worth while, the world is without meaning, knowledge strangleth," means that it is conventionally interpreted as representing Arthur Schopenhauer, the pessimistic philosopher *par excellence*). "Dost thou still hear nothing?", the old Prophet asked, "doth it not rush and roar out of the depth?" and so Zarathustra listened and heard a "long, long cry, which the abysses threw to one another and passed on; for none of them wished to retain it: so evil did it sound"—a cry that the old Prophet identified as the cry of the Higher Man, for he (that is, the Prophet) had come to seduce Zarathustra to his *last sin* (*letzte Sünde*), which is the sin of pity (*Mitleid*) (Z IV 2). It was, then, *this* cry that had originally motivated Zarathustra to go in search of the Higher Man (and to meet the various figures that he has done on this search, which constitutes the action of Part Four).

Now Zarathustra recalls this moment: "Here is indeed the stone," he says, stroking his beard: "'[...] on IT sat I yester-morn; and here came the soothsayer unto me, and here heard I first the cry which I heard just now, the great cry of distress" (Z IV 20). Now Zarathustra realizes that it was the distress (*Not*) of the Higher Men that the old Prophet has prophesied, and that his last sin was not just pity, but pity for the Higher Men — "FELLOW-SUFFERING! FELLOW-SUFFERING WITH THE HIGHER MEN!" (Z IV 20). But "THAT — hath had its time!" Zarathustra cries, and his face changes into brass (*sein Antlitz verwandelte sich in Erz*). Repeating his motto about setting aside "suffering and fellow-suffering" (*mein Leid und mit Mitleiden*) and about rejecting happiness (*Glück*) and striving after his work (*nach meinem Werke*), now he rejoices in this moment:

> "Well! The Lion hath come, my children are nigh,
> Zarathustra hath grown ripe, mine hour hath come:—

> This is MY morning, MY day beginneth: ARISE NOW, ARISE, THOU GREAT NOONTIDE!"—
>
> Thus spake Zarathustra and left his cave, glowing and strong, like a morning sun coming out of gloomy mountains. (Z IV 20)

In the final scene in *Faust II*, the Chorus and Echo sing, "Softly the lions, dumb- / Friendly about us come" (*Löwen, sie schleichen stumm- / Freundlich um uns herum*) (ll. 11850-51)—lines that Jung described in his letter to Baur-Celio as signifying an ἄδυτον (*adyton*, i.e., something "not to be entered," an "innermost sanctuary or shrine") (L1, 141). So too, here, the presence of the Lion announces the momentousness of this scene. In this final transformation, Zarathustra himself is said to be (as he was at the beginning of this chapter) "glowing and strong, like a morning sun coming out of gloomy mountains": Whereas before he simply left or "came out" of (*kam heraus*) his cave, this time he "leaves" (*verließ*) it—the implication being that he will never return. Thus begins Zarathustra's third (cf. Z I 22 §3) (or fourth?)—in any event, his *final—descent*: he has become like the sun, strangely akin to the transformatory moment associated with Moses descending from Mount Horeb (Exodus 34: 29-35); or with the account in Plutarch's account in "On the Sign of Socrates" (*De genio Socratis*) of Timarchus's descent into the cave of the oracle Triphonius, from which after two nights and a day he returned, emerging "in the morning with a radiant countenance" [§22]);[136] or indeed the transformation that is

[136] "De Genio Socratis," in Plutarch, *Moralia*, vol. 7, trans. Philip H. De Lacy and Benedict Einarson (London; New York; Heinemann; Putnam, 1959), pp. 361-509. Of the account given by Pausanias in his *Description of Greece* of what happened to those who descended to the oracle of Triphonius, Nietzsche might in particular have appreciated that those who reascend, while temporarily paralysed, subsequently "recover all their faculties, and the power to laugh will return" (Book 9, Chapter 39, §14; in Pausanias, *Description of Greece*, trans. W.H.S. Jones, vol. 4, *Books VIII (XXII) – X* (London; Cambridge, MA: Heinemann; Harvard University Press, 1935),

said by Lucius (in Apuleius's *Metamorphoses* or *The Golden Ass*) to have occurred in the initiatory rites of the Mysteries of Isis: "I came to the boundary of death and, having trodden on the threshold of Proserpina, I travelled through all the elements and returned. In the middle of the night I saw the sun flashing with bright light, I came face to face with the gods below and the gods above and paid reverence to them from close at hand."[137] (In other words, we have moved from an "ass-festival" to a *golden ass*.) Face to face with the gods … or in this case, perhaps face to face with the *Übermensch*?

In the light of such textual or symbolic highlights, it is surely no wonder that Jung was so intrigued by Nietzsche's *Zarathustra*. In Chapters 2, 3 and 4, we shall turn to considering how this fascination with *Zarathustra* played out in some of his central works, from *Transformations and Symbols of the Libido* and his early theoretical writings to his later studies of psychology and alchemy, including his late, great work *Mysterium Coniunctionis*.

---

p. 355).

[137] Apuleius, *Metamorphoses*, vol. 2, *Books VII-XI*, trans. J. Arthur Hanson (Cambridge, MA, and London: Harvard University Press, 1989), p. 341 (Book 11, §23). For further discussion, see Wytse Hette Keulen, Stefan Tilg, Lara Nicolini, Luca Graverini, S.J. Harrison, Stelios Panayotakis, D. van Mal-Maeder (eds.), *Apuleius Madaurensis Metamorphoses, Book XI, The Isis Book: Text, Introduction and Commentary* (Leiden: Brill, 2015), pp. 397-404.

Chapter 2

Nietzsche's *Zarathustra* in Jung's *Collected Works* [A]

In the early pages of *Transformations and Symbols of the Libido* (1911-12), Jung draws on Nietzsche as one of many sources which he uses to establish the intellectual framework of his study based on the fantasies of Miss Miller.[1] Correspondingly, Jung mainly refers to Nietzsche's early works rather than to *Thus Spoke Zarathustra*; in the second half of *Transformations and Symbols of the Libido*, however, this will radically change—and lengthy quotations from Nietzsche's late poetic works will move to the forefront of Jung's argumentation, as we shall see. In this second half, Jung admires the symbolism of his poetry as being of the "greatest richness" (PU §470), and he presents Nietzsche as articulating in poetic form what is, in fact, archetypal or mythological material:

> That which in Nietzsche appears as a poetical figure of speech is really a primitive myth. It is as if the poet still possessed a dim idea or capacity to feel and reactivate those imperishable phantoms of long-past worlds of thought in the words of our present-day speech and in the images which crowd themselves into his phantasy. (PU §471)

[1] For further information on Miss Miller, see the pioneering article by Sonu Shamdasani, "A Woman Called Frank," *Spring: A Journal of Archetype and Culture*, 50 (1990), 26-56.

Although Jung here says "as if," it is plain from his comments elsewhere and in particular from his seminar on *Thus Spoke Zarathustra* that he believes that Nietzsche really *did* possess that capacity. The first of the topics that establish Jung's argumentational framework in his study is—language.

Nietzsche's *Zarathustra* in *Transformations and Symbols of the Libido* (1911-12)

(a) *Thinking with Directed Attention, Language, and Dreams*

As he sketches out his distinction in the first chapter of Part One between two kinds of thinking, that is, between "directed thinking" and "dream or phantasy thinking" (PU §28), Jung cites Nietzsche in relation to this first category, "thinking with directed attention" (PU §16). Second, in addition to Christian Wolff (1679-1754), William James (1842-1910), and Hermann Lotze (1817-81), Jung refers in a footnote to Nietzsche's aphorism in *The Gay Science* where he states that "thoughts are the shadows of our feelings — always darker, emptier, and simpler" (GS §179; cf. PU §15, fn. 4). In a subsequent footnote, Jung refers to the equation of intelligence with speech made by Johann Georg Hamann (1730-88), the argument proposed by Fritz Mauthner (1849-1923) that there is no thought without speech (and so speaking *is* thinking), and to Nietzsche's view of intelligence as "speech metaphysics" (*Sprachmetaphysik*), perhaps thinking of the argument in *Twilight of the Idols* that "we are not rid of God because we still have faith in grammar" (TI "Reason" in Philosophy §5, cf. PU §17, fn. 5). Third, Jung points to Nietzsche's *Human, All-Too-Human* as a source for the idea that ontogeny recapitulates phylogeny: "In our sleep and in our dreams we pass through the whole thought of earlier humanity" (HA, vol. 1, §12); and: "I mean, in the same way that man reasons in his dreams, he reasoned when in the waking state many thousands of years. [...]" (HA, vol. 1, §13) (PU §37).

More generally, Jung places the entire question of the two kinds of thinking into a broader historico-intellectual context when he writes of such theological debates as how many angels could dance on the point of a pin or whether Christ could have carried out his work of redemption just as well if he had come into the world as a pea—and his specific reference point is Nietzsche:

> The possibility of such problems, to which belong the metaphysical problems in general, viz., to be able to know the unknowable, shows us of what peculiar kind that mind must have been which created such things which to us are the height of absurdity. Nietzsche had guessed, however, at the biological background of this phenomenon when he spoke of the "beautiful tension" [*prachtvolle Spannung*] of the Germanic mind which the Middle Ages created. Taken historically, Scholasticism, in the spirit of which persons of towering intellectual powers, such as Thomas of Aquinas, Duns Scotus, Abelard, William of Occam and others, have labored, is the mother of the modern scientific attitude, and a later time will see clearly how and in what Scholasticism still furnishes living undercurrents to the science of today. (PU §30)

The source of this remark, attributed to Nietzsche, is the Preface to *Beyond Good and Evil*—with its anti-Platonic invective, including its description of Plato's "invention of the pure spirit and the Good as such" as a "dogmatist's error" and its description of Christianity as "Platonism for 'the people'" (BGE Preface). On this account, the "fight against Plato or […] the fight against the Christian-ecclesiastical pressure of millennia […] has created in Europe a magnificent tension of the spirit the like of which had never yet existed on earth" (BGE Preface).[2]

Two points should be noted here: first, Nietzsche's use of a metaphor of the bow. Thanks to this "magnificent tension," Nietzsche writes, and "with so tense a bow we can now shoot for the most distant goals" (BGE Preface). Within our overall interpretative context, this metaphor of the bow links back to Wolfram's *Parzival* (see Volume 1, pp. 252-273), and his narrator's claim, "Nor my tale like the bow shall be bended, but straight as an arrow flies" (*ez ist niht krump alsô der boge, / diz mære ist wâr unde sleht*) (§805, ll. 14-15; vol. 2, p. 174). And it looks forward to Nietzsche's encomium in *Ecce Homo* of the historical Zoroaster: "Zarathustra has more pluck in his body than all other thinkers put together. To tell the truth and to aim straight: that is the first Persian virtue. Have I made myself clear? ... " (EH Why I Am a Destiny §2). Second, while Jung adduces the phrase in relation to the Middle Ages in general and Scholasticism in particular, there is no mention whatsoever of either in Nietzsche's text. Rather, Nietzsche refers to two occasions on which "attempts have been made in the grand style [*im grossen Stile*] to unbend the bow," namely: (a) Jesuitism; (b) the democratic Enlightenment, and in particular the free press.

So could it be in fact that Jung is thinking of the third of the *Untimely Meditations* on "Schopenhauer as Educator" (1874), in

[2] Compare with the following passages in Nietzsche's *Nachlass*, KSA 11, 34[163], 475-476: "The ecclesiastical pressure of millennia has created a magnificent tension of the bow, likewise the monarchical: the two attempted slackenings (instead of shooting with the bow) are 1) Jesuitism 2) democracy. Pascal is the glorious sign of that terrible tension: he laughed the Jesuits *to death*. — I am satisfied with despotic conditions provided that we are dealing with mixed races, where a tension exists anyway"; and KSA 11, 42[6], 696: "1 Dogmatists. Plato and the 'pure spirit.' the magnificent tension through the dogmatists. 2 Skeptics. The commanders rare. In the end the most mediocre rule in philosophy! Where does the will still exist?" (Nietzsche, *Unpublished Fragments (Spring 1885-Spring 1886)*, trans. Adrian Del Caro [*The Complete Works of Friedrich Nietzsche*, vol. 16] (Stanford, CA: Stanford University Press, 2020), pp. 48 and 244).

which Nietzsche wrote about his contemporary situation in relation to the Middle Ages as follows: "We live in the age of atoms, of atomistic chaos. In the Middle Ages the hostile forces were held together by the Church and, through the strong pressure it exerted, to some extent assimilated with one another. [...] We are [...] even now still in the ice-filled stream of the Middle Ages; it has thawed and is rushing on with devastating power. Ice-floes pile on ice-floe, all the banks have been inundated and are in danger of collapse. The revolution is absolutely unavoidable, and it will be the atomistic revolution [...]" (UM III §4)?[3] In his seminar on Nietzsche's *Zarathustra*, Jung told his listeners on 5 May 1937 that we have a sort of "reminiscence of what one might call a medieval or primitive world, in which the *numinosum* is outside of ourselves" (259) and he remarked on 19 October 1938 that the "consciousness of [hu]man[kind] has not increased very much since the Middle Ages" (324). In his *Red Book*, however, Jung himself had confessed: "I must catch up with a piece of the Middle Ages — within myself," adding: "We have only finished the Middle Ages of — others" (RB, 457).

An extensive footnoted quotation at the beginning of Chapter 2 in Part One, when Jung turns to consider the fantasies and dreams of Miss Miller, marks a change in his use of Nietzsche as well. In this footnote, drawn from Carl Albrecht Bernoulli's *Franz Overbeck und Friedrich Nietzsche: Eine Freundschaft*, vol. 1 (1908), Nietzsche himself serves as an example of the principle that recounting fantasies or dreams can reveal an individual's most painful problems:

> This author depicts Nietzsche's behavior in Basle society: "Once at a dinner he said to the young lady

[3] Friedrich Nietzsche, *Untimely Meditations*, trans. R.J. Hollingdale (Cambridge: Cambridge University Press, 1983), p. 150.

> at his side, 'I dreamed a short time ago that the skin of my hand, which lay before me on the table, suddenly became like glass, shiny and transparent, through which I saw distinctly the bones and the tissues and the play of the muscles. All at once I saw a toad sitting on my hand and at the same time I felt an irresistible compulsion to swallow the beast. I overcame my terrible aversion and gulped it down.' The young lady laughed. 'And do you laugh at that?' Nietzsche asked, his deep eyes fixed on his companion, half questioning, half sorrowful. The young lady knew intuitively that she did not wholly understand that an oracle had spoken to her in the form of an allegory and that Nietzsche had revealed to her a glimpse into the dark abyss of his inner self." (PU §58, fn. 1)

Jung goes on to quote Bernoulli's own interpretation of this conversation and his analysis of its significance: "One can perhaps see, behind that harmless pleasure of faultless exactness in dress, a dread of contamination arising from some mysterious and tormenting disgust," and Jung adds his own:

> Nietzsche went to Basle when he was very young; he was then just at the age when other young people are contemplating marriage. Seated next to a young woman, he tells her that something terrible and disgusting is taking place in his transparent hand, something which he must take completely into his body. We know what illness caused the premature ending of Nietzsche's life. It was precisely this which he would tell the young lady, and her laughter was indeed discordant. (PU §58, fn. 1)

In Chapter 7 of Part Two, Jung refers back to Bernoulli's account of this episode in the course of a quotation from the vision of the shepherd and the snake in *Thus Spoke Zarathustra*, noting in relation to the line, "Did I ever see so much disgust and pallid fear upon a countenance" (Z II 2 §2), that Nietzsche himself "must have shown at times a certain predilection for loathsome animals" (PU §595, fn. 112). Not the first time and (as we shall see) not for the last, Jung conflates Nietzsche the writer with Nietzsche the human individual, perhaps in the same way that Jung's own theory of self-transformation has its source in his own personal experiences in (or of writing) his *Red Book*.

Then, in Chapter 3 of Part One, Jung assimilates the biblical notion of God with the Freudian notion of libido, clinching his argument with an allusion to Goethe's *Wilhelm Meister*—[4] and an explicit reference to Nietzsche's *Zarathustra*:

> The attributes of the divinity are omnipotence, a sternly persecuting paternalism ruling through fear (Old Testament) and a loving paternalism (New Testament). These are the attributes of the libido in that wide sense in which Freud has conceived this idea empirically.

---

[4] See the second song sung by the harpist in *Wilhelm Meister's Apprenticeship*:

"Who never ate his bread in tears, Who never throughout sorrowful nights, Sat weeping on his bed, He knows not you, Heavenly Powers.	[*Wer nie sein Brot mit Tränen ass, Wer nie die kummervollen Nächte Auf seinem Bette weinend sass, Der kennt euch nicht, ihr himmlischen Mächte!*
You bring us into life, The poor man you let fall into guilt, Then leave him to his pain: For all guilt is suffered for on earth"	*Ihr führt ins Leben uns hinein, Ihr lasst den Armen schuldig werden, Dann überlasst ihr ihn der Pein: Denn alle Schuld rächt sich auf Erden.*]

(translated by Richard Stokes in *The Fischer-Dieskau Book of Lieder*, ed. Dietrich Fischer-Dieskau (New York: Knopf, 1977), p. 230).

> [...] As is easily understood, that which is valuable in the God-creating idea is not the form but the power, the libido. The primitive power which Job's Hymn of Creation vindicates, the unconditional and inexorable, the unjust and the superhuman, are truly and rightly attributes of libido, which "leads us unto life," which "lets the poor be guilty," and against which struggle is in vain. Nothing remains for [hu]mankind but to work in harmony with this will. Nietzsche's "Zarathustra" teaches us this impressively. (PU §111)

In a footnote further on in this chapter, Jung suggestively compares a passage from St. Augustine's *Confessions* (Book 10, Chapter 6) with the chapter from Part Four of Nietzsche's *Zarathustra* entitled "The Seven Seals" (*Die sieben Siegel*) (Z III 16), implicitly suggesting that Augustine's theology of interiority can be read as an anticipation of Nietzsche:

> "But what do I love when I love Thee, Oh God? Not the bodily form, nor the earthly sweetness, nor the splendor of the light, so dear to these eyes; nor the sweet melodies of the richly varied songs; not the flowers and the sweet scented ointments and spices of lovely fragrance; not manna and honey; not the limbs of the body whose embraces are pleasant to the flesh. I do not love these when I love my God, and yet the light, the voice, the fragrance, the food, the embrace of my inner man; when these shine into my soul, which no space contains, which no time takes away, where there is a fragrance which the wind does not blow away, where there is a taste which no gluttony diminishes and where harmony abides which no satiety can remove — that is what I love, when I love my God." (Perhaps a model for

Zarathustra: "Die sieben Siegel," Nietzsche's works, VI, p. 33 ff.) (PU §127, fn. 41)[5]

Jung returns to this chapter from *Zarathustra* in Part Two of *Transformations and Symbols of the Libido*; for now, we should note that the argumentational context in which Jung suggests this parallel is an argument about the psychological transformation wrought in different ways by, on the one hand, Mithraism and, on the other, Christianity—culminating in the Renaissance (represented here by Petrarch) and its "abundance of libido" (*diese Libidomenge*). For while Mithraic worship was a "nature religion in the best sense of the word," the primitive Christians "exhibited throughout an antagonistic attitude to the beauties of this world," and the abundance of libido "pursues with a budding Renaissance (for example, Petrarch) a course which outgoing antiquity had already sketched out as religious" (PU §127). (Of course, it is a passage from Augustine that Petrarch is said to have cited in his account of his ascent of Mont Ventoux on 26 April 1336.)[6]

---

[5] In the revised German Divine Office (or *Feier des Stundengebetes*), this passage from St Augustine is chosen on Wednesday of Week 15 in Ordinary Time of Year 2 as part of the second reading in the *Lesehore* (or *Vigil*) after a reading from the Book of Job (4:1-21); see *Monastisches Lektionar*, vol. II/2, *6.-34. Woche im Jahreskreis* (St. Ottlien: EOS Verlag, 1993), pp. 269-271.

[6] For the significance of Petrarch's ascent of Ventoux—whether it actually took place or should be read as an allegory—as a pivotal moment in the shift from the medieval to the modern period, see the remarks by Hans Blumenberg (1920-1996) in *Die Legitimität der Neuzeit* (Frankfurt am Main: Suhrkamp, 1966; [2]1996) (see *The Legitimacy of the Modern Age*, trans. Robert M. Wallace (Cambridge, MA, and London: MIT Press, 1983), pp. 341-342); and by Ernst Cassirer, Paul Oskar Kristeller, and John Herman Randall, Jr., *The Renaissance Philosophy of Man* (Chicago: University of Chicago Press, 1948), pp. 28-29 and 36-46. See also Michael O'Connell, "Authority and the Truth of Experience in Petrarch's 'Ascent of Mount Ventoux,'" *Philological Quarterly*, 62 (1983), 507-520; and Tomáš Nejeschleba, "Petrarch's Ascent of Mont Ventoux and Philosophy," *Archiwum Historii Filozofii i Myśli Społecznej = Archive of the History of Philosophy and Social Thought*, 64 (2019), 81-94.

(b) "Poetry means that behind words the primordial word is made to resound"

In Chapter 4 of Part One, Nietzsche moves from being buried in the footnotes of *Transformations and Symbols of the Libido* and is brought into the main body of Jung's text. The use made here of Nietzsche is correspondingly very different: as part of a discussion of the parallels between the ecstatic experiences of Mechthild von Magdeburg, Hildegard von Bingen, and Symeon the Theologian, Jung introduces as a further point of comparison Nietzsche's poem "Glory and Eternity" (*Ruhm und Ewigkeit*), where one is said to encounter an "essentially similar" symbol (PU §159):

> "Hush! I see vastness! — and of vasty things
> Shall man be done, unless he can enshrine
> Them with his words? Then take the night which brings
> The heart upon thy tongue, charmed wisdom mine!
>
> "I look above, there rolls the star-strewn sea.
> O night, mute silence, voiceless cry of stars![7]

[7] In this line, "*o todtenstiller Lärm*" ("oh deathly silent uproar"), Edith Düsing sees an echo of Pascal's *pensée*, "Le silence éternel de ces espaces infinis m'effraie" (201-*206*; Pascal, *Œuvres complètes*, ed. Louis Lafuma (Paris: Seuil, 1963), p. 528), and a response to Kant's famous remark in the conclusion to the *Critique of Practical Reason*, "Two things fill the mind with ever new and increasing admiration and reverence, the more often and more steadily one reflects on them: *the starry heavens above me and the moral law within me*" (Kant, *Critique of Practical Reason*, ed. and trans. Mary Gregor (Cambridge: Cambridge University Press, 2015), p. 129); see Edith Düsing, "»Der einzige logische Christ« — »Pascal, den ich beinahe liebe«! Streiflichter zu Pascal im Spiegel Nietzsches," in Steffen Dietzsch and Gian Franco Frigo (eds.), *Vernunft und Glauben: Ein philosophischer Dialog der Moderne mit dem Christentum: Père Xavier Tilliette SJ zum 85. Geburtstag* (Berlin: de Gruyter, 2006), pp. 297-314 (p. 309); and compare with this *Nachlass* fragment from Autumn 1881: "At night, when there is a starry sky, we begin to feel how wretched our capacity to listen is. Oh, this deathly silent noise! —" (KSA 9, 14[4], 624).

> And lo! A sign! The heaven its verge unbars —
> A shining constellation falls towards me." (cited PU §159)[8]

According to Jung, it should not be astonishing "if Nietzsche's great inner loneliness calls again into existence certain forms of thought which the mystic ecstasy of the old cults has elevated to ritual representation"; after all, one finds in the liturgy of the cult of Mithras "many similar representations which we can now understand without difficulty as the ecstatic symbol of the libido" (PU §160). After quoting (in Greek) a passage from Albrecht Dieterich's reconstruction of a Mithraic liturgy, Jung reflects on this passage in relation to Nietzsche's poem: "Silence is commanded," he says, "then the vision of light is revealed": "The similarity of the mystic's condition and Nietzsche's poetical vision is surprising" (PU §161). Where the Mithraic liturgy talks about "many five-pointed stars coming down from the sun and filling the whole lower air," enabling the neophyte to "see the Circle and fiery doors cut off from the opening disc of the sun" (PU §160, fn.*), Nietzsche simply talks about a "constellation" (*ein Sternbild*), and in addition, Jung notes that constellations are "chiefly therio- or anthropomorphic symbols," pointing out that the "whistling and snapping" sounds of which the Mithras liturgy also speaks are a "tasteless, archaic relic, an allurement for the theriomorphic divinity"—and "probably also an infantile reminisence" (PU §160, fn. 28).[9]

---

[8] Translated as "Fame and Eternity" in Friedrich Nietzsche, *Dithyrambs of Dionysus: Bi-Lingual Edition*, trans. R.J. Hollingdale (London: Anvil Press Poetry, 1984), pp. 61-67. This text has in common with "The Seven Seals" the ecstatic cry, "For I love thee, O Eternity!" (*Denn ich liebe dich, o Ewigkeit!*).

[9] For further discussion of the sounds associated with the experience of *katabasis*, see Pierre Bonnechere, "The Sounds of *Katabasis*: Bellowing, Roaring, and Hissing at the Crossing of Impervious Boundaries," in Gunnel Ekroth and Ingela Nilsson (eds.), *Round Trip to Hades in the Eastern Mediterranean Tradition: Visits to the Underworld from Antiquity to Byzantium* (Leiden and Boston: Brill, 2018), pp. 240-259.

The papyrus's reference to "five-fingered stars" (similar to the Homeric epithet of "rosy-fingered" Eos, the personification of the dawn) is equally an anthropomorphic image and marks the point at which Jung turns to another poem by Nietzsche, "The Beacon" (*Das Feuerzeichen*), in order to offer a "Mithraic" reading of this text in terms of *analogy*. "Accordingly," Jung argues, "one may expect from that, that by long gazing a living being would be formed out of the 'flame image,' a 'star constellation' [*ein «Sternbild»*] of therio- or anthropomorphic nature, for the symbolism of the libido does not end with sun, light and fire, but makes use of wholly other means of expression" (PU §162):

> "Here, where the island grew amid the seas,
> A sacrificial rock high-towering,
> Here under darkling heavens,
> Zarathustra lights his mountain-fires.
>
> "These flames with grey-white belly,
> In cold distances sparkle their desire,
> Stretches its neck towards ever purer heights —
> A snake upreared in impatience:
>
> "This signal I set up there before me.
> This flame is mine own soul,
> Insatiable for new distances,
> Speeding upward, upward its silent heat.
>
> "At all lonely ones I now throw my fishing rod.
> Give answer to the flame's impatience,
> Let me, the fisher on high mountains,
> Catch my seventh, last solitude!" (cited PU §162)[10]

[10] Translated as "The Fire-Signal" in Nietzsche, *Dithyrambs of Dionysus*, trans. Hollingdale (pp. 46-47). In the opening entry for 18 March 1914 in *Black Book 5*,

The core of Jung's complex response to this text may be summarized as follows: namely, that "here libido becomes fire, flame and snake" (PU §163). He goes on to unpack this idea, explaining that the Egyptian symbol of the "living disc of the sun," portrayed as a disc with two entwining snakes, offers the "combination of both the libido analogies" (PU §163). Indeed, the essential structure of this representation, and hence of Jung's interpretation, is *analogy*, inasmuch as the "disc of the sun with its fructifying warmth is analogous to the fructifying warmth of love" and the "comparison [*der Vergleich*] of the libido with sun and fire is in reality analogous [*ein wesentlich »analoger«*]" (PU §163).

At the same time, he recognized that there was also a "causative" element involved, insofar as "sun and fire as beneficent powers are objects of human love"; for instance, the sun-hero Mithras is called the "well-beloved," and in Nietzsche's poem the comparison is "also a causative one [*ein kausativer*], but this time in a reversed sense [*in umgekehrtem Sinne*]" (PU §164). For the comparison with the snake is said by Jung to be "unequivocally phallic, corresponding completely with the tendency in antiquity, which was to see in the symbol of the phallus the quintessence of life and fruitfulness," so that the phallus is the "source of life and libido," the "great creator and worker of miracles," and "as such it received reverence everywhere" (PU §164). Consequently, Jung reads the symbolic dimension of the poem as functioning on three different levels of comparison:

(i) a comparison by *analogy*, as sun and fire;

(ii) comparisons based on *causative relations*, as

(a) object comparison: the libido is designated by its object, for example, the beneficent sun;

(b) subject comparison, in which the libido is designated

Jung noted Nietzsche's use of the expression "ultimate solitude," and asked: "My soul, do you hear this expression?" (BB5, 203).

by its place of origin or by analogies of this, for example, by a phallus or (analogously) a snake;

(iii) a third comparison, in which the *tertium comparationis* is the *activity*; for instance, the libido is "dangerous when fecundating like the bull — through the power of its passion — like the lion, like the raging boar when in heat, like the ever-rutting ass, and so on" (PU §164-§165).

As a heuristic principle, it is useful when we turn to *The Red Book* to ask ourselves whether its symbolic argumentation is working by (i) analogy; (ii) causative relations; (iii) activity comparisons (*Tätigkeitsvergleiche*); or all three.

After an excursus on the way in which the "possibilities of comparison mean just as many possibilities for symbolic expression" (PU §166), Jung turns back to Nietzsche's poem "The Beacon," and summarizes his reading of this text. In this poem, Jung reminds us, we find the flame used as an "image of the libido, theriomorphically represented as a snake," but also as an "image of the soul," cf. "This flame is mine own soul" (PU §172). And we see that the snake is to be taken as a "phallic image of the libido"—cf. "upreared in impatience" (!)—and that "this image, also an attribute of the conception of the sun (the Egyptian sun idol), is an image of the libido in the combination of sun and phallus" (PU §172). In *The Red Book*, the abundance of snake imagery should be read in the light of Jung's interpretative approach to this poem.

Nietzsche then disappears from the pages of *Transformations and Symbols of the Libido* for a while, returning again in Chapter 4 of Part Two in connection with a significant methodological point. At the beginning of this chapter, Jung rehearses his core charge against Freudian psychoanalysis, noting how—for Freud—"taken at the roots in the case of our patients, the 'nuclear complex' [...] reveals itself as the *incest problem*" (PU §284). Here, the six-million-dollar question is what the incest problem itself is really all about. While the sexual libido regressing to the parents "appears as the incest tendency," the reason why this path is "so easily travelled" is due to the "enormous indolence of humankind, which will relinquish no object of the past, but will hold it fast forever" (PU §284). At this juncture, Jung has recourse to a striking expression used by Nietzsche in his Preface to the first volume of *Human, All-Too-Human*): "The 'sacrilegious backward grasp' [*der »tempelschänderische Griff rückwärts«*] of which Nietzsche speaks reveals itself, stripped of its incest covering, as an original passive arrest of the libido in its first object of childhood" (PU §284; cf. HA I Preface §3). (This highly metaphorical expression refers in its original context to Nietzsche's break with Wagner and with classical philology, although it could equally well be applied to the turmoil caused by Jung's break with Freud.)[11] This is by no means the most well-known of key terms or "catchphrases" used by Nietzsche, but Jung found it highly suggestive: so much so, in fact, that he uses it again later in his controversial essay on Joyce's *Ulysses* (cf. CW 15 §182). (Here Jung relates the expression to the novel's depiction of the condition of being "bereft of gods" (*»entgöttert«*) more than Nietzsche himself had ever dreamed of being.)[12]

After this invocation of Nietzsche in connection with this crucial methodological point, he disappears again from *Transformations and Symbols of the Libido* only to return in another important way in Chapter 6 of Part Two, entitled "The Battle for the Deliverance from the Mother." In Chapter 2 of Part One, Jung had quoted a passage from the biblical Book of Job where Job reflects on human injustice and divine justice (PU §91):

> God hath shut me up with the unjust man, and hath delivered me into the hands of the wicked.

[11] See Paul Bishop, *The Dionysian Self: C.G. Jung's Reception of Friedrich Nietzsche* (Berlin and New York: de Gruyter, 1995), pp. 108-109.
[12] Bishop, *The Dionysian Self*, p. 179.

> I that was formerly so wealthy, am all on a sudden broken to pieces: he hath taken me by my neck, he hath broken me, and hath set me up to be his mark.
>
> He hath compassed me round about with his lances, he hath wounded my loins, he hath not spared, and hath poured out my bowels on the earth.
>
> He hath torn me with wound upon wound, he hath rushed in upon me like a giant.
>
> (Job 16:12-15, DRV)[13]

Earlier, Jung had remarked that the "analogy of feeling" (*Gefühlsanalogie*) lies in the "suffering of the *hopeless struggle against the more powerful*" (PU §92; Jung's emphasis). The feeling is "analogous," because "it is as if this conflict were accompanied from afar by the sounds of 'creation'" (cf. Job 38:7, "When the morning stars sang together, and all the sons of God shouted for joy" [KJV]), and Jung follows up this auditory image with a visual one, referring to how this sound "brings up a beautiful and mysterious image belonging to the unconscious, and which has not yet forced its way to the light of the upper world" (PU §92). This battle or conflict (*Kampf*) is, Jung suggests—and he specifically says that this is something "we surmise, rather than know" (*wir ahnen mehr, als daß wir es wissen*)—"really something to do with creation, with the struggles between negations and affirmations" (*mit dem Ringen zwischen Verneinung und Bejahung*) (PU §92).

[13] The significance of the story of Job runs throughout Jung's life, from his initial (but superficial) encounter with the work as a child (see MDR, 59 and 64) to *Aion* (1951), where Job is seen as a kind of "prefiguration of Christ" (MDR, 243), and obviously *Answer to Job* (1952). For further discussion, see Peter Kingsley, *Catafalque: Carl Jung and the End of Humanity*, 2 vols. (London: Catafalque Press, 2018), vol. 1, pp. 354-355 and 714-716). Jung is by no means alone among 20th-century thinkers in sensing huge significance in the figure of Job; see, for example, René Girard's *La Route antique des hommes pervers* (1985), translated by Yvonne Freccero as *Job, the Victim of His People* (Stanford: Stanford University Press, 1987).

Now Jung says that we can read these lines in a fresh light, and understand its symbolism as an "expression for the soul torment caused by the onslaught of the unconscious desires," an onslaught in which the libido "festers in his flesh, a cruel god has taken possession of him and pierced him with his painful libidinal projectiles, with thoughts, which overwhelmingly pass through him" (PU §454). In this context, Jung cites the words of a *dementia praecox* patient who once said to him during his recovery: "Today a thought suddenly thrust itself through me" (PU §454) (but one thinks also of the images of crucifixion and torment that one finds in *The Red Book*, of course.) This anecdote from the consulting room or hospital ward serves as the starting point for establishing a parallel between this passage in the Book of Job and Nietzsche's poem from the chapter in *Zarathustra* called "The Magician" (and in the *Dithyrambs of Dionysus* called "Complaint of Ariadne"):

> Stretched out, shivering
> Like one half dead whose feet are warmed,
> Shaken alas! by unknown fevers,
> Trembling from the icy pointed arrows of frost,
> Hunted by Thee, O Thought!
> Unutterable! Veiled! Horrible One!
> Thou huntsman behind the clouds!
> Struck to the ground by thee,
> Thou mocking eye that gazeth at me from the dark!
> ——— Thus do I lie
> Bending, writhing, tortured
> With all eternal tortures,
> Smitten
> By thee, crudest huntsman,
> Thou unfamiliar God.

Smite deeper!
Smite once more:
Pierce through and rend my heart!
What meaneth this torturing
With blunt-toothed arrows?
Why gazeth thou again,
Never weary of human pain,
With malicious, God-lightning eyes,
Thou wilt not kill,
But torture, torture? (cited PU §454)[14]

What this comparison reveals—and Jung is confident, in a way that his critics usually are not, that "no long-drawn-out explanation is necessary to enable us to recognize [it]"—is the "old, universal idea of the martyred sacrifice of God," which one meets in the "Mexican sacrifice of the cross" and in the "sacrifice of Odin" (PU §455).[15] Again, the sacrifice of Odin is an explicit point of reference in Jung's *Red Book*: After all, in the chapter in *Liber Secundus,* which is itself called "The Magician," Jung at one point finds himself

[14] See "Ariadne's Complaint," in *Dithyrambs of Dionysus*, trans. Hollingdale, pp. 53-59.

[15] In the previous chapter, "Symbolism of the Mother and of Rebirth," Jung had cited the example of an Aztec Codex of central Mexico, known as the Codex Fejérváry-Mayer, mentioned by Johann Georg Müller in his *Geschichte der Amerikanischen Urreligionen* (1855; ²1867): "One finds the same cross in old, pre-Mexican [*vormexikanischen*] hieroglyphic manuscripts, such as, for example, in the Dresden Mexican Codex, but especially in the manuscript of Mr Fejérváry in Hungary, at the end of which there is a colossal cross, in the middle of which hangs a bleeding divinity, figures stand around a scaffolding in the shape of a T, in the middle of which a bird is nesting" (J.G. Müller, *Geschichte der Amerikanischen Urreligionen* (Basel: Schweighauser, 1855), p. 498; as his source, Müller cites Gustav Klemm's *Allgemeine Kulturgeschichte der Menschheit*, 10 vols. (1843-1852), vol. 5, pp. 142-143) (see PU §401). In the previous paragraph, Jung cites these lines from the *Hávamál*, an Old Norse Edda from the Viking age, containing verses attributed to Odin:

"I know that I hung on the windswept tree
Nine nights through,
Wounded by a spear, dedicated to Odin
I myself to myself" (PU §400).

"hang[ing] above the ground on the swaying branch of the divine tree [...] my hands are bound and I am completely helpless" (RB, 443), and a few pages later he cries out to ΦΙΛΗΜΩΝ, "Damned charlatan, you aped the mysteries for me, you lay the mantle of the stars on me, you played a Christ-fool's comedy with me, carefully and ludicrously, in the tree just like Odin" (RB, 449).

Similarly, Jung writes in *Transformations and Symbols of the Libido* that the same conception "faces us in the oft-repeated martyrdom of St. Sebastian, where, in the delicate-glowing flesh of the young god, all the pain of renunciation which has been felt by the artist has been portrayed," adding the aesthetic observation that an artist "always embodies in his artistic work a portion of the mysteries of his time" and that "in a heightened degree the same is true of the principal Christian symbol, the crucified one pierced by the lance, the conception of the man of the Christian era tormented by his wishes, crucified and dying in Christ" (PU §455). Similarly, in "First Day" in *Liber Secundus* of *The Red Book*, Jung urges the reader: "Bind the holy Sebastian to a tree and slowly and rationally shoot arrow after arrow into his twitching flesh" and "remind yourself that each arrow that strikes him spares one of your dwarfish and lame brothers" (RB, 288).

That it is not, as Jung puts it, "torment that comes from without" which befalls humankind, but rather that the human individual is the "hunter, murderer, sacrificer and sacrificial knife" is said to be shown in yet another of Nietzsche's poems, in "Between Birds of Prey" (*Zwischen Raubvögeln*). In this text, Jung writes, the "apparent dualism"—that is, of sacrificer and sacrificed—is "transformed into the soul conflict [*in den seelischen Konflikt*] through the use of the same symbolism":

> "Oh, Zarathustra,
> Most cruel Nimrod!
> Whilom hunter of God

The snare of all virtue,
An arrow of evil!
Now
Hunted by thyself
Thine own prey
Pierced through thyself,
Now
Alone with thee
Twofold in thine own knowledge
Mid a hundred mirrors
False to thyself,
Mid a hundred memories
Uncertain
Ailing with each wound
Shivering with each frost
Caught in thine own snares,
Self knower!
Self hangman!

"Why didst thou strangle thyself
With the noose of thy wisdom?
Why hast thou enticed thyself
Into the Paradise of the old serpent?
Why hast thou crept
Into thyself, thyself? ..." (cited PU §456)[16]

[16] See "Amid Birds of Prey," in *Dithyrambs of Dionysus*, trans. Hollingdale, pp. 41-45. In this poem, Edith Düsing has suggested, the undermining of the ego puts into question the mission of Zarathustra, while the motif of the Death of God acquires a suicidal aspect (Düsing, "»Der einzige logische Christ« — »Pascal, den ich beinahe liebe«! Streiflichter zu Pascal im Spiegel Nietzsches," p. 306).

In Jung's commentary on this poem (which again reads like an extended gloss on certain passages in *The Red Book*),[17] we read that the "deadly arrows" do not "strike the hero from without, but it is he himself who, in disharmony with himself, hunts, fights and tortures himself" and that "within himself will has turned against will, libido against libido —[[18]] therefore, the poet says, 'Pierced through thyself,' that is to say, wounded by his own arrow" (PU §457).

Again, one thinks back (or forward) to *The Red Book* when Jung tells us that "because we have discerned that the arrow is a libido symbol, the idea of 'penetrating or piercing through' consequently becomes clear to us" and is a "phallic act of union with one's self, a sort of self-fertilization (introversion); also a self-violation, a self-

[17] We need to remember, however, the chronology of these works: *Transformations and Symbols of the Libido* was published in the *Jahrbuch für psychoanalytische und psychopathologische Forschungen* in 1911 and 1912, while work on what was to become *The Red Book* did not begin until 1913, beginning with his vision of the flood in October 1913 (RB, 127) and his first entry in *The Black Books* on 12 November 1913 (BB1, 149-150). Thus, what appears to be a gloss on *The Red Book* could, in fact, be its actual source. On this point hinges the entire question of the collective unconscious as the "library within."

[18] Jung had worked out this dynamic of "libido against libido" in his letter to Freud of 26 June 1910, in which he justified the formulation, "Sexuality destroys itself," as used in a talk on symbolism given to a Meeting of Swiss Psychiatrists in Herisau on 16 May 1910 (which has not survived, and which we only know through Freud's—sometimes critical—notes). While conceding that this formulation was "extremely paradoxical," Jung justified it by arguing that "what it boils down to is a *conflict at the heart of sexuality itself*." In the symbolism found in one of the hymns of the Zoroastrian Avesta (which tells of a cosmic struggle between Tishtrya, a benevolent deity associated with rainfall, and Apaosha, a demon associated with drought, which took the form of a fight between a white horse and a black horse), the ancient Iranian astral myth (in which the sun languishes in winter, but returns triumphant in spring, just as one's own fruitfulness languishes yet finally blossoms), and the symbolism of Mithraism (and his sacrifice of the bull, whose testicles are attacked by a scorpion while a serpent and a dog leap up at the wound), Jung found evidence for his contention that the libido has to "free itself" from the "repression" of the "incest prohibition"—a central idea that emerges in *Transformations and Symbols of the Libido* and in *The Red Book* alike (see *The Freud/Jung Letters: The Correspondence between Sigmund Freud and C.G. Jung*, ed. William McGuire, trans. Ralph Manheim and R.F.C. Hull (Cambridge, MA: Harvard University Press, 1988), pp. 335-337).

murder; therefore, Zarathustra may call himself his own hangman, like Odin, who sacrifices himself to Odin" (PU §457). As well as noting the alignment between Odin, Nietzsche's Zarathustra, and Jung (in *The Red Book*), surely, we are also prompted to ask ourselves: Is this what Jung was doing (or believed himself to be doing) in *The Red Book*—enacting a phallic act of union with himself? Self-penetrating, self-fertilizing, giving birth to the self ... all striking and powerful ways of talking about self-*transformation*?

Here we can see how Jung already moves to cover up the radical, almost shocking experiment in self-transformation—his "most difficult experiments" (*schwerste Experimente*), as he once described them (BB2, 171)—that is going to be carried out in *The Black Books* and *The Red Book* by making space for those transformational experiences to be hidden behind the apparently neutral, oh-so-scientific term "introversion" (*Introversion*). But Nietzsche's poems, as they are used here by Jung, give us a taste of the almost visceral violence involved in this process—as we shall see in Volume 4—as well as the haunting sense of beauty that this experience leaves in its wake.

To begin with, Jung offers a quasi-scientific, psychological explanation of this symbolism: "The wounding by one's own arrow means," he says, the "state of introversion" (PU §458). He then translates this concept into the imagery of the poem, in which the libido "sinks into its 'own depths' [*»eigene Tiefe«*] (a well-known comparison of Nietzsche's)[[19]] and finds there below, in the

[19] Actually, not that common an expression in Nietzsche (see KSA, 13[1], 427), although there is a metaphorics of depth at work in *Zarathustra*; see "Calm is the bottom of my sea: who would guess that it hideth droll monsters! / Unmoved is my depth: but it sparkleth with swimming enigmas and laughters [*Unerschütterlich ist meine Tiefe: aber sie glänzt von schwimmenden Räthseln und Gelächtern*]" (Z II 13), and "O heaven above me, thou pure, thou deep heaven! Thou abyss of light! Gazing on thee, I tremble with divine desires. / Up to thy height to toss myself — that is MY depth! In thy purity to hide myself — that is MINE innocence! [*In deine Höhe mich zu werfen — das ist meine Tiefe! In deine Reinheit mich zu bergen — das ist meine Unschuld!*]" (Z III 4).

shadows of the unconscious, the substitute for the upper world, which it has abandoned: *the world of memories* ('mid a hundred memories' [*»zwischen hundert Erinnerungen«*]), the strongest and most influential of which are the early infantile memory pictures" (PU §458). On Jung's account, what Nietzsche is conjuring up—unconsciously, to be sure—is the "world of the child, this paradise-like state of earliest childhood, from which we are separated by a hard law [*ein hartes Gesetz*]"—presumably, in this context, the incest prohibition—and "in this subterranean kingdom slumber sweet feelings of home and the endless hopes of all that is to be" (PU §458). At this point Jung cites another literary parallel, and—at first sight—a surprising one: the German Naturalist writer Gerhart Hauptmann (1862-1946).

Yet the choice of text is apt: *The Sunken Bell* (*Die versunkene Glocke*) (1896) is a poetic drama in blank verse, perhaps best described as an example of *literarischer Jugendstil*. It tells the story of Heinrich, a master bellfounder who has fashioned a bell to be hung in a church on a mountain which is inhabited by sprites. When a cart carrying the bell is overturned by the sprites and the bell falls into a mountain lake, Heinrich is injured but is looked after by the half-child, half-fairy figure of Rautendelein. At one point in the work, Heinrich declares, in a passage quoted by Jung:

There is a song lost and forgotten,	*Es singt ein Lied, verloren und vergessen,*
A song of home, a love song of childhood,	*Ein Heimatlied, ein Kinderliebeslied,*
Brought up from the depths of the fairy well,	*Aus Märchenbrunnentiefen aufgeschöpft,*
Known to all, but yet unheard.	*Gekannt von jedem, dennoch unerhört.*

(cited PU §458)

In fact, on Jung's account, *The Sunken Bell* is itself an example of the solar myth in which bell = sun = life = libido (PU §266, fn. 42). Many years later, in his seminar on Nietzsche's *Zarathustra* (on 16 and 30 June 1937), Jung will return to this theme of childhood in relation to "The Grave Song" (in *Thus Spoke Zarathustra*, Part Two) and to J.M. Barrie's play *Mary Rose* about a child who vanishes twice on a remote Scottish island, the "island that wants to be visited" (SNZ, vol. 2, 1152 and 1201).[20] In these and other texts, Jung finds confirmation of the thesis propounded by Hauptmann himself in one of his more Neoromantic moods when he says, "Poetic rendering is that which allows the echo of the primitive word to resound through the form" (*Dichten heißt, hinter Worten das Urwort aufklingen lassen*).[21] In fact, one could say that, for Jung, literary interpretation pays attention to the formal surface while nevertheless remaining alert to the primal word struggling to emerge…

In the next paragraph, Jung links the Nietzschean image of the libido's "own depths" to Goethe's *Faust* in a way that clearly demonstrates the way that Jung's argumentation proceeds in places by means of a dense network of literary references and allusions. For Jung applies to these libidinal depths the warning given to Faust by Mephistopheles when he tells him about how to access the realm of the Mothers: "The danger is great" (*Die Gefahr ist groß*) (PU §459; cf. *Faust II*, l. 6291). Why are these depths so dangerous? Because

[20] In his seminar on Nietzsche's *Zarathustra*, one of Jung's participants (Heinrich H. Escher) notes how Gerhart Hauptmann's novel *The Fool in Christ* (*Der Narr in Christo Emanuel Quint*) (1910) describes an "identification with an archetype" (SNZ, vol. 1, 759). For further discussion of Nietzsche's influence on Hauptmann, see Klemens Dieckhöfer, "Gerhart Hauptmann (1862-1946) und Nietzsche: Nietzsches Einfluß auf Gerhart Hauptmann und dessen Erlebnis der Natur," *Medizinhistorische Mitteilungen: Zeitschrift für Wissenschaftsgeschichte und Fachprosaforschung*, 34 (2015), 123-128.

[21] Quoted by Wihelm Stekel from Gerhart Hauptmann's diary for 1912 in "Aus Gerhart Hauptmanns Diarium," *Zentralblatt für Psychoanalyse*, vol. 2, no. 6 (1912), 365.

they are "enticing; they are the mother — and death" (PU §459). They are "enticing," in part because they offer the possibility of transformation; they are "dangerous," in part because they involve death as a necessary stage to obtain renewal. Or as Jung puts it, in a passage whose imagery of liquid retreat and reemergence we find him using elsewhere to describe the trajectory of transformation:

> When the libido leaves the bright upper world, whether from the decision of the individual or from decreasing life force, then it sinks back into its own depths, into the source from which it has gushed forth, and turns back to that point of cleavage, the umbilicus, through which it once entered into this body. This point of cleavage is called the mother, because from her comes the source of the libido. Therefore, when some great work is to be accomplished, before which weak man recoils, doubtful of his strength, his libido returns to that source — and this is the dangerous moment, in which the decision takes place between annihilation and new life. If the libido remains arrested in the wonder kingdom of the inner world, then the man has become for the world above a phantom, then he is practically dead or desperately ill. But if the libido succeeds in tearing itself loose and pushing up into the world above, then a miracle appears. This journey to the underworld has been a fountain of youth, and new fertility springs from his apparent death. (PU §459)

In *Psychological Types* (1921), we find this energic metaphor linked to Parzival (or, in this case, Wagner's *Parsifal*). On Jung's account, this work's problem—the "tension of opposites represented by the Grail and [...] the holy spear"—is "solved" by a "primordial image," and he uncovers the following dynamic:

- Kundry symbolizes the "instinctive life-force or libido"
- Amfortas lacks libido but … he has the Grail
- Parsifal has neither libido nor the Grail, and so he is "*nirdvanda*, free from the opposites, and therefore the redeemer."

When the "bright, heavenly, feminine symbol of the Grail" is united with the "dark, earthly, masculine symbol of the spear," the libido is liberated—represented by the death of Kundry—from its "naturalistic, undomesticated form [and] falls away as a lifeless husk," while the "energy bursts forth as a new stream of life in the glowing of the Grail" (CW 6 §371).

And in *Psychological Types*, Jung also links the way in which the "divine images" of Paris and Helena "float up from the tripod of the Mothers" in *Faust*, Part Two, with how—out of the "regressive movement of libido toward the primordial and […] into the source of the first beginnings"—there arises the symbol, as a "living form" (*lebende Gestalt*) in Schiller's words or as a "God-image" (CW 6 §202). What appears externally as the image of the "rejuvenated pair" is at the same time the symbol of a "process of inner union"—and a process which Faust "passionately desires" for himself as a "supreme inner atonement" (*höchste innere Versöhnung*). (Let's not forget that, in 1922 and 1923, Jung will buy the land for his Tower at Bollingen and begin construction on its two-story round tower, carving over its gate the inscription, "Philemonis Sacrum—Fausti Poenitentia," i.e., "Philemon's Shrine—Faust's Penitence"….)

Here, in *Transformations and Symbols of the Libido*, Jung points to various mythological parallels for this pattern of transformative process: to the Hindu story of Vishnu and Brahma,[22]

[22] "Once upon a time, Vishnu sank into an ecstasy (introversion) and during this state of sleep bore Brahma, who, enthroned upon the lotus flower, arose from the navel of Vishnu, bunging with him the Vedas, which he diligently read. (Birth of creative thought from introversion.) But through Vishnu's ecstasy a devouring flood came upon the world. (Devouring through introversion, symbolizing the danger of entering

for instance, or the legend of Theseus and Peirithoos,[23] but in *Psychological Types* he might equally well have pointed (if he had not been keeping this work so private) to the narrative and imagistic dynamics in his own *Red Book*.

A further parallel between Nietzsche's poem "Between Birds of Prey" (*Zwischen Raubvögeln*) and Goethe's *Faust* is discovered (or invented, according to your point of view) when Jung considers the sources of the "reanimation of the mother-imago." One of these involves the "*willed introversion of a creative mind*, which, retreating before its own problem and inwardly collecting its forces, dips at least for a moment into the source of life, in order there to wrest a little more strength from the mother for the completion of its work," a situation which Jung associates with the Mothers Scene in *Faust* (PU §469) (see Volume 2, pp. 69-76 and 245-250). Jung describes this dynamic as a "mother-child-play with one's self, in which lies much weak self-admiration and self-adulation [...]; *a*

into the mother of death.) A demon taking advantage of the danger, stole the Vedas from Brahma and hid them in the depths. (Devouring of the libido.) Brahma roused Vishnu, and the latter, transforming himself into a fish, plunged into the flood, fought with the demon (battle with the dragon), conquered him and recaptured the Vedas. (Treasure obtained with difficulty.)" (PU §459).

[23] "This is also represented mythologically in the legend of Theseus and Peirithoos, who wished to capture the subterranean Proserpina. With this aim they enter a chasm in the earth in the grove Kolonos, in order to get down to the underworld, when they were below they wished to rest, but being enchanted they hung on the rocks, that is to say, they remained fixed in the mother and were therefore lost for the upper world. Later Theseus was freed by Hercules (revenge of Horus for Osiris), at which time Hercules appears in the rôle of the death-conquering hero" (PU §459, fn. 32); cf. Jung's letter to Freud of 25 February 1912, where he writes about his work on *Transformations and Symbols of the Libido*: "Essentially, it is an elaboration of all the problems that arise out of the mother-incest libido, or rather, the libido-cathected mother imago. This time I have ventured to tackle the mother. So what is keeping me hidden is the κατάβασις [i.e., *katabasis*, or 'descent to the Underworld'] to the realm of the Mothers, where, as we know, Theseus and Peirithoos remained stuck, grown fast to the rocks" (*Freud/Jung Letters*, p. 487). For further discussion, see Paul Bishop, "Introduction," in Paul Bishop, Terence Dawson, and Leslie Gardner (eds.), *The Descent of the Soul and the Archaic: Katábasis and Depth Psychology* (London and New York: Routledge, 2022), pp. 1-16.

Narcissus state, a strange spectacle, perhaps, for profane eyes," which Jung associates with the line "Among a hundred mirrors" (*zwischen hundert Spiegeln*) in Nietzsche's poem (PU §469). (Lacan is credited with having discovered the "mirror stage" in the development of the infant; should Jung perhaps be credited with discovering its archetypal equivalent in the development of the adult?) Thanks to the "separation from the mother-imago, the birth out of one's self [*die Geburt aus sich selber*]," a reconciliation of "all conflicts through the sufferings" is achieved, Jung says, and he refers us to further lines from Nietzsche's poem:

> "Why hast thou enticed thyself
> Into the Paradise of the old serpent?
> Why hast thou crept
> Into thyself, thyself? . . .
>
> "A sick man now
> Sick of a serpent's poison,
> A captive now
> Whom the hardest destiny befell
> In thine own pit;
> Bowed down as thou workest
> Encaved within thyself,
> Burrowing into thyself,
> Helpless,
> Stiff,
> A corpse.
> Overwhelmed with a hundred burdens,
> Overburdened by thyself.
> A wise man,
> A self-knower,
> The wise Zarathustra;
> Thou soughtest the heaviest burden

> And foundest thou thyself. ..."
> [*Du suchtest die schwerste Last:*
> *Da fandest du dich* ...] (cited PU §469)

It is this text which elicits from Jung the expression of his deepest admiration when he describes the "symbolism of this speech" as being of the "greatest richness" (PU §470).

Now the key idea here for Jung is that of being "buried in the depths of self, as if in the earth," a situation for which he finds several mythological parallels. First, there is Caeneus, a Lapith hero of Thessaly who, in the battle between the Lapiths and the centaurs, is mocked by one of them, the centaur Latreus, for his supposed lack of skill as a fighter when it is discovered that Caeneus was originally female. Caeneus strikes back at Latreus and is unharmed by the centaur's attempts to kill him. As an act of revenge, the centaurs pile tree trunks and stones on top of him to crush him to death, and accordingly, Caeneus is depicted as sinking into the earth; in this sense, Caeneus really is "overwhelmed with a hundred burdens" (*von hundert Lasten übertürmt*), as Nietzsche's poem puts it. Second, there is the so-called Taurophoria of Mithras, in which the divine hero takes his bull onto his back as a symbol for assuming his "love for his mother" as the "heaviest burden," and commences the so-called Transitus, an act described by the German classical archaeologist Wilhelm Gurlitt (1844-1895) as one of the difficult tasks performed by Mithras in the service of freeing humanity.[24] (In ancient Egyptian religion, Jung notes in parentheses, Apis (or

[24] In his seminar on *Zarathustra* of 10 October 1934, Jung considered the symbol of the *transitus* in some detail, exemplified by Christ's carrying of His cross, or the carrying of the tree in the cult of Attis, or the carrying of the dead bull in Mithraism, and applied by Jung to Zarathustra and his carrying of the dead rope-dancer. On this account, Zarathustra is "in the place of the god of the antique mysteries, [...] of Christ the man-god, or Mithras the hero god, or Attis the son god, the son of Astarte," because he is "carrying the human body, the corpse — or the humanity, one can say — which really carries him" (SNZ, vol. 1, 157 and 160-161).

Hapis), a sacred bull, came to be seen as a symbol for the king, and the title "strong bull of his mother Hathor" became a common title for Egyptian gods and kings). The Transitus, or this "path of passion," leads to the cave in which the bull was sacrificed, an act repeated in the subterranean temples of the Mithras cult.

And third, there is the Christian equivalent of the Transitus: the Way of the Cross, as Christ bore *his* "symbol of the love for the mother" in the form of the Cross, carrying it "to the place of sacrifice where the lamb was slain in the form of the God, the infantile man, a 'self-executioner' [*»Selbsthenker«*], and then to burial in the subterranean sepulchre" (PU §470). (It is no coincidence, Jung adds in a footnote drawing on the work of John M. Robertson (1856-1933), that in the three Synoptic gospels the figure of Simon of Cyrene is substituted for Christ as the bearer of the Cross, because Cyrene is in Libya, the site where Hercules carried his columns to Gades, the place of his death at the Western point where the sun sinks into the sea. In the Hebrew bible, a parallel figure is Samson, who dies between the columns of the Philistines' temple, and whose name is close both to Simon (i.e., Simson) and to Simon (i.e., Sermon or Sem), related to the old sun-god Semesch, identified with Baal. Could there be, as the work of Georg Thiele (1866-1917) suggested, a relation between the way Hercules carried his two columns under his arms so as to form a cross, and the wheel of the sun, represented by the Greeks in the symbol of the cross?).[25]

Jung tethers his earlier (and, in a sense, more scholarly) use of Nietzsche in the opening chapters of *Transformations and Symbols of the Libido* to his more imaginative and associative

[25] See Georg Thiele, *Antike Himmelsbilder: Mit Forschungen zu Hipparchos, Aratos und seinen Fortsetzern und Beiträgen zur Kunstgeschichte des Sternhimmels* (Berlin: Weidmann, 1898), p. 59. For discussion of the significance in relation to *Faust* of the parallel posited by Jung between the Hercules myth and the journey of the sun to the Western sea, where Hercules "discovered the straits of Gibraltar" (PU §461, fn. 36), see Volume 2, pp. 26-27).

response to Nietzsche's poetry in its later chapters by quoting *in extenso* the passage from the Preface to the first volume of *Human, All-Too-Human* in which we find the phrase about a "sacrilegious backward grasp" (*ein tempelschänderischer Griff und Blick rückwärts*) (see above, pp. 148-149). Typically, Jung introduces the passage with a plethora of mythological references, referring to how Horus "snatched from his mother her head adornment," that is, the power, and to how Adam's struggle for power is represented by his struggle with Lilith, the daimonic female figure in Jewish mythology and Gnosticism.[26] This struggle—ultimately, in Jung's view, the struggle for deliverance from our incestuous bond to the mother—is also expressed, he says, in these "very beautiful words" by Nietzsche from *Human, All-Too-Human,* where he proposes the notion of the "free spirit":

> One may suppose that a mind, in which the "type of free mind" is to ripen and sweeten at maturity, has had its decisive crisis in a great detachment, so that before this time it was just so much the more a fettered spirit and appeared chained forever to its corner and its pillar. What binds it most firmly? What cords are almost untearable? Among human beings of a high and exquisite type, it would be duties: that reverence, which is suitable for youth, that modesty and tenderness for all the old honored and valued things, that thankfulness for the earth from which they grew, for the hand which guided them, for the shrine where they learnt to pray: —their loftiest moments themselves come to bind them the firmest, to obligate them the most permanently. The great detachment comes suddenly for people so bound.

[26] For further discussion, see Siegmund Hurwitz, *Lilith – The First Eve: Historical and Psychological Aspects of the Dark Feminine*, trans. Gela Jacobson (Einsiedeln: Daimon, 1992).

> "Better to die than to live here" — thus rings the imperative voice of seduction: and this here, this "at home" is all, that it (the soul) has loved until now! A sudden terror and suspicion against that which it has loved, a lightning flash of scorn towards that which is called "duty," a rebellious, arbitrary, volcanic, impelling desire for travelling, for strange countries, estrangements, coolness, frigidity, disillusionments, a hatred of love, perhaps a sacrilegious touch and glance backwards [*ein tempelschänderischer Griff und Blick rückwärts*] there where just now it adored and loved, perhaps a blush of shame over what it has just done, and at the same time an exultation over having done it, an intoxicating internal joyous thrill, in which a victory reveals itself — a victory? Over what? Over whom? An enigmatic, doubtful, questioning victory, but the first triumph. Of such woe and pain is formed the history of the great detachment. It is like a disease which can destroy men, — this first eruption of strength and will towards self-assertion. (HA I Preface §3)

A passage which is usually read, in its Nietzschean context, as an expressive account of Nietzsche's journey of liberation away from cultural Wagnerianism, academic scholarship, and the Enlightenment in general, is subtly repurposed by Jung here as referring to liberation from the incestuous love for the mother.

In his footnotes, Jung highlights the motif of fettering (or *Fesselung*) (cf. PU §473); the perceived parallel between the "sacrilegious touch and glance backwards" and the sacrilegious assault of Horus upon Isis which so shocked Plutarch in *De Isis et Osiris* (see §20).[27] From Plutarch's expression of aghast disbelief,

[27] Plutarch, *Moralia*, Book 5, trans. Frank Cole Babbitt (Cambridge, MA, and London: Harvard University Press, 1936), p. 358.

Jung suggests one may surmise how pagan antiquity would have reacted to Christianity with its figure of the hanged god, and its emphasis on the family as the "foundation" of the state, and he tartly concludes, "The psychologist is not surprised" (PU §478, fn. 3); and finally (but once again) the fate of Theseus and Peirithoos (where the former escapes but the latter remains stuck in the underworld).

What Nietzsche—on Jung's account—so "brilliantly expresses" is how the "danger lies [...] in isolation in one's self," described by Nietzsche as a "solitude" which "surrounds and embraces him ever more threatening, ever more constricting, ever more heart-strangling, the terrible Goddess and *Mater saeva cupidinum*" (HA I Preface §3).[28] Jung's gloss on this passage is that the "libido taken away from the mother, who is abandoned only reluctantly, becomes threatening as a serpent, the symbol of death, for the relation to the mother must cease, must die, which itself almost causes man's death"—an idea which, in the Horatian formulation, *mater saeva cupidinum*, is said to attain "rare, almost conscious, perfection" (PU §480). Although Jung adds that he would never presume to "try to paint in better words than has Nietzsche the psychology of the wrench from childhood," in a sense this is *in nuce* precisely what he (that is, Jung) *is* doing on a theoretical level in *Transformations and Symbols of the Libido* (and on a more experiential-cum-expressive level in his *Black Books* and the resultant *Red Book*).

[28] For the original source of this expression, see Horace, *Odes*, Book 4, poem 1 (translated by John Conington):

Yet again thou wak'st the flame
That long had slumber'd! Spare me, Venus, spare!
Trust me, I am not the same
As in the reign of Cinara, kind and fair.
Cease thy softening spells to prove
On this old heart, by fifty years made hard,
Cruel Mother of sweet Love!

(Horace, *The Odes and Carmen Saeculare of Horace*, trans. John Conington (London: Bell, 1882), pp. 104-105).

Whereas the poems "Glory and Eternity," "The Beacon," "The Magician" (or "Complaint of Ariadne"), and "Between Birds of Prey" have been the main focus of Jung's attention in relation to Nietzsche so far, in the final chapter of *Transformations and Symbols of the Libido*—tellingly, called "The Sacrifice"—he returns to "Glory and Eternity" and cites two chapters from *Zarathustra*, as well as the poems "The Poverty of the Richest" and "Among the Daughters of the Desert." At the same time, echoes of "Between Birds of Prey" can still be heard in the footnotes: commenting on a stanza from Longfellow's *The Song of Hiawatha*, one of the influences on the visions of Miss Miller around which *Transformations and Symbols of the Libido* is constructed (PU §482), Jung repeats in a footnote the line, "Thou seekest the heaviest burden, there findest thou thyself" (*Du suchtest die schwerste Last:/ Da fandest du dich*) (PU §533, fn. 28); and in connection with the 52nd of the Orphic Hymns, where Trieterichus Bacchus is invoked as ὑποκόλπιε (that is, *hypokolpie* = "one beneath the lap") in order to indicate that the god enters into the individual as if through the female genitals,[29] Jung recalls in a footnote a similar image in Nietzsche, namely: *eingebohrt, im*

[29] For the text of this Orphic hymn in translation, see Thomas Taylor (trans.), *The Mystical Hymns of Orpheus* (London: Dobell; Reeves and Turner, 1896), pp. 108-110; and Apostolos N. Athanassakis, *The Orphic Hymns: Text, Translation and Notes* (Missoula, MT: Scholars Press, 1997), pp. 70-71:
"I call upon you, blessed, many-named and frenzied Bacchos,
Bull-horned Nysian redeemer, god of the wine-press, conceived in fire.
Nourished in the thigh, O Lord of the Cradle,
You marshal torch-lit processions in the night, O filleted and thyrsus-shaking [Eubouleus.
Threefold is your nature and ineffable your rites, O secret offspring of Zeus.
Primeval, Erikepaios, father and son of gods,
You take raw flesh, and, sceptered, you lead into the madness of revel and dance
In the frenzy of triennial feasts that bestow calm on us.
You burst forth from the earth in a blaze... O son of two mothers,
And, horned and clad in fawnskin, you roam the mountains,
O lord worshiped in annual feasts.
Paian of the golden spear, nursling, decked with grapes,
Bassaros, exulting in ivy, followed by many maidens...
Joyous and all-abounding, come, O blessed one to the initiates."

eigenen Schachte ("Piercing into one's own pit") (which is, in fact, a conflation of two sentences, "Jetzt — / von dir selber erjagt, / deine eigene Beute, / in dich selber *eingebohrt* [...]" and "im eignen *Schachte* / gebückt arbeitend, / in dich selber eingehöhlt, / dich selber angrabend") (PU §541).[30]

Jung also notes that, in a Greek papyrus kept in the British Museum, a prayer to Hermes asks, "Come to me, Lord Hermes, as the foetus into the womb of the mother" (PU §541). (However abstruse this reference to this Orphic hymn to Bacchus might seem, the subsequent reference to Hippolytus's account of the Eleusinian Mysteries and the exclamation, "the revered one has brought forth a holy boy, Brimos from Brimo,"[31] anticipates the reference made by the shadow of a dead woman in the *Scrutinies* (or *Prüfungen*) section of *The Red Book* to Brimo as the "old one [...] the one who bore the son [...]" and who, "above and below, envelops the son" (RB, 487; cf. BB5, 245-246).[32] And if, in the eyes of John M. Robertson, "the great and wonderful and most perfect Epoptic mystery" is "*a mown stalk of wheat*," Jung in turn will play with this image in *The Red Book*, closing "Murder of the Hero" in *Liber Primus* with the line, "The rain is the fructifying of the earth, it begets the new wheat, the young, germinating God" (RB, 164); and reflecting in "One of the

[30] "Now — / alone with yourself, / your own booty, / burrowed into yourself ..." and "labouring bowed / in your own mine, / self-excavated, / digging into yourself" (Nietzsche, *Dithyrambs of Dionysus*, trans. Hollingdale, p. 43).

[31] See Hippolytus, *Refutation of All Heresies* (5.8.40), "A holy Child is born to the Lady Brimo, Brimos" (in Marvin W. Meyer (ed.), *The Ancient Mysteries: A Sourcebook: Sacred Texts of the Mystery Religions of the Ancient Mediterranean World* (San Francisco: Harper & Row, 1987), p. 19).

[32] In ancient Greek mythology, the epithet Βριμώ (i.e., *Brimṓ*, meaning "angry", "terrifying") is associated with a variety of chthonic feminine deities, often associated with the land of the Dead, such as Hecate, Persephone, Demeter Erinyes (the "furious" or "vengeful"), or Cybele: in other words, with the archetypal mother. On Meyer's account, Lady Brimo the "Strong One" or "Terrible One") is Kore-Persephone (who, after intercourse with Zeus, gave birth to Dionysos, or Brimos), but he also notes that, in Clement of Alexandria's *Exhortation to the Greeks* (2.15), the epithet Brimo is applied to Demeter (Meyer (ed.), *The Ancient Mysteries: A Sourcebook*, p. 19).

Lowly" in *Liber Secundus*, "The knowledge of death came to me that night [...] I saw how we live toward death, how the swaying golden wheat sinks together under the scythe of the reaper, like a smooth wave on the sea-beach" [RB, 239].) In his *Zarathustra* seminar, Jung will later recall these verses from "Between Birds of Prey," saying:

> Nietzsche returned to himself, isolated himself from the whole world, crept into his own retort and underwent this processs. Then suddenly he discovered that he was filled with a new orgiastic enthusiasm which he called his experience of Dionysos, the god of wine. [...] In the latter part of *Zarathustra* there is a beautiful poem where Nietzsche describes how he was digging down into himself, working into his own shaft; there you can see how intensely he experienced the going-into-himself, till he suddenly produced the explosion of the most original form of spirit, the Dionysian. (SNZ, vol. 1, 368-369)

(As we shall see in Volume 4 in this series, this experience seems to have been Jung's in the creation of *The Red Book* as well; and one might go so far as to say that this process of isolation, introversion, and ecstatic transformation was the blueprint for Nietzsche and Jung alike.)

And commenting on a work by the eccentric Swiss mystic Anton Unternährer (1759-1824), the founder of the sect called the Antonians, who explained its "cult of nakedness" by arguing, "Now are the fig leaves and the covering removed, because thou hast turned to the Lord, for the Lord is the Spirit, and where the spirit of the Lord is, there is *freedom*," Jung wryly recalls in a footnote the following line from Nietzsche's *Zarathustra*, "Not a few who meant to cast out their devil, went thereby into the swine themselves" (Z I 13; cf. PU §593, fn. 106). (This quotation comes from a chapter in *Zarathustra* aptly called "Of Chastity"!) Yet this casual use of Nietzsche in a footnote to make a gently polemical point stands in stark contrast to the important role that he plays in how Jung now unfolds his argument in this chapter. For this argument turns around the image of the snake or the serpent, said by Jung to have a "phallic significance" which it negatively or mysteriously expresses (PU §595), and defined by him as representing the "introverting libido" (PU §596).

"History teaches in manifold examples," Jung declares, "how the religious mysteries are liable to change suddenly into sexual orgies because they have originated from an overvaluation of the orgy" (PU §594). In addressing the origin of the orgy, Jung is implicitly displaying his Nietzschean credentials: for in *Twilight of the Idols* Nietzsche had considered the concept "Greek" as it had been constructed by the likes of Winckelmann and Goethe — and found it "incompatible with that element out of which Dionysian art evolved — the orgy" (TI What I Owe to the Ancients §4). In fact, Nietzsche had argued, Goethe would doubtless have "utterly excluded anything of this kind from the possibilities of the Greek soul," which led Nietzsche to the devastating conclusion: "*Consequently Goethe did not understand the Greeks*" (TI What I Owe to the Ancients §4).

By contrast, of course, for his own part, Jung thought that he *did* understand the Greeks (and indeed every other ancient people) and so, without going down the route chosen by Nietzsche of defining the "psychology of the orgy as an overflowing feeling of life and energy within which even pain acts as a stimulus" and hence as providing a "key to the concept of the *tragic* feeling"—which moves the entire argument into the sphere of aesthetics, he did share with Nietzsche an interest in the "*sexual* symbol" as being "to the Greeks the symbol venerable as such, the intrinsic profound meaning of all antique piety" (TI What I Owe to the Ancients §5). Or, in short, an interest in the phallus, and the related theriomorphic symbol of the snake or the serpent. Accordingly, Jung argues that "it is characteristic that this priapic divinity returns again to the old symbol of the snake, which in the mystery enters into the faithful, fertilizing and spiritualizing them, although it originally possessed a phallic significance" (PU

§594). (In a footnote, Jung makes an observation about the pertinence of contemporary art by referring to the Belgian Symbolist Félicien Rops's fantasies around the theme of the crucified phallus.)[33] As Jung further explains, the "phallic significance is expressed negatively or mysteriously through the serpent, which always points to a secret related thought," and it turns out that this related thought "connects with the mother" (PU §595).

Figure 1. Félicien Rops, *Sainte Marie-Madeleine*.
Available through WikiArt. Image in the public domain.

[33] Although a number of works by the Belgian Symbolist Félicien Rops (1833-1898) display an erotic obsession with the theme of crucifixion, the work to which Jung is probably referring is entitled *Sainte Marie-Madeleine*, and depicts Mary Magdalen swooning in front of a crucified phallus. For further discussion, see "Allégories érotiques et sacrées: Une iconologie décadente," in Bernadette Bonnier, Véronique Leblanc, Didier Prioul, and Hélène Védrine (eds.), *Félicien Rops: Rops suis, aultre ne veulx estre* (Brussels: Éditions Complexe, 1998), pp. 171-216; and for a contemporary appreciation of Rops' *œuvre*, see Joris-Karl Huysmans, "Rops," in *L'Art moderne / Certains* (Paris: Union Générale d'Éditions, 1986), pp. 288-315).

Recalling the case of a patient or client with a "very strong introversion (catatonic state)" who complained to him that a snake was stuck in her throat, Jung recalls the line from "Among Birds of Prey"—"Why enticest thou thyself into the paradise of the old serpent?"—[34]as well as the more extensive symbolism used by Nietzsche in Zarathustra's "vision" of the shepherd and the snake in "Of the Vision and the Riddle" (Z III 2 §2). Over and above the specific echoes of Nietzsche's dream as earlier recounted in a footnote to Part One, Chapter 1, of *Transformations and Symbols of the Libido*, Jung identifies here not only the principle that the snake "represents the introverting libido," but in addition the fact (explored and exposed in considerable detail in *The Red Book*) that "through introversion one is fertilized, inspired, regenerated and reborn from the god," pointing to Hindu philosophy for evidence of how "this idea of creative, intellectual activity" has even "cosmogonic significance"—in other words, it creates a "world" (or what the ancient Greeks called κόσμος or *kosmos*) (PU §596) (see below, pp. 196-197).

This cosmogonic significance, exemplified in the close connection between the ideas of self-incubation, self-castigation, and introversion (PU §598), leads Jung to the following shattering insight: namely, that the "hero, who is to accomplish the rejuvenation of the world and the conquest of death, is the libido, which, brooding upon itself in introversion, coiling as a snake around its own egg, apparently threatens life with a poisonous bite, in order to lead it to death, and from that darkness, conquering itself, gives birth to itself again" (PU §600). (One might accuse Jung of many things, including of simply being wrong; but one cannot accuse him—on this point, at least—of not being eminently clear.) Immediately (indeed, almost instinctively), Jung turns to Nietzsche for corroborative evidence, claiming that he also "knows this conception" and quoting the opening lines from "Glory and Eternity" (*Ruhm und Ewigkeit*):

[34] See Nietzsche, *Dithyrambs of Dionysus*, trans. Hollingdale, p. 43: "Why did you lure yourself / into the old snake's garden?".

> "How long have you sat already upon your misfortune.
> Give heed! lest you hatch an egg,
> A basilisk egg
> Of your long travail." (cited PU §600)[35]

This stanza prompts Jung to remark that the "hero is himself a serpent, himself a sacrificer and a sacrificed" (PU §601). Consequently, the "hero himself is of serpent nature," a remark which casts significant light on much of the imagery of *The Red Book* and opens up a whole sequence of parallels: Christ, who compares himself to the serpent (cf. John 3:14); the serpent as the redeeming principle of the world in the Gnostic Ophite sect; the serpent as an *agathodaemon* and a *cacodaemon* (that is, an evil spirit and a good spirit); and, in Germanic saga, heroes are described as having serpents' eyes (PU §601).

Figure 2. Piero di Cosimo (Piero di Lorenzo), St. John the Evangelist, c. 1500. Available through Wikimedia Commons. Image in the public domain.

[35] See "Fame and Eternity," in Nietzsche, *Dithyrambs of Dionysus*, trans. Hollingdale, p. 61.

In some medieval pictures—such as the picture of St. John with Chalice and Serpent by Quinten Matsys (1466-1530),[36] or two pictures by an unknown Strasbourg master in the **Musée des Beaux-Arts de Strasbourg**—[37] the Communion cup contains a dragon or a snake (PU §589);[38] the dragon of the Tarpeian Rock (a steep cliff on the south side of the Capitoline Hill in Rome) is said to have had eyes "glittering like gems, fearful and terrible," just as, in the Book of Revelation, the eyes of the Son of Man are like a flame of fire (Revelations 1:15) (PU §582 and §584); while the idea that the "divine mystery of renewed rebirth in the maternal womb" was guarded by the "dragon [...] with changeful, serpent glances" prompts Jung to recall in a footnote two other verses by Nietzsche, taken from "The Sun Sets" (*Die Sonne sinkt*) and from *Nachlass* fragments from Summer 1888:

[36] This reference suggests Jung has in mind a detail of a Flemish altarpiece by Matsys in the Wallraf-Richartz Museum in Cologne, although the English translation of Jung's book reproduces as an illustration the painting by Piero di Cosimo (1462-1521) of St John the Evangelist (c. 1500-05) in the Honolulu Museum of Art. This latter work strikingly depicts the story from the apocryphal Acts of John, in which the Evangelist proves his faith by drinking from a cup of poisoned wine; when he blesses the cup, the poison takes on the form of a snake and slithers away.

[37] The works in question may be an altarpiece panel depicting Christ and three saints (including St John with a chalice and a snake) attributed to the Master of the Evangelists of Breisach, and an altarpiece from the workshop of Strigel on the predella of which is St John with the chalice, acquired by the Musée des Beaux-Arts in 1907 and now on display at the Musée de l'Œuvre Notre-Dame – Arts du Moyen Age. For assistance in identifying these works, I am grateful to Barbara Gatineau, Head of the Photo Library and Documentation, and Ludovic Chauvan, Collections Manager and Head Registrar, of the Musées de Strasbourg.

[38] For the apocryphal biblical source of this imagery, and the story of how St. John was challenged by Aristodemus, the chief pagan priest, to drink a cup of poisoned wine—but survived by blessing the cup, causing the poison to leave as a snake, see the Acts of John (*The Apocryphal New Testament*, ed. J.K. Elliott (Oxford: Clarendon Press, 1993), pp. 343-344; and Jacobus de Voragine, *The Golden Legend: Readings on the Saints*, trans. William Granger Ryan, 2 vols. (Princeton, NJ: Princeton University Press, 1993), vol. 1, p. 53).

"In the green light,
Happiness still plays around the brown abyss.
[…]
His voice grows hoarse,
His eye flashes verdigris!" (cited PU §601, fn. 121)[39]

Indeed, in another poem by Nietzsche, "The Poverty of the Richest" (*Vom Armut der Reichsten*), Jung believes that the "old, apparently long extinct idea"—the idea of the dragon guarding the divine mystery of rebirth— "is again revived":

"Ailing with tenderness, just as the thawing wind,
Zarathustra sits waiting, waiting on his hill,
Sweetened and cooked in his own juice,
Beneath his summits,
Beneath his ice he sits,
Weary and happy,
A Creator on his seventh day.

Silence!
It is my truth!
From hesitating eyes —
From velvety shadows
Her glance meets mine,
Lovely, mischievous, the glance of a girl.
She divines the reason of my happiness,
She divines me — ha! what is she plotting?
A purple dragon lurks
In the abyss of her maiden glance.
Woe to thee, Zarathustra,

[39] See "The Sun Sinks," in Nietzsche, *Dithyrambs of Dionysus*, trans. Hollingdale, p. 49; cf. KSA 13, 20[54], 559.

Thou seemest like some one
Who has swallowed gold,
Thy belly will be slit open." (cited PU §601)[40]

In turn, the line about the purple dragon who lurks in the girl's maiden glance prompts Jung to recall in a footnote some further fragments associated with Nietzsche's *Dithyrambs of Dionysos*:

"Heavy eyes,
Which seldom love:
But when they love, it flashes out
Like a gold mine
Where a dragon guards the treasure of love."
(cited PU §601, fn. 123)[41]

The final lines of "The Poverty of the Richest," in which Zarathustra is addressed as appearing like someone who has swallowed gold, and whose belly will be split open, impel Jung to remark in a footnote that "he is pregnant with the sun" (PU §601, fn. 124), thus linking Nietzsche's text back into the solar myth (cf. PU §323-§324). The density of allusion to Nietzsche here is, however, remarkable: One Nietzsche text is interpreted in the light of another, creating a kind of interpretative tessellation that reflects these texts into infinity.

Yet this technique of reading also opens up further mythological parallels. In "The Poverty of the Richest," one finds collected, Jung argues, "nearly all the symbolism which we have

[40] See "Of the Poverty of the Richest Man," in Nietzsche, *Dithyrambs of Dionysus*, trans. Hollingdale, pp. 71-73.

[41] See KSA 13, 20[61], 560. In Jung's case, he was citing from "Reden, Gleichnisse und Bilder (1882-1888)" from *Bruchstücke zu den Dionysos-Dithyramben (Lieder Zarathustra's), 1882-1888)*, in Friedrich Nietzsche, *Werke*, 16 vols. (Leipzig: C.G. Naumann, 1899-1911) — the so-called *Kleinoktavausgabe*—, vol. 8, *Der Fall Wagner. Götzen-Dämmerung. Nietzsche contra Wagner. Umwerthung aller Werthe I. Dichtungen* (1906), p. 401.

elaborated previously from other connections," but this does not prevent him from suggesting new ones: Cecrops, the founder and the first king of Athens, was said to have been born from the earth itself and to have been half-man, half-snake, and thus διφυής (*diphues*) or *of two natures*. As a buried god, Cecrops is like Erechtheus, the founder of the Athenian *polis* and associated with Poseidon, whose Erechtheion (an ancient Greek temple on the north side of the Acropolis) replaced the Kekropion, the grave of Cecrops and the serpent that embodied his spirit after it was destroyed in 480 B.C.E. during the Greco-Persian wars, above which rises on the Acropolis the Parthenon, the Temple of Athena dedicated to the virgin goddess (PU §602). Then again, in Mexican religion and its practice of human sacrifice, the gods were represented by criminals who were slaughtered, then flayed, while the subsequent wearing of the bloody skins represented the resurrection of the gods (PU §517; cf. PU §401). And Mani, the prophet and the founder of Manichaeism, is said to have been crucified, flayed, stuffed, and suspended over the city gate of the city of Gundeshapur, echoing "in another mythological form" the death of Christ (PU §602).

Drawing on the work of Sir James Frazer (1854-1941) in his *The Golden Bough* (1890; ²1900; ³1906-1915), Jung points to the further parallels with Marsyas, who was also skinned; the slaughter, skinning, and stuffing of slaves and horses whenever a Scythian king died; and the killing and skinning of representatives of the father-god in Phrygia, just as in Athens an ox was skinned, stuffed, and hitched again to the plough, and "in this manner the revival of the fertility of the earth was celebrated" (PU §604). The golden thread which runs through all these mythological references and links them to Nietzsche is the idea of the serpent that sloughs its skin in order to be "reborn" as an icon of transformation. And thus "in Nietzsche the old, apparently long extinct idea is again revived" (PU §601)—just as it was to be revived in *The Red Book*.

At the heart of this process of transformation lies this core development, in which the "active, fructifying (upward striving) form of the libido is changed into the negative force, striving towards death" (PU §606). In terms of iconographic representation, the hero, as zodiacal sign of spring (ram, bull) conquers the depths of winter; and beyond the summer solstice is attacked by the unconscious longing for death, and is bitten by the snake. "*However, he himself is the snake*" (PU §606; my emphasis). This means that the hero is caught up in an internal dialectical process or, to put in another way, he "is at war with himself, and, therefore, the descent and the end appear to him as the malicious inventions of the mother of death, who in this way wishes to draw him to herself" (PU §606). What "the mysteries" (or *das Mysterium*, the title of Chapter 9 of *Liber Primus* in *The Red Book*) consolingly declare(s) is that "there is no contradiction and no disharmony when life is changed into death" (PU §606): As an ancient Dionysian *symbolon* recorded by Clement of Alexandria and several other Christian writers text puts it, "the bull is father of the serpent, and the serpent father of the bull" (*tauros drakontos kai pater taurou drakon*).[42]

On Jung's account, this "mystery" (here, *Geheimnis*) is given expression by Nietzsche, too, in his strange poem, "Among the Daughters of the Desert" (*Unter Töchtern der Wüste*), sung by the Wanderer who calls himself Zarathustra's Shadow (in Z IV 16 §2):

> "*Here do I sit now,*
> […]
> That is, I'm swallowed down
> By this the smallest oasis —
> — It opened up just yawning,
> Its loveliest maw agape,
> […].

[42] See Meyer (ed.), *The Ancient Mysteries: A Sourcebook*, p. 19; cf. p. 65.

Hail! hail! to that whalefish,
When he for his guest's welfare
Provided thus!
[...]

Hail to his belly
If he had also
Such a lovely oasis belly —
[...]
The desert grows, woe to him
Who hides the desert!
Stone grinds on stone, the desert
Gulps and strangles.
The monstrous death gazes, glowing brown,
And *chews* — his life is his chewing . . .

Forget not, O man, burnt out by lust,
Thou — art the stone, the desert, thou art death!"
(cited PU §607)[43]

From here, there might at first sight seem to be quite a leap to be made to the Last Supper; yet what relates it to Nietzsche's poetry, however, is (in Jung's view) the "serpent symbolism" of the Last Supper (as reflected in the medieval depictions of the Communion cup discussed above, pp. 174-175) and the "identification of the hero with the serpent" (PU §608). Accordingly, "the god is buried in the mother," which means that "as fruit of the field, as food coming

[43] See "The Desert Grows: Woe to Him Who Harbours Deserts...", in Nietzsche, *Dithyrambs of Dionysus*, trans. Hollingdale, pp. 29-37. These lines prompted Martin Heidegger to make his remark about how Nietzsche "endured the agony of having to scream" and "screamed out into the world: 'The wasteland grows ...'" (Martin Heidegger, *What Is Called Thinking?* [1951/1952], trans. J. Glenn Gray (New York: Harper & Row, 1968), pp. 48-49).

from the mother and at the same time as drink of immortality he is received by the mystic [or initiate], or as a serpent he unites with the mystic" (PU §608). What all these symbols represent is—and by now this should come as no surprise—is the "liberation of the libido from the incestuous fixation through which new life is attained," but the following point is crucial: "The liberation is accomplished *under symbols*, which represent the activation of the incest wish" (PU §608; my emphasis). Hence the supreme importance for Jung of the symbol: For it is *through symbols* that liberation is accomplished, and the existence of a symbol should alert us to the presence of the incest wish—as a trigger or a device, so to speak, for the activation of unconscious resources.

After a brief, if polemical, excursus on Freudian psychoanalysis as a method of treatment (PU §609-§611) and on Act 3 of Wagner's *Siegfried* (PU §612-§614), Jung returns to his main thesis. In Wotan's words, "To the ever-young in gladness yieldeth the god!" Jung finds "wise words" that contain the "saving thought" (*den rettenden Gedanken*): namely, that "it is not the mother who has placed the poisonous worm in our path, but our libido itself wills to complete the course of the sun to mount from morn to noon, and, passing beyond noon, to hasten towards evening, not at war with itself, but willing the *descent and the end*" (PU §614; Jung's emphasis). This rhetoric is familiar; it is evidently Nietzschean, and Jung provides us with the source with a composite quotation from "Of Voluntary Death" (Z I 21) and "Of the Bestowing Virtue" (Z I 22 §3):

> "I praise thee, my death, the free death, which comes to me because I want it.
>
> "And when shall I want it? — He who has a goal and an heir wants death at the proper time for his goal and his heir.
>
> [...]

> "And this is the great noonday, when man in the middle of his course stands between man and superman, and celebrates his path towards evening as his highest hope: because it is the path to a new morning.
>
> "He who is setting will bless his own going down because it is a transition: and the sun of his knowledge will be at high noon." (cited PU §615)

Jung's subsequent pivot back to Wagner's *Siegfried* in this chapter cannot disguise his indebtedness in terms of argument and in terms of rhetoric to Nietzsche; nor, indeed, does Jung even try to disguise this indebtedness. For in this final (and climactic) chapter of *Transformations and Symbols of the Libido*, entitled "The Sacrifice," Jung summarizes his argument as follows:

> It is not to be forgotten that the *sexual phantasies of the neurotic and the exquisite sexual language of dreams* are regressive phenomena. The sexuality of the unconscious is not what it seems to be; *it is merely a symbol*; it is a thought bright as day, clear as sunlight, a decision, a step forward to every goal of life — but expressed in the unreal sexual language of the unconscious, and in the thought form of an earlier stage; a resurrection, so to speak, of earlier modes of adaptation. (PU §635; Jung's emphases)

This is a call to a Nietzschean outlook, as is underscored by Jung's explicit citation at this point from "Of the Way of the Creator" in *Zarathustra* (Z I 17):

> "Free dost thou call thyself? Thy dominant thought would I hear and not that thou hast thrown off a yoke.

> Art thou one who had the right to throw off a yoke? There are many who throw away their last value when they throw away their servitude." (cited PU §635)

And in the final pages of *Transformations and Symbols of the Libido*, Nietzsche emerges for a final time in the context of a dense set of references to Goethe, Hölderlin, and Nietzsche. (One might think of Friedrich Hölderlin as a kind of "Nietzsche-by-proxy" figure, given Nietzsche's admiration for this great German Romantic poet, described by Martin Heidegger as "one of our greatest, that is, most impending *thinkers* because he is our greatest *poet*" (*einer unserer größten, d.h. unser zukünftigster* Denker, *weil er unser größter* Dichter *ist*),[44] and by Norbert von Hellingrath as "the most German of poets" [*den deutschesten Dichter*].)[45]

For after citing a series of poems and texts by Hölderlin ("To the Rose," *Hyperion*, "Humanity," "To Nature," "Palinodia," "Empedocles," "Obituary" (*Nachruf*), and "Achilles"), Jung remarks that these works "describe more plainly than could be depicted with meagre words the persistent arrest and the constantly growing estrangement from life, the gradual deep immersion into the maternal abyss of the individual being" (PU §650). He then turns to consider the hymnic poem "Patmos," describing it in relation to these other "songs of retrogressive longing" as a "dismal guest surrounded by the mist of the depths, the gathering clouds of insanity, bred through the mother," in which the "primitive thoughts of the myth, the suggestion clad in symbols, of the sun-

[44] Martin Heidegger, *Hölderlins Hymnen "Germanien" und "Der Rhein"*, ed. Susanne Ziegler [*Gesamtausgabe*, Section II, vol. 39] (Frankfurt am Main: Klostermann, 1989), p. 6; translated in Fred Dallmayr, *Margins of Political Discourse* (Albany, NY: State University of New York Press, 1989), p. 213.

[45] See Norbert von Hellingrath's lecture *Hölderlin und die Deutschen*, in *Hölderlin: Zwei Vorträge* (Munich: Bruckmann, 1922), pp. 13-48 (p. 21); and see the note in Andrzej Warminski, *Readings in Interpretation: Hölderlin, Hegel, Heidegger* (Minneapolis: University of Minnesota Press, 1987), p. 209.

like death and resurrection of life, again burst forth" (PU §650).[46] Jung elides its famous arresting opening and its statement that "the God is near":

> "Near is the God
> And hard to comprehend,
> But where Danger threatens
> The Rescuer appears" (cited PU §651)

with an allusion to the Mothers Scene of *Faust*, Part Two, and the warning that "the danger is great" (l. 6291). He interprets first the stanza as a whole as suggesting that the libido "has now sunk to the lowest depths"—hence the danger, yet rescue is at hand, for if "the God is near," then "there we may find the inner sun, our own nature, sun-like and self-renewing, hidden in the mother-womb like the sun in the nighttime" (PU §652). Jung supports this reading with reference to the following lines:

> "... In Chasms
> And in darkness dwell
> The eagles, and fresh and fearlessly
> The Sons of the Alps pass swiftly over the abyss
> Upon lightly swinging bridges" (cited PU §652)

and notes that, "with these words, the dark phantastic poem passes on" (PU §652). Nevertheless, Jung's interpretative strategy is clear: By tracking the image of the eagle, as the "bird of the sun, [who]

[46] Likewise, Heidegger attached great significance to Hölderlin's "Patmos"-poem; see Martin Heidegger, *Erläuterungen zu Hölderlins Dichtung*, fourth edn.(Frankfurt am Main: Klostermann, 1971); and *Elucidations of Hölderlin's Poetry*, trans. Keith Hoeller (Amherst, NY: Humanity Books, 2000). For further discussion, see Andrzej Warminski, "'Patmos': The Senses of Interpretation," *Modern Language Notes*, vol. 91, no. 3 (April 1976), 478-500; and Michel Haar and Reginald Lilly, "Heidegger and the God of Hölderlin," *Research in Phenomenology*, vol. 19, no. 1 (1989), 89-100.

dwells in darkness," he discovers a symbol for how the libido has "hidden itself," while "high above it the inhabitants of the mountains pass, probably the gods ('Ye are walking above in the light')" (PU §653). In turn, these godlike inhabitants are "symbols of the sun wandering across the sky, like the eagle flying over the depths," as for Jung the following lines confirm:

> "... Above and around are reared
> The summits of Time,
> And the loved ones, though near,
> Live on deeply separated mountains.
> So give us waters of innocence,
> And give us wings of true understanding,
> With which to pass across and to return again."
>
> (cited PU §653)

In the course of these lines Jung detects another remarkable shift: from the "gloomy picture of the mountains and of time — although caused by the sun wandering over the Mountains," to the following picture of a "nearness, and at the same time separation, of the lovers," a picture which seems to hint at "life in the underworld" and to echo, he suggests, Book 11 of the *Odyssey* and Homer's account of the *nekyia* (PU §654). In a footnote, Jung reminds us of the passage in the account of his journey to Hades where Odysseus wishes to embrace his mother:

> "But I, thrilled by inner longing,
> Wanted to embrace the soul of my departed mother
> Three times I endeavored, full of passionate desire for the embrace
> Three times from my hands she escaped
> Like nocturnal shades and the images of dreams,
> And in my heart sadness grew more intense."
>
> (*Odyssey*, Book 11, ll. 204-208)

The underworld, or Hell, is defined by Jung as the "place of unfulfilled longing" (which is a useful definition to remember for the motif of Hell as it later recurrently appears in *The Red Book*) (PU §654, fn. 8). Here in the underworld, Odysseus is "united with all that once was dear to him, and yet cannot enjoy the happiness of reunion, because it is all shadows and unreal and devoid of life" (PU §654). In Hölderlin's poem, the familiar solar dynamic is in play, for as "here the one who descends drinks the waters of innocence, the waters of childhood, the drink of rejuvenation," so "wings may grow, and, *winged, he may soar up again into life, like the winged sun*, which arises like a swan from the water ('Wings, to pass across and to return again')" (PU §654; my emphases). Or in the words Jung quotes from Hölderlin's poem:

> "So I spoke, and lo, a genie [*ein Genius*]
> Carried me off, swifter than I had imagined,
> And farther than ever I had thought
> From my own house!
> It grew dark
> As I went in the twilight.
> The shadowy wood,
> And the yearning brooks of my home-land
> Grew vague behind me —
> And I knew the country no longer." (cited PU §654)

Throughout his reading of "Patmos," Jung is concerned to track the changing dynamic of the poem; in short, we could describe his interpretative strategy as a kind of voliciferic phenomenology.[47]

[47] "Velociferic" is a compound neologism derived from the Latin "velocitas" (speed) and "luciferic." It translates the term *veloziferisch*, composed of the Italian *velocità* and the German *luziferisch*, first coined by Goethe in a postscript to a letter addressed to the Prussian lawyer Nicolovius in 1825, and used in 1829 the second edition of Goethe's novel *Wilhelm Meister's Journeyman Years, or the Renunciants*. For further

Thus, after the "dark and obscure words of the introduction, wherein the poet expresses the prophecy of what is to come," Jung highlights how a new development takes place—and the "sun journey begins ('night journey in the sea') towards the east, towards the ascent, towards the mystery of eternity and rebirth" (PU §655). At this point, Jung pivots back to Nietzsche, for he, too, "dreams" of this mystery and (in "The Seven Seals," §2) expresses it in these "significant words":

> "Oh, how could I not be ardent for Eternity, and for the nuptial ring of rings — the ring of the return!
>
> Never yet have I found the woman from whom I wish children, unless she would be this woman whom I love; for I love thee, O Eternity." (cited PU §655)

Now what is this ring? (To be sure, it is not the "Ring" of Wagner, neither the object in question in the festival stage-play nor the cycle of the four operas.) This ring is, of course, the ring of eternal recurrence—one of the cornerstones (along with the doctrines of the *Übermensch* and of self-overcoming) of the late Nietzsche's philosophy, which Jung here deftly slides into the vast edifice that is *Transformations and Symbols of the Libido*.

"This same longing," Jung argues, or Zarathustra's longing for eternity, is expressed by Hölderlin in a "beautiful symbol, the individual traits of which are already familiar to us," and he quotes the following lines:

> "... But soon in a fresh radiance
> Mysteriously
> Blossoming in golden smoke,

discussion, see Manfred Osten, *"Alles veloziferisch" oder Goethes Entdeckung der Langsamkeit* (Göttingen: Wallstein Verlag, 2013).

With the rapidly growing steps of the sun,
Making a thousand summits fragrant,
Asia arose!
And, dazzled,
I sought one whom I knew;
For unfamiliar to me were the broad roads,
Where from Tmolus
Comes the gilded Pactol,
And Taurus stands and Messagis —
And the gardens are full of flowers.
But high up in the light
The silvery snow gleams, a silent fire;
And, as a symbol of eternal life,
On the impassable walls,
Grows the ancient ivy.
And carried by columns of living cedars and laurels
Are the solemn, divinely built palaces." (cited PU §656)

Wherein lies the familiarity of the symbol? In part, it lies in the fact that it is "apocalyptic," evoking the "maternal city in the land of eternal youth, surrounded by the verdure and flowers of imperishable spring" (PU §657). (The reference to "ancient ivy" prompts Jung to recall that the φάρμακον ἀθανασίας (i.e., *phármakon athanasías*, the "medicine for immortality"), exemplified by the *soma* (drink) in the Vedic tradition or the *haoma*, a divine plant in Zoroastrianism, might have been made from a species of shrub known as Ephedra vulgaris.)[48]

[48] As his source, Jung cites Friedrich Spiegel, *Erânische Alterthumskunde*, 3 vols. (Leipzig: Engelmann, 1871-1878), vol. 1, p. 433: "In both languages, the same word also refers to a beverage to which great healing powers are universally attributed; in both religions, Haoma is a remedy against illness and death; in both religions, this beverage is derived from a plant, and it is of little consequence if this plant is not the same for both peoples. However, in both religions, Soma or Haoma is not merely a plant or a beverage, but simultaneously a person, a god."

One thinks of earlier passages in *Transformations and Symbols of the Libido* where Jung discussed the city of Jerusalem in the biblical Apocalypse as a maternal symbol (see PU §319), and for a final time he quotes from the work of Gerhart Hauptmann, in this case his early play *The Ascension of Little Hannele* (*Hanneles Himmelfahrt*) of 1893, also known simply as *Hannele*. This Symbolist dramatic composition includes a dream sequence in which its child heroine, the eponymous Hannele, a poor peasant girl, experiences on her deathbed a vision of the divine:

> "Salvation is a wonderful city,
> Where peace and joy never end,
> Its houses are marble, its roofs are gold,
> But wine flows in silver fountains,
> Flowers are strewed upon the white, white streets,
> Continually from the towers sound the wedding bells.
> Green as May are the battlements, shining with the light of early morning.
> Giddy with butterflies, crowned with roses.
> […]
> There below, hand in hand,
> The festive people wander through the heavenly land,
> The wide, wide sea is filled with red, red wine,
> They plunge in with shining bodies!
> They plunge into the foam and the splendor,
> The clear purple covers them entirely,
> And they exulting arise from the flood,
> Thus they are washed by Jesus' blood." (cited PU §657, fn. 11)

In Hölderlin's text, the poetic voice is that of John, traditionally identified as the Apostle, son of Zebedee, and as the Evangelist, who was exiled to Patmos during the rule of Domitian in the late first century.[49] Jung reminds us that John was once associated with the "son of the Highest" (see Luke 1:32; cf. 1:76, with reference respectively to Christ and to John the Baptist) and that, on Patmos, it is said that he actually saw Him face to face:

> "There at the Mystery of the Vine they met,
> There at the hour of the Holy Feast they gathered,
> And — feeling the approach of Death in his great, quiet soul,
> The Lord, pouring out his last love, spoke,
> And then he died.
> Much could be said of it —
> How his triumphant glance,
> The happiest of all,
> Was seen by his companions, even at the last.
>
> [...]
> Therefore he sent the Spirit unto them,
> And the house trembled, solemnly,
> And, with distant thunder,
> The storm of God rolled over the cowering heads
> Where, deep in thought,
> The heroes of death were assembled.
> Now, when he, in parting,
>
> Appeared once more before them,
> Then the kingly day, the day of the sun, was put out,
> And the gleaming sceptre, formed of his rays,

[49] Other theories of authorship proposed by modern scholars identify John as (a) John the Baptist, (b) John Mark, the author of the second gospel, (c) an unknown prophet from Palestine called John, (d) John the Presbyter, a contemporary of the Apostle John in Ephesus, and (e) an unidentified author using the name of the apostle as a pseudonym, yet these proposals are problematic in their own right (see *The Ignatius Catholic Study Bible*, ed. Scott Hahn and Curtis J. Mitch (San Francisco: Ignatius Press, 2024), p. 2241).

> Was broken — and suffered like a god itself.
> Yet it shall return and glow again
> When the right time comes." (cited PU §657)

Here, the "fundamental pictures," Jung argues, are the "sacrificial death and the resurrection of Christ," events corresponding to the "self-sacrifice of the sun, which voluntarily breaks its sceptre, the fructifying rays, in the certain hope of resurrection" (PU §658). At the core of this mythological symbolism thus lies the solar drama, but phallic elements are said to be present, too: The solidity of these rays hints at their phallic associations, as represented mythologically by Thor's hammer, the bull's shoulder held by Mithras, or the missing phallus of Osiris (PU §658). Jung even draws a link to folk customs and beating fantasies that involve being struck with a rod:

> The blow of the hammer as a generating, fructifying, inspiring function is retained as a folk-custom and expressed by striking with the twig of life, which has the significance of a charm of fertility. In the neuroses, the sexual meaning of castigation plays an important part, for among many children castigation may elicit a sexual orgasm. The ritual act of striking has the same significance of generating (fructifying), and is, indeed, merely a variant of the original phallic ceremonial. (PU §658)[50]

[50] One thinks of the case discussed by Freud in "'A Child is Being Beaten': A Contribution to the Study of the Origin of Sexual Perversions" (1918), in Sigmund Freud, *The Standard Edition of the Complete Works*, vol. 2, trans. James Strachey and Alix Strachey (London: Vintage, 1999), pp. 179-181; or the punishment fantasies of Sabina Spielrein (see Zvi Lothane, "In Defense of Sabina Spielrein," *International Forum of Psychoanalysis*, vol. 5, no. 3 (1996), 203-207). The centuries-old tradition of "beating the bounds" used to take place during Rogationtide (i.e., the fifth week after Easter). Compare with Jung's discussion of pedagogical flagellation in his *Zarathustra* seminar, where he links initiation rites, schoolroom beatings, and the notion that the "idea becomes associated with the body" (SNZ, vol. 1, 197). This enthusiasm for the use of corporal punishment in an educational setting is perhaps surprising, but probably not untypical for Jung's times.

Here, too, there is a link back to the maternal: Hercules's club is made from the wood of the maternal olive tree, for instance, and Faust's key also "knows the Mothers" (cf. *Faust II*, ll. 6263-6264), confirming Jung's view that the libido "springs from the mother, and with this weapon alone can humankind overcome death" (PU §658).

Jung concludes his reading of "Patmos" by noting that, while in Hölderlin's poem, the passage from Asia through Patmos in Greece to the Christian mysteries is "apparently a superficial connection,"[51] in reality it demonstrates a "very ingenious train of thought": namely, the idea that the "entrance into death and the land beyond" is a "self-sacrifice of the hero, for the attainment of immortality," and that, "at this time, when the sun has set, when love is apparently dead," then the individual "awaits in mysterious joy the renewal of all life" (PU §660):

> "… And Joy it was
> From now on
> To live in the loving night and see
> The eyes of innocence hold the unchanging
> Depths of all wisdom." (cited PU §660)

What is this wisdom (*Weisheit*)? It is, of course, a Goethean wisdom—in the sense of a Faustian wisdom—namely the wisdom that "dwells in the depths, the wisdom of the mother" (PU §661). If we can identify this wisdom and become "one with it," then "insight is obtained into the meaning of deeper things, into all the deposits of primitive times, the strata of which have been preserved in the soul" (PU §661). This insight is, of course, at the very heart of the Jungian project and underpins the dynamics of those works exemplifying the epic of transformation.

[51] This shift from East to West (the movement of History) and from West to East (the flow of the river) informs another major poem by Hölderlin, *Der Ister*; see Martin Heidegger, *Hölderlin's Hymn "The Ister,"* trans. William McNeill and Julia Davis (Bloomington and Indianapolis: Indiana University Press, 1996).

What appears in Nietzsche "as a poetical figure of speech is really a primitive myth," and it is as if he "still possessed a dim idea or capacity to feel and reactivate those imperishable phantoms of long-past worlds of thought in the words of our present-day speech and in the images which crowd themselves into his phantasy" (PU §471). Correspondingly Hölderlin, "in his diseased ecstasy, feels once more the greatness of the things seen," albeit with this difference: namely, that "he does not care to bring up to the light of day that which he had found in the depths"—and in this crucial respect Hölderlin "differs from Faust":

> "And it is not an evil, if a few
> Are lost and never found, and if the speech
> Conceals the living sound,
> Because each godly work resembles ours;
> And yet the Highest does not plan it all —
> The great pit bears two irons,
> And the glowing lava of Aetna . . .
> Would I had the power
> To build an image and see the Spirit [*den Geist*] —
> See it as it was!" (cited PU §661)

In turn, these lines state Hölderlin's program, so close to Jung's: namely, to "build an image" (*ein Bild zu bauen*) and to "see the Spirit as it was" (*Zu schauen, wie er gewesen, den Geist*)![52] Hölderlin's work remains, however, suffused with a kind of self-

[52] As we noted in Volume 2, pp. 261-262, here Jung rewrites, whether consciously or unconsciously, the line *Zu schaun, wie er gewesen, den Christ*, replacing it with *Zu schaun, wie er gewesen, den Geist*. In the fragments of the later version, however, Hölderlin does write, "Therefore he sent them / The Spirit" (*Drum sandt er ihnen / Den Geist*) (Hölderlin, *Poems & Fragments*, trans. Michael Hamburger, 3rd edn. (London: Anvil Press, 1994), pp. 506-507). For an extensive commentary on this difficult and complex poem, see Hölderlin, *Sämtliche Gedichte*, ed. Jochen Schmidt (Frankfurt am Main: Deutscher Klassiker Verlag, 2005), pp. 969-1013.

doubt, a sense of the ultimate impossibility of this project, and in the end, what remains is not certainty, but hope. Or, as Jung puts it, Hölderlin "allows only one hope to glimmer through, formed in scanty words" (PU §662:

> "He wakes the dead;
> They who are not enchained and bound,
> They who are not unwrought
> . . . And if the Heavenly Ones
> Now, as I believe, love me —
> . . . Silent is his sign
> In the dusky sky. And one stands under it
> His whole life long — for Christ still lives." (cited PU §662)

Whose sign is it one sees in the thunderous skies? According to Jung, it is the sign "of the father" (PU §662, fn. 14)—as if to say that the attempt to accede to the feminine realm of the collective unconscious has failed and patriarchal authority has been restored. Here, as so often, Jung points to a mythological parallel, invoking the legend of Gilgamesh (or Izdubar, as he will be called in *The Red Book*), in a way that helps explain his reading of these lines.

Earlier (in Chapter 7 of Part Two on the dual mother role) Jung had compared Hiawatha's great battle with his father, Mudjekeewis, in order to avenge his dead mother, Wenonh, with the battle of Gilgamesh with the giant Humbaba and the subsequent conquest of Ishtar. Under this "figure of thought" (*Redefigur*) is hidden the thought that Hiawatha "slays the father, in order to take possession of the mother" (PU §518). Thus, in psychological terms, the father "represents the personification of the incest prohibition: that is to say, the resistance which defends the mother" (PU §518). Fearful animals can symbolize the father: a bear, a snake, a dragon, and so on. This is why the hero *is* a hero: because he "sees in every difficulty of life resistance to the forbidden treasure, and fights that resistance with the complete yearning which strives towards the treasure, attainable with difficulty or unattainable, and which paralyzes and kills the ordinary individual" (PU §518).

So, does the father here, too, represent the incest taboo? It would appear that Jung believes so. And there is another significant parallel: Further on in Chapter 7 of Part Two, Jung compares the way in which Hiawatha becomes the ruler of the home-wind with the way in which, in the epic that bears his name, Gilgamesh visits the sage Utnapishtim (the Noah-like figure who, at the command of the god Enki, created a giant ship to save all life from the Great Flood) who lives in the West and receives from him a magic herb with a promise of rejuvenation.[53] (By contrast, in *The Red Book,* Izdubar is squeezed by Jung into the size of an egg, popped into his pocket, and taken into the "welcoming house" where Izdubar "finds healing"—"And thus my god found salvation," Jung explains [RB, 295].) Returning home once more by sea to Uruk, Gilgamesh loses the magic herb (and hence the chance of immortality) to a serpent, which sheds its skin as it departs (PU §521). In psychological terms, Jung suggests, these events symbolize how, "when one has slain the father, one can obtain possession of his wife, and *when one has conquered the mother, one can free one's self*" (PU §522; my emphasis).

Likewise, just as Gilgamesh, when "bringing back the magic herb from the west land," was "robbed of his treasure by the demon serpent" (and weeps at the futility of his efforts to gain immortality), so too does Hölderlin's poem "die away in a painful lament, which betrays to us that no victorious resurrection will follow his descent to the shadows" (PU §663):

> "... Ignominiously
> A power tears our heart away,
> For sacrifices the heavenly ones demand." (cited PU §663)

[53] For further discussion, see Rivkah Schärf Kluger, *The Archetypal Significance of Gilgamesh: A Modern Ancient Hero*, ed. H. Yehezkel Kluger (Einsiedeln: Daimon, 1991).

In the case of Hölderlin (who, like Nietzsche, ended his days in madness or, as it is euphemistically called, *geistige Umnachtung*, i.e., mental darkness), this recognition—namely, that the individual "must sacrifice the retrogressive longing (the incestuous libido) before the 'heavenly ones' tear away the sacrifice, and at the same time the entire libido"—is something that "came too late to the poet" (PU §664).

Thus Hölderlin's problem was also Miss Miller's: Her visions, too, treat the "problem of the sacrifice of infantile longings," but Jung's extensive, cross-cultural analysis of them in *Transformations and Symbols of the Libido* has tried to show that they involve not just an "individual problem" but a "problem of humankind in general" (PU §665); in a word, they are *archetypal*. Hence the recurrence of the symbols employed: for example, the serpent that killed the horse (see Genesis 49:17, and the wish expressed in the prophetical blessings of Jacob that one of his sons, Dan, should be a "snake in the way, a serpent in the path, that biteth the horse's heels, that his rider may fall backward"), or the hero voluntarily sacrificing himself, or all the other "primitive figures of fantasies and religious myths streaming up from the unconscious" (PU §665). One can read *The Red Book* as Jung's own attempt deliberately to unleash and to engage with precisely such fantasies and religious myths.

The ubiquity of these myths and fantasies prompts Jung to the following reflection. Inasmuch as the world and everything that exists is "primarily a thought [*ein Gedachtes*], to which because of empirical necessity we attribute a transcendent 'substantiality' [*transzendente »Substantialität«*])," so the "sacrifice of the libido that looks back to all that is past gives rise to the creation of the world"—and, in psychological terms, the "world in general" (*überhaupt die Welt*) (PU §666). By "world" (*die Welt*) Jung means what the ancient Greeks called κόσμος or *kosmos*. And it is in this sense, too, that Faust uses the term *Welt* when he says at the outset of Part One that he wants to know "the mighty inmost tether/ […] that binds the world together" (*was die Welt / Im Innersten zusammenhält*), as opposed to the ordinary, everyday world as he knows it (in his book-filled, equipment-cluttered, dust-covered study), which he sarcastically dismisses in these words, "That is thy world! a world, good lack!" (*Das ist deine Welt! das heißt eine Welt!*) (ll. 328-383 and 409). For those who look backward, Jung says, "the world, and even the infinite starry sky, is the mother who bends over and encloses them on all sides," just as the ancient Egyptians represented the heavens as a woman and as a cow (PU §666). This, then, is the *mythical view* of the world, which we must heroically overcome: "From the renunciation of this image [*dieses Bild*] and from the longing for this image arises the image of the world [*das Weltbild*]," Jung says, as a way of describing how a dialectic of desire and renunciation of desire opens the way for us to see the world not just as a collection of random things but as a *cosmos*. This "most simple fundamental thought" appears strange to us, only because it emerges—in the Freudian categories, which have not yet been abandoned—from the pleasure principle (*Lustprinzip*) and not from the reality principle (*Realitätsprinzip*), and it reveals the "significance of the *cosmic sacrifice*" (PU §666).

At this point, Jung pivots, as he has done earlier, to the Rigveda and to the Upanishads,[54] before moving—via a whole series

[54] Given the remarkable richness of these pages, one example must suffice. Jung draws a highly suggestive link between, on the one hand, the account in the Brihadâranyaka-Upanishad, 3:3, of how those who come to offer up the sacrificial horse enter the narrowest fissure between where the shells of the world egg *unite* and where *they are divided* and, on the other, Plato's designation in the *Timaeus* of the "fissure" (in German, *Scheide*; in Latin, *vāgīna*) in the maternal world-soul by an X, or the symbol of the cross (PU §681); see *Timaeus*, 36 b-c, where Timaeus of Locri recounts how the Demiurge took a long band of soul-stuff and split it lengthwise into two strips, attaching them back together at the middle and bending them round into two circles or rings (cf. Francis MacDonald Cornford, *Plato's Cosmology: The "Timaeus" of Plato* (Indianapolis: Hackett, 1997), p. 72). Earlier in *Transformations and Symbols* Jung had referred to this myth, writing of how the "thought of 'union,' expressed by the symbol of the cross," informs the conception in the *Timaeus* of the world soul as "stretched out between heaven and earth in the form of an X [i.e., the

of mythological examples of sacrifice, including the catching and subduing of the bull in Mithraism (PU §682)—to conclude with the figure of Priapus (PU §697); the serpent as a symbol of the "repressed sexuality of youth" *and* the "repressed thought of death" (PU §699); an etymological reflection on the words *verstehen*, *comprehendere*, and *erfassen* (i.e., "to understand," "to comprehend") as originating in the idea of surrounding and unfolding, and the observation "there is no doubt that there is nothing in the world which so completely enfolds us as the mother"; and finally, the hauntingly beautiful lines from a sonnet by the French Symbolist poet Paul Verlaine (1844-96), *Mon rêve familier* (PU §700).

Buried in the footnotes to these final pages is one last, final reference to Nietzsche. Commenting on the Rigveda, Jung remarks that "thinking [*Denken*] and an image of the world [*Weltbild*] arose from a shrinking back from stern reality, and it is only after the individual has regressively assured himself again of the protective parental power that he enters life wrapped in a dream of childhood shrouded in magic superstititions; that is to say, 'thinking' [*»denkend«*], for he, timidly sacrificing his best and assuring himself of the favor of the invisible powers, step by step develops to greater power, in the degree that he frees himself from his retrogressive longing and the original lack of harmony in his being" (PU §676). In connection with this definition of "thinking," which brings us back to the two kinds of thinking discussed in Part One, Chapter 2 of *Transformations and Symbols of the Libido*, Jung refers to an aphorism in Nietzsche's *The Gay Science* entitled "Mentiri" (that is, "to lie" or "to make something up," derived from the word *mens,*

Greek letter *chi*]" (PU §406). In an entry in *The Black Books* for 3 January 1923, Jung recalled an epiphanic moment during his visit to North Africa in 1920—"that unforgettable night in the desert, where I saw the X for the first time and understood the Platonic myth"—when, "in the zenith, ~~where~~ there was a large radiant planet exactly at the intersection," an image which he interpreted as an "expression of the mystery of individuation" (BB7, 227).

or "mind," although Jung notes that the Indo-Germanic root *méntis*, *men*, is the same for *mentiri*, *memini* and *mens*:[55] in other words, to think is to lie): "Give heed! — he muses: immediately he will have a lie prepared. This is a stage of culture, upon which whole peoples have stood. One should ponder over what the Romans meant by *mentiri*!" (GS §157). Now, exactly how Jung intends us to interpret this text is not entirely clear, but from its context, it would appear to be seen as supporting Jung's claim about a necessary and ineluctable link between the sacrifice of (incestual) desire and civilizatory progress, or as he puts it: "Through the sacrifice a fulness of power was attained, which extends up to the power of the 'parents,'" and thus "the sacrifice has also the meaning of a psychological maturation process" (PU §678).

Even if this is the last explicit reference to Nietzsche, his presence nevertheless lingers on, right into the work's final paragraph. At the end of Miss Miller's drama, her hero figure, Chiwantopel, disappears when a volcano erupts and an earthquake shakes the ground, into which he disappears (cf. PU §631-§632). "As the volcano gave birth and name to the hero [cf. PU §297-§300], so at the end of the day it devours him again," Jung remarks (PB §700). In his footnote, Jung refers us to two examples: Hölderlin's poem "Empedocles," about the Presocratic philosopher who disappeared into Mount Etna;[56] and the journey to Hell of Zarathustra through the crater of the volcano in "Of Great Events." Aside from being an allusion to a chapter in *Zarathustra* that had long held Jung's attention (see below, pp. 205-206), this final reference to Nietzsche's *Zarathustra* anticipates Jung's own journey into the Underworld (as described in "Descent into Hell in the Future") in his *Red Book*.

---

[55] See Alois Walde, *Lateinisches etymologisches Wörterbuch*, 2nd edn (Heidelberg: Winter, 1910), entries for "mendax," "memini," and "mens."

[56] For the account of how Empedocles threw himself into Mount Etna, see Diogenes Laertius, *Lives and Opinions of Eminent Philosophers*, Book 8, Chapter 2, §66-§69.

In the image of the descent into a volcano, Jung's references to Nietzsche, Hölderlin, and Empedocles converge on a single point. For ever since he had been a young student, Jung had been fascinated—as Peter Kingsley has noted—with the story of how Empedocles had thrown himself into the volcano of Mount Etna in order to be reborn as a god and become immortal.[57] In his lecture to the Zofingia Society of 1898 entitled "Thoughts on the Nature and Value of Speculative Enquiry," Jung had spoken of "that ardent desire for truth which impetuously breaks down all barriers and is even capable of crushing the will to live" and exemplified it with the case of Empedocles (ZL §179). Did Empedocles leap into Mount Etna in order "to fathom the unfathomable"? Or had he—as the Roman lyric poet Horace suggested—desired to become an immortal god (cf. *Ars poetica*, ll. 464-466)? Jung was not sure. But he noted that "such Faustian beings whose life and death lies in the knowledge of truth" were not restricted to classical antiquity; Heinrich von Kleist was a case in point, shattered by his reading of Kant's critical philosophy (ZL §180).

In 1912, in *Transformations and Symbols of the Libido,* Jung cited those same lines from Horace—"*deus immortalis haberi / dum cupit Empedocles, ardentem frigidus Aetnam / insiluit*" ("Empedocles, eager to be thought / a god immortal, coolly leapt into burning Aetna")—[58] when he interpreted Hölderlin's poem "Empedocles," quoting the text in its entirety (PU §646). Here he read the poem as "betraying the secret longing for the maternal

[57] Peter Kingsley, *Catafalque: Carl Jung and the End of Humanity*, 2 vols. (London: Catafalque Press, 2018), vol. 1, p. 197. For further discussion, see Raymond Furness, "Nietzsche and Empedocles," *Journal of the British Society for Phenomenology*, vol. 2, no. 2 (1971), 91-94; and Karen Sieben, "Empedocles: Nietzsche's Failed Reformer," in Heather L. Reid, John Serrati, Tim Sorg (eds.), *Conflict and Competition: Agon in Western Greece: Selected Essays from the 2019 Symposium on the Heritage of Western Greece* (Sioux City, IA: Parnassos Press – Fonte Aretusa, 2020), pp. 251-266.

[58] Horace, *Satires, Epistles and Ars Poetica*, trans. H. Rushton Fairclough (London; Cambridge, MA: Heinemann; Harvard University Press, 1942), pp. 488-489.

depths" (PU §647) and, more precisely, the wish to "be sacrificed in the chalice, dissolved in wine like pearls"; or, in other words, to be transformed in the "*kratēr* of rebirth" (PU §648). Kingsley describes the Gnostic vessel of the *kratēr* as the "primordial symbol" of Jung's psychology, and he notes how Jung himself linked the symbol of the *kratēr* with the mystery of the Grail as the secret of individuation—that abandoned Grail vessel, the recovery of which he had decided to make his central task.[59] In his seminar on Nietzsche's *Zarathustra* of 20 May 1936, for instance, Jung linked the Grail to the *kratēr* as follows. His starting point was the "Gnostic interpretation" that the serpent in Paradise was the "son of the spiritual god who really tried to help [humankind] from the state of *anoia*, unconsciousness, and to give him *ennoia*, consciousness" (SNZ, vol. 2, 936). We find this same idea, he continues, "in the pagan Hermetic philosophy in the *kratēr*, the mixing jar, the famous vase of Hermes that was made by God after the creation":

> After he had created human beings in a state of *anoia*, he made that marvelous vessel, filled it with *nous*, and sent it down to the earth in order that those many human beings who felt the need of increasing consciousness could dip into that mixing jar, and [...] attain to *ennoia*. That is the origin probably of the Grail [...], and it appears also in alchemistic philosophy; this idea was widespread quite outside of biblical tradition. (SNZ, vol. 2, 936)[60]

[59] Kingsley, *Catafalque*, vol. 1, p. 197. For further discussion of this ambition to recover the Grail, see Volume 1, pp. 195-210.

[60] For further references to the likely Gnostic and Hermetic origins of the Grail, see CW 6 §396-§409 and CW 12 §246, fn. 125; as well as Kingsley, *Catafalque*, vol. 2, pp. 601-602.

In his lectures on "Psychology and Religion" given the following year in 1937, Jung repeats this account—which he attributes to the commentary (in Volume 6 of the *Theatrum Chemicum*) by Andreas Ortelius (1600-57) on *Novem Lumen Chemicum* (1656), a work by the Polish alchemist Michael Sendivogius (1566-1636)—that "the 'saviour' does not come down from heaven but out of the depths of the earth"—that is, from that which "lies below consciousness" (CW 11 §150). (For the alchemists, a "spirit" was imprisoned in the earth "in the vessel of matter," sometimes depicted as a "white dove," comparable to the *nous* (i.e., "intellect," "mind," "intelligence") in the *kratēr* of Hermes; Jung quotes from the *Corpus Hermeticum* (ed. Scott, vol. 1) where Hermes Trismegistus says, "Plunge into this *kratēr*, if thou canst, by recognizing to what end thou wast created, and by believing that thou wilt rise up to Him, who hath sent the *kratēr* down to earth" (CW 11 §150).[61] This *nous,* or spirit, is said to be the alchemical Mercurius [CW 11 §151].)

Yet Jung, on Kingsley's account, also recognized "with his fine eye for the sense of words"—a fine eye which Jung is not always credited as having, even by his friends—[62] that the old Greek term *kratēr* did not just mean "some pretty mixing-bowl or carefully crafted vessel." Instead, the term referred to the "crater

[61] See *Hermetica: The Ancient Greek and Latin Writings which contain Religious or Philosophic Teachings ascribed to Hermes Trismegistus*, ed. Walter Scott, 4 vols. (Oxford: Clarendon Press, 1924-1936), vol. 1, pp. 150-151, where the passage is translated: "Hearken, each human heart; dip yourself in this basin, if you can, recognizing for what purpose you have been made, and believing that you shall ascend to Him who sent the basin down" (cf. vol. 2, pp. 140-142); cf. "Immerse yourself in the mixing bowl if your heart has the strength, if it believes you will rise up again to the one who sent the mixing bowl below, if it recognizes the purpose of your coming to be" (Brian P. Copenhaver, *Hermetica: The Greek "Corpus Hermeticum" and the Latin "Asclepius" in a new English translation* (Cambridge: Cambridge University Press, 1992), pp. 15-16; cf. p. 134).

[62] See, for instance, Anthony Storr, who described Jung as "severely hampered [...] by his own difficulty in expressing his thoughts with clarity," a view with which Gary Lachman agrees (Anthony Storr, *Jung* (London: Fontana, 1973), p. 3; cf. Gary Lachman, *Jung the Mystic: The Esoteric Dimensions of Carl Jung's Life and Teachings* (New York: Penguin, 2010), p. 97).

of a magnificent volcano seething with lava and water and fire"—and, as such, "one of the most terrifying examples on earth of nature's utterly inhuman power to destroy, *transform*, give birth."[63] In fact, the image of the *kratēr* takes us to the heart of Jung's argumentation in *Transformations and Symbols of the Libido* and to his understanding of Nietzsche in that work.

Drawing on Franz Cumont's *Textes et monuments figurés relatifs aux mystères de Mithra* (1896-1899), in his final chapter, Jung refers to the Mithraic symbol of a crater (or mixing bowl) encoiled by a serpent, sometimes accompanied by a lion, which, as an antagonist, opposes the serpent (PU §692). Thanks to his exhaustive argumentation earlier in *Transformations and Symbols of the Libido*, Jung finds this symbol relatively easy to decode:

- the crater = the mother
- the serpent = the resistance defending the mother
- the lion = the greatest strength and strongest will (PU §692)

On Jung's account, the "struggle is for the mother" and the serpent —thanks to its mutual relationship in the Mithraic religion with the bull = the "living hero, the shining sun"—represents the "dead, buried or chthonic hero, the invisible sun," while also being the "symbol of the fear of death, the sign of the devouring mother" (PU §692).

Correspondingly, the sacrifice of the bull to the serpent signifies a "willing renunciation of *life*, in order to win it from *death*," after which "wonderful fertility results," and the antagonism between the serpent and the lion over the crater is thus interpreted by Jung as a "battle over the fruitful mother's womb" (PU §692; my emphasis). Yet we have also already met some of these symbols in Nietzsche:

- the serpent (together with the eagle, around whose neck it is wrapped) as one of Zarathustra's animals;

[63] Kingsley, *Catafalque*, vol. 1, p. 197 (my emphasis).

- the lion as the second of the transformations of the spirit;
- and the image of the mixing bowl in Zarathustra's ecstatic affirmation of eternal recurrence in "The Seven Seals."

In this discourse, Zarathustra declares:

> If ever I have drunk a full draught of the foaming spice- and confection-bowl in which all things are well mixed:
>
> If ever my hand hath mingled the furthest with the nearest, fire with spirit, joy with sorrow, and the harshest with the kindest:
>
> If I myself am a grain of the saving salt which maketh everything in the confection-bowl mix well: —
>
> — For there is a salt which uniteth good with evil; and even the evilest is worthy, as spicing and as final over-foaming: —
>
> Oh, how could I not be ardent for Eternity, and for the marriage-ring of rings — the ring of the return?
>
> Never yet have I found the woman by whom I should like to have children, unless it be this woman whom I love: for I love thee, O Eternity! (Z III 16 §4)

Thus, Empedocles—celebrated in Hölderlin's poem of that name and by Jung in his *Zofingia Lectures*, as well as one of Nietzsche's own favourite philosophers (as noted above, p. 200)—also represents the "root" of Jung's psychology: historically, as the "ultimate source of its lineage and pedigree"; and symbolically (and in every other sense) as the "primordial origin of its unstoppable vitality" and the "source of its raw, *transformative* power."[64]

---

[64] Kingsley, *Catafalque*, vol. 1, p. 198 (my emphasis). For further discussion of the relation between Presocratic thought and psychoanalysis, see Arthur M. Arkin, "A Short Note on Empedocles and Freud," *American Imago*, vol. 6, no. 3 (September 1949), 197-203; and Garfield Tourney, "Empedocles and Freud, Heraclitus and Jung," *Bulletin of the History of Medicine*, vol. 30, no. 2 (March-April, 1956), 109-123.

In his seminar on Nietzsche's *Zarathustra*, Jung affirms the significance of Empedocles for Nietzsche on two occasions. On 4 May 1938, he rehearses Horace's argument that Empedocles had leapt into the volcano on Etna in his quest for divine immortality, but he suggests two other reasons for why the philosopher leaped into the fiery crater: perhaps in order to get away from the crowds of people who followed him and to get a bit of peace; or perhaps as an enactment of a mythological motif—the motif that, after all the "greatness" when Nietzsche felt himself to be the "savior of the world" or the "one who tells all the boys what to do in order to get salvation" (!), he would "have to make the descent into utter destruction" (SNZ, vol. 2, 1217). The context of these remarks is Jung's reading of "On Great Events," whose opening narrative had struck Jung when he read *Zarathustra* as a student as remarkably similar to a passage from Justinus Kerner's *Blätter aus Prevorst* (translated by Catherine Crowe as *The Seeress of Prevorst*). (Jung had gone so far as to write to Nietzsche's sister, Elisabeth Förster-Nietzsche, for confirmation that Nietzsche had read the book, and discussing the case as an example of cryptomnesia in his doctoral dissertation published in 1902).[65] For Jung, the episode represents Zarathustra's descent into Hades: There is a volcano, an entrance to the interior of the earth, and even Cerberus, the fire dog; in psychological terms, the episode is said to mark a moment of

[65] See SNZ, vol. 2, 1217-1218; and for further discussion, see Paul Bishop, "The Jung/Förster-Nietzsche Correspondence," *German Life and Letters*, 46 (1993), 319-330; and "The Descent of Zarathustra and the Rabbits: Jung's Correspondence with Elisabeth Förster-Nietzsche," *Harvest: Journal for Jungian Studies*, 43 (1997), 108-123. In *Transformations and Symbols of the Libido*, Jung refers in a footnote in its final pages to the "journey to hell of Zarathustra through the crater of a volcano" (PU §700, fn.). Jung discussed Justinus Kerner's *Die Seherin von Prevorst* at some length in his ETH lectures on the History of Modern Psychology (see C.G. Jung, *History of Modern Psychology: Lectures delivered at the ETH Zurich*, ed. Ernst Falzeder, trans. Mark Kyburz, John Peck, and Ernst Falzeder (Princeton, NJ, and Oxford: Princeton University Press, 2019), pp. 38-41, 46-48, 53-60, 62-69).

enantiodromia, a moment of descent in which one will be "burned up" and "dissolve" (SNZ, vol. 2, 1217).

Puzzled by Nietzsche's lack of an explicit reference to Empedocles (although there was no explicit reference to Justinus Kerner either, so perhaps not so surprising), Jung equivocates about whether Nietzsche had been "conscious at all of the example of Empedocles," before conceding that he "might have been" and then strongly suspecting that "he *must* have been aware of it" (SNZ, vol. 2, 1217 and 1220). Yet how far was Jung aware of his *own* indebtedness to Empedocles? As the source of one of his favorite expressions, *pharmakon athanasias* (that is, the "medicine of immortality"), Jung cited the study *Die hellenistischen Mysterienreligionen: Ihre Grundgedanken und Wirkungen* (1910; ^{3}1927) by the German classical philologist Richard Reitzenstein (1861-1931) (cf. CW 12 §125, fn. 3), but the idea itself goes back, as Kingsley has shown, to Empedocles.[66]

As offering direct access to the underworld, the *kratēr* plays a role that is, as Kingsley notes, "absolutely central to the dynamics" of *The Red Book*.[67] For the scene of the mystery play that takes place in "Mysterium. Encounter" in *Liber Primus* on the night when Jung "considered the essence of the God" is described as a "deep place like the crater of a volcano" (RB, 174 and 178-179). In the second scene, the following night in "Instruction," Jung is standing "in the rocky depth that seems to me like a crater" (RB, 184). And in the final chapter of *Liber Primus* called "Resolution" on the third night when he was seized by "deep longing to continue to experience the mysteries"—after he witnesses the fight of two snakes, and before he transforms into Christ, standing with "outstretched arms like someone crucified [...] and horribly entwined by the serpent" like

[66] Kingsley, *Catafalque*, vol. 2, p. 602; cf. Kingsley, *Ancient Philosophy, Mystery and Magic: Empedocles and Pythagorean Tradition* (Oxford: Oxford University Press, 1995), pp. 218-223.
[67] Kingsley, *Catafalque*, vol. 2, p. 603.

a *Deus Leontocephalus* (RB, 194 and 197)—the setting in which Jung finds himself undergoes a sudden metamorphosis as the "walls enlarge into a huge mountain" and Jung finds himself "below on the foundation of the crater in the underworld" (RB, 196).[68] It is in this context, in a setting said (in Jung's seminar on Analytical Psychology given on 8 June 1925) to be comparable to the Gnostic symbol of the two cones and to the cosmological model of Dante's *Inferno* (RB, 196, fn. 210; cf. AP, 96-97), that Jung finds himself in front of the house of the prophet Elijah—the significance of whom we shall discuss in greater detail in Volume 4 in this series.

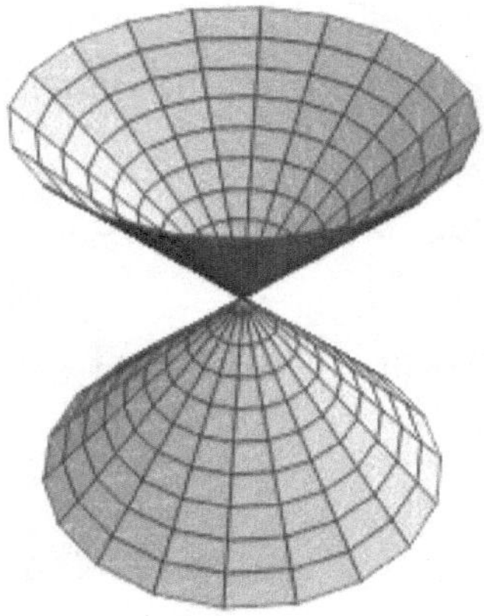

Weisstein, Eric W. "Double Cone." From MathWorld—A Wolfram Web Resource. https://mathworld.wolfram.com/DoubleCone.html. Used with permission

Excursus: The Grail in Jung's Seminar on Nietzsche's *Zarathustra*

In his Seminar on Nietzsche's *Zarathustra* (held between 1934 and 1939), Jung links Zarathustra's journey into the underworld in "Of Great Events" with the legend of the Grail. He does so through

[68] Cf. Jung's own commentary on this episode in the Appendices (see RB, 567).

noting the motif of flying or suspension, associating it with the *hamsa,* or heavenly swan, in Hindu mythology, which—because of its pure sunlight-white color—represents the "universal soul or supreme spirit."[69] In the legend of the Grail, the Grail itself is held in a state of suspension, held suspended by angels between heaven and earth (SNZ, vol. 1, 186-187). The motif of suspension has significance in a further context, being an aspect of crucifixion or the "unconscious aspect of transfiguration" (ibid., 187). While it is undergoing transformation, the "subtle body" (using a term found in a variety of religious and esoteric traditions) undergoes a kind of "martyrdom," appearing in a "sort of crucifixion" or a "state of suspension" which "precedes birth or creation" (ibid., 187). At this point, Jung recalls a passage from the *Runenkunde* of the Edda,

> I know that I hung on the windswept tree
> Nine nights through,
> Wounded by a spear, dedicated to Odin
> I myself to myself,

that passage which he had also quoted in *Transformations and Symbols of the Libido* (PU §400) and to which he had alluded in *The Red Book* when he finds himself "hang[ing] above the ground on the swaying branch of the divine tree [...]" (RB, 443), and he cries out to ΦΙΛΗΜΩΝ, "damned charlatan, [...] you played a Christ-fool's comedy with me, you hanged me, carefully and ludicrously, in the tree just like Odin" (RB, 449).

[69] See the entry for हंस (Hamsa), in Monier Monier-Williams, *A Sanskrit-English Dictionary: Etymologically and Philologically arranged with special reference to Cognate Indo-European Languages* (Oxford: Clarendon Press, 1899), p. 1286; and the entry for "haṁsa" in Margaret and James Stutley, *A Dictionary of Hinduism: Its Mythology, Folklore and Development, 1500 B.C.-A.D. 1500* (London and New York: Routledge, 2019), p. 108. For the link between the haṁsa and the phoenix, see Volume 1, pp. 157 and 164.

Many months later we find the motifs of the Grail, Odin/ Wotan and his spear, and the unconscious constellated again by Jung when discussing these lines from "The Child with the Mirror": "And when I want to mount my wildest horse, then doth my spear always help me up best: it is my foot's ever ready servant:— / The spear which I hurl at mine enemies! How grateful am I to mine enemies that I may at last hurl it!" (Z II 1). For Jung, the spear is a "symbol for the intellect on account of its piercing, discriminating, dissecting character," and this symbolism connects with the earlier line where Zarathustra declares, "Wounded am I by my happiness" (SNZ, vol. 2, 865). Jung goes on to argue that "th[is] happiness is the consequence of his identification with the spirit [...] by way of the intellect, so by that *détour* it is of course the spear by which he is wounded," a motif that he associates with the "Amfortas problem"—or the dolorous stroke, as explained by Trevrizent to Parzival in Book 9—[70] and with the "idea of the suffering god" (ibid., 866).

On Jung's very peculiar, even idiosyncratic, reading of the story of the Crucifixion (which sheds a good deal of light on the use of this motif in *The Red Book*), Christ represents the human

---

[70] "When he died, Frimutel, our father, they chose them his eldest son
As Lord of the Grail and Its knighthood, thus Anfortas his kingdom won,
And of riches and crown was he worthy, and we were but children still —
When he came to the years of manhood, when love joyeth to work her will
On the heart, and his lips were fringèd with the down of early youth,
Frau Minne laid stress upon him who for torment hath little ruth.
But if love the Grail King seeketh other than he find writ,
'Tis a sin, and in sorrow and sighing full sore shall he pay for it!
[...]
"One day as the king rode lonely, in search of some venture high
(Sore trouble it brought upon us,) with love's payment for victory,
For love's burden lay heavy on him, in a joust was he wounded sore
With a poisoned spear, so that healing may be wrought on him nevermore.
For thine uncle, the King Anfortas, he was smitten thro' the thigh
By a heathen who with him battled, for he jousted right skilfully. [...]"
(§478, ll. 1-16 and §479, ll. 3-14; vol. 1, p. 275)

being that was "wounded by the overwhelming fact of the spirit, which carried him away and killed his humanity" (SNZ, vol. 2, 866). ("Of course we worship that fact," Jung—tellingly—adds, "but not all of us worship it.") On the one hand, this experience of the spirit has a "very marvelous side," inasmuch as "it is [...] really very wonderful to be like a wild river rushing into the wide plains inundating everything and enjoying the play" but, on the other, its corollary is that "there is any amount of destruction linked up with it" (ibid., 867). We can see precisely this ambivalence, Jung believes, in the case of Nietzsche here: It is a "very wonderful experience to be identical with the spirit, in spite of all sorts of indications that it is not such a particularly happy event," as is reflected in Zarathustra's words that he is *wounded by his own happiness*, that he *hurls a spear against his enemies*, and that he is *grateful that he has enemies*, someone upon whom he can inflict the wound again (ibid., 867).

So if the spirit manifests itself as a "one-sided thing," then the unconscious mind foresees "some compensating truth"—something shown, Jung believes, "in the symbolism of the Grail and in similar symbolism of the unconscious," such as is embodied in the symbolism of Wotan's spear and his host roaring through the forest, as expressed in the following lines: "Too great hath been the tension of my cloud: 'twixt laughters of lightnings will I cast hail-showers into the depths. / Violently will my breast then heave; violently will it blow its storm over the mountains: thus cometh its assuagement. / Verily, like a storm cometh my happiness, and my freedom! But mine enemies shall think that THE EVIL ONE roareth over their heads" (Z II 1; cf. SNZ, vol. 2, 867). In Jung's view, these lines from "The Child and the Mirror" demonstrate the fact that if there is a "thing from which one always suffers," one "is always led to inflict the wound upon others" (ibid., 867). Thus people who are "caught or overcome by the power of the spirit" have a tendency to "do the same to others": Just as they have "been overcome and wounded," so they in turn will "overcome and wound" others—because they are "not themselves," because they are "filled with the spirit," and because they are "inhuman or supermen, whatever you like to call it" (ibid., 867).

In his discussion of "The Bedwarfing Virtue," Jung returned to this point, emphasizing how Nietzsche "often liked to think of himself as a religious reformer" and that "not in vain did he take the name of Zarathustra to express his historical role" (SNZ, vol. 2, 1364). Thus, Nietzsche presented Zarathustra as a "Saoshyant, a new savior," who has "come back in order to heal the wound he caused" (SNZ, vol. 2, 1364). Consequently, Nietzsche's idea of an *Übermensch* would be the "man who was beyond that wound, who had healed that wound," and here lies for Jung the link to the Grail mystery—the figure of the "suffering king who is to be cured by a savior," representing an analogy of the "Christian man who carries that moral wound" as well as the "Persian man [who] was rent asunder" by (the historical) Zoroaster's teaching about the "idea of good and evil" and the "moral opposites" (ibid., 1364). According to Jung, Nietzsche believed that "his task in the history of the world" had been to "cure Man of that incurable wound he has suffered from hitherto"; in other words, Nietzsche saw himself as a kind of Parzival, healing not just an individual but the community, even the entire human race. On this point Jung is insistent: Nietzsche had not been "simply playing" with this idea, he emphasizes, but rather it grew into a "deep-rooted conviction in him amounting to a sort of mystical experience"—hence the quasi-reality of the figure of Zarathustra as "more than a speech metaphor," and as a "more or less real figure" (ibid., 1364-1365).[71]

This background, Jung believes, explains why it was precisely the opera *Parsifal* (1882) that caused the "bitterest estrangement"

[71] For further discussion of the mystical aspects of Nietzsche, see Herbert Theierl, *Nietzsche — Mystik als Selbstversuch* (Würzburg: Könighausen & Neumann, 2000).

between the two former friends, Wagner and Nietzsche. As a contemporary of Nietzsche, it was "not without meaning" that Richard Wagner chose to occupy himself precisely with the story of Parzival, which "contains this very problem," namely: how to heal the wound? Yet when Nietzsche accused Wagner, "seemingly the all-conquering," of actually being a "decaying, despairing decadent" who "suddenly sank down helpless and shattered before the Christian cross,"[72] this was—according to Jung, playing with the idea of the spear—a "bitter shaft," because "in his consciousness Nietzsche could only see the so-called Christian gesture or the Christian sentimentality" and hence he was "not aware of the deeper meaning of that whole fact," namely: that Wagner was asking exactly the same questions as Nietzsche was and indeed providing similar solutions to his own (SNZ, vol. 2, 1365).

Hence, Jung sees Wagner's *Parsifal* as "practically the parallel of Zarathustra," and regards Nietzsche's *Zarathustra* as the "other aspect of the same thing, only expressed in entirely different terms" (SNZ, vol. 2, 1365).[73] For Jung, the main difference between Wagner and Nietzsche lies in their differing historical perspectives: Whereas Wagner had used a legend which was "well known and still much appreciated" and so he "only went back to the Middle Ages," Nietzsche had made a "much further regression," going back into the eighth or ninth centuries B.C.E. in order to find "his figure or analogy, his myth" (ibid., 1365). Nevertheless, Jung insisted that the "actual ideas are very much the same": namely, the "idea of the cure of the incurable wound" (ibid., 1365).[74] Seen in this light,

[72] "Richard Wagner, apparently most triumphant, but in truth a decaying and despairing decadent, suddenly sank down, helpless and broken, before the Christian cross ..." (NCW How I Broke Away from Wagner §2).

[73] In this respect Jung anticipates the core argument of Roger Hollinrake's seminal study: *Nietzsche, Wagner, and the Philosophy of Pessimism* (London: Allen and Unwin, 1982).

[74] In his *Letters on the Aesthetic Education* (1795), Friedrich Schiller uses the image of culture or civilization itself as inflicting a wound, arguing that "it was civilization

one might be tempted to ask: If Nietzsche's Zarathustra is a parallel to the legendary Grail figure of Parzival, we should not also see Wolfram's Parzival himself as a kind of Saoshyant figure? Indeed, is this not a precise description of Parzival's role as an agent of transformation?

One of Jung's seminar participants had a different question, however. A certain Mrs. Jay asked Jung about the parallels between Parsifal/Zarathustra and Wagner/Nietzsche; about the wound of Amfortas and the spear which healed it; and about whether both Parsifal and Zarathustra become "wise through compassion" (SNZ, vol. 2, 1376-1377).[75] At this point, Jung pauses, exclaiming, "that is a chapter in itself"! For in order to answer that question, he adds by way of explanation, they would have to be reading *The Case of Wagner* instead of *Zarathustra*; as a result, the parallel

itself which inflicted this wound upon modern man" and that "it must be open to us to restore by means of a higher Art the totality of our nature which the arts themselves have destroyed" (Letter 6, §6 and §15; Friedrich Schiller, *On the Aesthetic Education of Man: In a Series of Letters*, ed. and trans. Elizabeth M. Wilkinson and L.A. Willoughby (Oxford: Clarendon Press, 1982), pp. 33 and 43).

[75] See the words introduced by Amfortas, picked up by Gurnemanz—*Durch Mitleid wissend, der reine Tor* —and subsequently echoed by the Four Squires, by the Squires and Knights, and finally the Alto Voice from on high in Wagner's *Parsifal*, Act 1, Scene 1. As Peter Bassett has pointed out, the expression "made wise through compassion" sounds very much like the way in which Brünnhilde is "made wise through love" — in Act 3, Scene 3, of *Siegfried*, she tells Siegfried, "What you would know, know it from me, for I am wise because I love you!" (*Was du nicht weisst, / weiss ich für dich; / doch wissend bin ich / nur — weil ich dich liebe!*), and later he reminds her: "Didn't you tell me," Siegfried says, "that all of your wisdom came by the light of your love for me?" (*Sangst du mir nicht, / dein Wissen sei / das Leuchten der Liebe zu mir?*) (Act 3, Scene 3), — and at the first rehearsals of Wotan's final scene with Erda in Act 3, Scene 1, of *Siegfried* when he expresses his new-found wisdom in accepting he must "will" the coming of a new order, Wagner himself is reported to have said, "It must sound like the proclamation of a new religion" (Heinrich Porges, *Wagner Rehearsing the "Ring": An Eye-Witness Account of the Stage Rehearsals of the First Bayreuth Festival*, trans. Robert L. Jacobs (Cambridge: Cambridge University Press, 1983), p. 103; cf. Peter Bassett, *The Nibelung's Ring: A Guide to Wagner's "Der Ring der Nibelungen"* (Kent Town: Wakefield Press, 2003), pp. 119 and 121). For further discussion of this ethical aspect of the Grail legend, see Kim Samuel, "Re-Imagining the Grail Quest: The Grail of Compassion," *Temenos Academy Review*, 19 (2016), 78-95.

between the mystery of the Grail and the meaning of *Zarathustra* must "remain a mere allusion for the time being"; and he takes issue with the suggestion that both Nietzsche/Zarathustra and Parsifal become "wise through compassion." Rather, this statement is said to mark a crucial point of difference between Wagner and Nietzsche, as Jung shrewdly observes: "As a human being Wagner was not compassionate at all, while Nietzsche surely suffered from his great compassion for the world; therefore he curses compassion and Wagner praises it" (ibid., 1377).

Chapter 3

Nietzsche's *Zarathustra* in Jung's *Collected Works* [B]

Nietzsche in Jung's Early Systematic and Typological Writings

It would be fair to describe Jung's use of Nietzsche in *Transformations and Symbols of the Libido* as allusive, even allegorical: He is attracted to Nietzsche primarily, it seems, by the complexity and density of symbolism in *Zarathustra* and in the *Dithyrambs of Dionysos*, rather than by the other part of Nietzsche's *œuvre*, his aphoristic and essayistic writings. Not surprisingly, therefore, Nietzsche was able to serve as a model in some respects for what Jung was to undertake in his *Red Book* (as we shall see in Volume 4 in this series).

Yet Nietzsche also played an important role in Jung's various attempts, after his break with Freud announced in public by *Transformations and Symbols of the Libido* (and his struggle, in private, to come to terms with his *Auseinandersetzung* or "confrontation" with the unconscious in *The Red Book*), to offer a systematic formulation of what he now began to call *analytical psychology* (rather than *psychoanalysis*), particularly in regard to the notion of typology. As a result, the first such text we should briefly consider is Jung's second major monograph, published in 1921, called *Psychological Types*.

(a) *Psychological Types* (1921)

Given its modest and somewhat dry title, it is easy to overlook the amazing intellectual range and historical scope of *Psychological*

Types: from its discussion of the problem of types in the history of classical and medieval thought (the Gnostics, Tertullian, and Origen; the theological disputes in the ancient Church; the problem of transubstantiation; nominalism and realism; and the controversy about Holy Communion between Luther and Zwingli), via Friedrich Schiller's *Letters on the Aesthetic Education of Humankind* (1794) and *On Naïve and Sentimental Poetry* (1795-1796) and Nietzsche's *The Birth of Tragedy* (1872) and its concepts of the Apollonian and the Dionysian, to his discussions of John Furneaux Jordan (1830-1911), Carl Spitteler (1845-1924), and William James. Yet here and there indications of what Jung had experienced when working on *The Red Book* flicker through …[1]

Concluding the first part of his discussion of Schiller's idea on the type of problem as found in his *Letters on the Aesthetic Education of Humankind* and in the correspondence between Goethe and Schiller, Jung highlighted Schiller's formulation of one of the "two fundamental laws of humankind's sensuo-rational nature" (*die zwei Fundamentalgesetze der sinnlich-vernünftigen Natur*): namely, that human beings should "externalize all within and shape everything without" (*alles Innre veräussern und alles Äussere formen*) (Letter 11, §9).[2] On Jung's account, this formula represents the ideal of the introvert's conscious attitude. It assumes two things: the ideal range of an inner world of concepts and formal

[1] Just as *Transformations and Symbols of the Libido* can be seen as anticipating or looking *forward* to *The Red Book*, so *Psychological Types* can be seen, in places, as explicating or looking *back* at it.

[2] These two laws are:

- turn everything which is mere form into world, and make all our potentialities [*Anlagen*] fully manifest (*alles zur Welt machen, was bloss Form ist*), i.e., "absolute reality"
- destroy everything in ourselves which is mere world, and bring harmony into all our changes (*alles in sich vertilgen, was bloss Welt ist*), i.e., "absolute formality"

(Letter 11, §9). Cited here by letter and paragraph number from Friedrich Schiller, *On the Aesthetic Education of Man: In a Series of Letters*, ed. and trans. Elizabeth M. Wilkinson and L.A. Willoughby (Oxford: Clarendon Press, 1982).

principles as well as a way of employing the sensory principle (or, as Schiller would call it, the *Sinntrieb*, that is, the sensory drive) as an active power. As long as human beings are merely sensuous or merely feel, they are "nothing but world" (*nichts als* Welt); and "in order not to be mere world" (*um also nicht bloss Welt zu sein*), human beings must "impart form to matter" (*der Materie Form erteilen*) (Letter 11, §8); thereby, in Jung's view, reversing the passive, receptive sensuous principle (and turning it into something active) (CW 6 §149).

("Somewhere or other the individual must be related, must be subject to something, otherwise he would be really godlike," Jung adds. Why does he say this? Because Schiller begins his argumentation at this point by introducing the notion of the Godhead (*Gottheit*), and defining its "unending task" as the realization of its "most characteristic attribute" as:

- "absolute manifestation of potential" (or the "actualization of all that is possible")
- "absolute unity of manifestation" (or the "necessity of all that is made actual")

Schiller goes on to say that human beings carry within them a "disposition to the divine" (*die Anlage zu der Gottheit*) — it is in the personality, but the "way to the divine" (if, he gnomically adds, we can call a way that which never leads to the goal …) "is opened up" to us "through the senses" (*in den* Sinnen) (Letter 11, §7).[3]

[3] In his poem "The Ideal and Life" (*Das Ideal und das Leben* (1804), originally called when written in 1795 "The Kingdom of the Shadows" (*Das Reich der Schatten*) and changed in 1800 to "The Kingdom of the Forms" (*Das Reich der Formen*), Schiller alludes to the myth of Persephone (l. 13), going on to say that, whereas the body is subject to the "dark fate" (*das dunkle Schicksal*) (l. 22), beyond it lies the "divine image of humanity" (*der Menschheit Götterbild*) (l. 33) (Schiller, *Sämtliche Gedichte und Balladen*, ed. Georg Kurscheidt (Frankfurt am Main and Leipzig: Insel, 2004), pp. 117-118). This "divine image" is, as Frank Fowler explains, both the image of the blessed dead who wander the Elysian Fields *and* the Platonic image of original perfection from which we descend to this life (Schiller, *Selected Poems*, ed. Frank M. Fowler (London; New York: Macmillan; St. Martin's Press, 1969), p. 160). For

Hence, the twin tasks of "absolute reality" and "absolute formality"—"conceived," that is, "in their highest fulfilment"—lead back to this initial concept of *Gottheit*. Thus, in this letter, Schiller sets out the basis for the program that Jung will carry out in *The Red Book*: namely, to realize the God within.)[4]

Yet how—to return to the problematic of the *Aesthetic Letters*—can we give our world of ideas that extraordinary range necessary to impose a congenial form on the material world and to convert our passive, sensuous nature into something active in order to bring it up to the level of our world of ideas? Must we not, in one respect or another, be related, or so to speak, "subjected" (*unterlegen*), for otherwise *we* would be godlike? Schiller writes that we ought to "destroy" (*vertilgen*) everything in ourselves that is "mere world" (*bloss Welt*) (Letter 11, §9), and Jung suggests that this would mean going so far as to allow "violence to be done to the object" (*dem Objekt Gewalt anzutun*) (CW 6 §149). If so, then in so doing, Schiller would be conceding to the "archaic, inferior function" an unrestricted right to existence, something which Schiller himself nowhere consciously expresses. By contrast, in Jung's view, Nietzsche did—or at least he did in theory (CW 6 §149). Here, then, lies a crucial difference between Schiller and

further discussion of this text, see Paul Bishop, *On the Blissful Islands with Nietzsche and Jung: In the Shadow of the Superman* (London and New York: Routledge, 2017), pp. 143-181; and Owen Ware, *Return of the Gods: Mythology in Romantic Philosophy and Literature* (New York: Oxford University Press, 2024), pp. 24-46.

[4] In his essay "On Grace and Dignity" (1793), Schiller had defined love as "*absolute greatness* itself, that finds itself imitated in grace and beauty and affirmed in the ethical […] the legislator himself, the *God* in us [*der Gott in uns*], who plays with his own image in the world of senses" (Friedrich Schiller, *Schiller's "On Grace and Dignity" in its Cultural Context: Essays and a New Translation*, ed. Jane V. Curran and Christophe Fricker (Rochester, NY: Camden House, 2005), p. 166). This turn of phrase is echoed by Jung when, in *The Relations between the Ego and the Unconscious* (1928), he writes of the Self as something "strange to us and yet so near, wholly ourselves and yet unknowable, a virtual centre [*ein virtueller Mittelpunkt*] of so mysterious a constitution that it can claim anything […] without moving us to wonder," and adding, in Schillerian terms: "It might equally well be called the 'god within us' [»*der Gott in uns*«]." (CW 7 §398-§399).

Nietzsche: For Schiller's formula about "externalizing all within and shaping everything without" is said to exhibit a "thoroughly naïve and idealistic character that was quite consistent with the spirit of his time [*mit dem Geist seiner Zeit*]"—with what, in *The Red Book*, he had called the "spirit of this time" (*der Geist dieser Zeit*)—"which was not yet infected by that deep mistrust of human nature and of human truth as was the epoch of psychological criticism [*Epoche des psychologischen Kritizismus*] inaugurated by Nietzsche" (CW 6 §149). In short, Schiller = idealism, Nietzsche = criticism!

On Jung's account, this Schillerian principle of "externalizing all within and shaping everything without" was one which, in order to be realized, would require a "ruthless power standpoint" that cared neither about justice nor reasonableness for the object nor about its own competence (CW 6 §150). Does this not sound like *our* world? It should—for, despite (or because of) Schiller, an epochal shift took place in the 18th century: "In this way the archaic [*das Archaische*] asserted itself naively, unconsciously, and decked out for the moment in the splendour of great words and beautiful gestures, and helped to build our present 'civilization' [*»Kultur«*], about the nature of which humankind is at the moment"—that is, in the 1920s—"in some measure of disagreement" (CW 6 §150). The cause of this disagreement, or presumably what Freud was to call a sense of "discontent" (*Unbehagen*) in civilization, was that the "archaic power drive" (*der archaische Machttrieb*), previously "hidden behind the façade of cultured gestures," now "came to the surface in its true colours" in the form of the French Revolution and its subsequent Terror, thereby "prov[ing] beyond question that we 'are still barbarians'" (CW 6 §150; citing Letter 8, §4). In this development Jung sees an example of the law of complementarism, in the sense that "in the same measure as the conscious attitude can, on the basis of its lofty and absolute standpoint, make a claim to a certain god-likeness, so an unconscious attitude develops, whose god-likeness is however oriented downwards — toward an archaic god [*nach einem archaischen Gotte*] whose nature is sensuous and brutal" (CW 6 §150). Moreover, in accordance with Heraclitus's principle of enantiodromia, Jung foresees a time "when this *deus absconditus* shall also rise to the surface and press the God of our ideals to the wall" (CW 6 §150).

Toward the end of the 18th century, however, people seem not to have really seen what was taking place in Paris but instead "persisted in a certain aesthetic [*schöngeistigen*], enthusiastic [*schwärmerischen*], or trifling [*spielerischen*] attitude," in order to delude themselves about the "glimpse into the abysses of human nature" (CW 6 §150)—those abysses to which Schiller's poem, "The Diver" (*Der Taucher*), chillingly alludes:

"May the horror below never more find a voice —
Nor Man stretch too far the wide mercy of Heaven!
Never more — never more may he lift from the sight
The veil which is woven with Terror and Night!"

Da unten aber ist's fürchterlich,
Und der Mensch versuche die Götter nicht,
Und begehre nimmer und nimmer zu schauen,
Was sie gnädig bedecken mit Nacht und mit Grauen.[5]

Whereas, on Jung's account, in Schiller's lifetime, the moment for coming to terms with that underworld had not yet come, it was something that was much closer to Nietzsche, for whom it was "certain that we were approaching an epoch of unprecedented struggle" (CW 6 §151). And consequently, it fell to Nietzsche, as the "only true pupil of Schopenhauer," to tear through the "veil of naïveté" and—in his *Zarathustra*—to "conjure up some of the things that were destined to be the most vital content of the coming

[5] *The Poems and Ballads of Schiller*, trans. Edward Bulwer Lytton, 2 vols. (Edinburgh and London: Blackwood, 1844), vol. 1, p. 5.

age" (CW 6 §151). Of course, the "coming age" for Nietzsche had, by the 1920s, become the "present age" for Jung and his contemporaries—and, arguably, for ourselves.

Further on, in his discussion of those eminently Nietzschean categories of the Apollonian and the Dionysian (CW 6 §223-§242), Jung links Schiller to Nietzsche once again. Obviously, the central text here for Jung is *The Birth of Tragedy*, but he takes Nietzsche to task for seeing the struggle between Apollo and Dionysos and their eventual reconciliation in *aesthetic*, rather than *religious*, terms (CW 6 §231). (This move is made in the opening section of *The Birth of Tragedy*, where Nietzsche introduces the two deities as "artistic deities" (*Kunstgottheiten*), then "artistic worlds" (*Kunstwelten*), namely: dreams and ecstasy, respectively.) Indeed, Jung writes that "aestheticism" (*der Ästhetismus*) is actually a "modern pair of glasses through which the psychological mysteries of the cult of Dionysos are seen in a light in which they were certainly never seen and experienced by the ancients," and that "with Nietzsche, as with Schiller, the religious point-of-view is entirely overlooked and is replaced by the aesthetic viewpoint" (CW 6 §231). (Of course, this leaves open the entire question of the sense in which the Greeks, as Paul Veyne put it, may—or, indeed, may not—have believed in their gods…)[6]

While Jung nevertheless concedes that the religious does have an aesthetic dimension and, in a footnote, adds that the aesthetic can even replace the religious, he notes that Nietzsche's later "conversion" (*Bekehrung*) to Dionysos suggests that the aesthetic substitute he had proposed "did not stand the test of time" (CW 6 §231, fn. 14). So both the historical approach, as critiqued by Nietzsche in the second of his *Untimely Meditations* entitled "On the Uses and Disadvantages of History for Life" (1874), and the aesthetic approach, which regards the relation of the Apollonian and

[6] Paul Veyne, *Les Grecs ont-ils cru à leurs mythes? Essai sur l'imagination constituante* (Paris: Seuil, 1983).

the Dionysian as a "problem with horns" (as Nietzsche described it in his "Attempt at a Self-Criticism" of 1886 [BT Attempt §2]), fail to do justice to the religious aspect. Whereas Nietzsche wrote *The Birth of Tragedy* in 1872 while moved by aestheticism, he wrote his "Attempt at a Self-Criticism" (1886) and *Thus Spoke Zarathustra* (1883-92) while moved by Dionysos, as is reflected in his comment, "Indeed, what is Dionysian? — This book contains an answer: one 'who knows' is talking, the initiate and discipline of his god" (BT Attempt §4), and in the passage from "On the Higher Man" with which he concluded his "Attempt at a Self-Criticism," "Lift up your hearts, my brethren, high, higher! And do not forget your legs! Lift up also your legs, ye good dancers, and better still, if ye stand upon your heads!" ("On the Higher Man," §17). Indeed, Jung goes so far as to talk about Dionysos having "taken his revenge" on Nietzsche—as if the Dionysian had some agency of its own (or were an actual deity…) (CW 6 §232). This same Dionysian spirit, described on Jung's account by Nietzsche as an "unfolding," as a "streaming upward and outward," or (in Goethean terms) as a "diastole," is presented by Schiller in his famous ode "To Joy" (written 1795) as a "motion embracing the world":

Be embraced, Millions!	*Seid umschlungen, Millionen,*
This kiss to all the world!	*Diesen Kuss der ganzen Welt.*
[…]	[…]
All creatures drink of joy	*Freude trinken alle Wesen*
At nature's breasts.	*An den Brüsten der Natur*
[…]	[…]
Lust was given to the worm	*Wollust ward dem Wurm gegeben*
And the cherub stands before God.	*Und der Cherub steht vor Gott.*[7]

[7] Schiller, *Sämtliche Gedichte und Balladen*, ed. Kurscheidt, pp. 192-193, cf. pp. 321-322. Text and translation available online HTTP <https://de.wikisource.org/wiki/An_die_Freude_(Schiller)>.

Both Nietzsche's *Zarathustra* and Schiller's ode are interpreted by Jung as depicting "Dionysian expansion" as a "flood of the most powerful universal feeling, which bursts forth irresistibly and like the strongest wine intoxicates the senses"; indeed, it *is* "intoxication in the highest sense" (CW 6 §135).

In terms of Jungian typology, the Dionysian is the attitude of *extraversion,* and the Apollonian is *introversion*; more precisely, the Dionysian is *extraverted sensation,* and the Apollonian is *introverted intuition* (CW 6 §235-§238). Thus, beyond the typological categories of extraversion and introversion and the functional categories of thinking (*Denken*) and feeling (*Fühlen*), the Dionysian and the Apollonian point to two further functional categories: sensation (*Empfindung*) and intuition (*Intuition*). On Jung's account, ideas (*Ideen*) are just as much feeling (*Gefühl*) as they are thought (*Gedanke*), that is, inasmuch as their elaboration is rational and logical. *Beyond* logico-rational elaboration, however, lies another standpoint, but it is now a standpoint that Jung himself tellingly does not describe as religious but as *aesthetic*: this aesthetic standpoint "dwells in introversion on the contemplation [*Anschauung*] of ideas, it develops intuition [*die Intuition*], the inner contemplation [*die innere Anschauung*]; in extraversion it dwells on sensation [*Empfindung*] and develops the senses, instinct, affectivity" (CW 6 §239). In fact, the functions of intuition and sensation are said to be *prior to* thinking and feeling, inasmuch for the aesthetic standpoint "thinking is by no means the principle of inner perception [*Wahrhehmung*] of ideas, just as little as feeling is; instead, thinking and feeling are mere derivatives of inner contemplation [*Anschauung*] or sensory sensation [*Sinnesempfindung*]" (CW 6 §239).

So maybe Nietzsche was not so wrong in his aesthetic approach after all. As always, with Jung, the answer is never an "either-or" but always "it depends"; in this case, it depends on Nietzsche's own personal psychology, which Jung describes here as introverted intuition (CW 6 §242).[8] Whereas earlier Jung contrasted the aesthetic approach of *The Birth of Tragedy* with the Dionysian approach of the "Attempt at a Self-Criticism" (see above), he now points to the continuity in terms of the "predominantly intuitive-artistic [*intuitiv-künstlerische*] mode of production" across *The Birth of Tragedy* and *Thus Spoke Zarathustra* as opposed to the "introverted-intellectual" aspect of his aphoristic writings (CW 6 §242).

On this account, *Zarathustra* is a breakthrough precisely for aesthetic rather than religious reasons. (At the same time, Jung has been careful to ensure that the former does not entirely exclude the latter…) Thanks to his intuitive attitude, Nietzsche is said by Jung to have been able to gain "deep insight into the Dionysian qualities of his unconscious, the crude form of which, so far as we know, reached the surface of his consciousness only with the outbreak of his illness, after it had previously revealed itself in various erotic allusions in his writings" (CW 6 §242). Thus, the breakthrough of *Zarathustra* is seen by Jung in light of Nietzsche's *breakdown* in Turin—surely a kind of biographical reductionism?—along with an expression of regret for the fact that the "very significant fragments of writing" found in Turin after the onset of his insanity (although what exactly Jung means by these "fragments" is unclear—presumably the so-called *Wahnbriefe* or *Wahnzettel* sent by Nietzsche to various correspondents early in 1889 …?) should have met with destruction "out of moral and aesthetic scruples" (CW 6 §242).

Chapter 5 of *Psychological Types* on the type problem in poetry is an extensive discussion of the allegorical prose poem *Prometheus und Epimetheus* (1880-81) by Jung's fellow Swiss, Carl Spitteler. In the course of his discussion, Jung notes that Epimetheus's raging

[8] Cf. CW 6 §540, but in CW 6 §632 he appears to describe Nietzsche as an introverted thinking type?

fury against an obvious caricature of traditional Christianity in the shape of the "little lamb" (*Lämmchen*) represents an outburst of an affect comparable to what happens in the Ass Festival in Part Four of *Thus Spoke Zarathustra*—and hence expresses a "contemporary tendency" (CW 6 §312). Spitteler's poem explores the contrasts between ideals and dogmas through the two mythological figures of its title in a way which makes it, Jung argued, a work of great importance (although today, it must be said, it is little read).[9]

At its core lies the redemptive significance of the deed of Prometheus (or "forethought"), who defied the gods by stealing fire and giving it as a gift to humanity, for which he was sentenced by Zeus to eternal torment as a punishment; the downfall of his brother, Epimetheus (or "afterthought"), who accepted the gift of Pandora from the gods, with disastrous consequences; the reconciliation of the two brothers; and the revenge taken by Epimetheus on the "little lamb" (the cruelty of which, Jung suggests, recalls the scene between Ugolino and Archbishop Ruggieri in Canto 32 of Dante's *Inferno*)—all these plot details are said by Jung to "prepare a solution of the conflict that involves a bloody revolt against traditional collective morality" (CW 6 §321). As such, the work reveals Spitteler's place among those true poets who can "fathom and read the collective unconscious," who are "always the first in their time to divine the darkly moving mysterious currents and express them [...] in more or less eloquent symbols," and who, "like true prophets, make known what is happening in the unconscious, or in the language of the Old Testament 'what the will of God is' [...]" (CW 6 §321). (Using these criteria, one might say that *The Red Book* reveals Jung's own status as a true poet *and* a true prophet alike...)

[9] A significant exception is John Beebe and Steve Myers, "The transcendent function in Spitteler's *Prometheus and Epimetheus*," *Journal of Analytical Psychology*, vol. 66, no. 5 (November 2021), 1139-1158.

In other words, Spitteler's work "transcends his personal destiny" and, in this respect, there is said to be "only one step" between Spitteler and Nietzsche's *Zarathustra* (a work written only a few years later, we should remember) (CW 6 §322). Casting his net more widely to include philosophers, Jung suggests that Arthur Schopenhauer (with his world-negating philosophy of pessimism in *The World as Will and Representation* [1818; [2]1844]) and Max Stirner (with the nihilistic anarchism of his *The Ego and its Own* [1844]), as well as Spitteler, can all be seen to have anticipated Nietzsche's *Zarathustra*, hailed here as a work which above all "brings to light the contents of the collective unconscious of our age" and, in particular, the "iconoclastic revolt against the conventional moral atmosphere and the acceptance of the 'Ugliest Man'"—something which in Nietzsche "leads to the shattering unconscious tragedy presented in *Zarathustra*" (CW 6 §322).

At this point, Jung makes an unexpected move—unexpected, that is, in the light of his comments about the aesthetic (see above, pp. 223-224). For now, he reverts to his earlier position and goes on to explain that the solution to the problem of the opposite types "in *Faust*, in Wagner's *Parsifal*, in Schopenhauer, and even in Nietzsche's *Zarathustra*, is *religious*" (CW 6 §324). In this respect, then, there lies a profound contrast to Spitteler, for while he, too, is drawn to a religious setting, the profusion of its "mythological texture" is said to complicate the work. Consequently there is a crucial difference between, on the one hand, Spitteler's *Prometheus und Epimetheus*, and, on the other, *Faust* and *Zarathustra*: in the case of the latter, the "conscious participation of the poet in the meaning of the symbol" is said to be greater, so that the "mythological profusion" of *Faust* (one thinks of the Classical Walpurgis Night or the Helena Act, for example) and the "intellectual profusion" of *Zarathustra* (with its *Übermensch*, death of God, doctrine of eternal recurrence) are said to be "reined in" (or "pruned back") "in favour of the desired solution" (CW 6 §324). This "reining in" (or "pruning back") has another effect: *Faust* and *Zarathustra* are said to be "far more *beautiful*" than Spitteler's *Prometheus*, which is said to be "more *true* as a more or less faithful depiction of the actual processes in the collective unconscious" (CW 6 §324). (Here we find another rare admission on Jung's part as to the *aesthetic* dimension of *Faust* and *Zarathustra*, as well as their alleged *religious* significance.)

As a consequence, *Faust* and *Zarathustra* are said to be "helpful to a high degree" in the "individual mastery" of the problem of the opposite types, while Spitteler's *Prometheus und Epimetheus* offers a "more general insight into the problem and its collective manner of appearance, thanks to the profusion of mythological material" (CW 6 §325). At the same time, *Prometheus und Epimetheus* also points forward to Spitteler's later work, his allegorical epic poem in iambic hexameters called *Olympischer Frühling* (*Olympic Spring*) (1900-05), and its portrayal of unconscious religious contents in the "*symbol of the God-renewal*" (CW 6 §325). Here, the solution to the problem of the opposite types in the form of a "renewal of the general attitude" is expressed in the "language of the unconscious" as a "renewal of the God" (CW 6 §325).

In a passage that recalls his famous letter to Freud of 15 November 1909 about the dying and the resurgent god in the Mysteries of Orpheus and the cult of Dionysos,[10] but also the transformational dynamic of his *Red Book*, Jung writes that "the renewal of the God is a familiar primordial image [*urtümliches Bild*], which one finds almost everywhere," adding: "I need only mention the entire complex of the dying and the resurgent God

[10] "Now to better things — mythology. [...] The dying and resurgent god (Orphic mysteries, Thammuz, Osiris [Dionysus], Adonis, etc.) is everywhere phallic. At the Dionysus festival in Egypt the women pulled the phallus up and down on a string: 'the dying and resurgent god'" (*The Freud/Jung Letters: The Correspondence between Sigmund Freud and C.G. Jung*, ed. William McGuire, trans. Ralph Manheim and R.F.C. Hull (Cambridge, MA: Harvard University Press, 1988), p. 263).

and all its precursors all the way to the re-charging of fetishes and churingas with magical force." As an image, this complex "expresses that the attitude has changed and as a result a new potential of energy has arisen, a new possibility for the manifestation of life, a new fruitfulness" (CW 6 §325). Evidently, the central idea here in this analysis of Spitteler's *Olympic Spring* is the emphasis on *transformation*—given here, as in the other works in this series, epic form.

In Chapter 8 of *Psychological Types*, Jung turns to the problem of the opposite types in modern philosophy, and specifically in the work of William James, in which the drama of the confrontation between nominalism and realism in the Middle Ages is said to be repeated. Jung concludes his discussion by pausing for a moment to consider the "intuitive method" of Henri Bergson (1859-1941). Dismissing the suggestion that Bergson's notions of *élan vital* and *durée créatrice* are products of intuition (and suggesting that they were, anyway, current in Neoplatonism), Jung proposes Nietzsche as a far stronger candidate for an "intuitive" thinker. On this account, Nietzsche made "in an incomparably greater measure use of the intuitive source" and, in so doing, "freed himself from the mere intellect in the construction of his philosophical outlook, albeit in such a way and to such a degree that his intuitionism went far beyond the limits of a *philosophical* worldview and led him to an artistic deed [*zu einer künstlerischen Tat*], whose greatness is largely inaccessible to philosophical critique" (CW 6 §540). (Again, we should note the emphasis on the *aesthetic* dimension of Nietzsche's thought.)

While this description does not apply to his aphoristic writings, which, because of their "predominantly intellectual method," *are* accessible to philosophical critique, it applies preeminently to the achievement which is Nietzsche's *Zarathustra*. Indeed, Jung goes so far as to describe *Zarathustra* as the "best example" of a so-called "intuitive method," and one that has strikingly demonstrated "the possibility of a non-intellectualistic, yet philosophical way of grasping a problem" (CW 6 §540). Surprisingly, Jung cites Schopenhauer and G.W.F. Hegel—a pair of names one rarely sees together, except as forming a contrast—as "forerunners" of Nietzsche's intuitionism: Schopenhauer, because of the "*feeling-intuition*" (*Gefühlsintutition*) that is so influential on his outlook, and Hegel, because of the "*ideal* intuition" (*ideelle Intuition*) that underpins his system. (Schopenhauer and Hegel are usually considered as philosophical antipodes, not least because of the personal enmity of the former for the latter; for Jung, the two philosophers may have more in common than is usually realized.) Yet if, in the case of both Schopenhauer and Hegel, intuition was placed *below* intellect, in the case of Nietzsche, intuition was placed *above* it.

Jung acknowledges the solution to the problem of the opposite types proposed by James's pragmatism, but nevertheless, he insists on its limitations: for ultimately, he argues, the solution to the conflict of the opposites lies neither in (a) a logico-intellectualistic compromise as in conceptualism, nor in (b) a pragmatic assessment of the practical value of logically irreconcilable worldviews, but only in (c) a positive creation or deed which assimilates in itself the opposites as necessary elements of coordination (CW 6 §541). Although Jung gives as an example of this third approach the fact that a coordinated muscle movement always involves the innervation of antagonistic muscle groups (so that some extend or stretch, while others contract or squeeze), perhaps another, more revealing example of this "positive creation or deed" would be *The Red Book*. On Jung's account, Jamesian pragmatism is a transitional attitude, something that "prepares the way for the creative deed by the removal of prejudices" (CW 6 §541). Thus, pragmatism prepares for, Bergson points toward, and German philosophy outside the academy has already trodden this "new way"; above all, it is Nietzsche who, "with his own peculiar violence, has burst open this closed door." His creative act, that is, his *Zarathustra*, "leads beyond what is unsatisfying about the pragmatic solution and it does so as thoroughly as the pragmatic acknowledgement of the vital value of a truth has overcome the arid one-sidedness of the unconscious conceptualism of philosophy after Abelard — and there is still more to be overcome" (CW 6 §541).[11] (What Jung ascribes here to the transformational achievement of Nietzsche's *Zarathustra* also applies, *mutatis mutandis*, to his own *Red Book*, as we shall see in Volume 4 in this series.)

Finally, in his lengthy discussion of the symbol in the "Definitions" section of *Psychological Types*, Jung notes how indications of the "symbol-forming process" can be found in the sparse accounts of the initiation period undergone by religious founders: for example, the conflicts experienced by Jesus and Satan, by Buddha and Mara, by Luther and the Devil, by Zwingli and his previous worldly life, or by Goethe's Faust in his rejuvenation as a result of his pact with the Devil. And Jung gives one final example: Nietzsche's *Zarathustra*, toward the end of which one finds an "excellent example" of the repression of the antithesis in the figure of the "Ugliest Man" (CW 6 §829). (This and other gnomic allusions to the Ugliest Man are best explained with reference to Jung's discussion of this figure in his Seminar on *Zarathustra*.)

(b) Jung's paper, "Psychological Typology" (1936)

In its Appendix, Volume 6 of the *Collected Works* republishes four much shorter papers on typology from 1913, 1923, 1931, and 1936. (Although these papers are often overlooked, they provide concise theoretical statements of Jung's view of typology and

[11] The medieval scholastic philosopher Peter Abelard (1079-1142), a proponent of conceptualism in the debate over universals, features earlier in *Psychological Types* in Jung's discussion of the problem of types in classical and medieval thought (CW 6 §68-§79 and §94-§95).

reveal how it developed over time.) In the last of these shorter works, entitled "Psychological Typology" (and first published in *Süddeutsche Monatshefte*) Jung notes how "primitives"—that is, prephilosophical human individuals—lived and experienced the world "in the grip of their emotions [*Gemütszuständen*]" (CW 6 §963). As other commentators have pointed out (for example, the classicist R.B. Onians (1899-1986) in his study *The Origins of European Thought: About the Body, the Mind, the Soul, the World, Time and Fate* [1951; ^{2}1954]), the ancient Greeks (such as, for instance, Homer) located the soul, not in the head, but in the diaphragm or the lungs (*phrenes*). At this stage of human development, consciousness means to be seized (*Ergriffenheit*) and to experience everything as a unity: The Homeric heroes cried, laughed, raged, outwitted, and killed "in a natural world that was self-evidently divine and human, and the Olympian gods amused themselves in immortal lack of responsibility" (CW 6 §962)—Zeus himself being, in this regard, a particularly bad offender.

On this account, only with the rise of philosophy did the seat of reason begin to be assigned to the head, and so this people of serenity and tragedy (*dieses Volk der Heiterkeit und der Tragödie*)—that is, the Greeks—invented, with the advent of thinking, a division—a division, the responsibility for which Nietzsche laid at the door of the ancient figure of Zoroaster: namely, the invention of the pairs of opposites (CW 6 §963). (In "Why I am a Destiny" [§3] in *Ecce Homo*, Nietzsche himself makes precisely this point about the "tremendous uniqueness of that Persian in history.") The separation of even and odd, of above and below, of good and evil: This was (also) the work of the ancient Pythagoreans, and thanks to the spread of the Orphic-Pythagorean Mysteries, the doctrine of moral responsibility and the serious metaphysical consequences of sin penetrated throughout all levels of the population; in fact, in the sixth century B.C.E., Pythagoreanism was almost like a state religion in Graecia Magna. And so, the ancient Mystery cults proclaimed the doctrine of a reward in the hereafter for the good and the punishment of hell for the wicked; in his *Phaedrus* (246, 253-254), Plato used the parable of the white and black horses to express the intractability and polarity of the human psyche. And, in the second century B.C.E., the philosophical renaissance of the ideas underlying the Mysteries exercised great influence on the Alexandrian world of thought, colliding with the Jewish prophecy of the Old Testament in a way that led to the beginnings of Christianity as a world religion (CW 6 §963).

Thus, when Nietzsche, in *Thus Spoke Zarathustra*, dismisses these doctrines of moral responsibility and of postmortem punishment as no more than the psychological hairsplitting and nitpicking of philosophical "backwoodsmen" (*Hinterweltler*), Jung hesitates; *he* is not so quick to dismiss them. In a sense, the entire *Red Book* is an expression of this hesitation—can good and evil be simply dismissed? Is God sick, or even dead, or is He "as alive as ever"?—and in some of his early theoretical writings, Jung hints at his reservations about Nietzsche and what his fate can teach us.

(c) "The Psychology of the Unconscious" (1917; ^{3}1926; ^{5}1943)

In 1912, Jung wrote a short theoretical paper published in the Rascher Yearbook entitled "New Paths in Psychology" (*Neue Bahnen der Psychologie*), which he subsequently revised and enlarged as "The Psychology of the Unconscious Processes" (*Die Psychologie der unbewussten Prozesse*) (1917), then as "The Unconscious in the Normal and the Pathological Mind" (*Das Unbewusste im normalen und kranken Seelenleben*) (1926), and finally as "The Psychology of the Unconscious" (*Über die Psychologie des Unbewussten*) (1943).[12] This text has become one of the most popular starting

[12] C.G. Jung, *Two Essays on Analytical Psychology*, trans. H.G. and C.F. Baynes (London: Baillière, Tindall and Cox, 1928). Page references to this edition are given in brackets.

points for learning about Jungian psychology. In it, Jung used Nietzsche to challenge Freud, opposing the "will to power" to the "eros theory" and describing it in the title of Chapter 3 as the "other point of view."

Jung's starting point is grim and foreboding, for there is much about Freud's view of humankind that is true. "Eros is a mighty daimon," as Diotima tells Socrates (*Symposium*, 202d-e), and the sexual theory of psychoanalysis is "entirely correct up to a certain point"; however, it is "one-sided," and so "it would therefore be just as false to repudiate it as to accept it as universally valid" (27). It is precisely its truth to which "our pride, our cultural consciousness said no, though something in us said yes," and even to admit to this conflict is said to be "terrible," for it means a "yea-saying to instinct" (28). But what does it mean to say yes to instinct? This is where Nietzsche comes in, for it turns out that a "yea-saying to instinct" is *exactly* what he "desired and taught":

> [Nietzsche] made, with a rare passion, the sacrifice of himself, of his whole life, to the idea of the super-man — to the idea of the man who through obedience to instinct transcends himself. And what was the course of his life? It was as Nietzsche himself prophesied in Zarathustra, in that foreboding vision of the fatal fall of the rope-dancer, the man who would not be '"surpassed." To the dying rope-dancer Zarathustra said: "Thy soul will be sooner dead than thy body." And in a later passage the dwarf says to Zarathustra: "Oh, Zarathustra, thou stone of wisdom! High thou flingest thyself, but every stone that is flung must fall! Condemned of thyself and to thine own stoning: O Zarathustra, far indeed flingest thou the stone — but upon thyself will it fall.'" When he cried his "Ecce Homo" over himself, it was again too late, as once before when this saying went forth,

> and the crucifixion of the soul began before the body was dead. (28-29)

Here we find an approach to *Thus Spoke Zarathustra* that we shall see again in his extensive seminar on this work: the suggestion that *Zarathustra* is in some sense a prophetic work, both in terms of Nietzsche's personal biography and indeed of Germany as a whole, in relation to the First and Second World Wars. (Needless to say, such an approach is usually regarded by most commentators as highly problematic.)

While Nietzsche's *teaching* may have been a "yea-saying to instinct," what about Nietzsche's *life*? Here, Jung detects a tension between what Nietzsche *taught* and how he *lived*, a tension so great that he describes Nietzsche as a pathological personality (CW 7 §37):

> Nietzsche lived beyond instinct, in the lofty heights of heroic "sublimity" —heights that he could maintain only by the help of a most meticulous diet, a carefully selected climate, and many aids to sleep — until the tension of this living shattered his brain. He spoke of yea-saying and lived the nay. His loathing for man, for the animal living by instinct, was too great. He could not swallow the toad, of which he so often dreamed, and which he feared must be swallowed. The roaring of the lion of Zarathustra drove back into the cavern of the unconscious all the "higher" men who had aspired to live with him. Hence his life does not convince us of his teaching. The "higher" man would fain be able to sleep without chloral, be able to live in Nuremburg and Basel despite "fogs and shadows" [*»Nebel und Schatten«*]. He would desire wife and offspring, standing and reputation among his own group,

> innumerable commonplace realities and not least, those of the philistine. This side of instinct Nietzsche did not see — the animal urge to Life. (29)

To understand Nietzsche, we have to understand instinct; and, in particular, to understand that instinct is not just sexual (or the instinct for the preservation of the species) but also the instinct for *self*-preservation or, in other words, the will-to-power. In the case of Nietzsche, the problem was not so much the repression of sexuality as the repression of the will-to-power (and the subsequent return of the repressed):

> The case of Nietzsche shows, on the one hand, the consequences of neurotic one-sidedness, and, on the other, the dangers that lurk in this leap beyond Christianity. Nietzsche undoubtedly felt the Christian denial of animal nature very deeply indeed, and therefore he sought a higher human wholeness beyond good and evil. But he who seriously criticizes the basic attitude of Christianity also forfeits the protection which these bestow upon him. He delivers himself up unresistingly to the animal psyche. That is the moment of Dionysian frenzy, the overwhelming manifestation of the "blond beast," which seizes the unsuspecting soul with nameless shudderings. The seizure transforms him into a hero or into a godlike being, a superhuman entity. He rightly feels himself "six thousand feet beyond good and evil." (CW 7 §40)

This state is known, in Jungian terms, as "identification with the shadow," and it arises in those moments when there is a "collision" with the unconscious (CW 7 §41). In such moments, Jung (as the author of *The Red Book*) advises, the only thing that helps is "cautious self-criticism" (CW 7 §41). But what, Jung asks, did Nietzsche's collision with the unconscious, his encounter with the shadow, or perhaps even his inflation reveal?

> The case of Nietzsche faces us with the question: What did the collision with the shadow, namely the will to power, reveal to him? Is it to be regarded as something bogus, a symptom of repression? Is the will to power genuine or merely secondary? If the conflict with the shadow had let loose a flood of sexual fantasies, the matter would be perfectly clear; but it happened otherwise. The "Kern des Pudels" was not Eros but the power of the ego. From this we would have to conclude that what was repressed was not Eros but the will to power. There is in my opinion no ground for the assumption that Eros is genuine and the will to power bogus. The will to power is surely just as mighty a daemon as Eros, and just as old and original. (CW 7 §42)

Yet here Jung urges caution, suggesting that it would be wrong to be reductive in one's approach to Nietzsche in respect of the will-to-power as Nietzsche himself was wrong in his approach to Wagner in respect of the sexual drive:

> A life like Nietzsche's, lived to its fatal end with rare consistency to the nature of the underlying instinct for power, cannot be simply explained away as inept. So to belittle it would be to fall victim to the same unfair prejudice that caused Nietzsche to say of his polar opposite, Wagner: "Everything in him is false. What is genuine is hidden or else disguised. He is an actor, in every bad and good sense of the word." Why this judgment? It is simply because Wagner is

> a representative of that other elemental urge which Nietzsche overlooked, and upon which Freud's psychology is built. (30)

True, in Freudian psychoanalysis, there is a recognition of the will-to-power in the form of the notion of the "ego-instinct." Yet this term hardly seems adequate in comparison with the space given by Freud to the sexual factor, and Jung argues that, in reality, "human nature bears the burden of a terrible and almost endless conflict between the principle of the ego and that of formless instinct — the ego all barriers and restraint, the instinct limitless, and both principles of equal might" (30-31). From this perspective, "an individual may count himself happy if he is conscious of only one instinct, and therefore it is a shrewd device to guard against knowing the other"—alluding to Faust's advice to Wagner, *Du bist dir nur des einen Triebs bewusst, / O lerne nie den andern kennen!* (ll. 1110-1111). But what if he does, after all, learn to know the other? Then "it is all up with him," and he "then enters upon the Faustian conflict":

> Goethe has shown us in the first part of *Faust* what the acceptance of instinct means, and in the second part what it means to accept the ego, with its weird unconscious world. All that is insignificant, paltry, and cowardly in us cowers and shrinks from this acceptance — and there is an excellent means of avoiding it. The discovery is made that the "other" in us is indeed an "Other" — a live man, who actually thinks, does, feels, and desires all the things that are despicable and odious. In this way the bogey is seized [*den Popanz erfaßt*] and war declared against him to our satisfaction. Thus arise those chronic idiosyncrasies of which the history of morals provides many examples. (31)

Indeed, Nietzsche himself is regarded by Jung as being one such example, reflected in Nietzsche's opposition to Wagner, to St. Paul, and to almost anyone else around, as it sometimes seems; and even "daily life abounds with such cases," as Jung acerbically adds. (Acerbically, but surely not incorrectly.) But "by this ingenious device," he goes on to say, "an individual may save himself from the catastrophe that befell Faust, before which indeed his courage and strength might fail," for a "true individual, however, knows that his most bitter foe, or indeed a whole host of enemies, does not equal that one worst adversary, that 'other self,' who 'bides within his breast'" (31). Hence, Jung sums up the case of Nietzsche as follows:

> Nietzsche had Wagner *in himself*; and that is why he envied him *Parsifal*. But, what was worse, he, Saul, had also Paul within himself. That is why Nietzsche became stigmatized by the spirit. Like Saul he had to experience Christification, when the "other" presented him with the challenge: "Ecce Homo." Which was it who "broke before the cross," Wagner or Nietzsche? (31)

Now, as fate would have it, Jung adds (by way of conclusion), one of Freud's earliest disciples, Alfred Adler (1870-1937), had formulated a theory of neurosis that was based exclusively on the power principle. Yet, Jung does not associate himself here with Adler; rather, he uses Adler in order to relativize Freud, arguing that the question— "which of the two points of view is right?"—is a "question which might lead to much brain-racking": "The two explanations cannot simply be laid side by side, for they absolutely contradict each other. In the one, love and its destiny is the chief and decisive fact; in the other, the power of the ego. In the first case the ego is merely a kind of appendage to the passion of love; whereas in the second case love appears merely as a means to the end of gaining ascendency. Whoever has most at heart the power of the ego will revolt against the first conception, but he who cares most for love will never be reconciled to the second" (38).

Jung's final reckoning with Adler—as with Freud—in relation to Nietzsche can be found in *Memories, Dreams, Reflections* in its chapter on Freud (cf. JLW, 232-2333 and 287). Here, Jung seems to take at face value Freud's repeated claims that he had never read Nietzsche, suggesting that Freudian psychoanalysis had been an "adroit move on the part of intellectual history, compensating for Nietzsche's deification of the power principle" (MDR, 176). Consequently, the history of psychoanalysis was not so much "Freud versus Adler," as "Freud versus Nietzsche." (In this formula, Adler simply falls out of the equation altogether!) And now Jung (or Jaffé, on his behalf) makes his move: Could it be that Eros and the power principle were in a sense like the "dissident sons of *a single* father"—in other words, like the rebellious sons of the primal horde envisaged in *Totem and Taboo* (1913), Freud's riposte to Jung's *Transformations and Symbols of the Libido*—or like the products of a "single, motivating psychic force, which manifested itself—like positive and negative electrical charges—empirically in opposing forms: one of them as a *patiens*, eros, and the other as an *agens*, the power drive—and vice versa" (MDR, 176)? If so, then surely Freud had shown "how the object succumbs to the drive," while Adler had shown "how the individual uses the drive in order to force his will upon the object [*um das Objekt zu vergewaltigen*]" (MDR, 177)? So where does this leave Nietzsche? "Exposed to his destiny and subjected to it," Jung suggests, Nietzsche had had no choice other than "to create a 'superman' for himself" (MDR, 177).

And now Jung (or, on his behalf, Jaffé) twists the knife. Had Freud, Jung wonders, been so "deeply influenced" by the power of Eros that he had actually wished to elevate it like a religious *numen* into a dogma, something *aere perennius* (MDR, 177)? (This is an allusion to one of Horace's *Odes* (Book 3, §30), which opens with lines about the monument that he, as a poet, has left.)[13] Far from Jung wanting to be a prophet, it had been *Freud* who wanted to be the prophet! And the incontrovertible sign of this was surely that Freud, in trying to compete with the Church by canonizing doctrines, had ended up following Nietzsche, whose Zarathustra *is* "the proclaimer of a gospel," and who really had been a prophet (MDR, 177)! If only Freud had listened more to Diotima in the *Symposium*! For if, as Jung (or Jaffé on his behalf) reflected, he had "given greater consideration to the psychological truth that sexuality is something numinous — it is a god and a devil," then he would not have "ended up getting stuck within the narrow confines of a biological concept" (MDR, 177). And there was a lesson here for Nietzsche, too: If only he could have "held more firmly to the foundations of human existence," then perhaps—just perhaps—he would not "have been carried over the brink of the world with his exuberance [*Überschwang*]" (MDR, 177).

This thought-provoking argument was by no means the only time that Nietzsche crops up in *Memories, Dreams, Reflections*, to which we shall now briefly turn before moving to consider the role of Nietzsche in Jung's later writings—namely, an essay on the archetype of rebirth and, in Chapter 3, in his extensive writings on alchemy.

---

[13] Horace, *Odes and Epodes*, ed. and trans. Niall Rudd (Cambridge, MA: Harvard University Press, 2004), pp. 216-217:

> *Exegi monumenum aere perennius*
> *Regalique situ pyramidum altius,*
> *Qupd non imber edax, non Aquilo impotens*
> *Possit diruere aut innumerabilis*
> *Annorum series et fuga temporum.*
>
> [I have finished a monument more lasting than bronze,
> more lofty than the regal structure of the pyramids,
> one which neither corroding rain nor the ungovernable North Wind
> can ever destroy, nor the countless
> series of the years, nor the flight of time.]

Excursus: Nietzsche and *Zarathustra* in *Memories, Dreams, Reflections*

In *Memories, Dreams, Reflections*, the first mention of Nietzsche is a reference to his absence—his absence, that is, from the conversation of his uncle (the pastor of St. Alban's in Basel) and his cousins at lunch on Thursdays to which Jung was invited when he was attending the Gymnasium. These relatives were, it seems (and perhaps not surprisingly) much happier discussing the dogmas and doctrines of the Church Fathers than discussing Nietzsche, whom they did not mention, or Jacob Burckhardt (1818-97), dismissed as a "liberal" and a "bit of a freethinker"; while their praise for Kant could not disguise the fact he was only used to bolster their own views and discredit opposing ones (MDR, 92-93). By contrast, in his school years Jung was drawn to the Presocratics and Plato, to Meister Eckhart, and above all to Schopenhauer and, as one of the most important sources of Schopenhauer's philosophy, to Kant (MDR, 87-89; cf. JLW, 59-60 and 167-169).

Yet the encounter with Nietzsche had to wait until Jung's time as a student at Basel, at a time in the city's history when, as Jung later recollected, the old bridge over the Rhine was still half made of wood, the old chapter house still stood behind the cathedral, and Bachofen and Burckhardt could be seen walking in the streets … (MDR, 133).[14] (In the Protocols, Jung is recorded as recalling that he often came across them, contrasting Burckhardt, who "shuffled so and looked rather awkward" and was "not exactly dressed very elegantly" in a "large cravat and high collar," to Backofen, "who travelled in a wonderfully elegant coach" [JLW, 154-155].) In his Nietzsche seminar of 26 February 1936, Jung spelled out

[14] See Lionel Gossman, *Basel in the Age of Burckhardt: A Study in Unseasonable Ideas* (Chicago and London: University of Chicago Press, 2000); and Kathrin Schaeppi, *C.G. Jung — The Basel Years: A Walking Guide* (Einsiedeln: Daimon, 2025).

the implications of these reminiscences, telling his audience about Franz Overbeck (1837-1905) and Burckhardt: "I wish I could show you old man Burckhardt as I saw him practically every day, walking near the Cathedral coming from the University library"—the symbolic significance of these buildings is evident—adding: "And Zarathustra! — you could not imagine anything more different than those two" (SNZ, vol. 2, 862). Yet although Nietzsche was on his list of books to read at that time, Jung is said to have hesitated. Why? As a former colleague of Nietzsche in Basel, Burckhardt was in a position to make critical comments about Nietzsche, and other academics who had known Nietzsche personally were able to trade in negative gossip about him, too. But this was not what put Jung off reading Nietzsche; on the contrary.

Rather the problem lay, it seems, in what is described in *Memories, Dreams, Reflections* as a "secret fear" that Jung might have been in some way *like Nietzsche*; that Nietzsche might have had a "secret" of the kind that he himself had; that he might be, in the words of the title of famous novel by Friedrich Theodor Vischer (1807-77), *Auch Einer* (i.e., "One of Them").[15] Despite the differences between them—Nietzsche was German, while Jung was Swiss; Nietzsche spoke High German, knew Latin and Greek, and probably spoke French, Italian, and Spanish as well, while Jung was fluent only in the Waggis-Basel dialect—did they have more in common than Jung would have wanted to admit? In the Jaffé Protocols, Jung is recorded as saying that his earliest insight into how visions of the kind he had elaborated in *The Red Book* were "dangerous experiences" and the "material that destroys people" was Nietzsche, who showed how someone can be "destroyed by the plenitude," despite—or because of—the "fullness of power and of imaginative possibility contained in those images" (JLW, 152).

[15] For further discussion of Jung and F.T. Vischer, see Paul Bishop, "Jung's *Red Book* and its relation to aspects of German Idealism," *Journal of Analytical Psychology*, vol. 57, no. 3 (June 2012), 335-363; and Domenici, *Jung's Nietzsche* (pp. 33-65).

One fact was incontestable: Nietzsche had been, like Jung, the son of a clergyman; a fact to which, in his seminar on *Zarathustra*, he had attached great significance.

In the end, Jung's curiosity won out, and the first book he read by Nietzsche was his *Untimely Meditations*, the four essays published between 1873 and 1876 in which Nietzsche launched a savage attack on David Friedrich Strauss (1808-74); compared different approaches to history; praised Schopenhauer as an educator; and celebrated Wagner's achievements at Bayreuth. Next up was *Thus Spoke Zarathustra*—and if Jung had been enthusiastic about the *Untimely Meditations*, he was overwhelmed, as so many other readers have been, by *Zarathustra*. (As the German Modernist poet Gottfried Benn (1886-1956) put it, everything that his generation "had discussed, had thought out inside itself, one might say: suffered, one might also say: done to death — all that had already been expressed and exhausted in Nietzsche, had found definitive formulation; all the rest was mere exegesis.")[16] And there could be no higher praise for *Zarathustra* than to compare this "tremendous experience"—*ein stärkstes Erlebnis*—to that of reading Part Two of Goethe's *Faust* (MDR, 123). In passages like these, we see how Jung builds his canon: a canon of works to which he himself was to contribute in the form of his transformational *Red Book*.

Zarathustra was brilliant—but it was also morbid. Was there something morbid about Jung, too? Likewise, Nietzsche had been brilliant—but had he been so brilliant that he had not noticed that something was amiss? After all, Nietzsche had spoken carelessly about his *arrheton*, the term for the "unspeakable" in the ancient Greek mystery cults, as if it were quite in order to do so.[17]

[16] Gottfried Benn, "Nietzsche — nach fünfzig Jahren" [1950], in *Gesammelte Werke*, ed. Dieter Wellershoff (Wiesbaden: Limes, 1968), vol. 4, pp. 1046-1057 (p. 1046).

[17] Note the following distinction: "The ancient Greek language has two words for 'that which is not to be spoken of': *arrheton* and *aporrheton*. The first translates

(Presumably, Jung means by this those elements in *Zarathustra* that he would identify elsewhere as Dionysian.) In this respect, however, Jung believed he himself had been cleverer—and had quickly noticed that to speak the unspeakable led to "bad experiences" (MDR, 123). This forms the basis for the critique of Nietzsche, which then follows.

Like the educated Philistines or *Bildungsphilister,* which, tragicomically, he criticized—tragicomically, because he himself was one—Nietzsche did not understand himself when he "fell into the mystery"—*das Mysterium*, the same term used by Jung in his *Red Book*—"and into the unspeakable [*das Nichtzusagende*]," and when he wanted to "sing its praises" (that is, of falling into the mystery or the unspeakable) "to the crowd that had been forsaken by all the gods" (MDR, 124).[18] Although Nietzsche had wanted to "find people who could share his ecstasy and could understand the 'revaluation of all values,'" this was nothing but a "childish hope" (MDR, 123). This failed ambition to find an audience that would listen to his praise for his *arrheton* was the reason for the "bombastic language, the metaphors that got carried away, the hymnlike enthusiasm, that tried in vain to make itself audible to a world that

as 'the ineffable': that which, in principle, *cannot* be brought to speech; the second refers to that about which discourse is *forbidden*. The prohibition against speaking or writing of the ineffable may be statutory, as in classical Athens, or self-imposed, following from religious conviction" (Charles Stein, "Ancient Mysteries," in Glenn Alexander Magee (ed.), *The Cambridge Handbook of Western Mysticism and Esotericism* (Cambridge: Cambridge University Press, 2016), pp. 3-12 [p. 3]). For further discussion, see the study in Polish by Krzysztof Bielawski, "Arrheton: niewypowiadalne w greckich kultach misteryjnych" [Arrheton — Unspeakable in the Greek Mystery Cults], *Filozofia Chrześcijańska*, 13 (2016), 37-52.

[18] Note the etymology of the term *mysterion*: "The word 'mysteries' (*ta mysteria*) comes to us directly from the Greek *mysterion*, 'a secret rite,' which derives from two linked verbs: *myo* and *myeo*. *Myo* means to close up or conceal, as in closing the eyes and stopping the ears or as when a flower closes itself at nightfall. *Myeo* means to initiate — for example, to initiate someone into the mysteries. The mysteries in Ancient Greece concealed initiatory secrets that were both incapable of being rendered verbally and of which the initiate was forbidden to speak" (Stein, "Ancient Mysteries," p. 3).

has sold its soul to a disconnected knowledge that only knows what is worth knowing"—*dieser Welt, die sich dem zusammenhanglosen Wissenswerten verschrieben hatte*, as Jung puts it, using a phrase which is often used in the sense of *sich dem Teufel verschreiben*, to "sell oneself to the devil" (MDR, 124). And so, Jung concludes (thereby eliding fictional events with biographical facts—as he so often does), Nietzsche "fell—this rope-dancer—even beyond himself" (*sogar noch über sich selbst hinaus*).

Among Jung's circle of friends at this time, most of them simply did not understand the appeal of *Zarathustra*; two who did (and who were, Jung notes but without explaining why, both homosexual) and who declared themselves to be Nietzscheans, met a sticky end: One committed suicide, the other went to the dogs as a "misunderstood genius" (MDR, 124). And so Jung's relation to Nietzsche is said to have been characterized by huge ambivalence: On the one hand, *Zarathustra* had been a "tremendous experience" like *Faust*, Part Two; on the other, just as *Faust* had "opened a door" to Jung, so *Zarathustra* "slammed another one shut"—and it would "remain shut for a long time to come." In a delightful and typically Jungian aside, Jung compares his situation to that of an old peasant farmer who discovered that, presumably as a result of witchcraft, two cows had got their heads in the same halter and who replied to his son's question "How did that happen?" by responding, "One doesn't talk about such things" (MDR, 124)!

Yet maybe Jung was right to be worried. After all, his characterization of Nietzsche's language in *Zarathustra* as "bombastic," its metaphors as "getting carried away," its enthusiasm as "hymnlike," recalls his later account (in the chapter entitled "Confrontation with the Unconscious") of the fantasies that underpinned the creation of *The Red Book* and his description of the language of the archetypes. Here, Jung characterized their style with reference to their "elevated" or "high-flown" language (*gehobene Sprache*), adding that archetypes speak in a way that is "full of pathos" (*pathetisch*) and even "pompous" (*schwülstig*). As a style, Jung admits, it is not pleasant, and he compares it to the sound of someone scratching his or her nails down a plaster wall or scraping their knife across a plate (MDR, 202; cf. JLW, 149). Yet as a description of the style of *The Red Book*, it is really quite an accurate one, and *Memories, Dreams, Reflections* emphasizes how the language of *The Red Book*, how "the style chosen by the unconscious itself," was something that *happened to him*: "Sometimes it was as if I were hearing it with my ears. Sometimes I was feeling it with my mouth, as if my tongue were formulating words; and sometimes it happened that I heard myself whispering aloud" (ibid., 202; cf. JLW, 149-50).

This description inevitably invites comparison with Nietzsche's account in *Ecce Homo* of the composition of *Zarathustra*. "Has any one at the end of the nineteenth century any distinct notion of what poets of a stronger age understood by the word *inspiration*?" Nietzsche asked in *Ecce Homo*, and he went on: "If not, I will describe it. If one had the smallest vestige of superstition left in one, it would hardly be possible completely to set aside the idea that one is the mere mouthpiece, or medium of an almighty power. The idea of revelation, in the sense that something which profoundly convulses and upsets one becomes suddenly *visible* and audible with indescribable certainty and accuracy — describes the simple fact. One hears — one does not seek; one takes — one does not ask who gives: a thought suddenly flashes up like lightning, it comes with necessity, without faltering — I have never had any choice in the matter" (EH Z §3).[19] It would seem that, from the composition of *The Red Book*, Jung would have had a pretty good idea of what poets understood by the word "inspiration," and

[19] For further discussion of this passage as exemplifying a "mysticism" of "apotheosis" — defined as the identification of the ego with a unity underlying all reality —, see Brett Carollo, "Nietzsche and the Mysticism of Apotheosis," *Journal for Continental Philosophy of Religion*, 6 (2924), 241-262.

it seems that *he* did not have any choice in the matter either. In fact, in the Jaffé Protocols, Jung expressly says: "And so I had absolutely no choice" (JLW, 149).

Tellingly, *Memories, Dreams, Reflections* uses exactly the same verb to describe Jung's experience and Nietzsche's: namely, as *falling*. Nietzsche, this tightrope walker, "*fell* [...] even beyond himself," Jung writes, and when describing the decisive step he took during Advent of the year 1913 on 12 December when he resolved to embark on his confrontation with the unconscious, he says: "Then I let myself drop" (*dann ließ ich mich fallen*) (MDR, 203). From a Jungian perspective this motif of descent is, of course, an archetypal one, corresponding to the *katabasis* of ancient Greek myth (a transliteration from the ancient Greek κατάβασις, derived from κατὰ (= "down") and βαίνω (= "to go"), and thus indicating some kind of descent, some sort of journey or voyage to the depths).[20] More important—or, at least, *as important*—as this archetypal dimension is the way in which Jung's self-identification with Nietzsche reflects itself (or repeats itself), whether consciously or unconsciously, in his description of Nietzsche's style in *Zarathustra*, which coincides with the style of his own *Red Book*. Hence, it should come as no surprise that Jung should describe *Zarathustra* as "mostly unpopular, ambiguous, and dangerous"; as a "voyage of discovery to the other pole of the world"; and as part of an *aurea*

[20] For previous studies of the phenomenon of *katabasis*, see Albrecht Dieterich, *Nékyia: Beiträge zur Erklärung der neuentdeckten Petrusapokalypse* (Leipzig: Teubner, 1893, ²1913); Richard Ganschinietz, "Katabasis," in Pauly-Wissowa, *Realencyclopädie der classischen Altertumswissenschaft*, 85 vols. (Stuttgart: Metzler, 1890-1980), vol. 10, cols 2359-2449; Joseph Kroll, *Beiträge zum Descensus ad Inferos* (Königsberg: Hartung, 1922); Joseph Kroll, *Gott und Hölle: Der Mythos vom Descensuskampfe* (Leipzig and Berlin: Teubner, 1932; reprinted 1963); Wolfgang Fauth, "Katabasis," in Konrat Ziegler and Walther Sontheimer (eds.), *Der kleine Pauly: Lexikon der Antike*, 5 vols. (Stuttgart: Metzler, 1964-1975), vol. 3, pp. 152-153; Pierre Bonnechere and Gabriela Cursaru, "Katábasis," *Cahiers des études anciennes*, 53 (2016), 7-14; and Gunnel Ekroth and Ingela Nilsson (eds.), *Round Trip to Hades in the Eastern Mediterranean Tradition: Visits to the Underworld from Antiquity to Byzantium* (Leiden and Boston: Brill, 2018).

catena, that is, a golden (or Homeric) chain, which has existed from the very beginnings of philosophical alchemy and Gnosticism and to which the second part of *Faust* belongs (MDR, 213-214)—and, one might add, to which Jung's own *Red Book* belongs, too.

Without *The Red Book*, one cannot appreciate the full extent of Jung's affinity with Nietzsche—despite the fact that (or because of the fact that) *Memories, Dreams, Reflections* is at pains to emphasize the differences between them. In the chapter on the "Confrontation with the Unconscious," Nietzsche is portrayed, somewhat unfairly, as a "piece of paper blowing around in the winds of the spirit," as "having lost the ground under his feet," and as being possessed more *by* his thoughts than he possessed *them*, in effect disappearing into his "inner world." Despite the Zarathustrian cry "remain true to the earth!" Nietzsche is here presented as having "lost his rootedness" (*entwurzelt*) and as "floating above the earth," as someone who fell or succumbed (*verfiel*) to exaggeration and unreality (*der Übertreibung und der Unwirklichkeit*) (MDR, 214). Jung, on the other hand, was eminently "rooted": with a medical diploma from a Swiss university, with a wife (one of the richest women in Switzerland), and with five children; and with a splendid house at 228 Seestrasse in Küsnacht—quite a contrast to the small, sad rented rooms in which Nietzsche lived for most of his life, wandering across Europe.

Such a "lack of reality" (*Unrealität*) was, as Jung somewhat tartly remarked, the quintessence of horror (*Grauen*), since Jung was very much someone who "aimed" fairly and squarely "at *this* world and *this* life" (MDR, 214); thereby echoing his words in the first chapter of *The Red Book*, "the one thing I have learned is that one must live this life" (RB, 128). (Both sentences are a succinct statement of Jung's remarkable combination of intellectual ambition and existential pragmatism, even canniness—in the Scottish sense.) Consequently, Jung regarded his personal and his professional life as a source of stability—as a "joyful reality" as well as a "guarantee" that he had a "normal, real existence" (MDR, 214). Now, just how "normal" or "real" that existence was must surely be put in question by *The Red Book*, but it underscores the point that the kind of transformation in which Jung was interested was something *concrete*, something *real*; not empty, feel-good psychobabble or *faux* mysticism. (Does this make Jung sound bourgeois? Perhaps it does. But then, as Goethe put it, *Wo kam die schönste Bildung her, Und wenn sie nicht vom Bürger wär?*)[21]

The remaining references in *Memories, Dreams, Reflections* to Nietzsche demonstrate the breadth of his significance, as Jung saw it, in four main respects. First, there is the political dimension. On 18 January 1871, Wilhelm I of Prussia was proclaimed Kaiser Wilhelm in the Hall of Mirrors in the Palace of Versailles. During the Franco-Prussian War of 1870 between the Second French Empire and the German states of the North German Confederation, led by the Kingdom of Prussia, the South German states had joined the North German Confederation, and the country now called itself the German Empire (*Deutsches Reich*). The date had been chosen by his minister president, Otto von Bismarck, as the coronation date of the first Prussian king in 1701, and for many, the coronation of Wilhelm carried associations with the restoration of the Holy Roman Empire. But not for all; according to Jung, Jacob Burckhardt regarded the coronation as the end of Germany (*Das ist der Untergang Deutschlands*, i.e., "That is the doom of Germany"). Looking back at his youth, Jung saw himself as having been "unconsciously caught up" in "this spirit of the age" (*Zeitgeist*), in this remark echoing the "spirit of this age" that is contrasted to the "spirit of the depths" at the outset of *The Red Book* (RB, 119-120). In *Memories, Dreams, Reflections*, this spirit is seen as being symbolized by the "archetypes" of Wagner, "knocking

[21] "And whence came the best culture, if it was not from the burgher?" (Goethe, *Werke: Vollständige Ausgabe letzter Hand*, vol. 47 [*Nachgelassene Werke*, vol. 7] (Stuttgart and Tübingen: Cotta, 1833), p. 222).

at the door"; and by the "Dionysian experience" of Nietzsche—an experience which should, it is suggested, be more accurately ascribed to Wotan. On a larger scale, the *hubris* of the Wilhelmine era (or so Jung argues) succeeded in alienating the rest of Europe from Germany and "prepared the way for the catastrophe of 1914," or the First World War (MDR, 263).

Yet there was a second, *sociocultural* context of which Nietzsche was also an important part. In a passage of impassioned *Zeitkritik*, Jung castigates the modern age: his age—and ours. Despite what our psyches may pretend, we are "very far from being finished with the Middle Ages, antiquity, and the primitive" (MDR, 239), echoing Jung's words at the conclusion of *Liber Secundus* that "we have only finished the Middle Ages of — others" and his recognition, "I must catch up with a piece of the Middle Ages — within myself" (RB, 457).[22] Plunged down into a "cataract of progress," we are swept with ever greater violence into the future, the further we are torn away from our "roots." This loss of a contextual connection or this "uprootedness" produces the "discontent" (*Unbehagen*) of Freud's *Civilization and its Discontents* (*Das Unbehagen der in der Kultur*) so eloquently speaks, but it does more: It produces a "hastiness," such that one lives less "in the present" and more "in the future and its chimerical promise of a golden age" (MDR, 263). Here it is hard not to hear an echo of Nietzsche's lament in *The Gay Science* for the loss of leisure and idleness: "One thinks with a watch in one's hand, even as one eats one's midday meal while reading the latest news of the stock market [...]. One no longer has time or energy for ceremonies, and for any *otium* at all" (GS §329). Virtue has come to consist in "doing something in less time than someone else"; "hours in which

[22] For discussion of Jung's essay on "The Spiritual Problem of Modern Man" (1928; [2]1931), see Paul Bishop, "Where Is Soul? A 'Spiritual Problem' for Jung's Time and our Own?", in Greg Mogenson and Pamela J. Power (eds.), *Where Is Soul? Psychology in Modernity* (London, Ontario: Dusk Owl Books, 2025), pp. 115-130.

honesty is *permitted* have become rare"; and one wishes to "*stretch out* as long and wide and ungainly as one happens to be" when writing letters, and "the style and spirit of letters will always be the true 'sign of the times' [*»Zeichen der Zeit«*]" (or, one might say, "spirit of the times") (GS §329). In *Memories, Dreams, Reflections*, Jung's critique of modernity sounds as if it might almost have been written for us; and, in a way, it was:

> One rushes impetuously into novelty, driven by an increasing feeling of inadequacy, dissatisfaction, and restlessness. One no longer lives on what one possesses, but on what is promised, no longer in the light of the present day, but in the darkness of the future, where we await the proper sunrise. One refuses to believe that everything better is purchased at the price of something worse. (MDR, 263)

The less we understand of what our ancestors sought—or, one might say, the less we understand such foundational works as Wolfram's *Parzival*, Goethe's *Faust*, and Nietzsche's *Zarathustra*—the less we understand *ourselves*; and this lack of understanding fuels the individual's "lack of instinct and of roots," turning the individual into a mass particle, mindlessly following the "spirit of heaviness" (*Geist der Schwere*), to use Nietzsche's phrase from *Zarathustra*.

The third of the four aspects of Nietzsche's significance in *Memories, Dreams, Reflections* might be described, surprisingly enough, as his religious significance. There is a huge contrast between the critique of modernity that we have just been considering and the insights Jung believed he had gained from discovering other cultures, as recalled in his accounts of his travels. In the case of the Pueblo peoples of New Mexico in the southwestern United States, for instance, where Jung was engaged in dialogue with one of their chiefs, Ochwiay Biano (Mountain Lake), their lives are said to be "cosmologically meaningful"; the statement, "all life comes from the mountain," is said to reflect their belief in a world that is close to God (MDR, 280-281). At this point, Jung pauses to reflect on an important intercultural principle of Analytical Psychology: for the holiness of the mountains in the Pueblo tradition, the revelation of Yahweh on Mount Sinai to the Israelites, or the inspiration that Nietzsche experienced in the Engadine (presumably, the thought of eternal recurrence) are all, in Jung's eyes, saying more or less the same thing. For they form an answer to Parzival's question, "what is God?"; they confirm the existence of an essential relation between humankind and divinity, or what Jung calls "God and us" (*"Gott und wir"*), and remind us that the acts in religious rites and cults of humankind are a reaction and a response to the effect (*Einwirkung*) of God on humankind. As well as representing the desire to exercise some kind of coercion (*Bewirkung*) on the divinity in the form of magic, religious ritual marks a significant change in the status of humankind, for it "raises the human being to the dignity of a metaphysical factor" (MDR, 281). Precisely the consequences of this loss of metaphysical dignity are at stake in Nietzsche's exploration of what it means to live in a world where God is dead; and, *mutatis mutandis*, Jung's exploration in *The Red Book* of what it means to live in a world where "God is not dead" but "He is as alive as ever" (RB, 516).

At the same time, Jung's visit to the Puebloans also contains some of his severest anticolonialist strictures. During his conversation with Ochwiay Biano, Jung has a kind of intuitive vision of the history of the West: the Roman legions entering Gaul, and the faces of Julius Caesar, Scipio Africanus, and Pompey; the *aquila* or Roman eagle on the standards of Roman legions, crossing the North Sea and planted on the banks of the White Nile; St. Augustine, bringing Christianity to the Britons on the tips of Roman lances; Charlemagne forcing the heathens to convert; the rape, pillage, and murder of the Crusaders; Columbus, Cortes, and the conquistadors bringing fire, sword, torture, and Christianity to the Puebloans; and the peoples on the Pacific Islands decimated by the diseases spread by the missionaries. The face of colonization, Jung concludes, is the face of an eagle, a rapacious bird of prey.

And yet Jung feels curiously close to this colonialized Other, and the sense of proximity is for reasons that are strangely, if only implicitly, Nietzschean. For with the Pueblo peoples, Jung notices the utmost secrecy with which they guard their religious practices, which reminds him of the ancient Greeks; in other words, it reminds him of *arrheton*. The strange situation where the air was filled with a secret gave Jung, we are told, a sense of what it must have been like at Eleusis, the site of arguably the most famous of the ancient Mystery Cults, the *Eleusinia*, celebrated in honor of the goddesses Demeter and Persephone. When Pausanias or Herodotus says that he was not permitted to name the name of a god,[23] now Jung

[23] See Pausanius, who records that the crest of a hill above the city of Pallantium has a sanctuary identified as belonging to the *katharoi*, i.e., the "Pure Ones," where it is customary to take the "most solemn oaths," adding that "the names of the gods either they do not know, or knowing will not divulge" (*Description of Greece*, Book 8, Chapter 44, §5-§6), while he himself writes of the goddess worshipped in the Eleusinan Mysteries as the daughter of Demeter and Poseidon and known by the epithet *Despoina* (i.e., "the Mistress") that he is "afraid" to write her "real name" to the "uninitiated" (book 8, chapter 37, §9; cf. chapter 25, §7) (Pausanias, *Description of Greece*, trans. W.H.S. Jones, vol. 4, *Books VIII (XXII) – X* (London; Cambridge, MA: Heinemann; Harvard University Press, 1935), pp. 125, 89, and 25). And see Herodotus, *Histories*, Book 2, §170-§171: "Also in the sanctuary of Athena at Sais is the tomb of one whose name I consider it religiously offensive to mention in this context. […] It is on this lake that they have nocturnal performances reenacting the sufferings of the god, which the Egyptians call the mysteries. Now, although I know all the details of these rites, may my reverence ensure that they remain unspoken. I feel the same way about the rite of Demeter which the Hellenes call the Thesmophoria, so may my reverence ensure that they also remain unspoken, except for that which one can say without offense to religion" (*The Landmark Herodotus: The Histories*, ed. Robert B. Strassler (London: Quercus, 2008), p. 198). In his commentary, Strassler suggests that "May my reverence ensure that they remain unspoken" is a metrical phrase, possibly part of a hymn or ritual prayer (p. 198). As Daniela Bonanno has noted, "to call upon the gods by name is tantamount to identifying them, giving them an anchor in time and space and, in a way, overcoming their otherness in order to establish communication with them," whereas there may be "different reasons

understands why: It is not mystification, but rather the preservation of a vital mystery (MDR, 278).

Indeed, Nietzsche had presented himself as having had unique insight into these Mysteries when, in *Twilight of the Idols*, he wrote: "As the key to understanding the older, inexhaustibly rich and even overflowing Greek instinct, I was the first to take seriously that wonderful phenomenon which bears the name of Dionysos, which is only explicable in terms of excess of force" (TI What I Owe to the Ancients §4). Taking issue with the work of such scholars as Christian Lobeck (1781-1860) (in his *Aglaophamus* of 1829), J.J. Winckelmann, and even Goethe, Nietzsche argued that "it is only in the Dionysian mysteries, in the psychology of the Dionysian state, that the basic fact of the Hellenic instinct finds expression—its 'will to life'":

> What was it that the Hellene guaranteed himself by means of these mysteries? Eternal life, the eternal return of life, the future promised and hallowed in the past; the triumphant Yes to life beyond all death and change; *true* life as the continuation of life through procreation, through the mysteries of sex. For the Greeks a sexual symbol was therefore the most sacred symbol, the real profundity in the whole of ancient piety. Every single element in the act of procreation, of pregnancy, and of

for failing to name a god," viz. "because of a genuine uncertainty as to the identity of the deity; because the prayer takes place in the context of mysteries, in which both *legomena* and *dromena* had to remain secret; or because the prayer is an appeal to the infernal gods, whom one would always approach with a measure of dread" ("Memory Lost, Memory Regained: Considerations on the Recovery of Sacred Texts in Messenia and in Biblical Israel: A Comparison," in Nicola Cusumano, Valentino Gasparini, Attilio Mastrocinque and Jörg Rüpke (eds.), *Memory and Religious Experience in the Greco-Roman World* (Stuttgart: Franz Steiner Verlag, 2013), pp. 63-80 [p. 67]). For further discussion, see Robert Parker, *Greek Gods Abroad: Names, Natures, and Transformations* (Oakland, CA: University of California Press, 2017), especially "Names and Epithets," pp. 1-32.

> birth aroused the highest and most solemn feelings. In the doctrine of the mysteries, *pain* is pronounced holy: the pangs of the woman giving birth consecrate all pain; and conversely all becoming and growing — all that guarantees a future — *involves* pain … That there may be the eternal joy of creating, that the will to life may eternally affirm itself, the agony of the woman giving birth *must* also be there eternally. (TI What I Owe to the Ancients §4)

For Nietzsche, this insight was captured in symbolic form in the figure of Dionysos, the dying-and-resurgent god *par excellence*. In Jungian terms, the myth of Dionysos serves as a symbol of how the ego must be ripped apart and die—it must be *transformed*—in order that the Self might be born, a Self that one might therefore even describe as a "Dionysian Self":

> All this is meant by the word Dionysos: I know of no higher symbolism than this *Greek* symbolism, the symbolism of the Dionysian festivals. Here the most profound instinct of life, that directed toward the future of life, for the eternity of life, is experienced *religiously* — the actual road to life, procreation, as the *sacred road* … (TI What I Owe to the Ancients §4)

Hence Nietzsche was able to identify himself as the "teacher of the eternal recurrence"—and as the "last disciple of the philosopher, Dionysos" (TI What I Owe to the Ancients §5).

Finally, the fourth (and final) aspect of Nietzsche's significance has to do with the deep and pressing existential issues that Jung feels life has addressed to *him*—the question of the meaning of his life. (Equally, says Jung, who always thinks in terms of a reciprocity between Self and World, *he* is a question that is addressed to the world, which the world itself must answer!) Either way, to answer this question is the task that exceeds an individual lifetime (*eine überpersönliche Lebensausgabe*), and which consequently cost Jung himself much effort to realize (MDR, 350). In the end, Jung wonders, is it even his *own* question, or is it rather the question of his ancestors, which he, because they were unable to answer it, has inherited? And Jung casts this existential question in the form of four specific questions as follows:

- first, does this explain why he is so fascinated by the fact that the conclusion of *Faust* contains no real solution?
- second, does it explain why he is so fascinated by the problem that led to Nietzsche's downfall, namely: the experience of the Dionysian, which seems to have been lost to the Christian individual?
- third, is it related to the challenging riddles posed to him by the restless Wotan-Hermes archetype of his Alemannic and Frankish ancestors (MDR, 350)?
- or fourth, as Richard Wilhelm once jokingly suggested, does it suggest that, in a previous life, Jung had been a rebellious Chinese man, who for his punishment would have to discover his Eastern soul in Europe (ETG, 350)? (Perhaps not surprisingly, this joke is removed from the English translation…)

On the one hand, one can read the "ancestors" evoked in *Memories, Dreams, Reflections* as biological ones (and this is, to be sure, a legitimate reading). On the other, they raise the question of a filiation, which is not so much biological as intellectual-historical, and in this sense, Jung's entire *œuvre* is an attempt to respond to these questions:

- as Wolfram's Parzival put it, "What is God?"
- in terms of Goethe's Faust, how does one discover the Eternal Feminine (or Magna Mater)?
- is it true that, as Zarathustra declared, God is dead?

The answer to all three questions is what Jung was trying to work out in his *Red Book*, which is why *The Red Book* can rightly be described as the latest installment in the epic of transformation that we are tracing in these four volumes.

(d) Nietzsche and *Zarathustra* in "On Rebirth" (1939)

In the fourth (and final) part of *Thus Spoke Zarathustra*, we come across a curious chapter (in this most curious of books), entitled "At Midday" (or "Noontide").[24] Occupying a central position in Part Four, it relates how Zarathustra falls asleep beneath an old tree embraced by a grapevine and has a dream, or a vision, or an ecstatic experience of some sort, described as a "strange drunkenness." (In this respect, the chapter acts as an anticipation of the "Drunken Song," or the "Night-Wanderer's Song," sung by Zarathustra in the penultimate chapter.) Our attention is drawn to this passage by Jung in his paper on the archetype of rebirth (CW 9/i §199-§258). This paper is particularly important because it addresses a chapter in Part Four, which Jung's seminar on *Zarathustra* never reached.

First given as an Eranos lecture in 1939, Jung's paper considers five different kinds of rebirth, namely:

- (a) metempsychosis
- (b) reincarnation
- (c) resurrection
- (d) rebirth (*renovatio*); and
- (e) "participation in the process of transformation" (§199-§205).

[24] For further discussion, see Paul Bishop, "Just a Moment? Or, The Archaic as an Expression of the Eternal in Time," in Angeliki Yiassemides (ed.), *Time and the Psyche: Jungian Perspectives* (London and New York: Routledge, 2017), pp. 87-105; and "High Noon on Zarathustra's Mountain: Zarathustra's Midday Vision," in George A. Dunn and Mango Telli (eds.), *A New Politics for Philosophy: Perspectives on Plato, Nietzsche, and Strauss* (Lanham, MD: Lexington Books, 2022), pp. 201-221.

As is clear from this list, this paper is an unusual one, inasmuch as it considers an archetype that is not a figure (as is the Anima or the Animus, the Mother or the Wise Old Man, the Trickster or the Shadow), but a *process*, yet Jung insists on its archetypal dimension: “Rebirth is an affirmation that must be counted among the primordial affirmations of humankind,” he argued, and “these primordial affirmations are based on what I call archetypes” (CW 9/i §206). As an example of this fifth (and, it seems, for Jung, the most interesting) kind of rebirth, Jung mentions the ceremony of the Mass, but also the Eleusinian Mysteries. He cites, for instance, the Homeric Hymn to Demeter, “Happy is he among men upon earth who has seen these mysteries; but he who is uninitiate and who has no part in them, never has lot of like good things once he is dead, down in the darkness and gloom,”[25] and he refers to a text he identifies as one of the Eleusinian epitaphs: “Truly the blessed gods have proclaimed a most beautiful secret: / Death comes not as a curse, but as a blessing to men” (§205, fn. 2).[26]

In this way, Jung tries to resolve the problem of whether or how we can actually discuss the ancient Mysteries. For him, the basic proposition underlying his approach is that “there must be psychic events underlying these affirmations which it is the business of psychology to discuss — without entering into all the metaphysical and philosophical assumptions regarding their significance” (CW 9/i §207). In presenting what he thus conceives as a *phenomenology* of the archetypal experience of rebirth, Jung

[25] Hesiod, *The Homeric Hymns and Homerica*, trans. Hugh G. Evelyn-White (Cambridge, MA; London: Harvard University Press; Heinemann, 1982), p. 323.

[26] Jung also refers to this epitaph in *Transformations and Symbols of the Libido* (see PU §543), and on several other occasions; this same text (like the one from the Hymn to Demeter) is also cited by Ludwig Klages in *Vom kosmogonischen Eros*, end of Chapter 6 (*Of Cosmogonic Eros*, trans. Mav Kuhn, 2nd edn (Munich: Theion, 2022), p. 208). Its source appears to be Δ. Φίλιος, “ΕΠΙΓΡΑΦΑΙ ΕΞ ΕΛΕΥΣΙΝΟΣ” [Inscriptions from Eleusis], *Archaiologikē ephēmeris* (1883), 75-86 (p. 81).

distinguishes between two kinds of experience of archetypal rebirth, which in turn subdivides into further subcategories:[27]

- experience of the transcendence of life in general:
    - ritual-induced experiences
    - immediate experiences
- experience of one's own subjective transformation:
    - diminution of personality
    - enlargement of personality
    - change of internal structure
    - identification with a group
    - identification with a cult hero
    - magical procedures
    - technical transformation
    - natural transformation (individuation)

For Jung, the noontide vision experienced by Zarathustra in "At Midday" falls into two of these categories. First, it belongs in the former category of the transcendence of life, where it constitutes a "classic example" of the "spontaneous, ecstatic, or visionary experience." Indeed, Jung considered its details to be *so* accurate that he went so far as to proclaim that it was "just as if Nietzsche had been present" at a performance of the mysteries of Eleusis (CW 9/i §210).[28] "Nietzsche, as we know," Jung argues, "substitutes

[27] Jung's taxonomy in this paper can be usefully compared with that proposed by Richard Maurice Bucke (1837-1902) in his study, *Cosmic Consciousness: A Study in the Evolution of the Human Mind* (New York: Dutton, 1901).

[28] For further discussion of the significance of the Eleusinian Mysteries from a Jungian perspective, see C.G. Jung and Carl Kerényi, *Essays on a Science of Mythology: The Myth of the Divine Child and the Mysteries of Eleusis*, trans. R.F.C. Hull (Princeton, NJ: Princeton University Press, 1969). For more recent discussion, see Christiane Sourvino-Inwood, "Festival and Mysteries: Aspects of the Eleusinian Cult," in Michael B. Cosmopoulos, *Greek Mysteries: The Archaeology and Ritual of Ancient Greek Secret Cults* (London and New York: Routledge, 2003), pp. 25-49; Jennifer Larson, *Ancient Greek Cults: A Guide* (New York and London: Routledge, 2007), Chapter 6, "Mistresses of Grain and Souls: Demeter and Kore/Persephone," pp. 69-85; and Hugh Bowden, *Mystery Cults in the Ancient World* (London: Thames & Hudson, 2010), pp. 26-48, as well as the synthetic overview in Helene P. Foley,

for the Christian mystery the myth of Dionysus-Zagreus, who was dismembered and came to life again. His experience has the character of a Dionysian nature myth: the Deity appears in the garb of Nature, as classical antiquity saw it"—Jung refers to the opening paragraph about "an old, bent and gnarled tree, hung with grapes"—"and the moment of eternity is the noonday, sacred to Pan" (CW 9/i §210):

> — "[...] What hath befallen me: Hark! Hath time flown away? Do I not fall? Have I not fallen — hark! into the well of eternity?
>
> — What happeneth to me? Hush! It stingeth me — alas — to the heart? To the heart! Oh, break up, break up, my heart, after such happiness, after such a sting!
>
> —What? Hath not the world just now become perfect? Round and ripe? Oh, for the golden round ring — whither doth it fly? Let me run after it! Quick!
>
> Hush —" (and here Zarathustra stretched himself, and felt that he was asleep.)
>
> "Up!" said he to himself, "thou sleeper! Thou noontide sleeper! Well then, up, ye old legs! It is time and more than time; many a good stretch of road is still awaiting you —
>
> Now have ye slept your fill; for how long a time?
>
> A half-eternity! Well then, up now, mine old heart! For how long after such a sleep mayest thou—remain awake?"

"Background: The Eleusinian Mysteries and Women's Rites for Demeter," in Foley (ed.), *The Homeric "Hymn to Demeter": Translation, Commentary, and Interpretive Essays* (Princeton, NJ: Princeton University Press, 1994), pp. 65-75; and Marvin W. Meyer (ed.), *The Ancient Mysteries: A Sourcebook: Sacred Texts of the Mystery Religions of the Ancient Mediterranean World* (San Francisco: Harper & Row, 1987), pp. 15-45.

> (But then did he fall asleep anew, and his soul spake against him and defended itself, and lay down again) — "Leave me alone! Hush! Hath not the world just now become perfect? Oh, for the golden round ball! — [...]" (Z IV 10)

In the image of the "golden ring," or the "ring of return," Jung believes (and here he draws for support on the Nietzsche interpretation of Ernst Horneffer [1871-1954],[29] as he does also in his Seminar on *Zarathustra*) that Nietzsche saw a "promise of resurrection and life" (§211). According to Jung, this kind of "spontaneous, ecstatic, or visionary experience" can offer "all that the mystery drama represents and brings about in the spectator," and it is on the basis of his reading of "At Midday" that Jung confidently concludes that everything is "just as if Nietzsche had been present at a performance of the mysteries" (CW 9/i §210). In a sense, Jung is entirely correct to associate Nietzsche with the great Mysteries, inasmuch as Socrates remarks in the *Phaedo*, "many bear the emblems, but the devotees are few," and "these devotees are simply those who have lived the philosophical life in the right way" (*Phaedo*, 69d).[30]

By placing Zarathustra's vision in the category of immediate experiences, Jung reads the chapter as a transcript of an actual event and seems to endorse its validity. Elsewhere in "Concerning Rebirth," however, he sounds a note of caution. This is when he places Nietzsche's "encounter with Zarathustra" in the category of "subjective transformations" that involve the "enlargement of

[29] Ernst Horneffer, *Nietzsches Lehre von der ewigen Wiederkunft und deren bisherige Veröffentlichung* (Leipzig: Naumann, 1900). For further discussion, see Paul Bishop, *Jung's Seminar on Nietzsche's "Zarathustra": Birth of an Archetypal Hermeneutics* (Palgrave Macmillan, forthcoming).
[30] *Phaedo*, 69d; Plato, *The Collected Dialogues*, ed. Edith Hamilton and Huntington Cairns (Princeton, NJ: Princeton University Press, 1989), p. 52.

personality" (CW 9/i §215). Analogous to the conversion of Paul on the road to Damascus that turned the persecutor into a believer, this experience converted Nietzsche from being a "critic and aphorist" into a "tragic poet and prophet" (CW 9/i §216). From his allusion to the little poem "Sils Maria,"[31] it is clear that Jung regards the experience of "One becom[ing] Two" as the basis for nothing less than a revelation: "When a summit of life is reached, when the bud unfolds, and from the lesser the greater emerges, then, as Nietzsche says, 'One becomes Two,' and the greater figure which one always was but which remained invisible, appears to the lesser personality *with the force of a revelation*" (CW 9/i §217).

The awful ambiguity of this experience is emphasized by Jung through his powerful combination of Pauline and Nietzschean metaphors: "The man who is inwardly great will know that the long expected friend of his soul, the immortal one, has now really come, 'to lead captivity captive'"—a quotation from St. Paul's Letter to the Ephesians (4:8), itself a quotation from (and an adaptation of) Psalm 68:18, and a text associated liturgically with the Feast of the Ascension—"that is, to seize hold of him by whom this immortal had always been confined and held prisoner, and to make his life flow into that greater life—a moment of deadliest peril!" (CW 9/i §217). This emphasis on peril recalls Jung's words in *Transformations and Symbols of the Libido* about the danger of—like Theseus and Peirithoos—becoming stuck in the collective unconscious, as well as the sense of danger accompanying the dynamic of *The Red Book*. Nietzsche's "prophetic vision of the Tightrope-Walker"—and Zarathustra's words of comfort, "Thy soul will be dead even sooner than thy body"—are said to "reveal the awful danger that lies in having a 'tightrope-walking' attitude towards an event to which St. Paul gave the most exalted name he

[31] For further discussion, see Bishop, *Jung's Seminar on Nietzsche's "Zarathustra"* (forthcoming).

could find" (CW 9/i §217). As we shall see in Volume 4, Jung's claim here (as in "A Psychological Approach to the Dogma of the Trinity" [CW 11 §226-§233]) about the figure of Christ as the "perfect symbol of the hidden immortal within the mortal individual" (§218) can be retrospectively applied to the Christ symbolism of *The Red Book*.

Chapter 4

Nietzsche's *Zarathustra* in Jung's *Collected Works* [C]

On the face of it, Nietzsche's *Zarathustra* would seem to have very little to do with alchemy, and hence it would be surprising to find any references to *Zarathustra* at all in the three volumes in the *Collected Works* that contain most of Jung's writings on alchemy: *Psychology and Alchemy* (CW 12), *Alchemical Studies* (CW 13), and *Mysterium Coniunctionis* (CW 14). On further reflection, however, it is not surprising that we *do* find significant references to Nietzsche, both in the main body of Jung's text and tucked away in his scholarly footnotes. First, because Nietzsche himself does make use of alchemical images and metaphors in his *Zarathustra.*[1] And second, because *Zarathustra* is in a way entirely imbued with the spirit of alchemy, inasmuch as it is steeped in the idea of *transformation*. Piecing together Jung's comments in his writings on alchemy can thus enhance our appreciation of the extent to which Jung can be placed in the tradition of the epic of transformation. And, in and out of his commentaries on various sets of dreams, a distinctly Nietzschean thread emerges in Jung's argumentation about alchemy.

[1] See Richard Perkins, "Nietzsche's *opus alchymicum*," *Seminar*, 23 (1987), 216-26; Graham Parkes, *Composing the Soul: Reaches of Nietzsche's Psychology* (Chicago and London: University of Chicago Press, 1994); and Paul Bishop, "The Superman as salamander: symbols of transformation or transformational symbols?", *International Journal of Jungian Studies*, vol. 3, no. 1 (2011), 4-20.

Nietzsche and *Zarathustra* in *Psychology and Alchemy* (1944)

(a) "Individual Dream Symbolism in Relation to Alchemy" (1936)

In the first part of "Individual Dream Symbolism in Relation to Alchemy" (1936), Jung interprets a sequence of dreams and visual impressions by one of his analysands. (Although Jung preserves the dreamer's anonymity, we now know the dreamer in question was the theoretical physicist Wolfgang Pauli [1900-1958].)[2] In the 18th of these dreams, the dreamer is offered some golden coins by a man who stretches out his hand. But the dreamer rejects them indignantly and throws the coins to the ground, a gesture which, however, he immediately regrets; and a variety performance then takes place in an enclosed space. Interpreting the dream in alchemical terms, Jung reads it as a mistaken rejection of the *aurum philosophicum,* or the philosopher's gold. Expanding on why such a misunderstanding occurs, Jung explains that "it is so hard to find the *lapis*" because it is "*exilis*, uncomely,[[3]] it is thrown out into the

---

[2] See C.G. Jung and Wolfgang Pauli, *Atom and Archetype: The Pauli/Jung Letters, 1932-1958*, ed. C.A. Meier, trans. David Roscoe (Princeton, NJ, and Oxford: Princeton University Press, 2001), p. 10. After his lecture at Eranos in 1935, in 1944 Jung reworked this material into *Psychology and Alchemy*, but in 1936 and 1937 Jung gave a series of lectures, first in Bailey Island, Maine, and then in New York, in which he explored further the personal aspects of Pauli's dreams; see C.G. Jung, *Dream Symbols of the Individuation Process: Notes of C.G. Jung's Seminars on Wolfgang Pauli's Dreams*, ed. Suzanne Gieser (Princeton, NJ, and Oxford: Princeton University Press, 2019).

[3] Jung is echoing here Wolfram's understanding of the Grail as the *lapis exilis*:

> [...] Then know, by a *stone* they live,
> And that stone is both pure and precious — Its name hast thou never heard?
> Men call it *Lapis Exilis* [*lapsit exillis*] — by its magic the wondrous bird,
> The Phœnix, becometh ashes, and yet doth such virtue flow
> From the stone, that afresh it riseth renewed from the ashes glow,
> And the plumes that erewhile it moulted spring forth yet more fair and bright —
> [...] And this stone all men call the Grail
> [*der stein ist ouch genant der grâl*].
> (§469, ll. 2-13 and 28; vol. 1, p. 270)

For further discussion, see Volume 1, pp. lix-lx, 144, and 145-148.

street or on to the dung-hill,"—perhaps like the dung heap on which Jung perishes in "Death" in *The Red Book* (RB, 268)—and because it is the "commonest thing to be picked up anywhere," or as one text has it, *in planitie, in montibus et aquis* (i.e., "inside pastures, in mountains and waters") (CW 12 §103). In the biblical tradition, the alchemical stone is identified with "the stone which the builders has rejected, the same is become the head of the corner" (see Psalm 118:22, cf. Matthew 21:42, 1 Peter 2:4-8), while in Carl Spitteler's *Prometheus und Epimetheus,* it is identical with the jewel which was not recognized by the worldly-wise.

According to Jung, it is part and parcel of the banality of its external aspect that the gold is shaped into coins, stamped, and valued—or, in other words, minted. There is an important psychological aspect here, he argues: For to "give names to the virtues" is, Jung suggests, "just what Nietzsche refuses to do in his *Zarathustra*" (CW 12 §104). Yet this is a curious remark, for in "Of the Thousand and One Goals" Zarathustra says, "Loving ones, was it always, and creating ones, that created good and bad. Fire of love gloweth in the names of all the virtues, and fire of wrath" (Z I 15), but perhaps Jung is thinking of "On the Bestowing Virtue" where Zarathustra says:

> Upward soareth our sense: thus is it a simile of our body, a simile of an elevation. Such similes of elevations are the names of the virtues.
>
> Thus goeth the body through history, a becomer and fighter. And the spirit—what is it to the body? Its fights' and victories' herald, its companion and echo.
>
> Similes, are all names of good and evil; they do not speak out, they only hint. A fool who seeketh knowledge from them!
>
> Give heed, my brethren, to every hour when your spirit would speak in similes: there is the origin of your virtue. (Z I 22 §1)

At this point, Jung offers a thought-provoking reflection on what one might call the "monetization of the psyche."[4] By shaping and naming the life of the psyche, Jung argues, one breaks it down into coins or units of value. Yet this division and evaluation are, he goes on to suggest, only possible because the psyche itself is intrinsically a great plurality or variety, or an "accumulation of unintegrated hereditary parts" (CW 12 §104). As a consequence, the natural individual lacks an identity as a "self" but is rather a mere particle in the mass, and for this reason, "collective to such a degree" as to be "not even sure of the ego" (§104). (In *Memories, Dreams, Reflections*, Jung speaks of the modern individual's "lack of instinct and of roots," which turns the individual into a mass particle, mindlessly following the "spirit of heaviness" (*Geist der Schwere*), to use Nietzsche's phrase from *Zarathustra* [MDR, 263].) It is precisely for this reason, Jung argues, that the Transformation Mysteries were needed: for they turned the individual *into something*, rescuing the individual from the animal collective psyche (§104).

Consequently, Jung interprets the end of the dream as referring to the *temenos*, or a piece of land assigned as a domain dedicated to the gods. Although in the dream the performance is described as a variety performance, the satyr play, or the "play of goats," can easily become a tragedy: Arguing that the satyr play was in itself a kind of Mystery performance, Jung suggests that its function, too, was to "re-establish humankind's connection with its natural ancestry and thus with the source of life" (CW 12 §105). As parallels, he cites the obscene stories, or *aiskhologia* (abusive and foul speech), that were related by Athenian ladies at the Eleusinian Mysteries and were thought to promote earth's fertility, or the account given by Herodotus of the exhibitionistic behavior associated with the

[4] See Richard Seaford, *Money and the Early Greek Mind: Homer, Tragedy, and Philosophy* (Cambridge and New York: Cambridge University Press, 2004); and *Tragedy, Ritual and Money in Ancient Greece. Selected Essays* (Cambridge: Cambridge University Press, 2018).

festivities of Isis at Bubastis.[5] (Equally, Jung might have made mention of the "variety performance" of sorts that takes place in *Zarathustra*, when the tightrope walker begins his act across the marketplace, only to be leapt over by the clown or buffoon—and to fall to his death; or to the Ass-Festival of Part Four.)

In the 21st visual impression in the first series, the dreamer finds himself surrounded by nymphs, those minor female nature deities of classical antiquity, depicted as beautiful maidens and usually regarded as personifications of nature. The dreamer hears a voice which says, "We were always there, only you did not notice us" (CW 12 §114). And in the 22nd visual impression, a figure recurs from an earlier dream, the 14th, when the dreamer was in America, looking for an employee "with a pointed beard" (§86). In this 22nd visual impression, a large ape-man threatens to attack the dreamer with a club, until the man with the pointed beard appears and stares at the aggressor until he is spellbound, and a voice says, "Everything must be ruled by the light" (§117). In his interpretation of these two dreams, Jung suggests that the earlier entertaining variety performance of the 18th dream has begun to turn into something more disturbing.

For while we find it easy to accept the classical figures of the nymphs, so often portrayed as beautiful, graceful figures (one thinks, for example, of John William Waterhouse's painting on display in the Manchester Art Gallery, *Hylas and the Nymphs* (1896), where erotically enticing Naiads or freshwater nymphs abduct the fascinated youth), but "behind these gracious figures there lurks the Dionysian mystery of antiquity," a mystery embodied in the satyr play and its tragic implications. Ultimately, the Dionysian mystery depicts the bloody dismemberment of the god, who has been reduced to the condition of an animal. Over

[5] See Herodotus, *Histories*, Book 2, §58-§60 (in *The Landmark Herodotus: The Histories*, ed. Robert B. Strassler (London: Quercus, 2008), p. 144).

time, Jung is suggesting here, the West has lost the sense of what the ancient world was all about: Our attitude, he says, has become "feeble," like that of "a schoolboy," and it took a figure of the stature of Nietzsche to expose its feebleness. But, Jung asks, "what did Dionysos mean to Nietzsche?" (CW 12 §118). What Nietzsche says about Dionysos, Jung says, must be "taken seriously"; and what Dionysos "did to him" must be taken even more seriously. For in the preliminary stages of his fatal illness, Nietzsche could not but have known, Jung confidently asserts, that his fate would be that dismal one of Dionysos Zagreus, dismembered by the Titans in the *sparagmos* and subsequently reborn. Thus, Jung describes Dionysos as the "abyss of the passionate dissolution of all human particularity into the animal divinity of the primordial soul — a blessed and terrible experience" (CW 12 §118) and moreover an experience that modern civilization believes it can escape. And, up to a point, it can—until (as Jung puts it in a sentence which, he notes in a footnote, he wrote in the spring of 1935) civilization unleashes a "frenzied bloodletting that amazes all well-meaning people [*Wohlgesinnten*]," while all the while blaming high finance, the armaments industry, the Jews, and the Freemasons ... (§118).

This, then, is a political Dionysos—that is, Dionysos as a symbol of the destructiveness of the Second World War. Yet there is another aspect of Dionysos: an aspect one could describe as religious, which emerges in the second set of dreams (which refer to the mandala) analyzed in "Individual Dream Symbolism in Relation to Alchemy." This aspect is associated with the dream, for example, of a clergyman who dreamt that, entering his church one night, he found the wall of the choir had collapsed, the altar and ruins were overgrown by vines full of grapes, while the moon was shining in through a gap (CW 12 §179). Another man preoccupied with religious problems had a dream in which, in the middle of the celebration of High Mass in an immense, dark, Gothic cathedral, the wall of the aisle suddenly collapses, allowing blinding sunlight and a large herd of bulls and cows to burst into the interior (§180). And a third (and much more elaborate) dream—the 17th in the second series—is set in a church resembling the Hagia Sophia, in which a religious chorale is replaced by a loudspeaker blaring out a ragtime melody (§176). Referring the reader to his more detailed interpretation of the dream in his Terry Lectures of 1937 on "Psychology and Religion" (see CW 11 §40-§55), here Jung focuses on how the space of the *temenos* has become a sacred building, while the "grotesque-comic" aspect of the Dionysian mysteries emerges in the *gemütlich* part of the ceremony when it turns into a kind of party, wine is served, and a toast is proposed to the health of the Church! Jung interprets the "anti-ascetic tendency" to which a priest in the dream refers and the dream as a whole as a "regression" to pre-Christian Dionysos worship, but not simply as a fall into anarchy and chaos: Rather, it is a kind of descent *ad inferos* or a psychological *nekyia* (CW 12 §178).

In fact, Jung regards the dream as something quite positive and syncretistic, symbolized by the similarity between the church in the dream and the Hagia Sophia, an ancient Christian basilica which then served as a mosque, before it became a museum (and now, as of 2020, a mosque again). As such, the dream is said to represent for Jung a "combination of Christian and Dionysian religious ideas" (CW 12 §181). Referring back to the 22nd visual impression in the first series in which the large ape-man appears (§117) and the 16th dream in the second series in which people, who are seen walking to the left around a square, tell the dreamer that "a gibbon is to be reconstructed" (§164), Jung pauses to consider the possibly sacrilegious connotation of this symbolism, the leftward movement recalling the *diabolica fraus* and the gibbon as the devil or the "ape of god." Yet the unconscious has, he insists, no such "blasphemous intentions," but is rather trying to restore to the religious world the lost Dionysos—the sense of the Dionysian that modern humankind lacks (§181). Although the 22nd visual impression in the first series concludes with a voice saying, "everything must be ruled by the light" (§117 and §120), this everything must, Jung now adds, include the so-called Lord of Darkness with his horns and cloven foot (a figure who is jokingly described as a "Dionysian corybant who has unexpectedly been elevated to the rank of Prince"!) (CW 12 §181).

By the Dionysian, Jung explains, he means the capacity for emotions and affects which have, since the rise of predominantly Apollonian cult and ethos of Christianity, found "no suitable religious form" (CW 12 §182). In the Middle Ages, the Church abolished carnivals and ball games (*jeux de paume*) relatively early, and with the secularization of carnival, "divine intoxication disappeared from the sacred space" (§182). In this respect, Jung can be read as endorsing the theory of the "carnivalesque" as proposed by Mikhail Bakhtin (1895-1975) in his *Problems of Dostoevsky's Poetics* (1929; ^{2}1963) and explored further in *Rabelais and His World* (1965). For the carnivalesque is a literary mode that challenges and subverts the existing social order and structures of power in four main ways: first, by promoting interaction between people from different social classes; second, by encouraging eccentric or exaggerated behavior; three, by encouraging *mésalliances* between such archetypal opposites as young and old, upper and lower, heaven and hell; and licensing profanity, obscenity, and blasphemy.[6] In short, the carnivalesque is a form of the Dionysian.

So on Jung's account, the Church remained the privileged space for mourning, serious-mindedness, severity, and well-tempered spiritual joy, but where did this leave Dionysian intoxication (*Rausch*)? As the "most immediate and most dangerous form of possession [*Ergriffenheit*]," the intoxication of Dionysian *Rausch* was turned away from the gods, and its "exuberance [*Überschwang*]"

[6] For further discussion, see Richard Sheppard, "Tricksters, Carnival and the Magical Figures of Dada Poetry," in *Modernism – Dada – Postmodern* (Evanston, IL: Northwestern University Press, 2000), pp. 292-303.

and "pathos" embraced the human world instead. Two responses to these conditions were possible. First, pagan religions retained a place for ecstatic intoxication in their cults; Jung cites the saying of Heraclitus, "But Hades is that same Dionysos in whose honour they go mad and keep the feast of the wine-vat" (fragment 15; DK 22 B 15).[7] In line with this strategy, the orgy was granted license within the religious cult, thereby exorcizing the threatening danger that Hades posed. Second, Christianity sought to repress the Dionysian or the carnivalesque, but at the risk—and, in this respect, Jung *did* agree with Freud—that the repressed would return; or, as Jung puts it, his solution has "thrown open wide the gates of Hades" (CW 12 §182).

The 18th dream in this second series includes two snakes moving in opposite directions within a square space, then four snakes gliding into its four corners, and finally a huge reptile carried by two priests while a voice proclaims, "These are attempts at becoming" (*Das sind die Versuche des Werdens*) (CW 12 §183). The priests holding the reptile use it to touch the forehead of a shapeless animal-like life-mass, thereby transforming it into a human head, and this association between the snakes and their transformative effect immediately excites Jung's attention; not surprisingly, given the prevalence of snake imagery in his *Red Book*. According to Jung, the transfiguration of the shapeless life-

[7] For this translation, see John Burnet, *Early Greek Philosophy* (London: Black, 1908), pp. 155-156 (fragment 127); citing Clement of Alexandria, *Protrepticus*, Part Two, Chapter 34, §5, in Clement of Alexandria, *The Exhortation to the Greeks; The Rich Man's Salvation;* [...] *To the Newly Baptized*, trans. G.W. Butterworth (Cambridge, MA; London: Harvard University Press; Heinemann, 1960), pp. 72-73). Originally a vegetation god, Dionysos was thus—according to Butterworth—another form of Hades or Pluto, the "wealth-giver." (Under the guise of Plutus, the god of wealth—etymologically and conceptually related to Pluto, because "wealth [...] comes up from below out of the earth" [Plato, *Cratylus*, 403a]—is a figure we encounter in the Carnival in Act 1 of Goethe's *Faust*, Part Two, as well as in Dante's *Divine Comedy* in *Inferno*, Canto 7, where Pluto presides over the Hoarders and the Spendthrifts in the fourth circle of Hell.)

mass into a human head by the ceremonial use of a reptile or snake symbolizes the union of the mass of the inherited unconsciousness with consciousness, and the "idea of transformation [*Verwandlung*] and renewal [*Erneuerung*] by means of a serpent" represents a well-substantiated archetype (§184). On this account, the healing serpent represents the god, and Jung suggests numerous parallels: In the mysteries of Sabazios (who is, according to the 10th-century Byzantine Greek encyclopedia, the *Suda*, identical to Dionysos), a golden snake is let down into the lap of the uninitiated and taken away again; among the Ophites (a Christian Gnostic sect described by Hippolytus of Rome in his lost work, the *Syntagma*), Christ was identical with the Brazen Serpent lifted up in the wilderness; in Kundalini Yoga, serpent symbolism is connected with the renewal of the personality; and, of course, there is the famous episode of the shepherd and the snake in "Of the Vision and the Riddle" in *Zarathustra* (Z III 2 §2; see Chapter 1, pp. 57-62).

(In his discussion of this episode in his seminar given in 1936 on Bailey Island, Jung related this vision to the experiences in Kundalini Yoga, arguing that:

- "translated into religious language," Zarathustra's vision means that the god "really tried to enter the shepherd's consciousness in his sleep";
- the shepherd in *Zarathustra* represents Nietzsche himself;
- the archaic individual "knew that the Zarathustra experience was a religious experience," but the "exalted consciousness of Nietzsche, which was overwrought and identified with the figure of Zarathustra, advised him not to let the god in, but to bite his head off; but this was, of course, fatal";
- if Nietzsche had "accepted" the snake, it would have been an "illustration of that archaic form of initiation in which the god enters man," signifying that "the man becomes filled with god, he has god within"—equated by Jung to the "Kundalini experience."

By the "Kundalini experience," on which he had lectured with Jakob Wilhelm Hauer (1881-1962) in a seminar held in 1932, Jung means an experience of "everything that is above: all the lotuses or chakras, all higher states of consciousness, all religious experiences which have a healing effect.")[8]

Over and above these examples, one might point to the fact that some of the dreams recorded in the dream protocols of Theodor W. Adorno (1903-69), the great thinker of the Frankfurt School, also reveal a fascination with reptiles and, in particular, dinosaurs.[9] In a dream from Hamburg in May 1954, during which he thought he could feel his veins "swelling and hardening to bursting point," Adorno sees the following: "Some kind of disgusting little animals were creating havoc. A toy-size triceratops appeared so as to introduce order, but nothing happened and he finally became indistinguishable from the little animals" (52). And a dream of 16 June 1955 features "two giant, black triceratops, as if made of plastic, furious, horrifying animals" which attached an ankylosaurus (55-56). As we saw in Chapter 1 (pp. 15-16), in his seminars on dream analysis, Jung explains that snakes, crocodiles, and "cold-blooded relics" are "uncanny powers, because they symbolize the fundamental factors of our instinctive life, dating from Paleozoic times," and "so whenever life means business" and "things are getting serious," one is "likely to find a saurian on the way."[10]

---

[8] Jung, *Dream Symbols of the Individuation Process*, ed. Gieser, p. 218. See C.G. Jung, *The Psychology of Kundalini Yoga: Notes of the Seminar Given in 1932*, ed. Sonu Shamdasani (London: Routledge, 1996).

[9] Theodor W. Adorno, *Dream Notes*, ed. Christoph Gödde and Henri Lonitz, trans. Rodney Livingstone (Cambridge and Malden, MA: Polity, 2007). For the German original, see Theodor W. Adorno, *Traumprotokolle*, ed. Christoph Gödde and Henri Lonitz (Frankfurt am Main: Suhrkamp, 2005). For further discussion, see Stefan Müller-Doohm, "Traumprotokolle," in Richard Klein, Johann Kreuzer, Stefan Müller-Doohm (eds.), *Adorno-Handbuch: Leben – Werk – Wirkung*, 2nd edn. (Berlin: Metzler, 2019), pp. 19-22.

[10] C.G. Jung, *Dream Analysis: Notes of the Seminar given in 1928-1930*, ed. William McGuire (London: Routledge & Kegan Paul, 1984), pp. 645-646. For further discussion, see Paul Bishop, "Adorno and Jung, Bloch and Klages: Disorientation

In "Individual Dream Symbolism in Relation to Alchemy," Jung explains the dynamic of transformation in terms that assimilate alchemy and psychology. Thus, the "shapeless life-mass" in the dream symbolizes the alchemical "chaos," or the *massa* (or *materia*) *informis* (or *confusa*), which is transformed by a *circumambulatio*, that is, by an exclusive concentration on the *middle* or *center* as the place of creative transformation (*schöpferische Wandlung*) (CW 12 §185-§186). During this process, as is the case with the shepherd and the snake in *Zarathustra*, the dreamer is "bitten" by animals and is transformed, but what does this mean? Jung explains the significance of this dynamic in the following terms:

> One has to expose oneself to the animal impulses of the unconscious, but without identifying with them or "running away" from them; for to flee from the unconscious would be to nullify the purpose of the proceedings. One has to stick at it [*Man muß dabei bleiben*]; that means in this case that the process initiated by self-observation must be experienced in all its reversal or turning-points [*Peripetien*, cf. περιπέτεια] and incorporated with the unconscious by means of the best possible understanding. Of course this means an often unbearable tension between conscious life and the unconscious process, for the latter can only be experienced in the innermost psyche [*im innersten Gemüt*] and cannot touch the visible surface of life at any point. (CW 12 §186)

Leibniz's dictum, *nihil est in intellectu, quod non antea fuerit in sensu*, that is, "there is nothing in the understanding that was not

---

and Reorientation of Consciousness in the Totally Administered Society," *Eranos Yearbook* [The Disoriented Consciousness and the Thought of a New Habitability], vol. 76 (2022–2023–2024), 483-538.

previously in the senses," is identified by Jung as the "principle of conscious life." Against this, he sets the principle of the unconscious—namely, the autonomy of the psyche itself, the play of whose images (*Bilder*) does not reflect the world but *itself*, even if it uses the possibilities of representation provided by the sensory world in order to clarify those images (*Bilder*) (CW 12 §186). Jung emphasizes that the sensory data are not the efficient cause (*causa efficiens*) of these images, for they are freely selected and exploited by the psyche, thereby violating the rationality of the cosmos (*die Vernünftigkeit des Kosmos*). But when the sensory world does burst in on intrapsychic processes as a *causa efficiens*, it is equally destructive; so in order, on the one hand, not to upset rationality, and on the other, to avoid a clumsy or violent suppression of the creative play of the images, a careful and far-reaching process of synthesis is required in order to achieve the paradox of the union of irreconcilables (§186). Thus, alchemy offers a possibility of synthesis, something which is said ultimately to be missing from Nietzsche's *Zarathustra*.

In the terms of this 18th dream in the second series, the dreamer is in search of the elusive fourth function, a function that is "contaminated with the unconscious" (and hence, when made conscious, "drags the whole of the unconscious along with it"). This dynamic allows the dreamer to come to terms with the unconscious and to bring about a "synthesis of opposites," symbolized by the mandala (or, in its simplest form, the square) (CW 12 §193). Consequently, in the 22nd dream in the second series, the number 4 is hinted at in the detail of a lift that carries the dreamer "up" from the "sub"-conscious to "about the third or fourth floor," while the fact that the dreamer is part of a group of people indicates that the problem of the mysterious fourth is "not merely an individual but a collective problem" (§201). In fact, Jung remarks, linking back to his discussion in *Psychological Types* (see Chapter 3, pp. 215-230), the "noticeable revival of the unconscious in recent times" was something that Friedrich Schiller had foreseen and that raised questions of which the 19th century had never dreamed. Until, that is, Nietzsche in his *Zarathustra* decided to reject the snake and the "Ugliest Man," which led him, in Jung's curious phrase, to a "heroic cramp of consciousness" (*zu einem heroischen Bewußtseinskrampf*) and ultimately to the collapse that Jung regards as having been "foretold" in *Zarathustra* (§201).

(b) "Religious Ideas in Alchemy" (1937)

In "Religious Ideas in Alchemy" (1937), Jung offers a reading of a text by an ancient authority, the Persian alchemist Ostanes, as cited in the third century by Zosimos of Panopolis. This text begins as follows: "Go to the waters of the Nile and there you will find a stone that has a spirit [*pneuma*]. Take this, divide it, thrust in your hand and draw out its heart: for its soul [*psyche*] is in its heart [...]."[11] The quality of having a spirit—like all the other qualities associated with the lapis (it is the panacea, the universal medicine, the alexipharmic, the tincture transforming base metal into gold; it brings riches, power, health)—is a sign of its power as a symbol of the savior, of the Anthropos (in Gnosticism, the primeval Man), of immortality. Or, one might say, as a symbol of the *Übermensch*.

For Jung compares this text to the passage in "On the Blissful Islands" where Zarathustra says, "I see an image sleeping in the stone, the image of my visions! Ah, that it must sleep in the hardest, ugliest stone!" (Z II 2). Now in this exclamation one might hear an echo of the principle attributed to Michelangelo that "every block of stone has a statue inside it and it is the task of

[11] Cited from Marcellin Berthelot, *Collection des anciens alchimistes grecs*, 3 vols. (Paris: Steinheil, 1887-1888), vol. 2, *Les œuvres de Zosime*, section III.vi, §5, pp. 121 and 129); cf. CW 12 §405; SNZ, vol. 2, p. 949; "Psychology and Religion," in CW 11 §151; and "Transformation Symbolism in the Mass," in CW 11 §355.

the sculptor to discover it."[12] (And when Zarathustra announces, "Now my hammer rages fiercely against its prison. Fragments fly from the stone: what is that to me?" one might recall a further statement attributed to Michelangelo: "In every block of marble I see a statue as plain as though it stood before me, shaped and perfect in attitude and action. I have only to hew away the rough walls that imprison the lovely apparition to reveal it to the other eyes as mine see it.")[13] For his part, however, Jung sees the passage from *Zarathustra* about the image slumbering in the stone as saying the "same thing" as Ostanes—but the "other way round" (CW 12 §406). For in antiquity, Jung explains, the world of matter was seen as filled with the projection of a "psychic secret" (*eines seelischen Geheimnisses*), which from then on appeared as the "secret of matter" (*als Geheimnis des Stoffes*) in a way that persisted until the decline of alchemy in the 18th century (§406). But then Nietzsche, Jung continues, tried with his "ecstatic intuition" to wrest the secret of the *Übermensch* from precisely the stone in which it had been sleeping for such a long time. Accordingly Nietzsche wanted to create the *Übermensch* in the likeness of this image, and what Nietzsche called the *Übermensch* is said to correspond to what, in the language of antiquity, would have been called the "divine human being" (*den göttlichen Menschen*) (§406).

This approach was the *exact reverse* of the one taken by the alchemists. For the alchemists saw themselves as search of the marvelous stone that contained a "pneumatic essence," hoping thereby to win from it that substance that penetrates all material bodies, because it is the "spirit" (*Geist*) that has penetrated the stone.

---

[12] Cited in John Russon, "The Project of Hegel's *Phenomenology of Spirit*," in Stephen Houlgate and Michael Baur (eds.), *A Companion to Hegel* (Malden, MA, and Oxford: Blackwell, 2011), pp. 47-67 (p. 48).

[13] Cited in Russon, "The Project of Hegel's *Phenomenology of Spirit*," p. 63. For further discussion, see Paul Bishop, *On the Blissful Islands with Nietzsche & Jung: In the Shadow of the Superman* (London and New York: Routledge, 2017), pp. 79-142.

This substance, they believed, would enable them through a process of recoloring to transform (*verwandeln*) all base metals into noble ones. The "spirit-substance" (*Geiststoff*) is like quicksilver, lurking unseen in the ore and which must be expelled if one wishes to capture it *in substantia*. Anyone who might possess this penetrating Mercurius would be able to "project" it onto other substances and transpose them from an imperfect into a perfect state. (In a footnote, Jung expresses his amazement that alchemists actually used this term, *prioectio*, in order to describe the application of the philosophical Mercury to base metals!) This imperfect state is said to be like a state of slumber: It is in this state that material bodies lie, like "sleepers chained in Hades."[14] (In the words of Joseph von Eichendorff in his short poem, "Dowsing Rod" (*Wünschelrute*): "There is a song sleeping in all things / that dream on and on / and the world begins to sing / if only you can find the magic word" [*Schläft ein Lied in allen Dingen, / Die da träumen fort und fort, / Und die Welt hebt an zu singen, / Triffst du nur das Zauberwort*].)[15] Thanks to the "divine tincture" extracted from the marvelous stone pregnant with spirit (*geistesschwanger*), these material bodies can be awakened as from death to a new, more beautiful life. (Thus, there is an important sense in which the *alchemical* transformation is an *aesthetic* transformation, too.) In other words, the alchemists saw the "secret of psychic transformation" (*das Geheimnis der seelischen Wandlung*) as located in matter but also as offering a theoretical guiding principle that would bring about actual chemical changes (CW 12 §406).

While the alchemists aimed at looking for the divine *in* the stone in order to *project* it onto other substances, and Nietzsche was looking to wrest the "divine man," or *Übermensch, from* the stone

[14] *The Book of Comarius*, citing Ostanes's words to Cleopatra; in Berthelot, *Collection des anciens alchimistes grecs*, vol. 3, IV.xx, §8 (p. 281).

[15] Joseph von Eichendorff, *Sämtliche Gedichte und Versepen*, ed. Hartwig Schulz (Frankfurt am Main and Leipzig: Insel, 2007), p. 271.

in order to create it, Jung identifies this parallel: Just as Nietzsche made very sure that nobody would mistake the *Übermensch* for an ideal spiritual and moral individual, so the alchemists emphasized that the tincture or divine water does not just enable beneficial curative and ennobling changes but can also act as a deadly poison, penetrating other bodies just as much as it penetrates its own, that is, the stone.[16] In other words, it is, in Derridean terms, a *phármakon*: that is, it is not simply a "cure" *or* a "poison," it is *both* in a way that is radically indeterminable.[17] Likewise, the *Übermensch* is neither a good thing nor a bad thing: it is both good *and* bad, it is "*beyond* good and evil," and it cannot be circumscribed by existing moral categories.

(c) "Epilogue" to *Psychology and Alchemy*

In his important "Epilogue" to *Psychology and Alchemy* (written in 1944), Jung offers a synthesizing intellectual-historical account of the heyday and subsequent decline of alchemy. In so doing, however, he repeatedly links Nietzsche's *Zarathustra* back to Goethe's *Faust* in a way that highlights both the political and the religious significance of *Zarathustra*. Nowhere is this clearer than when Jung, declaring that in Goethe's *Faust* alchemy "reached its final summit, and thus its historical turning-point," turns to consider the scene in Act 1 of Part Two, when Faust conjures up Paris and Helena. When Faust *intervenes* in what he is watching, he identifies with Paris and brings the *coniunctio* back "from its projected state into the sphere of personal psychological experience and thus into consciousness" (CW 12 §559). Faust's identification with Paris

[16] *The Divine Zosimos on Virtue and Interpretation*; in Berthelot, *Collection des anciens alchimistes grecs*, vol. 3, III.vi, §8 (pp. 131-132).

[17] See Jacques Derrida, "Plato's Pharmacy," in *Dissemination*, trans. Barbara Johnson (Chicago and London: University of Chicago Press, 1981), pp. 63-17. The logic of the *pharmakon* underpins the dynamics of *The Red Book*, as we shall see in Volume 4.

is said to represent the "redemption [*Erlösung*] of a previously unconscious part of the personality" (§559), yet this in turn creates a problem for, in Jungian terms, every increase in consciousness "harbors the danger of *inflation*"—as is reflected in Faust's inclination to try and be an *Übermensch*! While Faust's death was "necessary" in his day and age as a consequence of his actions, it was not a "sufficient answer"; nor was his postmortal rejuvenation, for his rebirth and transformation that followed the *coniunctio* "take place in the hereafter, i.e., in the unconscious"—and this leaves the problem "hanging in the air" (*hier blieb ein Problem hängen*) (§559). And here, for Jung, lies the intimate connection between *Faust* and Nietzsche's *Zarathustra*.

For, according to Jung, Nietzsche "took up this problem again" in his *Zarathustra* in the form of the transformation into the *Übermensch* (*die Wandlungen zum Übermenschen*), but he did so in a way that brought the *Übermensch* into a dangerous proximity to the human being of *this* world, not the next. And, in doing so, he inevitably called up an anti-Christian *ressentiment*, for the *Übermensch* represents a "hybris of individual consciousness," which cannot avoid colliding with the "collective power" of Christianity—and leading to the "catastrophic destruction of the individual" (CW 12 §559). This destruction of the individual was, on Jung's account, to be Nietzsche's personal fate—a fate that affected him, in line with the ancient principle of alchemy, both morally and materially (*tam ethice quam physice*). (In so writing, Jung is echoing the alchemical principle, *aurum nostrum non est aure, vulgi tam ethice quam physice*, i.e., "our gold is not the common gold, as much moral as material.")[18]

[18] See *Rosarium philosophorum*, for "our gold is not the common gold" (*aurum nostrum non est aurum vulgi*); cited in CW 12 §99, fn. 30, and §342-§343; cf. "our gold is, of course, not the gold of the vulgar people. Our gold is a philosophical gold. It is a metaphorical gold" (Jung, *Dream Symbols of the Individuation Process*, ed. Gieser, p. 273).

Beyond Nietzsche, how did the next generation respond to this problem? How did it respond to the individualism of the Nietzschean *Übermensch*? (Jung's question is a legitimate one, given Gottfried Benn's observation (see Chapter 3, p. 243) about how everything his generation "had discussed, had thought out inside itself, one might say: suffered, one might also say: done to death — all that had already been expressed and exhausted in Nietzsche, had found definitive formulation; all the rest was mere exegesis.") On Jung's account, this following generation's answer was a "collectivism, a collective organisation, and a piling-up of the masses, 'both morally and materially,' that made a mockery of everything that had gone before" (CW 12 §559). In 1944, Jung drew up the following (rather gloomy) balance sheet of his time: on the one hand, the suffocation of the personality; on the other, an impotent, or perhaps even fatally wounded, Christianity. (Over three-quarters of a century later, one might ask: Does the balance sheet look so very different today…?)

At this point in his "Epilogue," Jung pivots to the devastating episode toward the end of Act 5 of *Faust*, Part Two: the murder of Philemon and Baucis. As always, we should remember that, in his Tower at Bollingen, Jung carved over the gate the inscription, "Philemonis Sacrum – Fausti Poenitentia" (that is, "Philemon's Shrine – Faust's Repentance"); and, a couple of years earlier, in a letter to Paul Schmitt in 1942, he had written that he had "taken over" Faust as his "heritage," and "moreover as the advocate and avenger of Philemon and Baucis, who, unlike Faust the superman, are the hosts of the gods in a ruthless and godforsaken age" (L1, 309-310). To understand what Faust's *repentance* is, we have first to understand what Faust's *sin* is (and, *mutatis mutandis*, Nietzsche's).

On the one hand, Jung tells us that Faust's sin was the "identification with what was to be transformed [*dem zu Wandelnden*] with what had been transformed [*dem Gewandelten*]" (§560), and similarly that Nietzsche's act of overreaching himself had been to identify (assuming, of course, that he really did) with the *Übermensch* in the form of Zarathustra, that is to say, with that part of Nietzsche's personality that was struggling or emerging into consciousness. On this account, Faust's sin and Nietzsche's sin had been identical: Both had identified with something archetypal and become inflated. But—and this is surely the six-million-dollar question—is it permissible to speak about a fictional character (Faust) and a historical person (Nietzsche) in the same way? For his part, Jung raises another pertinent question: Is it right to speak about Zarathustra as a "part of the personality" at all? Is not Zarathustra, he asks, rather something that is essentially superhuman (*das Übermenschliche*)? (Of course, another six-million-dollar question might be: can Zarathustra—the teacher of the *Übermensch* (Z Prologue §3) and, according to the animals in "The Convalescent," the teacher of eternal recurrence (Z III 13 §2)—really be identified, as Jung does twice in §560, with the *Übermensch* himself or with *das Übermenschliche*?) Here, however, Jung pursues an entirely different line of questioning: Is Zarathustra as *das Übermenschliche* something *in which* the human being can *participate*, but which the human being actually *is* not? Or to put it another way: Is God really dead? Is he dead, simply because Nietzsche (or, more accurately, the madman in the parable in *The Gay Science*) says that he has "gone missing"? Or is it possible that, under the guise or disguise of the *Übermensch*, God has found his way back to us…?

On the other hand, Faust's sin (and therefore Nietzsche's sin) was what happened as a consequence of this identification: the murder of Philemon and Baucis, committed by Faust (or, more precisely, at his behest) in "his blind urge for superhuman power" (*in blindem Übermenschendrang*) (CW 12 §561). In *Memories, Dreams, Reflections*, we read that Jung felt "personally implicated" in this episode: "When Faust, in his hubris and self-inflation, caused the murder of Philemon and Baucis, I felt guilty, quite as if I myself in the past had helped commit the murder of the two old people"

(MDR, 261; cf. JLW, 224). (Not only is this a "strange idea," but it becomes even stranger when Jung suggests that the "heroic myth" of *Faust* had in some way "prophetically anticipated the fate of the Germans.") As a consequence, we learn, Jung came to regard it as his responsibility to "atone for this crime [*diese Schuld zu sühnen*], or to prevent its repetition" (MDR, 261). In his "Epilogue" in 1944, however, Jung places emphasis on the *metaphysical* rather than the *political* dimension of the story of Philemon and Baucis, for he reminds us of who, according to Ovid (on whose account Goethe partially drew), this humble old couple was. It was they who, "when the world had become godless and no longer offered a hospitable retreat to the divine [*göttlichen*] strangers Jupiter and Mercury," nevertheless "received their superhuman [*übermenschlichen*] guests." And it was when Baucis was about to sacrifice their last goose for them that the "transformation [*die Wandlung*] happened: the gods made themselves known, the humble cottage became a temple, and the old couple became immortal servitors at the shrine" (CW 12 §561). On *this* account, then, Nietzsche is implicated both in the forgetting *and* in the unexpected return of the divine.

At this point, Jung returns to his broader intellectual-historical account of the role of alchemy. According to Jung, the old alchemists had been "nearer to the central truth of the psyche [*der seelischen Wahrheit*] than Faust when they strove to deliver [*erlösen*] the fiery spirit from the chemical elements," and treated the mysterium (*das Mysterium*) "as though it lay in the womb of dark and silent nature" (CW 12 §562). At this stage, the mystery (*das Mysterium*) was something located *outside* themselves. With the increasing development of consciousness, however, reflected in the age of the Enlightenment and in the era of scientific rationalism, this projection collapsed; the soul or psyche (*die Seele*) became identified with consciousness; and the contents of the unconscious, previously thought of as external, *now became internalized*. Thus, "previously projected contents" became "personal possessions," or the "chimerical fantasy-images of ego-consciousness"; put metaphorically, the fire cooled down and became air, which in turn became the stormy wind of Zarathustra—"Too great hath been the tension of my cloud: 'twixt laughters of lightnings will I cast hail-showers into the depths. [...] Verily, like a storm cometh my happiness, and my freedom! But mine enemies shall think that THE EVIL ONE roareth over their heads," as we read in "The Child with the Mirror" (Z II 1)—thereby causing an inflation of consciousness. This apparently ever-increasing inflation of consciousness could only be counteracted by the "most terrible catastrophes of civilization," or in other words the "deluge which the gods visited upon inhospitable humankind" (§562). We call these catastrophes of civilization—*wars*.

And so, Jung's account moves back from the metaphysical to the political; ultimately, these two aspects are, as far as he is concerned, not separate but intertwined. According to his diagnosis, the inflation of ego-consciousness has political and military consequences, such as the military conflict of the First World War, the backdrop to Jung's work on *The Red Book*. When Europe allowed a "war of grandiose frightfulness to play out for four years" (that is, between 1914 and 1918), and a war that "nobody wanted," why did no one ask, he wonders, who had caused this war and allowed it to continue? (One is reminded of Lord Palmerston's famous joke about the 1864 Danish-German war that only three people ever understood the reason behind it: one who had died, one who went mad, and the third who had forgotten ....). We should note, incidentally, that Jung at first specifically asks: "who" (*wer*), not "what," caused the war, as the Hull translation suggests. For no one took into account, Jung goes on, that the Europeans had been possessed (*besessen*) by something (*etwas*) that had "robbed" them of "all free will" (CW 12 §563). And this possessed, unconscious state is something that was going to continue, Jung grimly concluded in 1944, until the Europeans became "afraid of their god-almightiness" (*von seiner*

Gottähnlichkeit bange), alluding to the concluding words spoken by Mephistopheles in the second Study Scene in *Faust*, Part One (l. 2049-2050).[19]

In other words, we need another *transformation*, and this transformation (*Wandlung*) cannot begin with the masses, which Jung compares to "blind animals"; rather, it must begin *with the individual*. (Thus, Analytical Psychology *is* a political project, albeit one that shuns the collective to focus on the individual; or, more precisely, understands that the relation between the individual and the collective is a dialectical one.) And so Jung reckons it as a matter of some importance that at least a few individuals—he means, presumably, analytical psychologists, or at least those analytical psychologists who have understood the significance of Jung's project—have begun to realize that there are some contents (of consciousness) which do not belong to the ego-personality, but which belong to a "psychic non-ego," that is, the collective unconscious. The threat of inflation can, he insists, only be avoided if we realize this fact. But by no means do we stand alone: for we have the "useful and instructive models, which the poets and philosophers show us," models which he describes as *archetypi* and as "remedies for individuals and eras alike" (CW 12 §563). To this extent, Analytical Psychology is indeed a *cultural project*, and there can be no greater, no more useful and instructive models than Wolfram's *Parzival*, Goethe's *Faust*, and Nietzsche's *Zarathustra*.

And what we may learn from the great models of the past is this: namely, that the psyche or the soul (*die Seele*) holds contents or stands under influences, the assimilation into consciousness of which is connected with the greatest dangers. If, on the one hand, the ancient alchemists ascribe their secret to matter and, on the

[19] As the student exits, Mephisto mutters, "Follow the ancient saw, and follow the snake, my cousin; / God's image as thou art, thou'lt rue the way thou hast chosen!" (*Folg nur dem alten Spruch und meiner Muhme, der Schlange, / Dir wird gewiß einmal bei deiner Gottähnlichkeit bange!*) (ll. 2049-2050).

other, the examples of Faust and Zarathustra alike "do not really encourage us to embody this secret in ourselves," could there be a third way—a way that involves rejecting the "arrogant claim of consciousness" to be itself psyche or soul (*Seele*) and recognizing that the soul possesses a "reality which we cannot grasp with our present means of understanding" (CW 12 §564)? If so, what would this mean in practice? It would surely mean *turning to* the poets and the philosophers with their useful and instructive models, but it would also mean—at the right time, and in the right way—*turning away from them*. For, as Jung reminds us in the final paragraphs of his "Epilogue," alchemy described itself as an "art" (*Kunst*), for—rightly—it felt that was dealing with processes of giving shape (*Gestaltungsvorgänge*) which ultimately can be "described intellectually" (*intellektuell bezeichnet*) but "only really grasped in experience" (*nur im Erleben wirklich erfaßt*) (§564). (This is why Jung gave the advice to Christiana Morgenstern that she should create her own kind of *Red Book*, as a "cathedral for the soul"; Analytical Psychology involves a praxis, and an aesthetic one.)

Even the alchemists themselves, despite their insistence on study (as Jung reminds us), insistently warn: *Rumpite libros, ne corda vestra rumpantur* ("Rend the books, lest your hearts be rent asunder!") (CW 12 §564). (Or in the words of Gerhard Dorn, cited in "Individual Dream Symbolism in Relation to Alchemy," *Transmutemini in vivos lapides philosophicos!* ("Transform yourselves into living philosophical stones!") [CW 12 §187].[20] Or as Nietzsche's Zarathustra put it, "Write with blood, and thou wilt find that blood is spirit" [Z I 7].) *Au fond*, all this intellectual-historical analysis has to have some kind of experiential dimension—the six-million-dollar question involves what form this might take:

[20] For further discussion of Jung's reception of Gerhard Dorn, see Thomas Willard, "The Star in Man: C.G. Jung und Maire-Louise von Franz on the Alchemical Philosophy of Gerhard Dorn," *Psychological Perspectives*, vol. 64, no. 1 (2021), 9-36.

educational? political? mystical? spiritual? aesthetic? For the alchemists and Nietzsche alike realize that, as Jung puts it, "it is *experience* which leads one closer to understanding" (CW 12 §564); closer, one should note, but not necessarily leading to full, actual understanding itself! Hence, it is no coincidence that the final image in the "Epilogue"—and hence, the entire volume of *Psychology and Alchemy*—is taken from the *Symbolographia, sive De arte symbolica: sermones septem* (1702) of the 17th-century Jesuit Jacob Bosch (1652-1704), and depicts, as a symbol of resurrection, the phoenix—the archetypal bird of transformation.

Figure 1. "The phoenix as symbol of resurrection," in Boschius, *Symbolographia*. Image in the public domain.

(e) "Paracelsus as a Spiritual Phenomenon" (1942)

A few years before he wrote his "Epilogue" for *Psychology and Alchemy*, Jung had been involved in the commemorations in 1941 for the 400th anniversary of the death of the great Swiss alchemist and philosopher of the German Renaissance, Philippus Aureolus

Theophrastus Bombastus von Hohenheim (1493/4-1541), more simply known as Paracelsus. To mark the occasion, celebrations were held at Einsiedeln, the municipal town near to Egg, a village close to the Etzel Pass, where in 1493, Paracelsus was born (in a house next to the *Teufelsbrücke*, a bridge across the Sihl River); and on 5 October 1941, Jung gave a lecture entitled "Paracelsus as a Spiritual Phenomenon."[21]

As part of the cultural and intellectual context to his discussion of the significance of Paracelsus, Jung provided one of those thumbnail historico-intellectual sketches at which he excelled, linking Paracelsus to two of the key figures in the tradition of the epic of transformation which we are exploring—Goethe and Nietzsche. According to Jung, Paracelsus had been a prototype of Faust, a figure whom Jacob Burckhardt had described as a "great primordial image" (*ein großes urtümliches Bild*)—and one that lay in the soul of the Germans as Oedipus had lain in the soul of every Greek in classical times (CW 13 §154).[22] From Faust there leads,

[21] For an overview of Paracelsus, see Rudolf Steiner, "Agrippa of Nettesheim and Theophrastus Paracelsus," in *Mysticism at the Dawn of the Modern Age*, trans. Karl. E. Zimmer (Blauvelt, NY: SteinerBooks, 1960), pp. 190-207; and Philip Ball, *The Devil's Doctor: Paracelsus and the World of Renaissance Magic and Science* (London: Heinemann, 2006); and for discussion of his influence, see Paul Bishop, "Paracelsus, Goethe, Jung," *Spring: A Journal of Archetype and Culture* [*Histories*], 64 (Fall/ Winter 1998), 135-158; and Bruce T. Moran, "Paracelsianism," in Glenn Alexander Magee (ed.), *The Cambridge Handbook of Western Mysticism and Esotericism* (Cambridge: Cambridge University Press, 2016), pp. 156-170. For extracts from his writings, see *Paracelsus: Selected Writings* [1951], ed. Jolande Jacobi, trans. Norbert Guterman (Princeton, NJ: Princeton University Press, 1979); and Paracelsus, *Essential Readings*, ed. and trans. Nicholas Goodrick-Clarke (Berkeley, CA: North Atlantic Books, 1999).

[22] See the footnote in *Transformations and Symbols of the Libido*, where Jung invites us to consider Burckhardt's letter to Albert Brenner of 11 November 1855, cited in Volume 1, p. 27: "What would the ancient Greeks have said had a commentator interposed himself between them and the Oedipus legend? There was a chord of the Oedipus legend in every Greek which longed to be touched directly and respond in its own way. And thus it is with the German nation and Faust" (PU §56; see Hans Brenner-Eglinger, "Briefe Jakob Burckhardts an Albert Brenner," *Basler Jahrbuch 1901*, 87-110 [p. 92]).

Jung says, a "direct line," via Max Stirner (1806-56), the author of *Der Einzige und sein Eigentum* (i.e., *The Individual and His Own*) (1845) and a somewhat neglected figure in intellectual history,[23] to Nietzsche, whom Jung describes as "a Faustian individual, if ever there was one" (§154).

If we want to appreciate what is so "Faustian" about Nietzsche, then we have to look more carefully at what Jung says here about Paracelsus. He compares what Paracelsus says about the divine office of the physician in *De caducis*, "I under the Lord, the Lord under me, I under him outside my office, and he under me outside his office" (*ich under dem herren, der herr under mir, ich under im außerhalb meins ampts und er under mir außerhalb seins ampts*),[24] to what the mystic and religious poet, Angelus Silesius (c. 1624-77), wrote in his *Cherubinischer Wandersmann* (i.e., *The Cherubinic Wanderer* or *Pilgrim*), in the form of two couplets:

> I am as great as God,
> And He as small as me;
> He cannot be above,
> Nor I below Him be.[25]

---

[23] For further discussion, see Michel Onfray, *Les radicalités existentielles* [*Contre-histoire de la philosophie*, vol. 6] (Paris: Grasset, 2009), pp. 293-348; Jacob Blumenfeld, *All Things Are Nothing To Me: The Unique Philosophy of Max Stirner* (Alresford: Zero Books, 2018); and Tim Dowdall, *Max Stirner and Nihilism: Between Two Nothings* (Rochester, NY: Camden House, 2024).

[24] Paracelsus, *Von den hinfallenden Siechtagen* [*De caducis*, Book 1], in *Sämtliche Werke*, ed. Karl Sudhoff and Wilhelm Matthiessen, section 1, *Medizinische, naturwissenschaftliche und philosophische Schriften*, 14 vols. (Munich and Berlin: Oldenbourg, 1922-1933), vol. 8, pp. 263-308 (p. 265).

[25] *The Cherubinic Wanderer*, Book 1, §10 (cited CW 13 §151); translated from Angelus Silesius, *Cherubinischer Wandersmann: Kritische Ausgabe*, ed. Louise Gnädinger (Stuttgart: Reclam,1985), p. 28. For the theological background to this work, see Josef Schmidt, "Foreword," in Angelus Silesius, *The Cherubinic Wanderer*, trans. Maria Shrady (Mahwah, NJ: Paulist Press, 1986), pp. ix-xv.

For Jung, these words capture the spirit of the Renaissance—an affirmation of the affinity between the human ego and God, especially with respect to human might, power of judgment, and beauty (*Schönheit*) (CW 13 §151). Thus, the clause in the Athanasian Creed, *quia Dominus noster Iesus Christus, Dei Filius, Deus* [*pariter*] *et homo est* (i.e., "our Lord Jesus Christ, the Son of God, is God and Man"), acquires a strikingly new meaning! Yet the direction toward the "heights of modernity" (*moderne Höhe*) is already set with Paracelsus's older contemporary, the German Kabbalist and occult thinker Agrippa von Nettesheim (1486-1535) who, in his skeptical satire on the state of science, *De incertitudine et vanitate scientiarum atque artium declamatio invectiva* (i.e., *Declamation Attacking the Uncertainty and Vanity of the Sciences and the Arts*, 1527; Jung quotes from the final revised edition of 1584), declares:

> Agrippa spares no man.
> He condemns, knows, knows not, weeps, laughs,
> waxes wroth, reviles, carps at all things;
> being himself philosopher, daimon, hero, God,
> and all things.
>
> (cited CW 13 §152)[26]

Already here, it is suggested, one sees how the kind of equilibrium found in Paracelsus and Angelus Silesius was beginning to disappear; and in the centuries that followed (and in the 20th

[26] Heinrich Cornelius Agrippa von Nettesheim, *De incertitudine et vanitate scientiarum* (Cologne, 1584). For an overview of the significance of Agrippa, see Steiner, "Agrippa of Nettesheim and Theophrastus Paracelsus," in *Mysticism at the Dawn of the Modern Age*, pp. 190-207; Michaela Valente, [entry on] "Heinrich Cornelius Agrippa," in Wouter J. Hanegraaff et al. (eds.), *Dictionary of Gnosis & Western Esotericism* (Leiden and Boston: Brill, 2006), pp. 4-8; and Wouter J. Hanegraaff, "Heinrich Cornelius Agrippa," in Christopher Partridge (ed.), *The Occult World* (London and New York: Routledge, 2015), pp. 92-99.

century in particular), the balance between the human ego and God was to sink lower and lower—to the advantage of an increasingly godlike ego.

Alongside the "inner piety" and "touching, yet dangerous simplicity" of Paracelsus and Angelus Silesius in their relation to God, Jung notices, however, the presence of the spirit of the earth (*der Erdgeist*), a chthonic force that emerged in Paracelsus to an increasing and sometimes terrifying degree (CW 13 §154). It is not hard to identify this *Erdgeist*—a figure found in Goethe's *Faust*, Part One—at least in this form with what elsewhere Jung calls the Dionysian … and it is significant that Jung associates this *Erdgeist* with manticism and magic (*Mantik und Magie*), noting that "magic was and still is a fascinosum" (§154). Of course, Jung knew what he was talking about when it came to magic; after all, he had devoted Chapter 19 of *Liber Secundus* in *The Red Book* to "The Gift of Magic," where he discusses with his soul what to do with a magical rod that looks like a thyrsus, that is, a wand or staff covered with ivy vines and leaves, associated with Dionysos (or Bacchus) and his followers, the satyrs and maenads (or bacchants), and described by Jung as a "black rod, formed like a serpent — with two pearls as eyes — a gold bangle around its neck" (RB, 379). Likewise, at the end of Part One of *Thus Spoke Zarathustra* in "Of the Bestowing Virtue," Zarathustra's disciples present him with the thyrsus-like gift of "a staff, on the golden handle of which a serpent twined round the sun," embodying what Zarathustra describes as a "new virtue": "Power is it, this new virtue; a ruling thought is it, and around it a subtle soul: a golden sun, with the serpent of knowledge around it" (Z I 22 §1).

Further on in "Paracelsus as a Spiritual Phenomenon," Jung returns to Paracelsus's formula, "I under the Lord, the Lord under me"—or as Jung puts it this time, "I under God" (*ich unter Gott*) and "God under me" (*Gott unter mir*)—a formula in which the latter element is an expression for how the human individual takes the place of the Creator. In so doing, Jung argues, medieval alchemy had been preparing the way for the "greatest intervention in the divine world-order that humankind had ever attempted": On this account, alchemy was far from being opposed to science; rather, alchemy itself was the "*dawn of the scientific age*" (CW 13 §163). As a consequence of the rise of science, the daimon of the scientific spirit, as Jung put it, compelled nature and its forces into the service of humankind as never before: a development reflected for Jung in two iconic texts, Goethe's *Faust* and Nietzsche's *Zarathustra*. As if playing on the subtitle of Nietzsche's *The Birth of Tragedy*, i.e., *out of the Spirit of Music*, Jung declares that Goethe created the figure of that "superman," Faust, "out of the spirit of alchemy." In turn, out of the figure of the *Übermensch* Nietzsche's Zarathustra was able (a) to declare that God was dead; and (b) to announce the will to give birth to the *Übermensch* out of one's sense of power; or as Zarathustra himself puts it in "Of the Way of the Creating One," "to create a God for oneself out of one's seven devils" (Z I 17). Here, in Jung's view, lie the "true roots" or the "secular, psychic preparatory processes" leading to "those factors that are at work in the world today," a world that has been conquered by science—but, he suggests, at the expense of the psyche itself.

In a footnote, Jung expands his commentary on the passage from *Zarathustra*, providing the following extracts:

> Thou lonesome one, thou goest the way to thyself! And past thyself and thy seven devils leadeth thy way!
>
> [...]
>
> Ready must thou be to burn thyself in thine own flame; how couldst thou become new if thou have not first become ashes!
>
> Thou lonesome one, thou goest the way of the creating one: a God wilt thou create for thyself out of thy seven devils! (Z I 17)

In Jung's eyes, there is a clear parallel between the imagery found in this passage and the following from the alchemical work "Consilium coniugii" in the collection *Ars Chemica* (1566), "Our stone slays itself with its own dart" (*lapis noster proprio iaculo interficit seipsum*), as well as the more general notion of *incineratio* and the emblem of the phoenix among the alchemists (CW 13 §163).[27] (Tracing such parallels is, of course, the basis of Jung's entire methodology; rather than seeking to demonstrate influence, he hopes thereby to gain access to archetypal images that express themselves across times and cultures in an identifiable way.)

Given this parallel, one is tempted to apply Jung's subsequent remarks about Paracelsus in this section to the figure of Nietzsche himself. Paracelsus's preoccupation with alchemy (like Nietzsche's preoccupation with the Dionysian) exposed him to an influence that left its mark on his spiritual being (as it did on Nietzsche's). For the innermost striving of alchemy was a presumption (as was Nietzsche's project to create the *Übermensch*), the "daimonic grandeur" as well as the "psychic danger" of which ought not to be underestimated. (In the light of Nietzsche's mental collapse in Turin, the warning given by Olympiodorus of Alexandria that "in lead [i.e., Saturn] there is a shameless daimon [i.e., the *spiritus mercurii*] who drives men mad," seems particularly apposite.)[28] This combination of "daimonic grandeur" and "psychic danger" was, according to Jung, the source of that "proud arrogance and self-overestimation" which, in the case of Paracelsus, contrasted with "true Christian humility" (just as, in the case of Nietzsche,

[27] *Consilium Coniugii de massa solis et lunae*, in *Ars Chemica, quod sit licita recte exercentibus, probationes doctissimorum iurisconsultorum* (Strasbourg, 1566), pp. 48-263 (p. 186).

[28] Olympiodorus, *Commentary on Zosimus' "On Action*"; in Berthelot, *Collection des anciens alchimistes grecs*, vol. 1, II.iv, §43 (p. 104). For further discussion, see Cristina Viano, "Olympiodorus and Greco-Alexandrian Alchemy," in Albert Joosse (ed.), *Olympiodorus of Alexandria: Exegete, Teacher, Platonic Philosopher* (Leiden and Boston: Brill, 2021), pp. 14-30.

there was a striking contrast between the *Übermensch* emerging like a bolt of lightning from the thundercloud—and the shy, retired professor eating his lunch with the other guests at the *Pension* in Sils Maria). What erupted so volcanically in those lines by Agrippa von Nettesheim about himself as "daimon, hero, God," remained "hidden" in Paracelsus "beneath the threshold of a Christian consciousness," and only expressed itself in "certain exaggerated claims" and his "irritable sense of self-importance." (Jung explains this symptom as a result of a sense of inferiority, a sense that he claimed to have detected in Nietzsche too.) Nevertheless, Jung believed he could read between the lines and discern the ambiguous status of Paracelsus, sounding a critical note about his personality while paying tribute to the significance of his thought. On the occasion of the 400th anniversary of his death, these insights served as a fitting commemoration of this fascinating, if frequently overlooked, figure in the history of Western thought.

Nietzsche's *Zarathustra* in *Mysterium Coniunctionis* (1955-1956)

Now Jung's most extensive reckoning with alchemy was the two-volume work, *Mysterium Coniunctionis*, to which Marie-Louise von Franz contributed a third volume, a study of the 15th-century alchemical treatise *Aurora consurgens* (i.e., *Rising Dawn*) attributed to St. Thomas Aquinas.[29] (Without getting caught up in the complex arguments for or against Thomas's authorship of the *Aurora*, suffice it to say that while its author clearly knows biblical and liturgical texts in great detail, and alchemical literature

[29] Marie-Louise von Franz (ed.), *Aurora Consurgens: A Document Attributed to Thomas Aquinas of the Problem of Opposites in Alchemy* [1957], trans. R.F.C. Hull and A.S.B. Glover (New York and London: Bollingen Foundation, 1966); and C.G. Jung, *Mysterium Coniunctionis* [...]: *Ergänzungsband «Aurora Consurgens»: Ein dem Thomas von Aquin zugeschriebenes Dokument der alchemistischen Gegensatzproblematik von Dr. M.-L. von Franz* [*Gesammelte Werke*, vol. 14/iii] (Olten and Freiburg im Breisgau: Walter, 1971).

less so, which might support Thomasian authorship, its style is largely different from Aquinas's other writings.) The treatise's title, of course, reminds one of the title of Nietzsche's *Dawn of Day* (although, in this case. it is more likely to be a reference to the Rig Veda (Book 7, hymn 76, entitled "Dawn"), while in his Preface, Nietzsche makes a mysterious reference to "this seeming Trophonius and subterranean man," alluding to Plutarch's account in his "On the Sign of Socrates" (*De genio Socratis*) of Timarchus's ascent into the cave of the oracle Trophonius, from which after spending two nights and a day he emerged "in the morning with a radiant countenance" (§22).[30]

In his foreword to *Mysterium Coniunctionis,* Jung restates his basic theory of alchemy as developed in volumes 12, 13, and 14 of his *Collected Works*. On this account, alchemy as an "art" does not belong on the "rubbish heap of the past" but rather stands in a "very real and living relationship" to modern psychology and, more precisely, provides Analytical Psychology with a "meaningful historical basis" (CW 14 xiii).[31] Noting the pioneering work done in this respect by Herbert Silberer (1882-1923) in his 1914 study, *Problems of Mysticism and its Symbolism*, Jung argued that the alchemical saying, *solve et coagula* (that is, "dissolve and coagulate"), was the key to the so-called "spagyric" art (a term derived from σπάειν, i.e., "to rend, tear, stretch out," and ἀγείρειν, i.e., "to bring or collect together"). In other words, it involved a dual movement of (a) analysis and separation, as well as (b) synthesis and consolidation, in a process that regarded the initial state of conflict, or *chaos,* as the *prima materia* to be *transformed* … but

[30] "De Genio Socratis," in Plutarch, *Moralia*, vol. 7, trans. Philip H. De Lacy and Benedict Einarson (London; New York; Heinemann; Putnam, 1959), pp. 361-509.
[31] For her encouragement in engaging with this most challenging of Jung's works, and the suggestion that it completes the project begun in *The Red Book*, I am grateful to Pamela J. Power. For a helpful introduction to Jung's last *magnum opus*, see Edward F. Edinger, *The Mysterium Lectures: A Journey through C.G. Jung's "Mysterium Coniunctionis,"* ed. Joan Dexter Blackmer (Toronto: Inner City Books, 1995).

transformed into what? The goal or end-state could be described in numerous ways, including:

- its permanence (prolongation of life, immortality, incorruptibility)
- its androgyny
- its spirituality and corporeality
- its human qualities (the homunculus)
- and sometimes even in terms of its divinity.

In Jung's eyes, this process of transformation is *analogous* to the problem of the opposites in the psychic sphere, and the concomitant dissociation of the personality which inevitably arises from such a conflict of incompatible tendences within the ego. On his account, the alchemical motif of the "chymical wedding" corresponds to one of the chief dynamics of psychoanalysis, the "transference" (CW 14 xv). With its numerous synonyms, the "philosophers' stone" or *lapis philosophorum*, sometimes equated by the alchemists with Christ, corresponds to the Jungian conception of the Self.

Before examining more closely what Jung says about the *coniunctio* and how it relates to Nietzsche, we should remember that the very title of Jung's study acknowledges that the *coniunctio* is a *mysterium*. In Chapter 1, Jung examines the components of the *coniunctio*, while in Chapter 6, he delineates its various stages. Yet an extra dimension emerges if we recall that, in *Liber Primus* of *The Red Book*, Chapter 9 is entitled "Mysterium. Encounter," the action of which informs the concluding Chapters 10 and 11, entitled "Instruction" and "Resolution." Without neglecting the important differences in genre between these two works, it is safe to say that both *The Red Book* and *Mysterium Coniunctionis* are focused on the question of transformation. We might even go so far as to say that *Mysterium Coniunctionis* is a reformulation, using alchemical language and imagery, of the process that Jung had experientially traced in his *Red Book* four decades earlier. At the same time, it also gave him the opportunity to engage for one final time with

Nietzsche and his *Zarathustra*; here, as before, inserting Nietzsche into his overarching narrative account of the trajectory of Western intellectual history.

For instance, a prayer entitled the "Secret Inscription" contained in the Great Magic Papyrus of Paris invokes "the Spirit of the air [...], Spirit, that penetratest from heaven to earth [...], Spirit that penetratest into me, and shakest me," in such a remarkable way that it prompts Jung to consider its more general significance. (Once again, this prayer recalls the opening scene of *Faust* where Faust conjures up the Earth Spirit, albeit without much long-term success.) Jung calls the prayer a "magnificent description" of a spirit that is "apparently the exact opposite" to the *pneuma* of Christian doctrine (CW 14 §251-§252). (In Judaic and Christian usage, one may recall, *pneuma* (πνεῦμα) is the most common word used for "spirit" in the Septuagint and the Greek New Testament, used to translate the *ruach* of the Hebrew Bible and distinguishable from *psyche* (ψυχή), the "breath of life" or "soul.") This antique way of viewing the spirit is, according to Jung, also the "spirit of alchemy"; and, as such, a spirit which can nowadays be understood as a "projection of the unconscious into space and objects" (§252). Now while Christianity later came to explain this spirit as being the Devil, it is not, Jung argues, in fact identical with evil itself; rather, it has the "uncomfortable characteristic" of actually being "*beyond* good and evil," and of lending this quality as a "dangerous gift" (*das gefährliche Geschenk*) to anyone who identifies with it—Nietzsche and the "epidemic that followed him" being a telling case, he adds.

Yet being "beyond good and evil" is, Jung declares, emphatically *not* the same as being "six thousand feet beyond good and evil" (a reference to Nietzsche's account in *Ecce Homo* of the basic conception of *Zarathustra*, that is, the idea of eternal recurrence, as having occurred to him in August 1881 and being jotted down in a piece of paper with the inscription, "Six thousand feet beyond man and time" [EH Z §1; cf. KSA 9, 11[141], 494). Rather, it is the same distance "below" or, better, "before" it—in the sense that it is the "spirit of the chaotic watery depths [*Urgewässer*]" that were there before the second day of Creation, or in other words, before the division into opposites, and hence *prior* to consciousness (CW 14 §252). Consequently, it leads anyone who "succumbs" (*verfällt*) to it neither "upwards" nor "beyond," but only "back"—back into the "chaos of the primal world [*Urwelt*]" (§252).

This spirit—the spirit of alchemy, the spirit that is "beyond good and evil," and hence a spirit that sounds, to this reader at least, very Dionysian—corresponds on Jung's account to that part of the psyche which has "not yet been assimilated into the conscious individual," and whose transformation (*Wandlung*) and integration represented the objective of a long and laborious *opus* on the part of the alchemist (§252). (In fact, it surely sounds rather like the process of self-overcoming or *Selbstüberwindung* as Nietzsche conceived it.) According to Jung, the artifex (that is, the alchemist trying to bring about the union of the opposites) was conscious of the dangers involved in this work, and for this reason, many of the operations corresponded closely to the rituals of the Church—not an option, of course, that was available to Nietzsche. And yet the parallel still stands: The "return to chaos" was, Jung claims, understood by the alchemists to be part of the *opus*, and Nietzsche's Zarathustra insists on the importance of chaos: "I tell you: one must still have chaos in one, to give birth to a dancing star," he declares in the Prologue, "I tell you: ye have still chaos in you" (Z Prologue §5). In both cases, alchemical and Nietzschean, the interest in chaos is not in chaos for the sake of chaos, but in chaos as a preliminary to *transformation*.

Now the key to this transformation is the integration of the inferior part of the self, sometimes called the shadow. Yet it is precisely this part that is so often ignored: In alchemical terms, the part that is associated with coldness, heaviness, melancholy, etc. (CW 14 §330). The masculine, solar part of the self (occupying on the diagram below the right half of the quaternio) does not want to know anything about this other part, because it identifies "as closely as possible with consciousness," that is to say, with the "idea which one has of oneself" (§330). As a consequence, the shadow is left out of account: first, because no one likes to admit to anything inferior; and second, because logic itself forbids that anything white be called black. Our sense of prestige means that we remain silent.

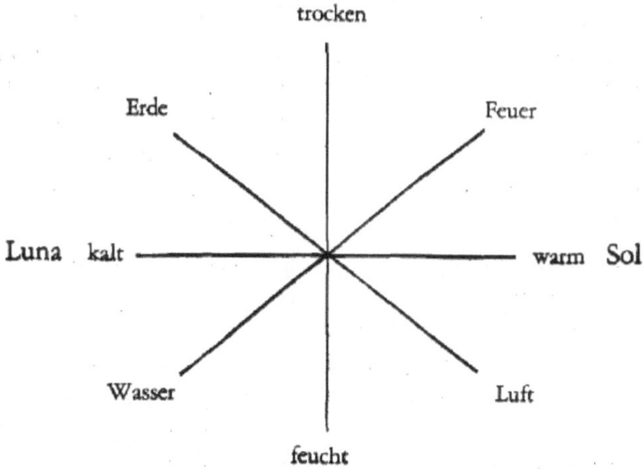

Yet, Nietzsche gives voice to this suppressed, forgotten, and allegedly inferior part of the self, but he does so in two different ways, depending on whether we read the English translation of *Mysterium Coniunctionis* or the original German. In the German original, Jung cites as an example of "masculine prejudice" Nietzsche's *Übermensch* and the "blond beast,"[32] an animal that he associates with the lion as a "gleaming, golden solar animal": in Christian terms, an *allegoria diaboli* and an emblem of paganism (and, for this reason, often depicted as forming the base of columns); and, in alchemical terms, the stage of warm-bloodedness which is reached after killing the *draco mercurialis*, and an emblem of

32 Cf. *On the Genealogy of Morals*, Essay 1, §11; Essay 2, §17; and *Twilight of the Idols*, 'The "Improvers" of Humankind', §2.

unbridled concupiscence (which is why his paws have to be cut off) (GW 14/i §324).

On Jung's account, the *Übermensch* seeks to resist (a) pity or compassion (*Mitleid*); and (b) the Ugliest Man, but only the Ugliest Man is mentioned in R.F.C. Hull's translation in the *Collected Works*, which excises the references to the blond beast. Now, who is the Ugliest Man? Here he is described by Jung as the "ordinary individual that everyone is," and this ordinary individual *is* in reality the shadow, something that "must not be seen" but must be denied (*geleugnet*), repressed (*verdrängt*), or twisted into something unusual (*in etwas Ungewöhnliches umgebogen*) (CW 14 §330). In the ordinary and everyday world (and isn't this so true?), the sun "is always shining" and everything "reflects its light back"; there is no space for any weakness that might reduce our prestige; and in alchemical terms, the *sol niger*, that is, the black sun (referring to the first stage of the alchemical magnum opus, the *nigredo* [i.e., the blackening, putrefaction, or decomposition]) is never to be seen; yet, Jung concludes, its presence is feared "in solitary hours" (§330). (In Heideggerian terms, what Jung is describing here is what, in *Being and Time*, is called *das Man*, or "the They" or "the un-owned self" as opposed to my "authentic self.")

Further on in *Mysterium Coniunctionis*, Jung discusses Nietzsche and his *Zarathustra* in a series of asides or footnotes as part of a larger discussion of the figures of the alchemical king and queen and, in particular, of a work by the English alchemist Sir George Ripley (c. 1415-90), his *Cantilena* (sometimes called *George Ripley's Song*). Because of the difficulty in locating this text, it is reproduced in full here (for convenience of reference, its stanzas are numbered):[33]

[33] The text is cited across a number of paragraphs in CW 14 and published in a collated form transcribed by Justin von Bujdoss on The Alchemy Web Site. Available HTTP: <https://www.alchemywebsite.com/cantilen.html>. Accessed 5 June 2024. See also F. Sherwood Taylor, "George Ripley's Song," *Ambix*, vol. 2, no. 3-4 (1946), 177-181.

Cantilena (George Ripley's Song)

[1] Behold! and in this Cantilena see
The hidden secrets of Philosophy:
What Joy ariseth from the Merry veines
Of Minds Elated by such dulcid Straines!

[2] Through Roman Countreys as I once did passe
Where Mercuries Nuptiall Celebrated was,
And feeding stoutly (on the Bride-Groomes score)
I learn'd these Novelties unknowne before.

[3] There was a certaine Barren King by Birth,
Composed of the Purest, Noblest Earth,
By Nature Sanguine (which is faire) yet hee
Sadly bewailed his Authoritie.

[4] Wherefore am I a King, and Head of all
Those Men and things that be Corporeall?
I have no issue, yet (I'le not deny)
Tis Mee both Heaven and Earth are Ruled by.

[5] Yet there is either a Cause Naturall
Or some Defect in the Originall:
For though the Wombe I never opened
I under Titan's wings was nourished.

[6] Each vegative which from the Earth proceeds
Ariseth up with its own proper Seeds:
And Animalls (at Seasons) speciously
Abound with Fruit, and strangly Multiply.

[7] But yet my Nature is so much Restrain'd
No Tincture from my Body can be gain'd:
And therefore it is Infoecund: nor can
It ought availe, in Generating Man.

[8] My Body's Masse is of a Lasting-Stuffe,
Exceeding Delicate, yet hard enough:
And when the Fire Assays to try my Sprite,
I am not found to weigh a grain too light.

[9] My Mother got me of a Sphaere, that I
Might contemplate the Globes Rotunditie;
And be more Pure of kind than other things,
By Right of Dignity Assisting Kings.

[10] Yet to my Griefe I know, unlesse I find
Forthwith Assistance out of my owne Kind
I cannot Generate; My Blood Growes Cold:
I am amaz'd to think I am so Old.

[11] Death me Assail'd, even in my Strength of yeares,
But yet Christ's voice did penetrate the Sphaeres,
And (to Amazement) told me from above
I should Revive ; I know well by whose Love.

[12] By other meanes I cannot enter Heaven:
And therefore (that I may be Borne agen)
I'le Humbled be into my Mother's Breast
Dissolve to what I was. And therein rest.

[13] Hereat the Mother Animates the King,
Hasts his Conception, and doth forthwith bring
And hide him closely underneath her Traine
Till (of herselfe) sh'had made him Flesh againe.

[14] 'Twas wonderfull to see with what a grace
This Naturall Union (made at one Imbrace)
Did looke; and by a League both sexes knitt,
Like to a Hill and Aire surrounding it.

[15] The Mother unto her Chast Chamber goes
Where in a Bed of Honour she Bestowes
Her weary'd selfe, 'twixt Sheets as white as Snow
And there makes Signes of her approaching woe.

[16] Ranke Poison issuing from the Dying Man
Made her pure Orient face look foule and wan:
Hence she commands all Strangers to be gone
Seals upp her Chamber doore, and lyes Alone.

[17] Meanwhile the Peacocks Flesh she kindly Eate,
And Dranke Greene-Lyons Blood (with that fine Meate)
Which Mercury (although in Passion:)
Brought in a Golden Cupp of Babilon.

[18] Thus great with Child, 9 months she languished
And Bath'd her with the Teares which she had shed
For his sweete sake, who should from her be Pluckt
Full-gorg'd with Milke which the Greene-Lyon suckt.

[19] Her Skin of divers Colours did appeare
Now Black, then Greene, annon 'twas Read, and Cleare:
Oft-times she would sitt upright in her Bed,
And then again repose her Troubled Head.

[20] Thrice Fifty Nights she lay in grievous Plight,
As many daies in Mourning sate upright:
The King Revived was in thirty more
Whose Birth was Fragrant as the Prim-Rose Flower.

[21] Her wombe which well proportion'd was at First
Is now Enlarg'd a Thousand fold at least:
That of his Entrance Men might witnesse this
The End, by Fires, the best approved is.

[22] Her Chamber's without Rocks, it smoothly stands,
With walls Erected like her Ivory Hands.
Or else the Fruit (for want of Fertile ground)
Had been nought worth, the Sonnes (to beare) unsound.

[23] One Staffe was placed underneath her Bed,
And on the same another Flourished:
Trimmed up with Art, and very Temperate,
Least her fine Limbs should freeze for lack of heate.

[24] Her Chamber doore was Lock'd and Bolted fast,
Admitting none to Trouble her, First, or Last:
The Furnace-Mouth likewise contrived, so,
That thence no vapourous Matter forth could goe.

[25] And when the Issue there was Putrifyed
The Fine from Filthy flesh she did Divide:
Ressembling Phoebe in her Fullest Light
And Breathing, Sol himselfe was not more Bright.

[26] Her time being come, what she conceiv'd before
Is now Re-borne, (sets ope her Chamber-door;
And being soe) resumes a Kingly State
Possessing fully Heaven's Propitious Fate.

[27] The Mother's Bed which erst stood in a Square
Is shortly after made Orbicular:
And on each side the Covering (as Round)
With Luna's Lustre Rightly doth Abound.

[28] Thus from a square, the Bed a Globe is made
Fair, white, and cleare emerges from the shade
Of Night, whence doth a Ruddy Nature spring
T'enjoy the Merry Scepter of a King.

[29] Hence God sett ope the Gates of Paradise,
Where Cynthia deckt him in Coelestiall Guise,
Sublim'd him to the Heavens, and when sh'had done,
Crown'd him in Glory, aequall with the Sun.

[30] Foure Elements, Brave Armes, and Polish'd well
God gave him : In the mid'st whereof did dwell
A Crowned Maid, ordained for to be
In the fifth Circle [of the Mystery]:

[31] With all delicious unguent flowed she
When Purg'd from Bloody Menstruosity:
On every side her Count'nance Brightly shone,
She being adorn'd with every Precious Stone.

[32] A Lyon Greene did in her Lapp reside
(the which an Eagle fed) and from whose Side
Blood gushed out: the virgin drunck it upp,
Whilst Mercury's Hand did th'Office of a Cupp.

[33] The Milk (admir'd) she hastened from her Breast
Bestow'd it frankly on the Hungry Beast,
And with a Sponge his face she likewise dry'd
Which her own Milke had often Madefy'd.

[34] Upon her Head a Diadem she did weare
With Fiery Feete sh'Advanced into the Aire;
And glittering Bravely in her Golden Robes
Tooke place ith' Middle of the Starry Globes.

[35] Thus Shee (by all the Planetes, Times, and Signes,
Dark, and Despised Clouds supported), Shines
and sits in Haire of Nett-worke, whilst the king
With his Glad Eyes, is, her Beleagreing.

[36] Thus she Triumphantly of kings is Chiefe
Of Body's sick the only Grand Reliefe:
Such a Reformist of Defects, that shee
is worshipped by Men of each degree.

[37] To Priests and Kings she yields an Ornament,
The sick and needy sort she doth content:
What Man is hee will slight so Rich a Store,
As drowns the very thought of being Poore?

[38] Wherefore (O God !) vouchsafe to graunt us this,
That through th' Encrease made of its species
And Second Birth, wee may ones and Agen
Enjoy its Firtile and Sweete Fruits. AMEN.

Without rehearsing in full Jung's extensive commentary on this text, let us focus on a few details in his interpretation of the *Cantilena* that form the backdrop to his discussion of Nietzsche.

To begin with, as a methodological aside in Chapter 4 on the alchemical King and Queen (or "Rex and Regina"), Jung notes that the "displacement and overlapping of images" in alchemy are as great as in mythology or folklore. He explains this displacement and overlapping with reference to the fact that, as "archetypal images," they are produced "directly by the unconscious" and hence "exhibit its contamination of content"—as illustrated in dreams by the "interconnection of everything with everything" —to a high degree (CW 14 §401). In fact, the reason why the "best instances" of this "interconnection of everything with everything," a phrase he also uses in his seminar on *Zarathustra* (86), are said to be found in dreams, is because they are very much closer to the unconscious than is myth (fn. 140).

The *Cantilena*'s use of the motif of the "sick King" reminds Jung of the Grail legend (and the ailing Fisher King), although he sets to one side the question of any influence (CW 14 §368). Nevertheless, he regards it as "conceivable" that, as an Englishman, Ripley would have been "acquainted" with this tradition, and that, apart from the evidence of the "*lapis exilis*" (or "*lapsit exillis*") in Wolfram von Eschenbach's *Parzival*, he had not been able to find any "more likely" traces of the Grail cycle in alchemical symbolism, aside from the parallel between the "mystic vessel of transformation" and the chalice in the Mass (see below, p. 336). (However, at this point Jung might have mentioned the frequent references to alchemy in Emma Jung's and Marie-Louise von Franz's study of the Grail legend …).

When discussing the decrepit condition of the alchemical king as depicted in stanza 10, for example, Jung notes that it was a "bold stroke" for Ripley, as an Augustinian canon, to identify the alchemical king with the "Ancient of Days," a figure from the Book of Daniel—"his garment was white as snow, and the hair of his head like clean wool: his throne like flames of fire: the wheels of it like a burning fire" (7:9). Jung offers a shrewd explanation of this identification, suggesting that Ripley-as-an-alchemist was speculating "over the head" of Ripley-as-a-cleric to express an idea that, in the context of the Middle Ages, can only have seemed like blasphemy—namely, that the "transformative substance" was God (CW 14 §374). To our way—that is, the modern way—of thinking, this older kind of thinking, which Jung describes as "allegory" or "symbolization," appears as absurd or unintelligible; as, indeed, it may well also have done in the Middle Ages themselves. And yet, Jung goes on, where allegory or symbolization does find acceptance—for example, in philosophical alchemy—this fact might explain the hymnlike, highly emotional language used. For on Jung's account, a new theology is emerging here: God is not only in the immaculate body of Christ and present in the consecrated Host but also hidden in the "cheap," the "despised," in the "uncleanness of this world, in filth" (*in immunditia huius mundi, in stercore*) (§374).[34] (Here again—one thinks of *The Red Book.*)

Thus, God is to be found only "through the art," that is, alchemy; indeed, God is the *object* of the art, and hence he is capable of "progressive transformation," in line with the motto, *Deo adjuvante* ("by the help of God"). This theology did *not* posit that God was "nothing but a substance that could be contained by chemical transformation," although this *is* a view that tends to be held by moderns, Jung believes, who "put matter or energy in the place of God" (CW 14 §374). In the case of the alchemists, many of whom were still pagans, their more mystical conception of God dated from late antiquity; as an example, Jung cites the case of Zosimos of Panopolis, the Egyptian-born Greek alchemist and mystic from the end of the third and the beginning of the fourth century C.E., whose outlook was essentially Gnostic. (Then again, some Christians held views that were strongly influenced by such pagan magical concepts as daimons, divine powers, and the *anima mundi*, that is, a part of God inherent in physical nature.)

The view that God could age and require renewal (which features so prominently in his *Red Book*) derives, Jung says, from ancient Egypt, but he professes ignorance about where Ripley, the so-called "Canon of Bridlington," could have discovered such a theology in the 15th century—other than in the Bible. A clue can be found, he suggests, in the alchemical tradition in its notion of a "corrupt arcane substance whose corruption is due to original sin" (CW 14 §375). After all, Jung reminds us again, a similar idea can

---

[34] See Johann Daniel Mylius, *Philosophia reformata* (Frankfurt am Main, 1622); compare with the alchemical dictum, *in stercore invenitur aurum nostrum* ("in the dung-heap our gold is found") ("Tractatus aureus," in *Ars Chemica*, p. 21).

be found in the Grail tradition, where the figure of the sick King is closely connected with the transformation mystery of the Mass. In the case of Parzival, for instance, the King is the ancestor of the hero, whom one could describe as a "redeemer figure," and in the alchemical tradition, the old King either has a son who is a redeemer or becomes a redeemer figure himself. (Symbolically, Jung suggests, this is represented by the fact that the *lapis* is said to be the same at the beginning and at the end of the alchemical procedure.)

A few paragraphs later, however, Jung answers his own question about the provenance of the motif of God's senescence, suggesting that it could have been an "autochthonous revival of the mythologem from the collective unconscious," or perhaps a modification of the conception of the "Ancient of Days" and his youthful son, the Logos—represented as a divine child or "naked boy" in the visions of the Gnostic theologian Valentinus and Meister Eckhart (CW 14 §378-§379).[35] Here Jung finds a parallel

[35] Cf. CW 11 §741; see one of the four legends about Eckhart called "The Naked Boy," which consists of the following short dialogue:

> He said, "I come from God."
> "Where did you leave Him?"
> "In virtuous hearts."
> "Where are you going?"
> "To God."
> "Where will you find Him?"
> "Where I abandoned all creatures."
> "Who are you?"
> "A king."
> "Where is your kingdom?"
> "Mind that no one shares it with you."
> "I will."
> Then he took the boy into his cell and said, "Take whichever coat you like."
> "Then I would not be a king!" And he vanished.
> It was God Himself having fun with him.

(Meister Eckhart, *Sermons & Treatises*, ed. and trans. Maurice O'Connell Walshe, 3 vols. (Longmead: Element Books, 1987), vol. 3, p. 138). For discussion of the status of this legend, see Dagmar Gottschall, "Eckhart and the Vernacular Tradition: Pseudo-Eckhart and Eckhart Legends," in Jeremiah M. Hackett (ed.), *A Companion to Meister Eckhart* (Leiden and Boston: Brill, 2013), pp. 509-551.

to Dionysos, as the youngest of the gods (according to Jane Ellen Harrison, the name Dionysos itself means "young Zeus,"[36] while the second element of his name, *-nūsos*, has been associated with Mount Nysa, the birthplace of the god in Greek mythology, where he was nursed by its nymphs, known as the Nysiads),[37] and to the Egyptian child god Horus, Hellenized as Harpocrates, and to Aion, the Hellenistic deity usually identified as a (semi)nude or young man within a circle representing the zodiac. As Jung emphasizes, with a footnote reference to a work by the Jesuit theologian and Church historian Hugo Rahner (1900-68) (and the elder brother of the famous theologian Karl Rahner), the step from the world of Christian ideas back to paganism is not so long at all.[38]

In his commentary on stanzas 11 and 12, Jung argues that, in order to enter the Kingdom of God, the alchemical King must "transform himself into the *prima materia* in the body of his mother," thereby returning to "chaos," as the alchemists called the "dark, initial state" (CW 14 §380). In the *massa confusa*, all the elements are in a state of mutual conflict; or as Jung puts it, "dissolution is the prerequisite for redemption" (§381). Likewise, in order to attain transformation, the celebrant of the Mysteries was said to have to undergo a figurative death. And in the Mysteries as

[36] Jane Ellen Harrison, *Myths of Greece and Rome* (Garden City, New York: Doubleday, Doran, 1928), p. 66. Despite his name, Harrison sees Dionysos as "essentially the son of his mother, Semele," and as later "affiliated to Zeus by a rebirth."

[37] "The word Dionysos is divisible into two parts, the first originally Διος (cf. Ζευς), while the second is of an unknown signification, although perhaps connected with the name of the Mount Nysa which figures in the story of Lykourgos: [...] when Dionysos had been reborn from the thigh of Zeus, Hermes entrusted him to the nymphs of Mount Nysa, who fed him on the food of the gods, and made him immortal" (William Sherwood Fox, *The Mythology of All Races*, vol. 1, *Greek and Roman* (Boston: Marshall Jones, 1916), p. 217.

[38] See Hugo Rahner, "Die Gottesgeburt," *Zeitschrift für katholische Theologie*, 59 (1935), 333-418 (pp. 341-342). Rahner lectured several times at the Eranos Conferences, including in 1944; see "The Christian Mystery and the Pagan Mysteries," in *The Mysteries: Papers from the Eranos Yearbooks*, ed. Joseph Campbell (London: Routledge & Kegan Paul, 1955), pp. 337-401.

in alchemy, the transformation being sought was a "miracle"—and as such could take place "only with God's help" (§381).

In stanzas 14-17, the focus shifts from the King to the figure of the alchemical Queen or mother, and Jung highlights her choice for her pregnancy diet, or the "feeding" of the "transformative substance" (CW 14 §388). Sometimes the material to be transformed had to be impregnated and saturated by "imbibing the tincture" (that is, the *aqua propria,* or its "own water," the soul), by eating its "feathers" or "wings" (that is, the volatile spirit), or by eating its own tail (that is, like the uroboros), or eating from the philosophical tree; here, in the case of Ripley's *Cantilena*, the substance is "peacock's flesh," associated with all the shimmering colors of its tail, and hence with the lapis itself (§388-§389). (Perhaps it is telling that, in "Of the Poets," Zarathustra relates the sea—read by Jung as a symbol of the unconscious—to the colorful peacock tail, saying: "They have learned from the sea also its vanity: is not the sea the peacock of peacocks? / Even before the ugliest of all buffaloes doth it spread out its tail; never doth it tire of its lace-fan of silver and silk" (Z II 17)? In the end, Zarathustra is suspicious of this poetic splendor, remarking: "What is beauty and sea and peacock-splendour to it! This parable I speak unto the poets. / Verily, their spirit itself is the peacock of peacocks, and a sea of vanity!" [Z I 17].)[39]

Commenting on Gerhard Dorn's remark—made in his *Of the Chymical Transmutation, Genealogy and Generations of Metals and Minerals* ["Congeries Paracelsicae chemicae de

[39] And he chooses to use the same imagery when angrily dismissing the Magician in Part Four, when he cries: "Flatter not, […] thou stage-player from the heart! Thou art false: why speakest thou — of truth! / Thou peacock of peacocks, thou sea of vanity; WHAT didst thou represent before me, thou evil magician; WHOM was I meant to believe in when thou wailedst in such wise?", to which the Magician replies: "THE PENITENT IN SPIRIT, […] it was him — I represented; thou thyself once devisedst this expression — / — The poet and magician who at last turneth his spirit against himself, the transformed one [*den Verwandelten*] who freezeth to death by his bad science and conscience" (Z IV 5 §2).

transmutatione metallorum"] (1581) included in Volume 1 of the *Theatrum chemicum* (1602)—that the "dead spiritual body" is the "bird without wings," which "changes into the raven's head and finally into the peacock's tail," after which it "attains to the whitest plumage of the swan" and, last of all, to the "highest redness, the sign of its fiery nature,"[40] Jung explains that this last detail alludes to the phoenix which (like the peacock) plays a significant role in the alchemical tradition as a "symbol of renewal and resurrection" (CW 14 §396). And, in a highly significant footnote, Jung cites the following quotation from the 12th-century theologian Honorius Augustodunensis (c. 1080-1154), commonly known as Honorius of Autun: "The phoenix is said to be red, and is Christ, of whom it is written: Who is this that cometh out of Edom, with dyed garments from Bosra? […] Edom, which means red, is the name given to Esau, from the red pottage with which he was fed by Jacob his brother."[41]

The significance of this footnote lies in the choice of biblical text cited here by Honorius, which also includes the lines: "Why then is thy apparel red, and thy garments like theirs that tread in the wine-press? […] and their blood is sprinkled upon my garments, and I have stained all my apparel" (Isaiah 63:2-3). For these verses are *identical* to those from the prophet Isaiah, which Jung cites at the beginning of *Liber Primus* in his *Red Book*; and so, through these textual references and allusions, Jung is signaling a continuity between his early work on *The Red Book* and his last great book, *Mysterium Coniunctionis*, both of which (albeit in their differing ways) place emphasis on the theme of transformation.

[40] See Gerhard Dorn, "Congeries Paraceliscae chemicae de transmutatione metallorum," in *Theatrum Chemicum*, 6 vols. (Ursel, 1602; Strasbourg, 1613-61), vol. 1, pp. 557-646 (p. 599).

[41] Honorius Augustodunensis, *Speculum de mysteriis Ecclesiae* (Jacques Paul Migne (ed.), *Patrologiae cursus completus* [Latin Series], 221 vols. (Paris: Petit-Montrouge, 1844-1864), vol. 172, cols 813-1108 [col. 936]).

As if to underscore this emphasis on transformation, Jung notes that the phoenix also plays a role in alchemy as a synonym for the lapis, and in his footnote Jung observes that Honorius adds, "On the third day the bird is restored, because on the third day Christ was raised again by the Father." Here, Jung reminds us that, in *Psychology and Alchemy*, he had shown how for 17 centuries the lapis was connected with the ancient idea of the Anthropos (that is, the Neoplatonic, Gnostic, and Christian notion of the "heavenly" or "original individual" and—for Jung—a symbol of the Self), and later with Christ as the Anthropos, the Son of Man, or the *logos* (CW 14 §397).

So much for the peacock whose flesh the Queen eats—what about the green lion, whose blood she drinks?[42] According to Jung, as the "royal" beast, the lion is a synonym for Mercurius; or, more precisely, for a stage in his *transformation* (CW 14 §404).[43] In a

[42] Cf. "The Hunting of the Greene Lyon" (1652), an alchemical text attributed to Abraham Andrewes:

> This *Lyon* maketh the *Sun* sith soone
> To be joyned to hys Sister the *Moone*:
> By way of wedding a wonderous thing,
> Thys *Lyon* should cause hem to begett a King:
> And tis as strange that thys Kings food,
> Can be nothing but thys *Lyons* Blood;
> And tis as true that thys ys none other,
> Than ys it the Kings Father and Mother.

(in *Theatrum Chemicum Britannicum*, ed. Elias Ashmole (London: John Grismond, 1652), pp. 278-290 [p. 279]). For further discussion of the green lion image in relation to Nietzsche, see Babette Babich, "Nietzsche's göttliche Eidechse: 'Divine Lizards,' 'Greene Lyons,' and Music," in Christa Davis Acampora and Ralph R. Acampora (eds.), *A Nietzschean Bestiary: Becoming Animal Beyond Docile and Brutal* (Lanham: Rowman & Littlefield, 2004), pp. 264-283; and in relation to Newton, see Betty Jo Teeter Dobbs, *The Foundations of Newton's Alchemy, or "The Hunting of the Greene Lyon"* (Cambridge: Cambridge University Press, 1975).

[43] As some commentators have noted, there exists a vast literature on the alchemical symbol of the Green Lion, especially by the early 20th-century French alchemist and esotericist known as Fulcanelli (see Captain NEMO and Fra' Cercone, *Philalethe Reveal'd: The Masterpiece of an English Adept*, 3 vols. (Rome: Nautilus Editions and Alla Via Jacobea Editions, 2015), vol. 1, p. 77). For the Green Lion is one of the most important representations of Mercury (ibid., p. 87), as Jung himself notes.

footnote, Jung describes Mercurius as the "master-workman" and the "artifex," quoting Johann Daniel Mylius's *Philosophia reformaia* (1622) which says that Mercurius is the green lion and "the whole elixir of the *albedo* [i.e., whiteness] and the *rubedo* [i.e., rednesss], and the *aqua permanens* [i.e., permanent water] and the water of life and death, and the virgin's milk, the herb of ablution [i.e., saponaria, berissa, and moly—according to Jung], and the fountain of the soul."[44] In fact, Mylius goes on to say, Mercurius is the "dragon who marries himself and impregnates himself, and brings to birth in due time, and slays all living things with his poison" (§401, fn. 138). While noting that, usually, Mercurius is also said to "slay himself" and thus "bring himself to life," Jung foregrounds another connection, linking Mercurius to the uroboros and its remarkable quality of "aseity" (i.e., its existence by self-origination)—a quality it shares with the Godhead, from which it "cannot be distinguished" (ibid.) In this respect, Jung's astonishing adventures in alchemical interpretation are, as much as anything, part of his ongoing investigation into the nature of God—and hence his search for an answer to Parzival's question, *waz ist got?*

According to Jung, the lion represents the "warm-blooded form" of the dragon as a "devouring, predatory monster" (CW

In the *Rosarium Philosophorum* the Green Lion is depicted as devouring the sun; a phylactery bears the inscription, "I am the true green and Golden Lion without cares, / In me all the secrets of the Philosophers are hidden," while the *Rosarium* itself comments on "our Mercury which is the Green Lion devouring the Sun": "Know that it is Mercury cold and moist and God hath created all minerals of it, for it is an airy element, flying from the fire" (ibid., p. 87; *Rosarium philosophorum*, originally published in a series of 20 woodcuts as Part Two of *De Alchemia Opuscula complura veterum philosophorum* (Frankfurt, 1550), transcribed from MS Ferguson 210 by Adam McLean; available online <https://www.alchemywebsite.com/rosary5.html>). In an article the Italian physicist and chemist Francesco Pannaria (1898-1994) added to this image the following caption, "The Lion of Alchemy, or the force of vitriol," i.e., sulfuric acid, a powerful solvent used as a catalyst for transformative change (ibid., p. 87).

[44] Mylius, *Philosophia reformata*, p. 303 (cited in CW 14 §401, fn. 138).

14 §404).[45] Its death and dismemberment are succeeded by the appearance of the lion, which in turn is followed by the eagle. (All these creatures—the dragon, the lion, the eagle—are, one will recall, found in various places in *Thus Spoke Zarathustra.*) In the *Chymical Wedding of Christian Rosenkreutz* (1616), attributed to Johannes Valentinus Andreae (1586-1654),[46] Jung adds, we find examples of the kind of transformation associated with Mercurius.[47] In Figure IV in *The Book of Lambspring*, the lion appears, like the Mercurius duplex, in a dual form as lion and lioness, while in Mylius's *Philosophia reformata,* the two lions are identified with the red sulfur (as the wingless lion) and the white sulfur (as the

[45] In his discussion of the Italian Renaissance polymath Girolamo Cardano in his seminar on *Dream Interpretation Ancient & Modern,* Jung comments on the order of the appearance of the dragon and the (green) lion as follows: "Usually the dragon guards the treasure — as a rule, the animal that comes after the dragon, mostly in double form. At first comes the *ouroboros*. Then comes the green lion. The difference between these two animals is that the lion is warm-blooded, the dragon cold-blooded. The lion is already on a higher level. And the greenness means that the positive life has already begun there. That's also why they talked about the *benedicta viriditas* [i.e., 'blessed greenness'], which appears simultaneously with lion power, sun power" (C.G. Jung, *Dream Interpretation Ancient & Modern: Notes from the Seminar Given in 1936-1941*, ed. John Peck, Lorenz Jung, and Maria Meyer-Grass, trans. Ernst Falzeder and Tony Woolfson (Princeton, NJ, and Oxford: Princeton University Press, 2014), p. 179).

[46] See Gerhard Wehr, *Die deutsche Mystik: Mystische Erfahrung und theosophische Weltsicht — eine Einführung in Leben und Werk der großen deutschen Sucher nach Gott* (Berne: O.W. Barth, 1988), pp. 273-286; and *Philosophie: Auf der Suche nach dem Sinn* (Augsburg: Pattloch, 1990), pp. 85-99.

[47] For example: "Now as soon as this was done, and silence had been kept for the space of five minutes, there came forth a beautiful snow-white unicorn with a golden collar (having on it certain letters) about his neck. In the same place he bowed himself down upon both his forefeet, as if hereby he had shown honour to the lion, who stood so immoveably upon the fountain, that I had taken him to be of stone or brass. The lion immediately took the naked sword which he had in his paw, and broke it in two in the middle, and the pieces of it, it seemed to me, sunk into the fountain; after which he roared for so long, until a white dove brought a branch of olive in her bill, which the lion devoured in an instant, and so was quieted. And so the unicorn returned to his place with joy" (cf. *Rosicrucian Trilogy*, trans. Joscelyn Godwin, Christopher McIntosh, and Donate Pahnke McIntosh (Newburyport, MA: Weiser Books, 2016), p. 107).

winged lioness) (§403). (Irrespective of whether green or red, both lions are said to be Mercurius [§405].) As a quarrelling couple of lions, these two lions prefigure the alchemical King and Queen; as a "fiery" creature, the lion expresses the outbursts of emotional passion that lead to the recognition of unconscious contents, as well as, yet again, the uroboros (§404).

In his *Symbola aureae mensae duodecim nationum* (1617), Michael Maier (1568-1622), quoting Raymund Lully (c. 1232-c. 1315/16), writes that "some have called this earth the green lion mighty in battle; others the serpent that devours, stiffens, and mortifies his own tail."[48] Arguing that, psychologically, emotion "unites as much as it divides," Jung points out that in *Gloria Mundi, alias Paradisi tabula* in the *Musaeum hermeticum* of 1678, Barcius (or Johann von Sternberg) defines the green lion as a mineral stone that "consumes a great quantity of its own spirit,"[49] which Jung identifies with the alchemical processes of *imbibatio*, *cibatio*, *nutritio*, *penetratio*, etc., or in other words, with "self-impregnation by one's own soul" (CW 14 §404).

In the later Middle Ages, the green lion was joined by a red lion, and both were identified as Mercurius; but why choose lions or, indeed, other animals at all? In Hellenistic times, Jung reminds us, the "king of beasts" represented a transformation stage [*Wandlungsstufe*] of Helios, the ancient Greek god and personification of the Sun, usually depicted with a radiant crown and as driving a horse-drawn chariot through the sky—and a figure who also recurs in *The Red Book* (see RB, 59). In the context of Ripley's *Cantilena*, the lion—who in Lorenzo Ventura's *De*

[48] Michael Maier, *Symbola aureae mensae duodecim nationum* (Frankfurt am Main, 1617), p. 427 (cited in CW 14 §404, fn. 148).

[49] Barcius, "Gloria mundi, alias Paradisi tabula," in *Musaeum hermeticum* (Frankfurt am Main, 1678), pp. 203-304 (p. 219); translated in *The Hermetic Museum Restored and Enlarged*, ed. and trans. Arthur Edward Waite, 2 vols. (London: J. Elliot, 1893), vol. 1, p. 178 (cited CW 14 §404, fn. 155).

ratione conficiendi Lapidis philosophici (1571) bears the title "Leo antiquus"—[50] can be said to represent the alchemical King in his *theriomorphic form* or *unconscious state*, in other words, as overcome by his "animal side" (CW 14 §405). On this account, emotions are essentially "animal reactions," symbolized by Apuleius of Madaura in the changing of Lucius into a golden ass, and in Christoph Martin Wieland's fairy tale "Der Stein der Weisen" by King Mark's transformation likewise into an ass; and, just as in Apuleius' *The Golden Ass* Lucius regains his human shape by eating roses, so does King Mark by eating a lily (§406).

In *De Chemia Senioris antiquissimi philosophi libellus* (1566), attributed to the early Muslim alchemist Muḥammad ibn Umayl al-Tamīmī (known in Latin as Senior Zadith) (c. 900 to c. 960),[51] an author called Marchos (mentioned in Arabic texts at Marqūš, king of Egypt, and identified by Jung as Marcus Graecus) describes a scene of a "lion-hunt" (CW 14 §409, cf. §386). Here—in contrast to Ripley's *Cantilena*—it is the lion, rather than the King, who is transformed. A trap is prepared for the lion with a sweet-smelling magic stone, which lures the lion into the trap and swallows it up. Jung identifies "the stone, which the lion loves" (and which Marchos himself describes as "a woman") with an eye-charm, pointing to the fact that the trap is covered by a "glass roof," while its interior, described by Senior as a "cucurbita" (that is, the still pot of the distilling apparatus containing the liquid to be distilled), is also called the "thalamus" (that is, the bridal chamber) (§409). This scene in which the lion falls, like a bridegroom, into the bridal chamber, where the magic stone—like a woman, "good for the eyes"—lies on a bed of coals, waiting to swallow (*transglutit*) the lion up so that "nothing more of him was to be

[50] Ventura, "De ratione conficiendi lapidis," in *Theatrum chemicum*, vol. 2, pp. 244-356 (p. 289) (cited in CW 14 §405, fn. 161).

[51] Also known by the honorific name of al-Sadik, this becomes in English "Zadith," while *ibn-Umail* is (mis)translated as "son of Hamuel."

seen," is interpreted by Jung as a scene of "royal incest," in which the incestuous love affair is projected onto the lion—that is, onto the animal nature (called the "accrescent soul") of the King—and unconsciously enacted as if in a dream (§410). This reading is itself a reenactment of one of the oldest disputes in psychoanalysis and one which led to the great falling-out between Jung and Freud: the role of incestuous desire in the psychosexual development of the individual and the question of its symbolic dimension.

In Freud's early works, incest fantasies are seen as repressed memories of real experiences and in his later works as expressions of imaginary desires. For Jung, however, incestuous desire is always symbolic, but nevertheless (or rather precisely for this reason), *real*: The tabooed incest is, he remarks, "imposed as a task and, as the wealth of allegories shows, it is always in some symbolical form and never concrete" (CW 14 §409). The location of this incestuous, yet "sacral" act in the cucurbita, or glass house, is taken as a sign of its recognition, *not* its repression; and Jung argues that we do not need so much to get "outside ourselves" (that is, as if into an external glass house) as merely "a little deeper *into* ourselves" (that is, into the microcosmic space of the psyche), in order to experience the "reality of incest," since "in each of us sleeps the 'beastlike' primordial individual [*der »bestialische« Primitive*]," something easily roused by the doves of Diana—as is the sleeping lion, according to Eleazar (Abraham the Jew), the pseudonym of Julius Gervasius of Schwarzburg, in his *Uraltes Chymisches Werk* (1760) (part 1, p. 86) (§410; cf. §408, fn. 168).[52]

This association in some alchemical texts of the lion with Venus, the goddess of love and beauty, is confirmed for Jung by the fact that in Gerhard Dorn's *Congeries Paracelsicae*,[53] as well as

[52] Abraham Eleazar, *Uraltes Chymisches Werk* (Leipzig, 1760), part 1, p. 86 (cited in CW 14 §408, fn. 168).
[53] Dorn, "Congeries Paracelsicae," in *Theatrum chemicum*, vol. 1, pp. 609-610 (cited in CW 14 §419, fn. 205 and 206).

in Heinrich Khunrath's *Von hylealischen Chaos* (1597),[54] the green lion is said to have rose-colored blood. The connection with the rose opens up for Jung a wide range of associations:

- with the *filius*, a well-known Christ parallel;
- with the "rosarium" (or rose garden);
- with the "Rosenkreuz" (i.e., the Rosie Cross);
- with the tincture "of a rosy colour," corresponding to the blood of Christ;
- and with the rose-garden as the *Hortus conclusus*, a sobriquet of the Virgin Mary as a parallel to the "locked" *prima materia;* as well as
- with the relation of the love-goddess to scarlet as the color of the Great Whore of Babylon;
- with red as the color of sin;
- and with the rose as an attribute of Dionysos (CW 14 §419-§420).

Nothing could prove better than does this list Jung's point about the acute dualism of certain symbols!

Because the peacock's flesh and lion's blood represent the goddess's own attributes, by consuming them as food and drink, the Queen or Mother may be said to be eating and drinking *herself.* Citing the line from the "Consilium coniugii," "And so at length it sinks down into one content through saturation with the one ferment, water, for water is the ferment of water,"[55] Jung detects in this formulation the old idea expressed by the ouroboros, the doctrine of *hen to pan* (ἓν τὸ πᾶν), that is, "the all is one," as found in the early alchemical text, *The Chrysopoeia of Cleopatra*, probably dating back to third-century Alexandria (CW 14 §422). Noting the antiquity of this symbol (it is suggested that it might go back to

[54] Heinrich Khunrath, *Vom hylealischen Chaos der naturgemässen Alchymiae und Alchymisten* (Magdeburg, 1597), pp. 93 and 196 (cited in CW 14 §419, fn. 207).
[55] "Consilium coniugii," in *Ars Chemica*, pp. 48-263 (p. 220) (cited in CW 14 §422, fn. 220).

ancient Egyptian theology and the doctrine of a *homoousia*—that is, consubstantiality—between Father-God and Pharaoh, the divine son), Jung argues that the idea of the self-generating, self-devouring being must surely predate Christianity, even though it later finds itself formulated in Christian terms by, for example, St. John Chrysostom or Tertullian. In fact, in his treatises on monogamy, Tertullian argues as follows in relation to a passage from the Letter to the Ephesians (1:10):

> In this same way the Lord applied to Himself two Greek letters, the first and the last, as figures of the beginning and end which are united in Himself. For just as *Alpha* continues on until it reaches *Omega*, and *Omega* completes the cycle back again to *Alpha*, so He meant to show us that in Him is found the course of all things from the beginning to the end and from the end back to the beginning, so that every divine dispensation should end in Him through whom it first began, that is, in the Word of God made flesh. Accordingly, it should also end in the selfsame *manner* in which it first began.[56]

For Jung, the analogy proposed by Tertullian between the self-generating, self-devouring being and Christ, who as the one God begets himself, voluntarily offers himself for sacrifice, and through the words of consecration in the Eucharistic rites, performs his own self-immolation, is "very striking" (CW 14 §421).

Continuing his exhaustive (and, it must be said, sometimes exhausting) analysis of stanzas 14-17 of Ripley's *Cantilena*, Jung summarizes the "animal" substances that the Queen, as the "accrescent soul," has to integrate: the peacock and the lion, together

[56] Tertullian, *Treatises on Marriage and Remarriage: To His Wife; An Exhortation to Chastity; Monogamy*, trans. William P. Le Saint (New York, NY; Ramsey, NJ: Newman Press, 1951), pp. 78-79.

with their positive and negative qualities; and the draught brought by Mercurius, bearing the "dart of passion," in the "golden cup of Babylon"—"full of abominations and filthiness of her fornication" (cf. Revelation 17:4), thus emphasizing further the erotic nature of the lion's lust and greed (CW 14 §426). Such an "unpalatable diet" is required, Jung suggests, because the old King was lacking something (and hence his senility): First, he was lacking the "dark, chthonic aspect of nature"; and second, he was lacking the "sense that all creation was in the image of God"—that "antique feeling" for nature which had, Jung asserts, become thought of in the Middle Ages as "a false track and an aberration" (which would seem to overlook the doctrine that God was the author of two texts, the Book of God—i.e., the Bible—and the Book of Nature) (§427). For his part, Jung insists that, however "dark and unfathomable" the earth is, its theriomorphic symbols are "paradoxical," inasmuch as they do not only have a "reductive" meaning, but one that is "prospective and spiritual," pointing "upward and downward at the same time" (§427). Even more paradoxically, by integrating these contents and widening her consciousness, the Queen will benefit the regeneration of the King by supplying what he lacks: not only the "darkness" of the animal sphere, but also a "spiritual nature" or "natural spirit," something which is even analogous (in the alchemists' eyes) to the mystery of faith (§427).

If stanza 18 reminds Jung of a couplet by Angelus Silesius about how human things have "humanized" God (CW 14 §429),[57] stanza 25 prompts Jung to reflect on the position held by the miracle of transubstantiation performed daily at Mass in the mind of the alchemist during the alchemical transformation (§435). Canon

[57] See Angelus Silesius, *Cherubinischer Wandersmann*, Book 3, §11 (p. 112); cf. "God drinks humanity's milk, leaves His divinity's wine, / How could He then not be immersed in His mankind?" (*The Cherubinic Wanderer*, trans. Shrady, p. 72). In Hull's gifted translation, the second line is translated thus: "How human things have humanized divine."

Ripley is, for Jung, a case in point, for here alchemical interests and religious conceptions seemed to be mixed in equal measure. Consequently, in his *Cantilena,* the Queen is not so much a wife or a mother as a "tutelary madonna" who has adopted the King as her son—a son who dies and is buried as if in consecrated ground, awaiting resurrection (§435). Likewise, the elevation of the "matrix" (or the chemical solution) out of the state of materiality and upward to Luna (the moon) is, as Jung surmises, that Ripley would have known well, the "classic allegory" of the Church (§436). In the *Cantilena,* Luna naturally stands for the Virgin and/or the Church, because the *senex-puer* (that is, the old man-youth—or the King who must be rejuvenated) is described by Ripley in biblical terms (as we saw in stanza 10) as the "Ancient of Days" (§436). Elsewhere, Jung explains that Ripley's inclusion of Luna as the maternal aspect of night in the transformatory apotheosis of the King reminds us of another apotheosis—that of Faust at the end of Part Two of the drama (§498).

In his commentary on stanza 29, where the rejuvenation of the King and the birth of the son are described—strangely enough, by a medieval ecclesiastic—in terms of the manifestation of a new redeemer (CW 14 §443), Jung rehearses his conjecture that medieval alchemy (with its roots in the Arabic tradition from which it emerged in the 13th century) was ultimately a development of those aspects of the doctrine of the Holy Spirit for which the Church could find no room (§444). For the likes of an Angelus Silesius, that the descent of the Paraclete upon the single individual thereby draws the believer into the Trinitarian process, was, as Jung remarks, an "obvious conclusion" (§444, fn. 245), citing four couplets from the *Cherubinischer Wandersmann* (Book 2, §101-§104). Equally, if the spirit of procreation and life can dwell within the individual, then God can be born in that individual—as Meister Eckhart had noted in his famous (Christmas Day) sermon on a text from the Wisdom of Solomon (18:14).[58] What Angelus Silesius and Meister Eckhart express in terms of *religious and psychological experience*, is what alchemy describes in (and through) terms of *matter* and what Ripley describes in *allegorical* terms—even if somewhat "tortuous" ones (§445). The nature of this experience was such, Jung adds, that it explains the "rapt language" (*die gesteigerte Sprache*) of certain verses in the *Cantilena*, and the same could be said of certain verses in *Thus Spoke Zarathustra*—as well as *The Red Book*.

Here lies the answer to the six-million-dollar question that Jung daringly goes on to pose: *How could those alchemists have retained such enthusiasm for their art, when a miraculous transformation never took place in the retort? When they never succeeded in making gold? When they never produced the elixir of life? And when no homunculus ever emerged from the furnace?* (CW 14 §445). The answer, he shrewdly suggests, is not simply that, after many centuries of endeavor, alchemy gave birth to chemistry and its staggering discoveries, but rather has more to do with the "emotional dynamism" of alchemy, as a result of which its practitioners' "chronic failure" did not detract from its "psychic effect of a positive nature," something which Jung described as akin to "satisfaction"—or even a "perceptible increase in wisdom" (§446). The real achievement of alchemy, then, was to have produced in the course of the chemical procedure certain "psychic projections," enabling "unconscious contents" to be brought to light—sometimes in the form of "vivid visions" (§446). Whereas nowadays Analytical Psychology brings unconscious contents into consciousness by the method of "active imagination," the alchemists produced *projections*—which proved to be of the "greatest therapeutic value." Because the Middle Ages couldn't provide an outlet for such unconscious contents, it was inevitable that the unconscious would generate projections—and

[58] See Eckhart, Sermon One, in *Sermons & Treatises*, trans. Walshe, vol. 1, pp. 1-13 (= Pfeiffer #1, Quint [1955] #57).

yes, even "neurotic symptoms." Thus the legacy of alchemy was twofold: First, it gave rise to the world of natural science; and second, it also gave rise, in parallel to the empiricism of scientific research, to that "particular religious spirit" (*jener gewisse religiöse Geist*) one encounters in so many alchemical treatises (§446)—and in the epic tradition as well.

Once again, Jung turns to Meister Eckhart as an example of this spirit, referring again to his sermon for Christmas Day and the idea of the birth of the Son in the human individual as well as the resulting affiliation of humankind to God.[59] According to Jung, this religious spirit realized itself in four ways: first, in the Protestant Reformation; second, in the mystical tradition after Jacob Boehme and, in particular, Angelus Silesius (whose work Jung celebrates in *Mysterium Coniunctionis* more fully than he does elsewhere); third, in the empirical sciences; and fourth, in the transmission of the religious philosophies of the East to the West (CW 14 §447). And one could add that it realized itself in a fifth and sixth way as well: namely, in the tradition of the quest for the Grail and in the philosophy of Friedrich Nietzsche (and his attempt to overcome nihilism and to achieve antinihilism in the form of the threefold teaching of the *Übermensch*, self-overcoming, and eternal recurrence).[60] And one might even add a seventh way: namely, in the Analytical Psychology of Jung and its own attempt to embrace Nietzsche's solution of non-metaphysical transcendence.

Via a brief, if unexpected, excursus on the *Hexastichon* of Sebastian Brant (1458-1521) (a mnemonic system published

[59] Meister Eckhart, *Sermons & Treatises*, trans. Walshe, vol. 1, pp. 5-9.

[60] For further discussion of nihilism as an aspect of Nietzsche's thought, see Michael Allen Gillespie, *Nihilism Before Nietzsche* (Chicago and London: University of Chicago Press, 1995); Eike Brock, *Nietzsche und der Nihilismus* (Berlin, Munich, Boston: de Gruyter, 2015); Paul van Tongeren, *Friedrich Nietzsche and European Nihilism* (Newcastle upon Tyne: Cambridge Scholars Publishing, 2018); and Jon Stewart, *A History of Nihilism: Confrontations with Nothingness* (Cambridge: Cambridge University Press, 2023).

in 1503 consisting of 15, somewhat bizarre-looking—in Jung's own words, "freakish beyond belief"—woodcut images to help remember the events in the four Gospels) and on James Joyce's great Modernist novel *Ulysses* (CW 14 §454-§455), Jung moves toward distinguishing between two kinds of alchemists: namely, between those who sought to combine revealed truth with a knowledge of God in nature (and hence hoped for a rebirth of dogma), and those for whom projecting their Christian faith into the physical world invested nature with mystical significance (and hence hoped for a new reincarnation of dogma and its transformation into a natural revelation) (§456).

In a methodological aside at this point, Jung explains why he places such great emphasis in his account of alchemy on the phenomena of assimilation; it is because, in his view, they constitute a prelude to the "modern approximation" between, on the one hand, empirical psychology, and, on the other, Christian dogma—an approximation, he adds, of the kind that Nietzsche had "clearly foreseen" (CW 14 §457). Although he does not explicitly explain how Nietzsche had done this, the rest of this paragraph nevertheless hints at some of the *methodological* parallels between Nietzsche and Analytical Psychology. To begin with, how does Jung see psychology as working? On his account, psychology "observes religious ideas from the standpoint of their psychic phenomenology without intruding on their theological content," and it puts "dogmatic images" into the category of "psychic contents" simply because they "constitute its field of research" (§457). Such a strategy is necessary, he argues, because of the very nature of the psyche itself: unlike alchemy, psychology does not try to explain "psychic processes" in "theological terms," but rather it seeks to "illuminate the darkness of religious images" by "relating them to similar images in the psyche" (§457). This approach can result, he admits, in a kind of "amalgamation of ideas of [...] the most varied provenance" and hence to "parallels and comparisons which [...]

may seem like a devaluation or a false interpretation," but only—and here Jung goes on the attack—to those with an "uncritical mind unacquainted with the epistemological method" (§457).

In fact, Jung's argument here recalls Nietzsche's insight as propounded in *The Anti-Christ*: namely, that "the most valuable insights are *methods*" (AC §13). Then again, in a programmatic aphorism in *Beyond Good and Evil*, Nietzsche declares that "psychology is now again the path to the fundamental problems" (BGE §23), and at the opening of this section, he begins to explain why. So far, Nietzsche says, psychology has "got stuck in moral prejudices and fears," because it has "not dared to descend into the depths" (BGE §23). In other words, psychology has to embark on a *katabasis* (κατάβασις)—that descent, that journey or voyage to the depths, for which of all the numerous literary-cum-mythical prototypes arguably the most famous is in Homer's *Odyssey* (where Odysseus follows the instructions of Circe and sails with his crew across the ocean until he reaches a harbor at the Western edge of the world, where he sacrifices to the dead and descends to the underworld). As we shall shortly see, Nietzsche himself uses a sailing metaphor in this passage.

In methodological terms, Nietzsche presents psychology here as "morphology," that is, as the "study of shape," a term used by Goethe to explain his own scientific approach;[61] and, more precisely,

[61] See *Goethe's Botany: The "Metamorphosis of Plants" (1790) and Tobler's "Ode to Nature" (1782)*, trans. Agnes Arber, *Chronica Botanica*, vol. 10, no. 2 (Summer 1946), 63-126; Johann Wolfgang von Goethe, *Goethe's Botanical Writings*, trans. Berthe Mueller (Honolulu: University of Hawaii Press, 1952); and *The Metamorphosis of Plants*, ed. Gordon L. Miller (Cambridge, MA, and London: The MIT Press, 2009). For further discussion, see Steen Brock, "Goethe's Contribution to Philosophy: The Morphology of Individuality," *SATS*, vol. 20, no. 1 (2019), 35-52; Oriane Petteni, "The Contemporary Legacy of Goethean Morphology: From *Anschauende Urteilskraft* to Algorithmic Pattern Recognition, Generation, and Exploration," *Goethe Yearbook*, 29 (2022), 43-72; and Claudia Nitschke, "Morphology," in Charlotte Lee (ed.), *Goethe in Context* (Cambridge: Cambridge University Press, 2024), pp. 216-224. Goethe's approach to morphology attracted the interest of Ernst Cassirer and Rudolf Steiner alike.

as the "doctrine of the development of the will to power" (BGE §23). Nietzsche's approach is avowedly one that is "beyond good and evil," inasmuch as it proposes a "doctrine of the reciprocal dependence of the 'good' and the 'wicked' drives," even if this approach has to contend with "unconscious resistance in the heart of the investigator" (BGE §23). Indeed, it proposes a "doctrine of the derivation of all good impulses from wicked ones," regarding such affects as "hatred, envy, covetousness, and the lust to rule" simply as "conditions of life" and as "factors which, fundamentally and essentially, must be present in the general economy of life" (BGE §23). Even if such a view may initially induce "seasickness," Nietzsche encourages us to "clench our teeth! let us open our eyes and keep our hand firm on the helm!" (BGE §23). For we must, he says, "sail right *over* morality," and then we shall discover that "never yet did a *profounder* world of insight reveal itself to daring travellers and adventurers"; furthermore, "the psychologist who thus 'makes a sacrifice' [...] will at least be entitled to demand in return that psychology shall be recognized again as the queen of the sciences" (BGE §23).

In this final remark, Nietzsche is playing on the medieval dictum, *philosophia ancilla theologiae* (that is, "philosophy as the handmaiden of theology"), and it is a trope that Jung knew as well. For in "Psychology and Literature," his contribution to a collection of papers edited by Emil Ermatinger (1873-1953), a Swiss professor for Germanic philology, published in 1930 (and expanded and revised by Jung in 1950), Jung began by noting that psychology, which had previously led a "modest existence in a small and highly academic backroom," had in recent decades—and in fulfilment of Nietzsche's prophecy (presumably the passage from *Beyond Good and Evil* cited above)—developed into an "object of public interest" and "burst the framework assigned to it by the universities" (CW 15 p. 84). Across three main areas, psychology had made its presence felt: in industry, in the form of psychotechnics (i.e., the use of psychological techniques for assessing human behavior, for example, in the form of the Myers-Briggs type indicator); in medicine, in the form of psychotherapy; and in philosophy, the field to which it has made the greatest contribution. For Jung sees psychology as having carried on the work of Schopenhauer and of Eduard von Hartmann (1842-1906), the author of *Philosophy of the Unconscious* (1869); as having rediscovered—thanks in large measure, one might add, to Ludwig Klages (1872-1956)—the legacies of Johann Jakob Bachofen (1815-87) and Carl Gustav Carus (1789-1869);[62] and as having driven new insights in the field of anthropology (or as Jung, with the political incorrectness of his day, puts it: in the psychology of "primitives"), as well as opening up new paths in comparative religion and even being applied by some theologians to the cure of souls. Could it be, Jung wondered, that Nietzsche will be proved right with his slogan, *scientia ancilla psychologiae* (i.e., "science as the handmaiden of psychology")? (Although Nietzsche writes in *The Birth of Tragedy* that "Plato has given to all posterity the model of a new art form, the model of the *novel*—which may be described as an infinitely enhanced Aesopeian fable, in which poetry holds the same rank in relation to dialectical philosophy as this same philosophy held for many centuries in relation to theology: namely, the rank of *ancilla*" (BT §14), in terms of sense it is more likely that Jung is thinking of the description in *Beyond Good and Evil* of psychology as the "queen of the sciences.")

In *Mysterium Coniunctionis*, Jung makes the point that objections to parallels and comparisons arising from this so-called "epistemological method" might also be made about the Church Fathers and their hermeneutics—which are said to be "often very

[62] See Johann Jakob Bachofen, *Versuch über die Gräbersymbolik der Alten*, 2nd edn., ed. Carl Albrecht Bernoulli, with an appreciation by Ludwig Klages (Basel: Helbing & Lichtenhahn, 1925); and Carl Gustav Carus, *Psyche*, ed. Ludwig Klages (Jena: Diederichs, 1926).

risky indeed"—or indeed about the "dubious nature" of textual criticism (*Textkritik*) (CW 14 §457). But of course, this is precisely the sort of objection that Nietzsche *did* make. In an aphorism in *Daybreak* (1881), for example, he launches an excoriating attack on the "philology of Christianity," opening with an assertion and a series of questions: "How little Christianity cultivates the sense of honesty can be inferred from the character of the writings of its learned men. [...] Their continual cry is: 'I am right, for it is written' — and then follows an explanation so shameless and capricious that a philologist, when he hears it, must stand stock-still between anger and laughter, asking himself again and again: Is it possible? Is it honest? Is it even decent?" (D §84).[63] Nietzsche chooses to focus on the way in which this "dishonesty" is practiced in Protestant pulpits—"in what a clumsy fashion the preacher takes advantage of his security from interruption; how the Bible is pinched and squeezed; and how the people are made acquainted with every form of the art of false reading"—but at the same time, he highlights how this philological practice is inherent in Christianity in its earliest forms, or what Nietzsche describes as a "religion which, during the centuries when it was being firmly established, enacted that huge philological farce concerning the Old Testament," and he goes on to elaborate this charge: "However strongly Jewish savants protested, it was everywhere sedulously asserted that the Old Testament alluded everywhere to Christ, and nothing but Christ, more especially His Cross [...]" (D §84).

The kind of interpretation that Nietzsche has in mind here is the one in which "wherever reference was made to wood, a rod, a ladder, a twig, a tree, a willow, or a staff, such a reference could not but be a prophecy relating to the wood of the Cross" (D §84), and he goes on to allude to a number of biblical episodes—"even

[63] For further discussion, see Paul Bishop, *Discourses of Philology and Theology in Nietzsche: From the "Untimelies" to The Anti-Christ* (Cham: Palgrave Macmillan, 2023).

the setting-up of the Unicorn and the Brazen Serpent, even Moses stretching forth his hands in prayer, indeed the very spits on which the Easter lambs were roasted: all these were allusions to the Cross, and, as it were, preludes to it!" (D §84).[64] The fundamental question that Nietzsche puts to his readers is this: "Has anyone who asserted this ever *believed* it?" (D §84).[65]

Ultimately, however, Jung and Nietzsche are perhaps not so far apart. After all, Jung's method of *amplification*—the search for an "Ariadne thread [...] through the labyrinth of symbolistic parallels" which is "absolutely essential" if one wishes to establish the "meaning of the archetypal context" (CW 5 p. xxv)—is not markedly different from what Nietzsche calls a *semiotic* approach (AC §32; TI "Improvers" of Humankind §1; EH UM §3). And as he moves in *Mysterium Coniunctionis* toward the conclusion of his analysis of Ripley's *Cantilena*, Jung expresses the wish for a *rapprochement* between, on the one hand, empirical science, and, on the other, religious experience. In his view, alchemy sits uneasily between these two, and he recognizes that it is not easy to defend alchemy "against the charge of unconsciousness" (CW 14 §457). Did Ripley ever, Jung wonders, reflect on his "theological enormities"? And if so, what did he think of them? The coronation of the Virgin and the heavenly marriage in stanzas 36 and 37 (with

[64] For the image of the unicorn or one-horned beast, see Deuteronomy 33:17, where Moses blesses the tribes and says of Joseph, "His beauty as of the firstling of a bullock, his horns as the horns of a rhinoceros," read by such Church Fathers as St. Augustine as applying to Jesus Christ as the first-born of creation and lifting up the nations on his cross, as it were with horns (Haydock, 257); for the Brazen or Bronze Serpent, see Numbers 21:4-9, read as a figure of the crucified Christ and of the efficacy of faith in him against the serpent from hell (Haydock, 184); and for the instructions of the preparation of the paschal lamb, seen as a prefiguration of Jesus Christ as redeeming through his death, see Exodus 12:1-14. In yet another philological turn, Nietzsche derived these examples from Moritz von Engelhardt's *Das Christenthum Justins des Märtyrers* (1878) (see NK, vol. 3/1, pp. 167-169).

[65] For Jordan B. Peterson, this correspondence between the Brazen Serpent and Christ is an amazing one, and to be taken at face value; see *We Who Wrestle with God: Perceptions of the Divine* (London: Allen Lane, 2024), pp. 445-451.

its apotheosis of the *filius regius*, and the triumph of the reborn king) brings Ripley's *Cantilena* to its triumphant conclusion in stanza 38. As a work, it is, Jung asserts, one of the "most perfect parables of the renewal of the King," although for elaboration of its mythical development it cannot compare with Christian Rosenkreutz's *Chymical Wedding*—nor for the variety of levels on which the motif of transformation is treated with Goethe's *Faust II*, Part Two (§462).

Returning to his defense in his methodological excursus of the "parallels and comparisons" of the "epistemological method" and to the fundamental question underpinning it—"tradition or spontaneous generation?" (CW 14 §397; cf.§378), Jung is arguably on stronger ground when he suggests that the psychologist approaches religious symbols as empirical material, and hence in a significantly different way from how the theologian would (§457). An example of how Jung approaches a symbol (and the kind of "parallels and comparisons" which he tries to discern) can be found a mere few paragraphs later when, in a section discussing the "dark side" of the King and the critical phase of the *nigredo* (that is, the phase of decay and death), he focuses on the alchemical symbol of the serpent or the snake. Here the association between the snake and the earth-gods (as well as such deities as Hermes and Asklepios) prompts Jung to recall in a footnote the question asked in "Of the Bite of the Adder" by Zarathustra to the snake that had bitten him, "When did ever a dragon die of a serpent's poison?" (Z I 19), describing Zarathustra as "a hero of the race of dragons" and hence rightly addressed in "Of the Vision and the Riddle" as "thou stone of wisdom" (Z III 2 §1).

Similarly, reflection on the comparison between the god and the snake—a comparison elaborated in considerable detail in Jung's *Red Book*—and how it reminds us of the god's chthonic form in the underworld prompts Jung to consider how the worm stands for the "most primitive and archaic form of life," out from which emerged the bird, that is, the direct opposite of the earthbound creature (CW 14 §483). Consequently, the snake and the bird as a pair is a classical representation of the pair of opposites. In the case of *Zarathustra*, the eagle and the snake are the two animals of Zarathustra: At the conclusion of the Prologue, the eagle sweeps through the air in wide circles, and coiled around its neck hangs the serpent (Z Prologue §10). In "The Convalescent" in Part Three, the animals sing to Zarathustra, "For thine animals know it well, O Zarathustra, who thou art and must become: behold, THOU ART THE TEACHER OF THE ETERNAL RETURN, — that is now THY fate!" (Z III 13 §2), while eternal recurrence itself is symbolized in "The Seven Seals" by the "ring of the return" (Z III 16 §1) and as "alpha and omega" (Z III 16 §6).

Likewise, the shepherd into whose mouth the serpent has crawled in "Of the Vision and the Enigma" (Z III 2 §2) is also connected with the idea of eternal recurrence, for with the snake, he forms the circle of the uroboros (that is, the serpent or dragon eating its own tail). Quoting a fragment from the *Nachlass*, "the circle is not something that has become, it is the primal law" (*der Kreislauf ist nichts Gewordenes, er ist das Urgesetz*) (KSA 9, 11[157], 502), which he cites from Horneffer's study, *Nietzsches Lehre von der ewigen Wiederkunft und deren bisherige Veröffentlichung* (Leipzig, 1900), Jung seeks to clinch this set of associations by referring to two ancient authors. First, the teaching of the early Gnostic Christian, Saturninus of Antioch (active 100-120 C.E.), as quoted by Irenaeus of Lyon (c. 130-c. 202 C.E.) in his *Adversus Haereses* (or *Against Heresies*), that the angels first created a man who could only crawl like a worm (Book 1, Chapter 24, §1); and second, the remark of Hippolytus of Rome (c. 170-c. 235 CE) in his *Refutation of All Heresies* (also called the *Elenchus* or *Philosophumena*) that, because of the weakness of the angels who created him, man "grovelled like a worm" (Book 7, Chapter 28, §3) (CW 14 §483 fn. 328).

Whatever one thinks of Jung's technique of "parallels and comparisons," this is as good (or as bad) a set as one can find in his writings, and they clearly illustrate his intention to set Nietzsche's *Zarathustra* in the broadest possible intellectual-historico-cultural context. Not surprisingly, then, these associations also remind Jung of the fact that the rejuvenated phoenix is said first to take the form of a worm (CW 14 §483; cf. §472); or, more precisely (in the words of a Gnostic manuscript in the Nag Hammadi Library), that the "worm that has been born out of the phoenix is a human being as well," because the "phoenix first appears in a living state, and dies, and rises again, being a sign of what has become apparent at the consummation of the age" (*On the Origin of the World*, §122).[66] Given the borrowings from Egyptian religion made by Christianity, Jung regards it as "not surprising" that the allegory of the snake marks a meeting point between Christian and alchemical traditions (§483).

The final reference to Nietzsche in *Mysterium Coniunctionis* occurs in the context of an argument where Jung recapitulates what he had suggested in his "Epilogue" to *Psychology and Alchemy*. The decline of alchemy during the Enlightenment, he argues, resulted in the descent for Europeans of their "dogmatic images" into "the underworld" (CW 14 §509). (Likewise, in an earlier epochal shift, the disappearance—thanks to the rise of Protestantism—of the feminine element in the cult of the Mother of God had "detached" the "spirituality" of the "dogmatic image" from the earthly individual human being and allowed it to "sink into the unconscious" [CW 14 §509].) Just as, so Jung had argued in *Psychology and Alchemy* (CW 12 §38 and §56), the decay of the "conscious dominant" on the level of the individual is followed by an eruption of chaos, so on the collective level, it erupts in such forms as the Peasant Wars, the rise of the Anabaptists, the French Revolution, and the unleashing of bloodthirstiness and lust for murder—all instances

[66] See "On the Origin of the World (II,*5* and XIII,*2*)," trans. Hans-Gebhard Bethge, Bentley Layton, and Societas Coptica Hierosolymitana, in *The Nag Hammadi Library in English*, ed. James M. Robinson, 3rd edn. (Leiden: Brill, 1988), pp. 170-189 (p. 186).

of the "sickness" described in Ripley's *Cantilena* (CW 14 §510).

(Jung saw this "sickness" as vividly portrayed in the *Cantilena* in the figure of the "sick King." Leaving again on one side the question of how far this idea may itself have been influenced by the legend of the Grail, he noted that, apart from the notion of the *lapis exilis* (or, in the case of Wolfram's *Parzival*, the *lapsit exillis*), there were no other likely traces of the influence of the Grail cycle in alchemical symbolism, with the exception of the "mystic vessel of transformation," analogous equally to the chalice used in the Mass [CW 14 §369]—implicit to all three traditions of the Grail, alchemy, and the Catholic rite of the Mass being the idea of *transformation*.)

Now such a loss of "eternal images" (*der Verlust der ewigen Bilder*) is, Jung writes, "no light matter for anyone of discernment," but because there are infinitely many more people of *no* discernment, no one has apparently noticed that the "truth expressed by the dogma" had suddenly vanished; but the "discerning" individual (*der Einsichtige*) knows—and *feels*—that something is missing. The "undiscerning" person (*der Uneinsichtige*, i.e., ἄνοος) "misses nothing" and only realizes this loss once it is too late: that is, when "alarming symptoms" have become "real" in the "outside world"—because they were "not perceived before inside, in oneself," just as the "presence of the symbol" (*die Gegenwart des Symbols*) was not noticed (CW 14 §510). If, however, these symptoms *had* been noticed, Jung suggests, then a veritable threnody for the "lost god" would have arisen—as it did, according to Plutarch's account in §17 of "The Obsolescence of Oracles" (*De defectu oraculorum*) on the death of Great Pan (§510).

In a footnote, Jung explicitly equates the cry of Thamus, the Egyptian pilot, to the people of Palodes, "Great Pan is dead"—that "ancient cry which came echoing over the sea to mark the end of the nature gods," as he puts it elsewhere (CW 11 §145)—with Zarathustra's cry, "God is dead!" describing it as its "modern equivalent" (CW 14 §510, fn. 392). By the stage of late antiquity, Jung goes on to explain, Pan was no longer the grotesque pastoral deity that he had been—the god of the wild, shepherds, and flocks, the god of fields, groves, and wooded glens, a god with the hindquarters, legs, and horns of a goat, and a god of fertility and the season of spring. Instead, Pan had acquired a distinctly philosophical significance and was regarded (according to the *Elenchos* or *Refutation* of Hippolytus) by the Christian Gnostic sect called the Naassenes as one of the forms of the "multiform Attis" (Book 5, Chapter 4) and as synonymous with numerous figures, including Osiris, Wisdom (Sophia), Adam, Corybas, Papa, Bacchus, and so on (§510, fn. 392).[67]

The problem, Jung realizes, is that "well-meaning people" (*die Wohlmeinenden*) keep assuring us that one has only to believe that He—presumably the Judeo-Christian God, not Pan—is still there, a gesture which merely serves to reinforce the lack of consciousness (CW 14 §510). (In fact, throughout this entire discussion, Jung operates with a distinction between the "well-meaning" or "undiscerning" person [*der Uneinsichtige*] and the "discerning" person [*der Einsichtige*].) Moreover, once the symptoms are "really outside" in the form of some kind of "sociopolitical insanity," then

[67] "Therefore, he says, when, on the people assembling in the theatres, any one enters clad in a remarkable robe, carrying a harp and playing a tune (upon it, accompanying it) with a song of the great mysteries, he speaks as follows, not knowing what he says: Whether (you are) the race of Saturn or happy Jupiter, or mighty Rhea, Hail, Attis, gloomy mutilation of Rhea. Assyrians style you thrice-longed-for Adonis, and the whole of Egypt (calls you) Osiris, celestial horn of the moon; Greeks denominate (you) Wisdom; Samothracians, venerable Adam; Haemonians, Corybas; and them Phrygians (name you) at one time Papa, at another time Corpse, or God, or Fruitless, or Aipolos, or green Ear of Grain that has been reaped, or whom the very fertile Amygdalus produced — a man, a musician. This, he says, is multiform Attis, whom while they celebrate in a hymn, they utter these words: I will hymn Attis, son of Rhea, not with the buzzing sounds of trumpets, or of Idaean pipers, which accord with (the voices of) the Curetes; but I will mingle (my song) with Apollo's music of harps, '*evoe, evan*,' inasmuch as you are Pan, as you are Bacchus, as you are shepherd of brilliant stars" (Hippolytus, *Refutation of All Heresies*, trans. J.H. MacMahon, in *Ante-Nicene Fathers*, vol. 5, edited Alexander Roberts, James Donaldson, and A. Cleveland Coxe (Buffalo, NY: Christian Literature Publishing, 1886), pp. 56-57. [Available online HTTP: <http://www.newadvent.org/fathers/050105.htm >.]

it is too late—and it becomes impossible to convince people that the *real* conflict is now taking place in the psyche of all individuals. While in the case of the "discerning person" the conflict remains an intrapsychic one, in the case of the *undiscerning,* it is acted out on the plane of projection in the form of "political tension and murderous violence" (§510). What happens in the case of these undiscerning individuals is, however, described in distinctly Nietzschean tones. Here is how Nietzsche describes the "blond beast" in *On the Genealogy of Morals*—and how Jung describes what happens when the unconscious "takes the lead":

Once [these noble, powerful men] go outside, where the strange, the *stranger* is found, they are not much better than uncaged beasts of prey. There they savour a freedom from all social constraints, they compensate themselves in the wilderness for the tension engendered by protracted confinement and enclosure within the peace of society, they go *back* to the innocent conscience of the beast of prey, as triumphant monsters who perhaps emerge from a disgusting procession of murder, arson, rape, and torture, exhilarated and undisturbed of soul [...]. One cannot fail to see at the bottom of all these noble races the beast of prey, the splendid *blond beast* prowling about avidly in search of spoil and victory; this hidden core needs to erupt from time to time, the animal has to get out again and go back to the wilderness [...]. (GM I §11)

Desirousness overpowers him, and illusory goals set up in place of the eternal images [*anstelle der ewigen Bilder*] excites his greed. The beast of prey [*Der Raubtier*] seizes hold of him and soon makes him forget that he is a human being. His animal affects hamper any reflection that might stand in the way of his infantile wish-fulfilment, filling him imstead with a feeling of a new-won right to existence and intoxicating him with the lust for booty and blood [*mit Beute- und Blutgier berauscht*]. (CW 14 §510)

In other words, Jung draws a clear causal line between, on the one hand, the proclamation of the "Death of God" and, on the other, the outbreak of world wars and the rise of National Socialism. If Jung is right—*if*—then what are we to do?

The answer can surely lie only in the notion of *transformation.* Jung declares that the "living presence of the eternal images"[68] alone can lend the human psyche the requisite dignity, making it "morally possible" for us as individuals to "stand by [our] own soul" (*bei* [*unserer*] *Seele auszuharren*) (CW 14 §511). For only then, Jung argues, will we realize that the conflict is *in us*: as a result, "discord and tribulation" are *our* riches, not to be "squandered" on attacks on others, and even the debt of *guilt* that we pay to ourselves makes us recognize the worth of our own psyche. If, however, we lose our own values, then we are transformed into a robber, a wolf, a lion, or some other ravening (and, more likely than not, blond) beast, as symbolized in alchemy by the black waters of chaos (that is, the unconsciousness of projection), which "swallow up" the alchemical King (§511).

Whereas in the "lion-hunt" of Marchos, it is not the King who is transformed but the lion (see above, pp. 319-320), in Ripley's *Cantilena,* the pregnant Mother eats the peacock's flesh and drinks the lion's blood—"Meanwhile the Peacocks Flesh she kindly Eate, / And Dranke Greene-Lyons Blood (with that fine Meate) / Which Mercury (although in Passion:) / Brought in a Golden Cupp of Babilon"—in this way feeding on the "transformative substance" (CW 14 §387). In a footnote, Jung explains that, due to his fiery nature, the lion is the "affective animal" *par excellence* (§512, fn. 393). To drink the blood of the lion (that is, the lion's essence) is, he adds, akin to assimilating one's own emotions and affects. The

[68] In *Black Book* 7, Jung's soul tells him that her "other half, which is on the side of the earth, is another soul" and that she is "between things and [Jung]," while she herself is "between the eternal images and [Jung]"; if Jung's soul is light, this other soul is dark—and "if she were released from the symbol, she would give form, substance, and actual life to the eternal images" (BB7, 186).

wounding of the lion allows it, so to speak, to be "tapped"—or, in psychological terms, the well-aimed thrust of the weapon of "insight" pierces the affect; or, in alchemical terms, the wounding or mutilation of the lion signifies the subjugation of concupiscence (§512, fn. 393).

In the *Cantilena*, the peacock's flesh and the lion's blood, which still the Mother's pregnancy cravings are, in fact, her *own* flesh and blood (CW 14 §512). On Jung's reading, this means that, in order to bring healing to the conflict that is projected, the conflict must first be returned to the place where it originally had its unconscious beginnings: that is, in the psyche of the individual. Using the image of liturgical Christianity, it means that we must "celebrate a Last Supper" with ourselves, eating our *own* flesh and drinking our *own* blood; in other words, recognizing and accepting the Other in ourselves.[69] If, however, we persist in our "one-sidedness," the two lions will tear each other to pieces. Is this, then, what Christ's teaching means, that we must each of us bear our own cross? (For if we have to endure ourselves, how would we be able also to rend [*zerreißen*] others?)

In this way, we can see how Jung is trying, in a post-Nietzschean age, to reinterpret the imagery of Christianity afresh, using the imagery of alchemy to do so. The miraculous feeding with one's own substance, represented in the Last Supper and reenacted in the Mass, means in psychological terms the "integration of those parts of the personality [...] outside ego-consciousness" (CW 14 §513), and this task of integration lies at the heart of Jung's own epic, his *Red Book*. Or in alchemical terms: the lion and the peacock, those emblems of concupiscence and pride, represent the "overweening pretensions" of our old friend, the human (all-too-human) shadow—a shadow which we so gladly project onto those

[69] For evidence of the continuity of Jung's interest in the notion of a "Last Supper with ourselves," compare with the "horrifying, sweet thought" in *Black Book* 4 of being "both guest and dish at this meal," a "Last Supper" (BB4, 237; RB, 415).

around us in order to visit on them with apparent justification our *own* sins.

In emblematic terms, *we* are the uroboros, the serpent or dragon that eats its own tail, and this thought of devouring oneself and turning oneself into a circulatory process revealed to the "more astute" alchemists the insight that the *prima materia* of the alchemical process was actually none other than *ourselves*, as human individuals. On this account, the uroboros is a "dramatic symbol" for the process of integrating and assimilating our own opposite—that is, the shadow. At the same time, it is a "symbol of immortality," for the uroboros slays itself and thereby brings itself to life; it fertilizes itself and thus gives birth to itself (CW 14 §513). In his interpretation of Nietzsche's *Zarathustra* in *Transformations and Symbols of the Libido*, it was precisely this mechanism that Jung had sought to uncover, a transformation that results in the triumphant cry, "I love you, O Eternity," and is symbolized by the golden ring, the ring of eternal return. Therefore, the circle, the ring, the uroboros all symbolize "the One"—the One that emerges from the clash and conflict of the opposites and thus constitutes the "secret" of the *prima materia,* which, although (or rather because) it is projected, has its origins in the unconscious of the human individual.

Conclusion (A)

In the epic opening of Stanley Kubrick's *2001: A Space Odyssey*, the arousing opening chord of Richard Strauss's tone poem *Also sprach Zarathustra* accompanies the famous majestic shot of the Earth, the moon, and sun aligned in one line. If we are to believe *The Black Books*, Jung experienced a similar epiphanic moment during his visit to North Africa in 1920 when—in an "unforgettable night in the desert"—he "saw the X for the first time and understood the Platonic myth" (BB7, 227). And 10 years later, in his essay on

"The Stages of Life" (1930; 1931), Jung had recourse to the daily course of the sun to illustrate his thesis of the midlife crisis—a sun "ensouled with human feeling and human temporal consciousness," to be sure (CW 8 §778). In the morning, Jung tells us, the sun rises "out from the nocturnal sea of unconsciousness" and climbs steadily into the "wide, bright world" of the sky. Eventually, the sun reaches its "unforeseen zenith"—and at the stroke of noon, the descent begins, and along with it the "reversal of all the values and ideals" of the morning (§778).

Likewise, the ascent and descent of the sun form the governing *Gleichnis,* or "allegory," of *Thus Spoke Zarathustra*: in an unpublished note from 1881, entitled "**MIDDAY AND ETERNITY**: *GUIDE-POSTS TO A NEW WAY OF LIVING,*" Nietzsche wrote the following:

> "Zarathustra born on lake Urmi; left his home in his thirtieth year, went into the province of Aria, and, during ten years of solitude in the mountains, composed the Zend-Avesta."
>
> "The sun of knowledge stands once more at midday; and the serpent of eternity lies coiled in its light — : It is YOUR time, ye midday brethren."
>
> (KSA 9, 11[195-196], 519)

In the Prologue, Zarathustra addresses the sun as it begins to rise at dawn (§1), and when the sun stands at noontide, he espies his animals, "An eagle swept through the air in wide circles, and on it hung a serpent, not like a prey, but like a friend: for it kept itself coiled round the eagle's neck" (§10). In the concluding chapter of Part One, Zarathustra promises his disciples that he will return to celebrate the "great noontide" with them:

> And it is the great noontide, when man is in the middle of his course between animal and Superman,

> and celebrateth his advance to the evening as his highest hope: for it is the advance to a new morning.
>
> At such time will the down-goer bless himself, that he should be an over-goer; and the sun of his knowledge will be at noontide.
>
> "DEAD ARE ALL THE GODS: NOW DO WE DESIRE THE SUPERMAN TO LIVE." — Let this be our final will at the great noontide! — (Z I 22 §3)

In Part Two, the sun has been "long set" (Z II 10) before Zarathustra commences his journey to the Island of the Dead or his descent into the unconscious, as he sings his "Grave-Song" (Z II 11). In Part Three, Zarathustra addresses the sun again before dawn in "Before Sunrise" (Z III 4), and in "Of Old and New Law Tables," he learns from the sun that "when it goeth down, the exuberant one: gold doth it then pour into the sea, out of inexhaustible riches, — / — So that the poorest fisherman roweth even with GOLDEN oars! For this did I once see, and did not tire of weeping in beholding it. —," reaffirming: "Like the sun will also Zarathustra go down: now sitteth he here and waiteth, old broken tables around him, and also new tables — half-written" (Z III 12 §3). In "The Other Dance-Song" and in "The Drunken Song," a great bell strikes midnight (Z III 15 §3 and Z IV 19); halfway through Part Four, Zarathustra experiences his great midday vision in the chapter entitled "At Noontide" (Z IV 10); and in the concluding chapter, "The Sign," Zarathustra addresses the rising sun yet again and declares, "This is MY morning, MY day beginneth: ARISE NOW, ARISE, THOU GREAT NOONTIDE! —," and he leaves his cave a final time, "glowing and strong, like a morning sun coming out of gloomy mountains" (Z IV 20).

On the one hand, this solar imagery can be seen to look back to Homer's *Odyssey*, where the course of a battle is described as fluctuating with the course of the sun, serving as a symbolic image for the work as a whole and for Odysseus's discovery that a reliance on "ego power" will not solve the problems of his return journey[70] and to the description of the initiation into the Mysteries of Isis found in the concluding chapter of Apuleius's *Metamorphoses* (Book 11, §23): "I came to the boundary of death and, having trodden the threshold of Proserpina, I travelled through all the elements and returned. *In the middle of the night I saw the sun flashing with bright light.* I came face to face with the gods below and the gods above and paid reverence to them from close at hand" (my emphasis).[71] On the other, it also looks forward as a structuring principle to *The Red Book*: in "Descent into Hell in the Future," the sun shines "in the depths" (RB, 148 and 151-154; cf. 169, 199); the setting and the rising sun determines the desert life led by Ammonius in "The Anchorite" (RB, 248-249); in "Dies II," Jung tries to offer a morning prayer to the sun (RB, 252-253 and 259 and 261); in "Death," a "new sun" arises, described as "awful" and as a "reversal of what we call day"—after which, when Jung has "comprehended" his "darkness," a "truly magnificent night" comes over him, his dream "plunges" him into the "depths of the millennia," and from them his phoenix "ascends" (RB, 265); at the end of "The Remains of Earlier Temples," Jung hastens "toward the East" and his "rising" (RB, 277); in "First Day," the sun sinks in the West "into the lap of glowing clouds in bright crimson" (RB, 279); in "The Opening of the Egg," Izdubar becomes "*completely sun* [...] *sun, completely sun. I am the sun,*" while Jung realizes that

[70] Homer, *The Odyssey*, Book 9, ll. 39-60; cf. Edward F. Edinger, *The Eternal Drama: The Inner Meaning of Greek Mythology*, ed. Deborah A. Wesley (Boston, MA: Shambhala Publications, 1994), pp. 102-104.

[71] Apuleius, *Metamorphoses*, vol. 2, *Books VII-XI*, ed. and trans. J. Arthur Hanson (Cambridge, MA; London: Harvard University Press, 1989), p. 341. For further discussion, see Marie-Louise von Franz, *The Golden Ass of Apuleius: The Liberation of the Feminine in Man* (Boston and London: Shambhala, 1992), pp. 187-210; and Wytse Hette Keulen, Stefan Tilg, Lara Nicolini, Luca Graverini, S.J. Harrison, Stelios Panayotakis, D. van Mal-Maeder (eds.), *Apuleius Madaurensis Metamorphoses, Book XI, The Isis Book: Text, Introduction and Commentary* (Leiden: Brill, 2015), pp. 517-528.

he had "captured the sun without knowing it" and carried it in his hand, becoming Izdubar's "nocturnal mother" who "incubated the egg of the beginning," so that Izdubar "rose up, renewed, reborn to greater magnificence" (RB, 307-309).

After the reborn Izdubar spreads his wings and flies up and away, in "The Sacrificial Murder" Jung declares that after the God has departed, we "need the sun" and must "regenerate ourselves" (RB, 323); in "Nox Tertia," Jung has a vision of the sun rising "in red glory, solitary and magnificent," while the World Clock strikes twelve o'clock midday (RB, 351); and in "Nox Quarta," the mysterious figure called the "son of the earth"—embodying, perhaps, Zarathustra's cry, "*remain true to the earth*" (Z Prologue §3)—is described as being "arisen," as "behold[ing] the light of the sun," and as "dwell[ing] among the living," while within him rise up "restlessness and division," "doubt" (*Zweifel*)—or *zwîvel*, that opening theme of the Prologue to Wolfram's *Parzival*—[72] and at the same time the "fullness of life" (*die Fülle des Lebens*). It is precisely this "fullness of life" that is represented by the Grail, is sought after so ardently by Faust, and is embodied in the *Übermensch*—and which lies at the core of Jung's *Red Book*, the final work in our survey of the epic of transformation to which, in Volume 4, we shall turn.

Conclusion (B)

L'Individu se fond dans le Monde et le Monde se fond dans l'Individu[[73]]

At the outset of his Seminar on Nietzsche's *Zarathustra* (1934-1939), Jung was insistent on the world-historical nature of *Thus*

[72] "If unfaith in the heart find dwelling, then the soul it shall reap but woe" (§1, l. 1-2; vol. 1, p. 3), where *zwîvel* can be variously translated as "unfaith" (Weston), "vacillation" (Hatto), or "doubt;" cf. DKV, vol. 2, pp. 445-446.

[73] Source unknown; cited in <https://fr.wikipedia.org/wiki/Ainsi_parlait_Zarathoustra_(Strauss)>.

Spoke Zarathustra, claiming that Zarathustra "appears in the moment when something has happened which made his presence necessary" and that what had happened is what Nietzsche calls the "death of God" (SNZ, 24). For when God dies, Jung continued, then humankind needs a "new orientation," and it is precisely at this moment that the "father of all prophets"—or, in the language of Analytical Psychology, the Wise Old Man—is supposed to "appear" in order to give a "new revelation" and to "give birth to a new truth" (24). *And, in this case, he did*—in the form of *Zarathustra*, a book which is an "extraordinary experience of that phenomenon, a sort of enthusiastic experience surrounded by all the paraphernalia [. . .] of true revelation" (24). And the "great revelation" that Nietzsche, in the guise of Zarathustra, brings ultimately involves the "union of the pairs of opposites, spirit and body" (192). Thus, for Jung, this is what *Zarathustra* is—nothing less than a revelation, anticipating the later revelation of *The Red Book*, and, in this sense, the next step in the epic of transformation.

Thus Spoke Zarathustra is the book *par excellence* about transformation, and "when Nietzsche declares that God is dead, instantly he begins to transform," embarking upon the "process of that archetype of rebirth" (SNZ, 37). Even Nietzsche himself did not realize that, when he said God was dead, it meant he would "get into the mill, into the alchemical pot where he is cooked and transformed" (38). In Jungian terms, the process of transformation inevitably involves God, inasmuch as those "vital powers" in us which we call "God" are "powers of self-renewal, powers of eternal change" (37). In this respect, however, *Zarathustra* has an important antecedent: Goethe's *Faust*, which contains the "beautiful verse" about the "kingdom of the Mothers," where everything is in a "continuous state of self-renewal, a continuous rearrangement"; alluding, of course, to the famous Mothers Scene in Part Two, where Mephistopheles describes them as "Formation, transformation, / The Eternal Mind's eternal recreation, / And round them float forms of all things that be" (ll. 6287-6289).[74] This kingdom of the Mothers is described by Jung as the "abyss of the deity," and as the "darkness of the good," the "*deus absconditus*," the "*auctor rerum*," the "dark father of created things," and as the "original mother" (37).

At the same time, Jung does not think that the death of God is nearly so interesting as the (re)birth of God:

> Then through the revelation of the Christian symbolism, we learned the most important fact that the deity had found a means in the human psyche to be reborn, to be born through man. That is the message, the great symbolic teaching; and that of course increases the conscious psyche of man to an extraordinary degree. It becomes the divine cradle, the womb, the sacred vase

[74] This passage had a particular significance for Jung: in the chapter of *Memories, Dreams, Reflections* suggestively entitled "Visions," he recorded the deliriums and visions that accompanied his recovery from slipping on an icy path and, in losing his step, breaking a foot in the early months of 1944 and subsequently having a heart attack. Over a period of some weeks, Jung experienced—in what has been called his final *metanoia*—see Michael Flanagin, "The Kabbalah and Jung's Final Metanoia [Review of: Sanford L. Drob, Kabbalistic Visions: C.G. Jung and Jewish Mysticism]," *Jung Journal*, vol.18, no. 1 (2024), 113-117—various forms of mystic union or *hierosgamos*:

- the Kabbalistic wedding of (masculine) Tiferet with (feminine) Malchuth in the Pardes Rimonim, the garden or orchard of pomegranates (alluding to the title of a classical Kabbalistic work by Moses ben Jacob Cordovero);
- the wedding in the afterlife of Rabbi Simon ben Yochai, said to be the author of the Zohar (and whose death was described by his friends as his wedding celebration);
- the "Marriage of the Lamb" in a festively bedecked Jerusalem, as found in the Book of Revelation (19, vv. 5-9); and
- the consummation of the mystic marriage of All-father Zeus and Hera (as celebrated at the Heraion of Samos), described in *The Iliad*, Book 14, ll. 292-351.

For further discussion, see Sanford L. Drob, *Kabbalistic Visions: C.G. Jung and Jewish Mysticism*, 2d edn. (London and New York: Routledge, 2023). All these experiences are said to have been "glorious" (*herrlich*), and the state of "purest bliss" in which, night after night, he floated is compared to being "thronged round with images of all creation" (*umschwebt von Bildern aller Kreatur*) [MDR, 325-326; JLW, 197].)

> in which the deity itself will be locked in, carried and born. This is really an *euangelion*. (SNZ, 243-244)

(Euangélion [εὐαγγέλιον], of course, means "good news," or as Christians would call it, "gospel.") Elsewhere, Jung placed Nietzsche's declaration of the "death of God" in the context of Nietzsche's identification with Zarathustra:

> It makes a great deal of difference with what one identifies, and Nietzsche was not fully aware with what he identified. He did not realize that his declaration, "God is dead", meant something which he did not quite grasp; to him the existence of God was an opinion or a kind of intellectual conviction, so one only needed to say God was not and then he was not. But in reality God is not an opinion. God is a psychological fact that happens to people. (SNZ, 258)

The problem, as Jung saw it, is that Nietzsche was at once a great psychologist yet someone who lacked psychological knowledge:

> Nietzsche, not knowing of psychology at all — though he was really a great psychologist — behaved with that concept of God as if it were purely an intellectual concept and thought that if he said God was dead, then God didn't exist. But the psychological fact remains and then the question is in what form that fact will appear again. In this case, it appeared again in Nietzsche's own dissociation: namely, when Zarathustra came up in him [...]. (SNZ, 258)

It comes as something of a surprise to see Nietzsche—who, after all, declared in *Beyond Good and Evil* that "psychology is now again the path to the fundamental problems" (BGE §23)—described as "not knowing of psychology at all"! And clearly, Nietzsche knew a great deal about psychology in another sense, inasmuch as his case illustrated, as Jung once put it, why "at this time, when a large part of mankind is beginning to discard Christianity, it is worth while to understand clearly why it was originally accepted" (PU §349).[75]

As Jung argued in "The Psychology of the Unconscious" (1917; 1926; 1943), the case of Nietzsche "shows, on the one hand, the consequences of neurotic one-sidedness, and, on the other hand, the dangers that lurk in this leap beyond Christianity" (CW 7 §40-§41). On this account, Nietzsche "undoubtedly felt the Christian denial of animal nature very deeply indeed, and therefore he sought a higher human wholeness beyond good and evil," but whoever "seriously criticizes the basic attitudes of Christianity also forfeits the protection which these bestow upon him" (§40-§41). Hence in *The Red Book,* Jung begins a lengthy debate in "Divine Folly" with the librarian about the value of Nietzsche. Nietzsche's "truth," Jung maintains, is "too agitated and provocative," and is only good for those "who are yet to be set free." Instead, he continues, we also need a "truth for those who are forced into a corner," for those who need a "depressive truth" which makes them "smaller and more inward" (RB, 330). It is to those who "need more freedom" that Nietzsche speaks, while to those who "clash strongly with life," who "bleed from wounds," and who "hold fast to actualities," he has nothing to say (RB, 330).

And in "Nox Tertia" Jung—now in the mental asylum—encounters another of the inmates, a man with a black beard, a tousled head of hair, and "dark shining eyes" (RB, 349). Previously

[75] Compare with Jung's urgent questions in "The Undiscovered Self" (as R.F.C. Hull imaginatively translated the title *Gegenwart und Zukunft*) of 1957: "Do we know that we are on the point of losing the life-preserving myth of the inner individual which Christianity has treasured up for us? Do we realize what lies in store should this catastrophe ever befall us?" (CW 10 §586).

lying "motionless" in bed with a "transfixed gaze" (RB, 338), this "fool" (*der Narr*) now identifies himself as "Nietzsche, only rebaptized," as well as "Christ, the Savior, and appointed to save the world" (RB, 338 and 349-350). "Why does my family always shut me in with crazy people [*mit Verrückten*]?" he cries—before lying down again and "sinking back" into his "lassitude"—"I'm the Savior," "I'm supposed to save the world!" (RB, 350). Despite—or perhaps because of—this implicit critique of Nietzsche, Jung then goes on to articulate a highly Nietzschean insight:

This — is now MY way,— where is yours? Thus did I answer those who asked me "the way." For THE way — it doth not exist! (Z III 11 §2)	Our life is the truth that we seek. Only my life is the truth, the truth above all. We create the truth by living it. (RB, 351)

To announce and to comprehend this truth, Nietzsche had recourse to writing *Thus Spoke Zarathustra*; while Jung, as we shall see in Volume 4, had recourse to creating his own version of *Zarathustra*—in the form of *The Red Book.*

Bibliography

Primary Texts and Editions

See *List of Abbreviations*, *Abbreviations of titles of Nietzsche's works*, *Editions of translations cited*, etc.

Other Works Cited

Acampora, Christa Davis, and Ralph R. Acampora (eds.). *A Nietzschean Bestiary: Becoming Animal Beyond Docile and Brutal* (Lanham, MD: Rowman & Littlefield, 2004).

Adler, Gerhard. "Aspects of Jung's Personality and Work," *Psychological Perspectives*, vol. 6, no. 1 (1975), 11-21.

Adorno, Theodor W. *Dream Notes*, ed. Christoph Gödde and Henri Lonitz, trans. Rodney Livingstone (Cambridge and Malden, MA: Polity, 2007).

Adorno, Theodor W. *Traumprotokolle*, ed. Christoph Gödde and Henri Lonitz (Frankfurt am Main: Suhrkamp, 2005).

Allison, David B. (ed.). *The New Nietzsche: Contemporary Styles of Interpretation* (Cambridge, MA, and London: MIT Press, 1985).

Anderson, Mark. *Plato and Nietzsche: Their Philosophical Art* (London and New York: Bloomsbury, 2014).

[Andreae, Johann Valentin]. *Rosicrucian Trilogy*, trans. Joscelyn Godwin, Christopher McIntosh, and Donate Pahnke McIntosh (Newburyport, MA: Weiser Books, 2016).

Angelus Silesius. *Cherubinischer Wandersmann: Kritische Ausgabe*, ed. Louise Gnädinger (Stuttgart: Reclam, 1985).

Angelus Silesius. *The Cherubinic Wanderer*, trans. Maria Shrady (Mahwah, NJ: Paulist Press, 1986).

Ante-Nicene Fathers, vol. 5, ed. Alexander Roberts, James Donaldson, and A. Cleveland Coxe (Buffalo, NY: Christian Literature Publishing, 1886).

Apuleius. *Metamorphoses*, vol. 2, *Books VII-XI*, trans. J. Arthur Hanson (Cambridge, MA, and London: Harvard University Press, 1989).

Aristotle. *Complete Works*, ed. Jonathan Barnes, 2 vols. (Princeton, NJ: Princeton University Press, 1984).

Arkin, Arthur M. "A Short Note on Empedocles and Freud," *American Imago*, vol. 6, no. 3 (September 1949), 197-203.

Ashmole, Elias (ed.). *Theatrum Chemicum Britannicum* (London: John Grismond, 1652).

Athanassakis, Apostolos N. *The Orphic Hymns: Text, Translation and Notes* (Missoula, MT: Scholars Press, 1997).

Bachofen, Johann Jakob. *Versuch über die Gräbersymbolik der Alten*, 2nd edn., ed. Carl Albrecht Bernoulli (Basel: Helbing & Lichtenhahn, 1925).

Baeumler, Alfred. *Männerbund und Wissenschaft* (Berlin: Junker & Dünnhaupt, 1934).

Ball, Philip. *The Devil's Doctor: Paracelsus and the World of Renaissance Magic and Science* (London: Heinemann, 2006).

Bambach, Charles. "Nietzsche's Madman Parable: A Cynical Reading," *American Catholic Philosophical Quarterly*, vol. 84, no. 2 (Spring 2010), 441-456.

Bassett, Peter. *The Nibelung's Ring: A Guide to Wagner's "Der Ring der Nibelungen"* (Kent Town, Australia: Wakefield Press, 2003).

Battistini, Matilde. *Symbols and Allegories in Art*, trans. Stephen Sartarelli (Los Angeles: The J. Paul Getty Museum, 2005).

Beebe, John, and Steve Myers. "The transcendent function in Spitteler's *Prometheus and Epimetheus*," *Journal of Analytical Psychology*, vol. 66, no. 5 (November 2021), 1139-1158.

Benedict XVI. *The Fathers* (Huntington, IN: Our Sunday Visitor Publishing, 2008).

Berthelot, Marcellin. *Collection des anciens alchimistes grecs*, 3 vols. (Paris: Steinheil, 1887-88).

Bielawski, Krzysztof. "Arrheton: niewypowiadalne w greckich kultach misteryjnych" [Arrheton — Unspeakable in the Greek Mystery Cults], *Filozofia Chrześcijańska*, 13 (2016), 37-52.

Bishop, Paul. "Adorno and Jung, Bloch and Klages: Disorientation and Reorientation of Consciousness in the Totally Administered Society," *Eranos Yearbook* [The Disoriented Consciousness and the Thought of a New Habitability: Uncertainties of Time and Spaces of Freedom / La coscienza spaesata e il pensiero di una nuova abitabilità: incertezze del tempo e spazi di libertà – Proceedings of the 2022, 2023, and 2024 Eranos Conferences and Eranos-Jung Lectures, Eranos & Monte Verità, Ascona, Switzerland / Atti dei Convegni di Eranos e delle Eranos-Jung Lectures del 2022, 2023 e 2024, Eranos e Monte Verità, Ascona, Svizzera], vol. 76 (2022–2023–2024), 483-538.

Bishop, Paul. *Discourses of Philology and Theology in Nietzsche: From the "Untimelies" to The Anti-Christ* (Cham, Switzerland: Palgrave Macmillan, 2023).

Bishop, Paul. *German Political Thought and the Discourse of Platonism: Finding the Way Out of the Cave* (Cham, Switzerland: Palgrave Macmillan, 2019).

Bishop, Paul. *Jung's Seminar on Nietzsche's "Zarathustra": Birth of an Archetypal Hermeneutics* (Cham, Swizerland: Palgrave Macmillan, forthcoming).

Bishop, Paul. *Nietzsche's Writing Against Religion and the Crisis of Faith: Twentieth-Century Reactions and Responses* (Cham, Switzerland: Palgrave Macmillan, 2024).

Bishop, Paul. *On the Blissful Islands with Nietzsche & Jung: In the Shadow of the Superman* (London and New York: Routledge, 2017).

Bishop, Paul. "Paracelsus, Goethe, Jung," *Spring: A Journal of Archetype and Culture* [*Histories*], 64 (Fall/Winter 1998), 135-158.

Bishop, Paul. *Reading Goethe at Midlife: Ancient Wisdom, German Classicism, and Jung* [Zürich Lecture Series, 3] [2011] (Asheville, NC: Chiron, 2020).

Bishop, Paul. "The Descent of Zarathustra and the Rabbits: Jung's Correspondence with Elisabeth Förster-Nietzsche," *Harvest: Journal for Jungian Studies*, 43 (1997), 108-123.

Bishop, Paul. "The Jung/Förster-Nietzsche Correspondence," *German Life and Letters*, 46 (1993), 319-330.

Bishop, Paul. "The Superman as salamander: symbols of transformation or transformational symbols?", *International Journal of Jungian Studies*, vol. 3, no. 1 (2011), 4-20.

Bishop, Paul, Terence Dawson, and Leslie Gardner (eds.). *The Descent of the Soul and the Archaic: Katábasis and Depth Psychology* (London and New York: Routledge, 2023).

Blumenberg, Hans. *Die Legitimität der Neuzeit* (Frankfurt am Main: Suhrkamp, 1966; [2]1996).

Blumenberg, Hans. *Höhlenausgänge* (Frankfurt am Main: Suhrkamp, 1989).

Blumenberg, Hans. *The Legitimacy of the Modern Age*, trans. Robert M. Wallace (Cambridge, MA, and London: MIT Press, 1983).

Blumenfeld, Jacob. *All Things Are Nothing to Me: The Unique Philosophy of Max Stirner* (Alresford, UK: Zero Books, 2018).

Boccassini, Daniela. "Down to the Father's Womb: Jung's and Dante's Encounters with the Dead," *Jung Journal: Culture and Psyche*, vol. 13, no. 2 (2019), 46-81.

Bonnechere, Pierre, and Gabriela Cursaru, "Katábasis," *Cahiers des études anciennes*, 53 (2016), 7-14.

Bonnier, Bernadette, Véronique Leblanc, Didier Prioul, and Hélène Védrine (eds.). *Félicien Rops: Rops suis, aultre ne veulx estre* (Brussels: Éditions Complexe, 1998).

Bowden, Hugh. *Mystery Cults in the Ancient World* (London: Thames & Hudson, 2010).

Brenner-Eglinger, Hans. "Briefe Jakob Burckhardts an Albert Brenner," *Basler Jahrbuch 1901*, 87-110.

Brock, Eike. *Nietzsche und der Nihilismus* (Berlin, Munich, Boston: de Gruyter, 2015).

Brock, Steen. "Goethe's Contribution to Philosophy: The Morphology of Individuality," *SATS*, vol. 20, no. 1 (2019), 35-52.

Browning, Robert M. (ed.). *German Poetry from 1750 to 1900* (New York: Continuum, 1984).

Bucke, Richard Maurice. *Cosmic Consciousness: A Study in the Evolution of the Human Mind* (New York: Dutton, 1901).

Burnet, John. *Early Greek Philosophy* (London: Black, 1908).

Calder, William M. III. "The Lion Laughed," *Nietzsche-Studien*, 14 (1985), 357-359.

Campbell, Joseph (ed.). *The Mysteries* [*Papers from the Eranos Yearbooks*, vol. 2], (Princeton, NJ: Princeton University Press, 1955).

Captain NEMO and Fra' Cercone, *Philalethe Reveal'd: The Masterpiece of an English Adept*, 3 vols. (Rome: Nautilus Editions and Alla Via Jacobea Editions, 2015).

Cardinal, Roger. *German Romantics in Context* (London: Studio Vista, 1975).

Carus, Carl Gustav. *Psyche*, ed. Ludwig Klages (Jena: Diederichs, 1926).

Cassirer, Ernst, Paul Oskar Kristeller, and John Herman Randall, Jr. *The Renaissance Philosophy of Man* (Chicago: University of Chicago Press, 1948).

Catechism of the Catholic Church (New York: Doubleday, 1995).

Cauchi, Francesca. *Zarathustra's Moral Tyranny: Spectres of Kant, Hegel and Feuerbach* (Edinburgh: Edinburgh University Press, 2022).

Clark, Maudemarie. *Nietzsche on Truth and Philosophy* (Cambridge: Cambridge University Press, 1990).

Clement of Alexandria, *The Exhortation to the Greeks; The Rich Man's Salvation;* [...] *To the Newly Baptized*, trans. G.W. Butterworth (Cambridge, MA; London: Harvard University Press; Heinemann, 1960).

Cooper, Laurence D. "Beyond the Tripartite Soul: The Dynamic Psychology of the *Republic*," *The Review of Politics*, vol. 63, no. 2 (Spring, 2001), 341-372.

Copenhaver, Brian P. (ed.). *Hermetica: The Greek "Corpus Hermeticum" and the Latin "Asclepius" in a new English translation* (Cambridge: Cambridge University Press, 1992).

Cornford, Francis MacDonald. *Plato's Cosmology: The "Timaeus" of Plato* (Indianapolis: Hackett, 1997).

Corriero, Emilio Carlo. *"The Gift" in Nietzsche's Zarathustra: Affirmative Love and Friendship*, trans. Vanessa di Stefano (London: Bloomsbury Academic, 2021).

Cosmopoulos, Michael B. *Greek Mysteries: The Archaeology and Ritual of Ancient Greek Secret Cults* (London and New York: Routledge, 2003).

Cusumano, Nicola, Valentino Gasparini, Attilio Mastrocinque and Jörg Rüpke (eds.). *Memory and Religious Experience in the Greco-Roman World* (Stuttgart: Franz Steiner Verlag, 2013).

Dallmayr, Fred. *Margins of Political Discourse* (Albany, NY: State University of New York Press, 1989).

Dastur, Françoise. "Who is Nietzsche's Zarathustra? A Note on the Iranian-Persian Background," *Comparative and Continental Philosophy*, vol. 1, no. 1 (2009), 39-54.

Davis, Bret W. (ed.). *Martin Heidegger: Key Concepts* (Durham: Acumen, 2010).

Derrida, Jacques. *Dissemination*, trans. Barbara Johnson (Chicago and London: University of Chicago Press, 1981).

Detienne, Marcel. *The Gardens of Adonis: Spices in Greek Mythology* [1972], trans. Janet Lloyd [1977] (Princeton, NJ: Princeton University Press, 1994).

Dieckhöfer, Klemens. "Gerhart Hauptmann (1862-1946) und Nietzsche: Nietzsches Einfluß auf Gerhart Hauptmann und dessen Erlebnis der Natur," *Medizinhistorische Mitteilungen: Zeitschrift für Wissenschaftsgeschichte und Fachprosaforschung*, 34 (2015), 123-128.

Dieterich, Albrecht. *Nékyia: Beiträge zur Erklärung der neuentdeckten Petrusapokalypse* (Leipzig: Teubner, 1893, ^{2}1913).

Dietzsch, Steffen and Gian Franco Frigo (eds.). *Vernunft und Glauben: Ein philosophischer Dialog der Moderne mit dem Christentum: Père Xavier Tilliette SJ zum 85. Geburtstag* (Berlin: de Gruyter, 2006).

Dobbs, Betty Jo Teeter. *The Foundations of Newton's Alchemy, or "The Hunting of the Greene Lyon"* (Cambridge: Cambridge University Press, 1975).

Dodds, E.R. (ed.). *Plato Gorgias: A Revised Text with Introduction and Commentary* (Oxford: Clarendon Press, 1959).

Dowdall, Tim. *Max Stirner and Nihilism: Between Two Nothings* (Rochester, NY: Camden House, 2024).

Drob, Sanford L. *Kabbalistic Visions: C.G. Jung and Jewish Mysticism*, 2nd edn. (London and New York: Routledge, 2023).

Dunn, George A. and Mango Telli (eds.), *A New Politics for Philosophy: Perspectives on Plato, Nietzsche, and Strauss* (Lanham, MD: Lexington Books, 2022).

Edinger, Edward F. *The Eternal Drama: The Inner Meaning of Greek Mythology*, ed. Deborah A. Wesley (Boston: Shambhala Publications, 1994).

Edinger, Edward F. *The Mysterium Lectures: A Journey through C.G. Jung's "Mysterium Coniunctionis"* (Toronto: Inner City Books, 1995).

Ehrman, Bart D. Ehrman (ed.). *The Apostolic Fathers*, vol. 1, *I Clement; II Clement; Ignatius; Polycarp; Didache* (Cambridge, MA, and London: Harvard University Press, 2003).

Eichendorff, Joseph von. *Sämtliche Gedichte und Versepen*, ed. Hartwig Schulz (Frankfurt am Main and Leipzig: Insel, 2007).

Ekroth, Gunnel and Ingela Nilsson (eds.). *Round Trip to Hades in the Eastern Mediterranean Tradition: Visits to the Underworld from Antiquity to Byzantium* (Leiden and Boston: Brill, 2018).

Elliott, J.K. (ed.). *The Apocryphal New Testament* (Oxford: Clarendon Press, 1993).

Fauth, Wolfgang. "Katabasis," in Konrat Ziegler and Walther Sontheimer (eds.), *Der kleine Pauly: Lexikon der Antike*, 5 vols. (Stuttgart: Metzler, 1964-1975), vol. 3, pp. 152-153.

Fischer-Dieskau, Dietrich (ed.). *The Fischer-Dieskau Book of Lieder* (New York: Knopf, 1977).

Flanagin, Michael. "The Kabbalah and Jung's Final Metanoia [Review of: Sanford L. Drob, Kabbalistic Visions: C. G. Jung and Jewish Mysticism]," *Jung Journal*, vol. 18, no. 1 (2024), 113-117.

Fogelin, Robert J. "Three Platonic Analogies," *The Philosophical Review*, vol. 80, no. 3 (July 1971), 371-382.

Foley, Helene P. (ed.). *The Homeric "Hymn to Demeter": Translation, Commentary, and Interpretive Essays* (Princeton, NJ: Princeton University Press, 1994).

Fox, William Sherwood. *The Mythology of All Races*, vol. 1, *Greek and Roman* (Boston: Marshall Jones, 1916).

Franz, Marie-Louise von (ed.). *Aurora Consurgens: A Document Attributed to Thomas Aquinas of the Problem of Opposites in Alchemy* [1957], trans. R.F.C. Hull and A.S.B. Glover (New York and London: Bollingen Foundation, 1966).

Franz, Marie-Louise von. *C.G. Jung: His Myth in Our Time*, trans. William H. Kennedy (New York: Putnam, 1975).

Franz, Marie-Louise von. *The Golden Ass of Apuleius: The Liberation of the Feminine in Man* (Boston and London: Shambhala, 1992).

Freud, Sigmund and C.G. Jung, *The Freud/Jung Letters: The Correspondence between Sigmund Freud and C.G. Jung*, ed. William McGuire, trans. Ralph Manheim and R.F.C. Hull (Cambridge, MA: Harvard University Press, 1988).

Freud, Sigmund. *Standard Edition of the Complete Psychological Works of Sigmund Freud*, ed. James Strachey and Anna Freud,

24 vols. (London: Hogarth Press; Institute of Psycho-Analysis, 1953-1974).

Furness, Raymond. "Nietzsche and Empedocles," *Journal of the British Society for Phenomenology*, vol. 2, no. 2 (1971), 91-94.

Ganschinietz, Richard. "Katabasis," in Pauly-Wissowa, *Realencyclopädie der classischen Altertumswissenschaft*, 85 vols (Stuttgart: Metzler, 1890-1980), vol. 10, cols 2359-2449.

Georg, Jutta, Renate Reschke, and Vivetta Vivarelli (eds.), *Nietzsche im Horizont der Literatur* (Leiden: Brill; Fink, 2022).

George, Stefan. *The Works of Stefan George rendered into English*, trans. Olga Marx and Ernst Morwitz (Chapel Hill, NC: University of North Carolina, 1949).

Gillespie, Michael Allen, *Nihilism Before Nietzsche* (Chicago and London: University of Chicago Press, 1995).

Girard, René. *Job, the Victim of His People*, trans. Yvonne Freccero (Stanford, CA: Stanford University Press, 1987).

Goethe, Johann Wolfgang. *Goethe's Botanical Writings*, trans. Berthe Mueller (Honolulu: University of Hawaii Press, 1952).

Goethe, Johann Wolfgang. *Goethe's Botany: The "Metamorphosis of Plants" (1790) and Tobler's "Ode to Nature" (1782)*, trans. Agnes Arber, *Chronica Botanica*, vol. 10, no. 2 (Summer 1946), 63-126.

Goethe, Johann Wolfgang. *Maximen und Reflexionen*, ed. and trans. R.H. Stephenson (Glasgow: Scottish Papers in Germanic Studies, 1986).

Goethe, Johann Wolfgang. *Selected Poems*, ed. Christopher Middleton [Goethe Edition, vol. 1] (Boston: Suhrkamp/Insel, 1983).

Goethe, Johann Wolfgang. *Selected Poems*, trans. John Whaley (London: Dent, 1998).

Goethe, Johann Wolfgang. *The Metamorphosis of Plants*, ed. Gordon L. Miller (Cambridge, MA, and London: The MIT Press, 2009).

Gossman, Lionel. *Basel in the Age of Burckhardt: A Study in Unseasonable Ideas* (Chicago and London: University of Chicago Press, 2000).

Grene, David and Richmond Lattimore (eds.). *Greek Tragedies*, vol. 1 (Chicago and London: University of Chicago Press, 1960).

Haar, Michel and Reginald Lilly. "Heidegger and the God of Hölderlin," *Research in Phenomenology*, vol. 19, no. 1 (1989), 89-100.

Hackett, Jeremiah M. (ed.). *A Companion to Meister Eckhart* (Leiden and Boston: Brill, 2013).

Hadot, Pierre. *Plotinus or the Simplicity of Vision* [1989], trans. Michael Chase (Chicago and London: University of Chicago Press, 1993).

Hahn, Scott and Curtis J. Mitch (eds.). *The Ignatius Catholic Study Bible* (San Francisco: Ignatius Press, 2024).

Hanegraaff, Wouter J. et al. (eds.). *Dictionary of Gnosis & Western Esotericism* (Leiden and Boston: Brill, 2006).

Harrison, Jane Ellen. *Myths of Greece and Rome* (Garden City, NY: Doubleday, Doran, 1928).

Hegel, G.W.F. *Faith and Knowledge*, ed. and trans. Walter Cerf and H.S. Harris (Albany, NY: State University of New York Press, 1977).

Heidegger, Martin. *Being and Truth*, trans. Gregory Fried and Richard Polt (Bloomington and Indianapolis, IN: Indiana University Press, 2010).

Heidegger, Martin. *Elucidations of Hölderlin's Poetry*, trans. Keith Hoeller (Amherst, NY: Humanity Books, 2000).

Heidegger, Martin. *Erläuterungen zu Hölderlins Dichtung*, fourth edn. (Frankfurt am Main: Klostermann, 1971).

Heidegger, Martin. *Hölderlin's Hymn "The Ister,"* trans. William McNeill and Julia Davis (Bloomington and Indianapolis, IN: Indiana University Press, 1996).

Heidegger, Martin. *Hölderlins Hymnen "Germanien" und "Der Rhein"*, ed. Susanne Ziegler [*Gesamtausgabe*, Section II, vol. 39] (Frankfurt am Main: Klostermann, 1989).

Heidegger, Martin. *Nietzsche*, trans. David Farrell Krell, vols. 1-2 (San Francisco: Harper & Row, 1979).

Heidegger, Martin. *The Essence of Truth: On Plato's Cave Allegory and "Theaetetus"* [1932], trans. Ted Sadler (London and New York: Continuum, 2002; Bloomsbury, 2013).

Heidegger, Martin. *What Is Called Thinking?* [1951/1952], trans. J. Glenn Gray (New York: Harper & Row, 1968).

Heidegger, Martin. *Vorträge und Aufsätze* (Pfullingen: Neske, 1954).

Hellingrath, Norbert von. *Hölderlin: Zwei Vorträge* (Munich: Bruckmann, 1922).

Herman, Arthur. *The Cave and the Light: Plato versus Aristotle and the Struggle for the Soul of Western Civilization* (New York: Random House, 2013).

Herodotus. *The Landmark Herodotus: The Histories*, ed. Robert B. Strassler (London: Quercus, 2008).

Hesiod. *The Homeric Hymns and Homerica*, trans. Hugh G. Evelyn-White (Cambridge, MA; London: Harvard University Press; Heinemann, 1982).

Hölderlin, Friedrich. *Poems and Fragments*, trans. Michael Hamburger, 3rd edn. (London: Anvil Press, 1994).

Hölderlin, Friedrich. *Sämtliche Gedichte*, ed. Jochen Schmidt (Frankfurt am Main: Deutscher Klassiker Verlag, 2005).

Hollinrake, Roger. *Nietzsche, Wagner, and the Philosophy of Pessimism* (London: Allen and Unwin, 1982).

Homer. *The Iliad of Homer*, trans. Richmond Lattimore (Chicago and London: University of Chicago Press, 1961).

Horace. *Odes and Epodes*, ed. and trans. Niall Rudd (Cambridge, MA: Harvard University Press, 2004).

Horace. *Satires, Epistles and Ars Poetica*, trans. H. Rushton Fairclough (London; Cambridge, MA: Heinemann; Harvard University Press, 1942).

Horace. *The Odes and Carmen Saeculare of Horace*, trans. John Conington (London: Bell, 1882).

Horneffer, Ernst. *Nietzsches Lehre von der ewigen Wiederkunft und deren bisherige Veröffentlichung* (Leipzig: Naumann, 1900).

Hough, Sheridan. *Nietzsche's Noontide Friend: The Self as Metaphoric Double* (University Park, PA: Pennsylvania State University Press, 1997).

Houlgate, Stephen and Michael Baur (eds.), *A Companion to Hegel* (Malden, MA, and Oxford: Blackwell, 2011).

Hurwitz, Siegmund. *Lilith – The First Eve: Historical and Psychological Aspects of the Dark Feminine*, trans. Gela Jacobson (Einsiedeln: Daimon, 1992).

Huysmans, Joris-Karl. *L'Art moderne / Certains* (Paris: Union Générale d'Éditions, 1986).

Jacobus de Voragine. *The Golden Legend: Readings on the Saints*, trans. William Granger Ryan, 2 vols. (Princeton, NJ: Princeton University Press, 1993).

Jaffé, Aniela. *Streiflichter zu Leben und Denken C.G. Jungs* (Einsiedeln: Daimon, 2021).

Janné, Aniela. *Reflections on the Life and Dreams of C.G. Jung*, trans. Caitlin Stephens (Einsiedeln: Daimon, 2023).

Jantz, Curt Paul. *Friedrich Nietzsche: Biographie*, 3 vols. (Frankfurt am Main and Vienna: Hanser, 1978).

Johnson, Sarah Iles. *Restless Dead: Encounters Between the Living and the Dead in Ancient Greece* (Berkeley and Los Angeles: University of California Press, 1999).

Johnston, Sarah Iles. *Hekate Soteira: A Study of Hekate's Role in the Chaldean Oracles and Related Literature* [American Classical Studies, 21] (Atlanta, GA: Scholars Press, 1990).

Joosse, Albert (ed.). *Olympiodorus of Alexandria: Exegete, Teacher, Platonic Philosopher* (Leiden and Boston: Brill, 2021).

Jung, C.G. and Carl Kerényi, *Essays on a Science of Mythology: The Myth of the Divine Child and the Mysteries of Eleusis*, trans. R.F.C. Hull (Princeton, NJ: Princeton University Press, 1969).

Jung, C.G. and Wolfgang Pauli. *Atom and Archetype: The Pauli/Jung Letters, 1932-1958*, ed. C.A. Meier, trans. David Roscoe (Princeton, NJ, and Oxford: Princeton University Press, 2001).

Jung, C.G. *Dream Analysis: Notes of the Seminar given in 1928-1930*, ed. William McGuire (London: Routledge & Kegan Paul, 1984).

Jung, C.G. *Dream Interpretation Ancient & Modern: Notes from the Seminar Given in 1936-1941*, ed. John Peck, Lorenz Jung, and Maria Meyer-Grass, trans. Ernst Falzeder and Tony Woolfson (Princeton, NJ, and Oxford: Princeton University Press, 2014).

Jung, C.G. *Dream Symbols of the Individuation Process: Notes of C.G. Jung's Seminars on Wolfgang Pauli's Dreams*, ed. Suzanne Gieser (Princeton, NJ, and Oxford: Princeton University Press, 2019).

Jung, C.G. *History of Modern Psychology: Lectures delivered at the ETH Zurich*, ed. Ernst Falzeder, trans. Mark Kyburz, John Peck, and Ernst Falzeder (Princeton, NJ, and Oxford: Princeton University Press, 2019).

Jung, C.G. *Mysterium Coniunctionis* [...]: *Ergänzungsband «Aurora Consurgens»: Ein dem Thomas von Aquin zugeschriebenes Dokument der alchemistischen Gegensatzproblematik von Dr. M.-L. von Franz* [*Gesammelte Werke*, vol. 14/iii] (Olten and Freiburg im Breisgau: Walter, 1971).

Jung, C.G. *Psychology of Yoga and Meditation: Lectures delivered at the ETH Zurich*, ed. Martin Liebscher (Princeton, NJ, and Oxford: Princeton University Press, 2020).

Jung, C.G. *The Psychology of Kundalini Yoga: Notes of the Seminar Given in 1932*, ed. Sonu Shamdasani (London: Routledge, 1996).

Jung, C.G. *Two Essays on Analytical Psychology*, trans. H.G. and C.F. Baynes (London: Baillière, Tindall and Cox, 1928).

Jung, Emma, and Marie-Louise von Franz, *The Grail Legend*, trans. Andrea Dykes, 2nd edn. (Boston, London: Sigo Press; Coventure, 1986).

Kant, Immanuel. *Critique of Practical Reason*, ed. and trans. Mary Gregor (Cambridge: Cambridge University Press, 2015).

Kant, Immanuel. *Groundwork of the Metaphysics of Morals*, trans. Mary Gregor (Cambridge: Cambridge University Press, 1998).

Keulen, Wytse Hette, and Stefan Tilg, Lara Nicolini, Luca Graverini, S.J. Harrison, Stelios Panayotakis, D. van Mal-Maeder (eds.). *Apuleius Madaurensis Metamorphoses, Book XI, The Isis Book: Text, Introduction and Commentary* (Leiden: Brill, 2015).

Kim, Alan (ed.). *Brill's Companion to German Platonism* (Leiden: Brill, 2019).

Kingsley, Peter. *Ancient Philosophy, Mystery and Magic: Empedocles and Pythagorean Tradition* (Oxford: Oxford University Press, 1995).

Kingsley, Peter. *Catafalque: Carl Jung and the End of Humanity*, 2 vols. (London: Catafalque Press, 2018).

Klages, Ludwig. *Of Cosmogonic Eros*, trans. Mav Kuhn, 2nd edn. (Munich: Theion, 2022).

Klages, Ludwig. *Vom kosmogonischen Eros*, 2nd edn. (Jena: Diederichs, 1926).

Klein, Richard, Johann Kreuzer, and Stefan Müller-Doohm (eds), *Adorno-Handbuch: Leben – Werk – Wirkung*, 2nd edn. (Berlin: Metzler, 2019).

Kroll, Joseph. *Beiträge zum Descensus ad Inferos* (Königsberg: Hartung, 1922).

Kroll, Joseph. *Gott und Hölle: Der Mythos vom Descensuskampfe* (Leipzig and Berlin: Teubner, 1932; reprinted 1963).

Lachman, Gary. *Jung the Mystic: The Esoteric Dimensions of Carl Jung's Life and Teachings* (New York: Penguin, 2010).

Larson, Jennifer. *Ancient Greek Cults: A Guide* (New York and London: Routledge, 2007).

Lebeck, Anne. "The Central Myth of Plato's *Phaedrus*," *Greek, Roman, and Byzantine Studies*, 13 (1972), 267-290.

Lee, Charlotte (ed.). *Goethe in Context* (Cambridge: Cambridge University Press, 2024).

Liessmann, Konrad Paul. *Alle Lust will Ewigkeit: Mitternächtliche Untersuchungen* (Vienna: Szolnay, 2021).

Loeb, Paul S. *The Death of Nietzsche's Zarathustra* (New York: Cambridge University Press, 2010).

Lothane, Zvi. "In Defense of Sabina Spielrein," *International Forum of Psychoanalysis*, vol. 5, no. 3 (1996), 203-207).

Magee, Glenn Alexander (ed.). *The Cambridge Handbook of Western Mysticism and Esotericism* (Cambridge: Cambridge University Press, 2016).

Maillard, Christine (ed.). *Recherches germaniques* 8 (2011) [*Art, sciences et psychologie: Autour du "Livre Rouge" de Carl Gustav Jung (1914-1930)*; *Kunst, Wissenschaften und Psychologie. Über das "Rote Buch" von C. G. Jung (1914-1930)*.

Malcolm, John. "The Cave Revisited," *Classical Quarterly*, vol. 31, no. 1 (1981), 60-68.

Malcolm, John. "The Line and the Cave," *Phronesis*, vol. 7, no. 1 (1962), 38-45.

McDermot, Violet. *The Fall of Sophia: A Gnostic Text on the Redemption of Universal Consciousness* (Great Barrington, MA: Lindisfarne Books, 2001).

Mansfield, Harvey C. *Machiavelli's Virtue* [1996] (Chicago and London: University of Chicago Press, 1998).

Meier, Heinrich. *Nietzsche's Legacy: "Ecce Homo" and "The Antichrist," Two Books on Nature and Politics* [2019], trans. Justin Gottschalk (Chicago and London: University of Chicago Press, 2024).

Meister Eckhart. *Sermons & Treatises*, ed. and trans. Maurice O'Connell Walshe, 3 vols. (Longmead: Element Books, 1987).

Meyer, Marvin W. (ed.). *The Ancient Mysteries: A Sourcebook: Sacred Texts of the Mystery Religions of the Ancient Mediterranean World* (San Francisco: Harper & Row, 1987).

Mistry, Freny. *Nietzsche and Buddhism: Prolegomenon to a Comparative Study* (Berlin and New York: de Gruyter, 1981).

Mogenson, Greg, and Pamela J. Power (eds.). *Where Is Soul? Psychology in Modernity* (London, Ontario: Dusk Owl Books, 2025).

Monastisches Lektionar, vol. II/2, *6.-34. Woche im Jahreskreis* (St. Ottlien: EOS Verlag, 1993).

Mullahy, Patrick. *Oedipus: Myth and Complex: A Review of Psychoanalytic Theory* (New York: Hermitage Press, 1948).

Müller, J.G. *Geschichte der Amerikanischen Urreligionen* (Basel: Schweighauser, 1855).

Murphy, G. Ronald, S.J. *Tree of Salvation: Yggdrasil and the Cross in the North* (New York: Oxford University Press, 2013).

Nejeschleba, Tomáš. "Petrarch's Ascent of Mont Ventoux and Philosophy," *Archiwum Historii Filozofii i Myśli Społecznej = Archive of the History of Philosophy and Social Thought*, 64 (2019), 81-94.

Nietzsche, Friedrich. *The Anti-Christ*, trans. H.L. Mencken (New York: A.A. Knopf, 1920).

Nietzsche, Friedrich. *Basic Writings*, ed. and trans. Walter Kaufmann (New York: Modern Library, 1968).

Nietzsche, Friedrich. *Dithyrambs of Dionysus: Bi-Lingual Edition*, trans. R.J. Hollingdale (London: Anvil Press Poetry, 1984).

Nietzsche, Friedrich. *Ecce Homo (Nietzsche's Autobiography)*, trans. Anthony M. Ludovici (New York: Macmillan, 1911).

Nietzsche, Friedrich. *Ecce Homo*, trans. R.J. Hollingdale (Harmondsworth: Penguin, 1992).

Nietzsche, Friedrich. *Human, All Too Human*, trans. Alexander Harvey (Chicago: Kerr, 1908).

Nietzsche, Friedrich. *Human, All Too Human*, trans. R.J. Hollingdale (Cambridge: Cambridge University Press, 1986).

Nietzsche, Friedrich. *The Case of Wagner; Nietzsche Contra Wagner, The Twilight of the Idols; The Antichrist* [*Works*, vol. 3], trans. Thomas Common. (London: T. Fisher Unwin, 1899).

Nietzsche, Friedrich. *The Dawn of Day*, trans. J.M. Kennedy (London: Allen & Unwin, 1924).

Nietzsche, Friedrich. *The Gay Science*, trans. Walter Kaufmann (New York: Random House, 1974).

Nietzsche, Friedrich. *The Joyful Wisdom*, trans. Thomas Common (New York: Macmillan, 1924).

Nietzsche, Friedrich. *The Will to Power*, ed. Walter Kaufmann, trans. Walter Kaufmann and R.J. Hollingdale (New York: Random House, 1968).

Nietzsche, Friedrich. *Twilight of the Idols/The Anti-Christ*, trans. R.J. Hollingdale (Harmondsworth: Penguin, 1968).

Nietzsche, Friedrich. *Unpublished Fragments (Spring 1885-Spring 1886)*, trans. Adrian Del Caro [*The Complete Works of Friedrich Nietzsche*, vol. 16] (Stanford, CA: Stanford University Press, 2020).

Nietzsche, Friedrich. *Untimely Meditations*, trans. R.J. Hollingdale (Cambridge, UK: Cambridge University Press, 1983).

Nietzsche, Friedrich. *Writings from the Early Notebooks*, ed. Raymond Geuss and Alexander Nehamas, trans. Ladislaus Löb (Cambridge: Cambridge University Press, 2009).

Nietzsche, Friedrich. *Thus Spake Zarathustra: A Book for All and None*, trans. Alexander Tille (New York: Macmillan, 1896).

Nimis, Steve. "Aristotle's Analogical Metaphor," *Arethusa*, vol. 21, no. 2 (Fall 1988), 215-266.

Nisbet, H.B. (ed.). *German Aesthetic and Literary Criticism: Winckelmann, Lessing, Hamann, Herder, Schiller, Goethe* (Cambridge: Cambridge University Press, 1985).

Norman, Brian. *The Influence of Switzerland on the life and writing of Edward Gibbon* (Oxford: Voltaire Foundation, 2002).

O'Connell, Michael. "Authority and the Truth of Experience in Petrarch's 'Ascent of Mount Ventoux,'" *Philological Quarterly*, 62 (1983), 507-520.

Onfray, Michel and Maximilien Le Roy. *Nietzsche: Se créer liberté* (Brussels: Lombard, 2010).

Onfray, Michel. *Le crépuscule d'une idole: L'affabulation freudienne* (Paris: Grasset, 2010).

Onfray, Michel. *Les radicalités existentielles* [*Contre-histoire de la philosophie*, vol. 6] (Paris: Grasset, 2009).

Orlov, Andrei A. *Supernal Serpent: Mysteries of Leviathan in Judaism and Christianity* (Oxford: Oxford University Press, 2023).

Osborn, Ronald E. *Humanism and the Death of God: Searching for the Good After Darwin, Marx, and Nietzsche* (Oxford: Oxford University Press, 2017).

Owen, Ware. *Return of the Gods: Mythology in Romantic Philosophy and Literature* (New York: Oxford University Press, 2024).

Panofsky, Erwin. *Hercules am Scheidewege und andere antike Bildstoffe in der neueren Kunst* [Studien der Bibliothek Warburg, 18] [1930] (Berlin: Gebr. Mann, 1997).

Paracelsus, *Essential Readings*, ed. and trans. Nicholas Goodrick-Clarke (Berkeley, CA: North Atlantic Books, 1999).

Paracelsus. *Sämtliche Werke*, ed. Karl Sudhoff and Wilhelm Matthiessen, section 1, *Medizinische, naturwissenschaftliche und philosophische Schriften*, 14 vols. (Munich and Berlin: Oldenbourg, 1922-1933).

Paracelsus. *Selected Writings* [1951], ed. Jolande Jacobi, trans. Norbert Guterman (Princeton, NJ: Princeton University Press, 1979).

Parker, Robert. *Greek Gods Abroad: Names, Natures, and Transformations* (Oakland, CA: University of California Press, 2017).

Parkes, Graham. *Composing the Soul: Reaches of Nietzsche's Psychology* (Chicago and London: University of Chicago Press, 1994).

Partridge, Christopher (ed.). *The Occult World* (London and New York: Routledge, 2015).

Pascal, Blaise. *Œuvres complètes*, ed. Louis Lafuma (Paris: Seuil, 1963).

Pausanias. *Description of Greece*, trans. W.H.S. Jones, vol. 4 (London; Cambridge, MA: Heinemann; Harvard University Press, 1935).

Pausanias. *Description of Greece*, trans. W.H.S. Jones, vol. 4, *Books VIII (XXII) – X* (London; Cambridge, MA: Heinemann; Harvard University Press, 1935).

Peck, John. "*Etwas geschah:* Orphaned Event and Its Adoptions," *Spring* 84 (Fall 2010), 143-162.

Perkins, Richard. "Nietzsche's *opus alchymicum*," *Seminar*, 23 (1987), 216-26.

Peterson, Jordan B. *We Who Wrestle with God: Perceptions of the Divine* (London: Allen Lane, 2024).

Petteni, Oriane. "The Contemporary Legacy of Goethean Morphology: From *Anschauende Urteilskraft* to Algorithmic Pattern Recognition, Generation, and Exploration," *Goethe Yearbook*, 29 (2022), 43-72.

Φίλιος, Δημήτριος. "ΕΠΙΓΡΑΦΑΙ ΕΞ ΕΛΕΥΣΙΝΟΣ" [Inscriptions from Eleusis], *Archaiologikē ephēmeris* (1883), 75-86.

Plato. *The Collected Dialogues*, ed. Edith Hamilton and Huntington Cairns (Princeton, NJ: Princeton University Press, 1989).

Plato. *The Republic of Plato*, ed. and trans. Allan Bloom (New York: Basic Books, 1991).

Plutarch. *Moralia*, Book 5, trans. Frank Cole Babbitt (Cambridge, MA, and London: Harvard University Press, 1936).

Plutarch. *Moralia*, vol. 7, trans. Philip H. De Lacy and Benedict Einarson (London; New York; Heinemann; Putnam, 1959).

Plutarch. *Moralia*, vol. 15, *Fragments from Other Named Works*, trans. F.H. Sandbach (Cambridge, MA: Harvard University Press, 1969).

Porges, Heinrich. *Wagner Rehearsing the "Ring": An Eye-Witness Account of the Stage Rehearsals of the First Bayreuth Festival*, trans. Robert L. Jacobs (Cambridge: Cambridge University Press, 1983).

Priviero, Tommaso. "C.G. Jung's *Liber novus* and Dante's *Commedia*," *Phanês*, 1 (2018), 28-57.

Priviero, Tommaso. *Jung, Dante, and the Making of the "Red Book": Of Fire and Form* (London and New York: Routledge, 2023).

Raffoul, François and Eric S. Nelson (eds.). *The Bloomsbury Companion to Heidegger* (London: Bloomsbury, 2016).

Rahner, Hugo. "Die Gottesgeburt," *Zeitschrift für katholische Theologie*, 59 (1935), 333-418.

Reid, Heather L., John Serrati, and Tim Sorg (eds.). *Conflict and Competition: Agon in Western Greece: Selected Essays from the 2019 Symposium on the Heritage of Western Greece* (Sioux City, IA: Parnassos Press – Fonte Aretusa, 2020).

Rintelen, Fritz Joachim von. "Die Gottesidee bei Johann Wolfgang von Goethe," *Philosophisches Jahrbuch*, 60 (1950), 1-7.

Robinson, James M. (ed.). *The Nag Hammadi Library in English*, 3rd edn (Leiden: Brill, 1988).

Roob, Alexander. *Alchemy and Mysticism*, trans. Shaun Whiteside (Cologne and London: Taschen, 2001).

Rudnytsky, Peter L. *Freud and Oedipus* (New York: Columbia Press, 1987).

Sallis, John. *Crossings: Nietzsche and the Space of Tragedy* (Chicago and London: University of Chicago Press, 1991).

Samuel, Kim. "Re-Imagining the Grail Quest: The Grail of Compassion," *Temenos Academy Review*, 19 (2016), 78-95.

Schaeppi, Kathrin. *C.G. Jung — The Basel Years: A Walking Guide* (Einsiedeln: Daimon, 2025).

Schaff, Philip (ed.). *Nicene and Post-Nicene Fathers*, First Series, vol. 9, *Chrysostom: On the Priesthood, Ascetic Treatises, Select Homilies and Letters, Homilies on the Statutes* (Grand Rapids, MI: Eerdmans, 1889).

Schärf Kluger, Rivkah. *The Archetypal Significance of Gilgamesh: A Modern Ancient Hero*, ed. H. Yehezkel Kluger (Einsiedeln: Daimon, 1991).

Scheier, Claus-Artur. *Nietzsches Labyrinth: Das ursprüngliche Denken und die Seele* (Freiburg and Munich: Karl Alber, 1985).

Schiller, Friedrich. *On the Aesthetic Education of Man: In a Series of Letters*, ed. and trans. Elizabeth M. Wilkinson and L.A. Willoughby (Oxford: Clarendon Press, 1982).

Schiller, Friedrich. *Sämtliche Gedichte und Balladen*, ed. Georg Kurscheidt (Frankfurt am Main and Leipzig: Insel, 2004).

Schiller, Friedrich. *Schiller's "On Grace and Dignity" in its Cultural Context: Essays and a New Translation*, ed. Jane V. Curran and

Christophe Fricker (Rochester, NY: Camden House, 2005), p. 166).

Schiller, Friedrich. *Selected Poems*, ed. Frank M. Fowler (London: New York: Macmillan; St Martin's Press, 1969).

Schiller, Friedrich. *The Minor Poems of Schiller*, trans. John Herman Merivale (London: Pickering, 1844).

Schiller, Friedrich. *The Poems and Ballads of Schiller*, trans. Edward Bulwer Lytton, 2 vols. (Edinburgh and London: Blackwood, 1844).

Schmidt, Dennis J. *On Germans and Other Greeks: Tragedy and Ethical Life* (Bloomington and Indianapolis: Indiana University Press, 2001).

Scott, Walter (ed.). *Hermetica: The Ancient Greek and Latin Writings which contain Religious or Philosophic Teachings ascribed to Hermes Trismegistus*, ed. Walter Scott, 4 vols. (Oxford: Clarendon Press, 1924-1936).

Seaford, Richard. *Money and the Early Greek Mind: Homer, Tragedy, and Philosophy* (Cambridge and New York: Cambridge University Press, 2004).

Seaford, Richard. *Tragedy, Ritual and Money in Ancient Greece. Selected Essays* (Cambridge: Cambridge University Press, 2018).

Shamdasani, Sonu. "A Woman Called Frank," *Spring: A Journal of Archetype and Culture*, 50 (1990), 26-56.

Sharpe, Leslie. *Friedrich Schiller: Drama, Thought and Politics* (Cambridge: Cambridge University Press, 1991).

Sheppard, Richard. *Modernism – Dada – Postmodern* (Evanston, IL: Northwestern University Press, 2000).

Sparks, Jack Norman et al. (eds.). *The Orthodox Study Bible*, ed. Jack Norman Sparks, et al. (Nashville, TN: Nelson, 2008).

Spiegel, Friedrich. *Erânische Alterthumskunde*, 3 vols. (Leipzig: Engelmann, 1871-78).

St. Cyril of Jerusalem. *The Catechetical Lectures of S. Cyril, Archbishop of Jerusalem* [Library of Fathers of the Holy Catholic Church, vol. 2] (Oxford: Parker, 1839).

Stausberg, Michael. *Faszination Zarathushtra: Zoroaster und die Europäische Religionsgeschichte der Frühen Neuzeit*, 2 vols. (Berlin and New York: de Gruyter, 1998).

Stein, Murray. "How to Read *The Red Book* and Why," *Journal of Analytical Psychology*, vol. 57, no. 3 (June 2012), 280-298.

Steiner, Rudolf. *Mysticism at the Dawn of the Modern Age*, trans. Karl. E. Zimmer (Blauvelt, NY: SteinerBooks, 1960).

Stekel, Wihelm. "Aus Gerhart Hauptmanns Diarium," *Zentralblatt für Psychoanalyse*, vol. 2, no. 6 (1912), 365-366.

Stewart, Jon. *A History of Nihilism: Confrontations with Nothingness* (Cambridge: Cambridge University Press, 2023).

Storr, Anthony. *Jung* (London: Fontana, 1973).

Tauler, Johannes. *Sermons*, trans. Maria Shrady (New York and Mahwah, NJ: Paulist Press, 1985).

Taylor, F. Sherwood. "George Ripley's Song," *Ambix*, vol. 2, no. 3-4 (1946), 177-181.

Taylor, Thomas (trans.). *The Mystical Hymns of Orpheus* (London: Dobell; Reeves and Turner, 1896).

Tertullian. *Treatises on Marriage and Remarriage: To His Wife; An Exhortation to Chastity; Monogamy*, trans. William P. Le Saint (New York, NY; Ramsey, NJ: Newman Press, 1951), pp. 78-79.

Thatcher, David S. "Eagle and Serpent in *Zarathustra*," *Nietzsche-Studien*, 6 (1977), 240-260.

Theierl, Herbert. *Nietzsche — Mystik als Selbstversuch* (Würzburg: Königshausen & Neumann, 2000).

Thiele, Georg. *Antike Himmelsbilder: Mit Forschungen zu Hipparchos, Aratos und seinen Fortsetzern und Beiträgen zur Kunstgeschichte des Sternhimmels* (Berlin: Weidmann, 1898).

Tongeren, Paul van. *Friedrich Nietzsche and European Nihilism* (Newcastle upon Tyne: Cambridge Scholars Publishing, 2018).

Tourney, Garfield. "Empedocles and Freud, Heraclitus and Jung," *Bulletin of the History of Medicine*, vol. 30, no. 2 (March-April, 1956), 109-123.

Vergely, Bertrand Vergely. *Notre vie a un sens!* (Paris: Albin Michel, 2019).

Veyne, Paul. *Les Grecs ont-ils cru à leurs mythes? Essai sur l'imagination constituante* (Paris: Seuil, 1983).

Waite, Arthur Edward (ed. and trans.). *The Hermetic Museum Restored and Enlarged*, ed. and trans. Arthur Edward Waite, 2 vols. (London: J. Elliot, 1893).

Warminski, Andrzej. "'Patmos': The Senses of Interpretation," *Modern Language Notes*, vol. 91, no. 3 (April 1976), 478-500.

Warminski, Andrzej. *Readings in Interpretation: Hölderlin, Hegel, Heidegger* (Minneapolis, MN: University of Minnesota Press, 1987).

Wehr, Gerhard. *Die deutsche Mystik: Mystische Erfahrung und theosophische Weltsicht — eine Einführung in Leben und Werk der großen deutschen Sucher nach Gott* (Berne: O.W. Barth, 1988).

Wehr, Gerhard. *Philosophie: Auf der Suche nach dem Sinn* (Augsburg: Pattloch, 1990).

Weinert, Friedel. *Copernicus, Darwin, & Freud: Revolutions in the history and philosophy of science* (Chichester; Malden, MA: Wiley-Blackwell, 2009).

Widmann, Claudio (ed.). *Dante e Jung: Una relazione a distanza* (Rome: Magi Edizioni, 2021).

Wiles, Maurice F., Edward J. Yarnold, and Paul M. Parvis (eds.), *St Augustine and His Opponents* [*Studia Patristica*, vol. 38] (Louvain: Peeters, 2001).

Willard, Thomas. "The Star in Man: C.G. Jung und Maire-Louise von Franz on the Alchemical Philosophy of Gerhard Dorn," *Psychological Perspectives*, vol. 64, no. 1 (2021), 9-36.

Wilshire, Donna. *Virgin, Mother, Crone: Myths & Mysteries of the Triple Goddess* (Rochester, VT: Inner Traditions, 1994).

Wilson, A.N. *God's Funeral* (London: Murray, 1999).

Woodward, Linda H. (ed.). *Selections from the Prometheus Trust Conferences 2006-2010* (Dilton Marsh, Westbury: Prometheus Trust, 2013).

Woodward, Thomas (ed.). *Sophocles: A Collection of Critical Essays* (Englewood Cliffs, NJ: Prentice, 1966).

Yiassemides, Angeliki (ed.). *Time and the Psyche: Jungian Perspectives* (London and New York: Routledge, 2017).

Young, Frances Margaret, Michael Edwards, and Paul M. Parvis (eds.). *Augustine* [*Studia Patristica*, vol. 42] (Louvain: Peeters, 2006).

Young, Julian. *The Death of God and the Meaning of Life* (London and New York: Routledge, 2003).

Zaehner, R.C. (ed. and trans.). *Hindu Scriptures* (New York: Everyman, 1992).

Zajonc, Arthur. *Catching the Light: The Entwined History of Light and Mind* (New York and Oxford: Oxford University Press, 1993).